CHANGING MULTICULTURALISM

JOE L. KINCHELOE AND SHIRLEY R. STEINBERG

OPEN UNIVERSITY PRESS
Buckingham · Philadelphia

In Memory of Paulo Freire who
affirmed radical love in all cultures

Open University Press
Celtic Court
22 Ballmoor
Buckingham
MK18 1XW

and

325 Chestnut Street
Philadelphia, PA 19106, USA

First Published 1997
Reprinted 2001

A catalogue record of this book is available from the British Library

ISBN 0 335 19484 2 (hb)   0 335 19483 4 (pb)

Library of Congress Cataloging-in-Publication Data
Kincheloe, Joe L.
    Changing multiculturalism / Joe L. Kincheloe, Shirley R. Steinberg.
        p. cm. — (Changing education)
    Includes bibliographical references and index.
    ISBN 0-335-19484-2 (hc). — ISBN 0-335-19483-4 (pbk.)
    1. Multicultural education—United States.   2. Multiculturalism—
–United States.   3. Critical pedagogy—United States.
    I. Steinberg, Shirley R., 1952– . II. Title. III. Series.
LC1099.3.K55   1997
370.117—dc21
                                                          97-12933   CIP

Typeset by Type Study, Scarborough
Printed in Great Britain by Biddles Ltd, www.biddles.co.uk

CONTENTS

SERIES EDITORS' PREFACE

Around the world, schools, and the societies of which they are a part, are confronting the most profound changes – changes the like of which have not been seen since the last great global movement of economic and educational restructuring more than a century ago. The fundamental forms of public education that were designed for an age of heavy manufacturing and mechanical industry are under challenge and fading fast as we move into a world of high technology, flexible workforces, more diverse school populations, downsized administrations and declining resources.

What is to follow is uncertain and unclear. The different directions of change can seem conflicting and are often contested. Decentralized systems of school self-management are accompanied by centralized systems of curriculum and assessment control. Moves to develop more authentic assessments are paralleled by the tightened imposition of standardized tests. Curriculum integration is being advocated in some places, more specialization and subject departmentalization in others.

These complex and contradictory cross-currents pose real challenges to theoretical and practical interpretation in many fields of education, and constitute an important and intriguing agenda for educational change – and for this series, which is intended to meet a deep-seated need among researchers and practitioners. International, social and technological changes require a profound and rapid response from the educational community. By establishing and interpreting the nature and scope of educational change, *Changing Multiculturalism* will make a significant contribution to meeting this challenge.

We are delighted that Professors Joe Kincheloe and Shirley Steinberg have agreed to join the Series with a critical and far ranging account of ways of *changing multiculturalism*. The importance of the volume is highlighted clearly in Peter McLaren's introduction which follows and we do not want to rehearse his arguments here. However, what is important about the book is the clarity with which it defines a critical and genuinely innovative way of thinking about 'multiculturalisms'. Their work is among that of a group comprising very few scholars which begins to engage with the fact that the diaspora is the norm and the native born person living in her or his own land increasingly the exception. With such a diasporic force at work in this period of late capital, it is clearly vital that new critical perspectives engage with emerging subjectivities and actions at the local through to global level.

What is so distinctive about the work of Kincheloe and Steinberg not just in this volume, but elsewhere, is the fluidity and reflexiveness with which they engage the New Work Order. This contrasts elegantly with the rather static determinism of a good deal of not just right-wing, but left-wing thinking around issues of culture. We believe that it is important in this series to engage in a reflective and flexible manner with the emergent new patterns of global control. But we also are mindful that the contest over multiculturalisms takes place at a local and rooted level as well. The advantage of the gaze adopted by Kincheloe and Steinberg is that it works across this whole spectrum from the local to the global. In this sense, all of those involved in *changing education* will find help and sustenance in the messages contained in this valuable volume.

FOREWORD

Peter J. McLaren

Educational multiculturalists have been among the few who have chosen the path to self-knowledge unfettered by the dangerous claims of neo-liberal monoculturalists. Yet multiculturalists have not succeeded. For in their indictments of racism they have mimicked many of racism's foundations and presuppositions. While historically multiculturalists have attempted to address the authoring or the narrating of the anti-racist self, they have done so mainly at the level of discourse, in antiseptic isolation from the material flows and circuits of capital. In so doing, multiculturalism has too often become an alibi for an establishment consensus and a neo-liberal apologetics that forces people into global labour pools in the worldwide accumulation/consumer society predicated on profit alone. Numerous species of liberal multiculturalism are now participating in what E. San Juan calls 'the fetishism of normative plurality or the seriality of autonomous instances'.

An emphasis on multiple subjectivities that has resulted from the critique of the singular, autonomous ego and unitary identity has led to a preoccupation with weak theories of social constructivism that fail to locate agency in the larger social totality of advanced capitalist flows. Within some postmodernist articulations of multiculturalism, self-reflexivity has become a historical impossibility, replaced by syntagmatic chains, gesturing falteringly towards meaning. Within the discourse of facile forms of postmodernist theorizing, oppression is relativized as subjective feeling and reduced to communicative practices removed from larger social and economic structures of domination. Similarly, there appears to be a general lack of awareness that race, class, gender and sexuality are non-synchronous and criss-crossed by vectors of privilege and relations of inequality, and hence are constructed by a *materiality of forces*. Within the nation state such forces have been 'sublimated into the symbolic economy of national culture'. The symbolic economy of the nation has effectively constructed an artificial community in which race, class and gender issues are symmetricized (flattened out) into issues of voluntary associations, forms of cultural meaning-making and a consensus-seeking negotiation of discourses when, in fact, race, class and gender are informed by relations of power and social relations of production and reproduction. They exist as structural relations and dependent hierarchies that are reproduced to the advantage of those who are most favoured in the existing social division of labour. Liberal multiculturalism thus underwrites the continual exploitation of people of colour and the poor. In parading before the public the virtues of diversity, liberal multiculturalists have displaced the contextual specificity of difference, recycling colonialism under the guise of democracy.

Displaying a form of ethnic absolution, government bureaucrats and pundits hold up Asian immigrants as model minorities in order to encourage inter-ethnic rivalry based on the ethos of competitive individualism and individual success. However, this often lays the groundwork for 'gutting affirmative action, curtailing social services, and justifying "de-industrialization"' (San Juan). In this case the myth of meritocracy gets reinforced by the putative assumption that everyone in every group has an equal chance to become a model minority by conforming to group consensus. This perspective displaces asymmetrical relations of power into the background, as the issue of race becomes cleansed of issues of class antagonisms and capitalist relations of production, and inter-ethnic communication becomes the terrain upon which ethnic relations are to be worked out, again largely at the level of superstructural relations.

Consider the liberal individualism that has helped to shape the anti-affirmative action sentiment in the United States. The conservative argument that affirmative action not only constitutes preferential treatment for minorities and instances of 'reverse racism', but leads to a culture of victimization in which powerlessness among people of colour and women is reproduced, forgets that there are many social programmes already in place for white immigrants and that capitalist hegemony in the USA favours a white male corporate ownership and management. It also ignores the relationship between deindustrialization and the loss of jobs among the working class in general, leading to a white backlash against people of colour. Further, it ignores strategies used by the 'new disadvantaged' (mainly white people who have lost their jobs owing to economic restructuring and downsizing) to outmanoeuvre the 'old disadvantaged' (groups such as African-Americans, and native Americans, whose economic advancement has been impeded at the structural level for many generations).

Recent attacks on affirmative action – such as criticisms of the lack of efficiency surrounding many of its programmes – checkmate the possibility of considering affirmative action as a necessary social critique of whiteness. They also ignore the growing insecurity among white males, in particular in relation to the shifting demographics of recent decades, which reveal that whites will soon represent a numerical minority in the United States. But as Jan Nederveen Pieterse notes, 'By any standard of fairness, the rights of the old and the new disadvantaged are not equal.' Pierterse also remarks, correctly in my view, that multiculturalism must be linked to structural adjustment, complete with an emphasis on rebuilding social infrastructure and increasing asset development among low-income groups. Without economic redistribution, economic growth only exacerbates racist formations, rather than eliminates them.

Many Western countries deny the influences of their ethnic minority inhabitants, while appropriating and naturalizing their contributions and making them their own. At the same time that the contributions of minority groups are absorbed by the dominant culture, the dominant culture presents itself as a distinctly white social order into which minority groups are invited to adjust themselves through an assimilation into whiteness. Yet the price of admission into such a society is not only morally repugnant but historically inaccurate, since whites have set themselves up as arbiters of a culture already transformed by the contributions of its oppressed groups. Such contributions are either ignored or assumed to have emerged from the dominant culture.

Over recent years, it has become alarmingly clear that educational multiculturalists and anti-racist educators need a critical conception of multiculturalism whose problematic puts at centre stage the (re)production of capitalist hegemony and the international sets of social relations of production as well as regional ensembles of discourses and practices that are constituent of subjectivity and agency. In other words, multiculturalism has to be engaged from both local or regional and global perspectives, mindful of the contemporary disorganization of capitalism. It is at this juncture of analysis – what I call a 'critical multiculturalism' – that this volume takes on a distinctive shape and importance within the burgeoning literature on multiculturalism. Taking seriously the *aporias* in current conceptualizations of multiculturalism, the authors lay bare many of the inadequacies connected to contemporary formulations of multiculturalism and provide educators with an innovative and important framework for (re)doing multicultural education. This is a book that demands a serious reading among educators faced at this moment of history with the challenge of new diasporic movements and existing communities of struggle. It is a book that invites educators to consider new approaches to understanding and engaging in a politics of difference. With the exercise of a critical multicultural awareness and practice we no longer have to consider ourselves at the end of history, as it might seem to many neo-liberals, but rather at the edge of the future.

one

INTRODUCTION: WHAT IS MULTICULTURALISM?

Multiculturalism means everything and at the same time nothing. It has been used and misused so often and for so many conflicting reasons and agendas that no one at the end of the twentieth century can speak of multiculturalism or multicultural education without specifically delineating what he or she means or does not mean. In a book entitled *Changing Multiculturalism*, this introductory chapter attempts simply to accomplish this one objective: clarifying our meaning of multiculturalism. While we cannot be sure of what individuals are suggesting when they employ the term multiculturalism, we can reasonably guess that they are alluding to at least one of the following issues: race, socio-economic class, gender, language, culture, sexual preference or disability. While the term is used more in relation to race, it is commonly extended to other categories of diversity. In public conversation, multiculturalism is a term used as a code word for race, much in the way that 'inner-city issues' signifies that race is the topic being referenced. Among many conservatives multiculturalism is a term of derision, deployed to represent a variety of challenges to the traditional European and male orientation of the educational canon.

Used as a goal, a concept, an attitude, a strategy and a value, multiculturalism has emerged as the eye of a social storm swirling around the demographic changes that are occurring in Western societies. Western nations, including the USA, UK, Canada, Australia and New Zealand, have experienced immigration and various movements of racial and gender awareness that have forced them to confront questions concerning the ways they define themselves and other social institutions. In the process serious questions have been raised in relation to the degree to which such nations are in reality open and democratic societies. The result of these upheavals has been dramatic: no longer can the West speak with unexamined confidence about its cultural nature, its values and its mission. Indeed, in this new social situation Western societies have been forced to confront the cultural contradictions that refuse to be swept under the rug. In this context many Westerners are arriving at the conclusion that like it or not they live in multicultural societies. Thus, we argue, that they cannot choose to believe in or not believe in the concept of multiculturalism. From our perspective multiculturalism is not something one believes in or agrees with, it simply is. Multiculturalism is a condition of the end-of-the-century Western life we live in multicultural societies. We can respond to this reality in different ways, but the reality remains no matter how we might choose to respond to it.

Multiculturalism, as used in this book, involves the nature of this response. As we will delineate, there are numerous ways to respond to this racial, socio-economic class, gender, language, culture, sexual preference and disability-related diversity. Generally speaking, this response involves the formulation of competing definitions of the social world that correspond to particular social, political and economic interests. Thus, power relations play an important role in helping to shape the way individuals, organizations, groups and institutions react to the reality of multiculturalism. Multiculturalism education involves the nature of this response in educational contexts – in *Changing Multiculturalism* such contexts include both school and out-of-school cultural locales. Categorizing educational approaches to multiculturalism is nothing new, as scholars have developed typologies for at least twenty years. Christine Sleeter and Carl Grant (1994) have reviewed the history of such delineations and no need exists to repeat it here. Suffice it to say that as they focused on different issues, adopted competing values, operated from different social positions or employed conflicting theoretical models, analysts classified forms of multicultural education in very different ways (Carby 1992; Perry and Fraser 1993; Swartz 1993). While we recognize the radical importance of the various forms of diversity in our critical vision of multiculturalism, we delimit our focus in this book to issues of race, class and gender diversity. In no way should this be taken as a dismissal of other forms of diversity not included in this triad.

While we make no claim to offer a final and complete delineation of multicultural education – we agree with Ellen Swartz (1993) that all delineations are tentative and must be constantly reformulated and reconceptualized in light of changing conditions – this book speculates about what a democratic multiculturalism concerned with social justice and community-building might look like at the end of the twentieth century. We will be sure to provide an update on such a portrait in light of the social changes we experience in the first few years of the twenty-first century. As we understand it, the current debate about the multicultural nature of Western societies encompasses a set of identifiable positions. Influenced by Peter McLaren's (1994b) categorization of multicultural positions, we lay out five types of muticulturalism – number five being what we describe as a critical multiculturalism. Chapters 2–9 proceed to characterize this critical category. Obviously, the categorizations we present are designed heuristically to promote understanding of the issues at hand. In the reality of the lived world such categories rarely appear in the 'purity' implied here, as they blend and blur, undermining any effort to impose theoretical order.

Conservative multiculturalism/monoculturalism

In many ways, conservative multiculturalism or monoculturalism (the belief in the superiority of Western patriarchal culture) at the end of the twentieth century is a form of neo-colonialism – a new embrace of the colonialist tradition of white male supremacy. Though most adherents to this position attempt to protect themselves against accusations of racism, sexism or class bias, they are quick to blame those who fall outside the boundaries of the white, male, middle/upper-middle class for their own problems. Everyone, advocates of a conservative multiculturalism maintain, would be better off if they could be exposed to the glories of Western Civilization. Under this mantle, Manifest Destiny, political and economic imperialism and Christian missions to the heathen have marched. From this colonial mind-set Africans and indigenous peoples have been categorized as lower types of human beings devoid of the rights and privileges of the higher (European) types. In its new monoculturalist manifestation the neo-colonists of whiteness have attacked the liberation movements of the 1960s and their concerns with the ravages of racism, sexism and class bias. In this context monoculturalists have fought what they perceive as multiculturalist attacks on Western identity. Ignoring progressive concerns with social injustice and the suffering of marginalized groups in schools and other social institutions, conservatives have targeted multiculturalism as an enemy from within.

Individuals who accept the neo-colonial way of seeing will often view the children of the non-white and poor as deprived. A wide variety of opinions may exist as to the cause of the deprivation – is it a cultural or a genetic phenomenon? – but within monoculturalist circles most agree that non-whites and the poor are inferior to individuals from the white middle or upper-middle class. The expressions of this inferiority are rarely stated overtly in public, but surface in proclamations about family values and what constitutes excellence. In this context family values and excellence become racial and class codes for justifying the oppression of the marginalized: because they allegedly don't have family values many non-whites and poor people fail to succeed; an excellent school is one that is often predominantly white and middle class. Thus, a central feature of monoculturalism or a conservative multiculturalism involves the effort to assimilate everyone who is capable of assimilation to a white, middle-class standard. Many colonized peoples have seen this assimilationism as a violent effort to destroy the cultures of ethnic groups and render them politically powerless. This ideology of the melting pot never operated smoothly even for non-white people who wanted to melt – no matter how much they tried to assimilate, they were still marginalized on the basis of their colour. At its best this monoculturalist assimilationist impulse has consistently worked to erase the voices of those who on the basis of their race, class, and gender are oppressed (Sleeter and Grant 1994; Taxel 1994; McLaren 1996; Giroux 1997).

In monoculturalist education's deprivation model problems are located within the student – a viewpoint that moves our awareness away from the reality of poverty, sexism and racism and their effects on the educational process. The focus of any cultural inquiry in a monoculturalist model involves exploring the problems caused by social diversity. White supremacy, patriarchy or class elitism do not exist in this construction and, as a result, no need exists for individuals from the dominant culture to examine the production of their own consciousness or the nature of their white, male or class privilege. Males, for example, do not have to consider their complicity in the patriarchal marginalization of women or examine the competitiveness, depersonalization and violence that many times accompany patriarchal domination. Since Western societies are superior to all others, the last thing needed is widespread reform. Thus, the path we need to avoid involves the nurturing of social differences connected to language, worldview, culture or customs. Such differences are divisive, monoculturalists argue, and the only way to build a functional society is through consensus. This consensus model promotes the concept of a 'common culture' that is sanctified in a way that protects it from questions about its political shortcomings and democratic failures. The consensus and harmony implied by the appeal to the common culture is a manifestation of the cultural insulation of members of the dominant culture who do not have to experience the sting of oppression as a regular part of their everyday lives.

As they promote their notion of a common culture, conservative multiculturalists typically ignore the fact that a common culture where all social groups participate equally has never existed in the West. Because race, class and gender groups who fell outside the dominant cultural norm were relegated to a culture of silence, monoculturalists have confused their silence for concurrence with the prevailing norms. Indeed, a manifestation of the monoculturalists' cultural location and access to power involves their ability to define what constitutes the so-called common culture. Who determines who falls inside and outside the boundaries of the common culture? Who delineates the correct interpretation of the history of Western civilization?

Who dictates what is included in the educational curriculum? The mono-culturalists' power to provide answers to these and other questions provides insights into the larger conservative project of redefining what is meant by the terms, democracy, egalitarianism and the common good. Michael Apple (1996) heightens our awareness of the importance of what is happening in this context when he maintains that the conservatives' redefinition of politi-cal common sense is one of the largest public re-education projects of the twentieth century. The success it has achieved has been based on the ability of the monocultural advocates to peddle the common culture argument as a form of common sense that is intimately connected to the way people make meaning and live their everyday lives.

The re-education project which Apple describes is an international effort to rewrite history and re-create public memory in a manner that justifies educational, social and political policies that perpetuate the growing inequality of Western societies. Such policies are grounded on an effort to protect an uninhibited free market economics that is allowed to harm indi-viduals – the non-white and poor in particular – in the name of economic efficiency. Economic policies emanating from the free market model deem any form of government aid to the poor as harmful to the economic health of the larger society. At the same time, however, governments advocating such regressive policies have delegated billions of dollars to the war against Iraq and more than 500 billion dollars to bail out corrupt bankers. Indi-viduals are learning to accept the supreme importance of a market economy, the absurdity of egalitarian programmes, and the necessity of rolling back democracy in the informal curriculum (out-of-school education or cultural pedagogy) as well as the formal curriculum (in-school education) of the monoculturalists. The curriculum has helped right-wing politicians to wrestle power away from liberal and labour coalitions who were much more willing to work with liberationist movements emerging in the 1960s and 1970s. As a result of their victories, conservative multiculturalists have rejected any need to work with such organizations, effectively shutting the marginalized out of any role in the political domain of Western societies (Fiske 1993; Macedo 1994; McLaren 1994a; Sleeter and Grant 1994; Jones 1995; Yudice 1995; Giroux 1997a).

The monoculturalist view of the purpose of schooling, of course, is not new, as American schools of the nineteenth century viewed themselves as agents of the Americanization of deficient immigrant children. Mono-culturalists of the late twentieth century might benefit from the understand-ing that the attempt to teach a monolithic Anglo worldview in the nineteenth century was unsuccessful. Alienated from their parents and uncomfortable in the public schools, immigrant children resisted the monocultural cur-riculum by dropping out en masse – most never completed elementary school. Erasing such knowledge from the public memory, contemporary monoculturalists paint a portrait of depraved blacks and Latinos in need of the civilizing influence of an assimilationist education that is disturbingly similar to the nineteenth-century portrait of dangerous Irish, Jewish and Italian immigrants. Indeed, efforts such as ours to point out the limitations and problematic assumptions of monoculturalism are portrayed by conservatives as a form of racism – a new racism directed against whites and males in particular. Such an argument is possible only if structural and institutional aspects of race, class and gender oppression are ignored. Monoculturalists must dismiss power relations between different groups, their relative access to job opportunities and their relationships to socio-economic gatekeepers; for example, those who hire, promote, admit and punish individuals in workplaces and academic institutions.

In this decontextualized manner monoculturalists continue with renewed vigour their historical attempt to adjust poor and non-white students to an unjust society. Eliciting the complicity of some marginalized students, parents and community members by the argument that assimilation will open doors of economic opportunity, conservative multiculturalists offer a devil's pact where marginalized students sign over their cultural heritage for a chance at socio-economic mobility. Education in this conception has nothing to do with civic responsibility and social justice, as those who challenge unequal opportunity are labelled unpatriotic whiners and complainers. As a group that speaks often of its fear that pluralistic and critical forms of multiculturalism are divisive, are tearing apart the social fabric, it is ironic that monoculturalists employ the binary opposition of 'we' and 'they' so often. In the dualistic monocultural universe 'we' are the good citizens, the virtuous, the civic-minded, homogeneous individuals who must defend the Euro-fortress against a group of heterogeneous 'others'. 'They' are shiftless and inferior burdens to society who once may have been victims of discrimination but are no longer (Franklin and Heath 1992; McLaren 1994b; Allison 1995; Gresson 1995; Apple 1996; Giroux and Searles 1996).

The charge of divisiveness against pluralist and critical multiculturalism drew blood in the late 1980s and early 1990s, as monoculturalists such as Diane Ravitch and Arthur Schlesinger Jr implicitly accepted the deficiency model and publicly called for assimilation into the common culture. Tacit in the assimilationist argument is the tenet that before the advent of multiculturalism schools and universities were spaces where objective teachers and scholars uninterested in the political affairs of the day pursued and produced truth. These disinterested institutions, as the monoculturalists frame the story, were undermined by radical multiculturalists who in their politically correct orthodoxy attempted to destroy what Western scholars had worked so hard to build. Never mentioned in this construction is the racism, class bias, gender bias, anti-Semitism and other exclusionary practices that marked the mythical glory days of schools and universities. Rarely referenced are the demeaning textbook portrayals of non-whites that were routinely and uncritically taught to students. Non-whites and women who reject the assimilationist, deficiency, common cultural model of the monoculturalists are portrayed as unreasonable separatists, ethnocentrics and sometimes even as the new racists.

A central feature of the monoculturalist construction of the traditional consensus in Western societies involves fanning the white fear of non-whites. As blacks learn about racism and the historical injustice perpetrated against them in divisive multiculturalist classrooms, they will become so enraged that they will begin to attack white people indiscriminately. Such an argument could gain credence and plausibility only in a society where people of African descent were viewed as naturally violent. It is in this history of fear that the charge of racial separatism gains its meaning and symbolic power in the public conversation about multiculturalism. Any programme or curriculum that induces people of African descent to group themselves together in opposition to white policies must be squashed in the name of 'our' mutual safety as white people. Such fear does not allow many whites to understand separation as a manifestation of resistance to an increasing disparity of the distribution of resources and new forms of white racism towards non-whites in the past 25 years. From our perspective the amazing aspect of racial relations in late twentieth-century Western societies is the degree to which blacks, Latinos, Asians and indigenous peoples have not chosen separatist routes. Above all, the monoculturalists refuse to acknowledge that the best way to bring about social unity (and we're not so sure such unity is always desirable) in the West is not through the squelching of minority, feminine and poor people's voices but is instead through the exposure and eradication of various forms of racism, sexism and class bias found within the culture (Frankenberg 1993; Macedo 1994; Sleeter and Grant 1994; Taxel 1994).

Thus, we argue throughout this book that the monoculturalist position can be understood in terms of power relations. Indeed, monoculturalism in the form that it has taken over the past two or three decades of the twentieth century exists as a reaction to the growing clout of non-whites and women in education and other institutions as a result of the Civil Rights movement and the women's movement. After the 1960s white patriarchal power could no longer silence those who fell outside its boundaries as effectively as it once had. Thus, the disuniting impulse so often referenced by monoculturalists is not a result of the hate-generating work of critical multiculturalists but simply an understandable emergence of previously silenced cultural voices speaking out against the exclusionary practices of the dominant culture. The critical multiculturalist objective of understanding race, class and gender power relations in the larger quest for social justice is not, as Arthur Schlesinger Jr puts it, an activity that feeds prejudices and intensifies antagonisms. One can portray the movement for egalitarianism, a democratic notion of excellence and social justice as a form of hate mongering, only if one is attempting to protect the privilege of a powerful group. Whenever cultural hegemony is threatened, dominant groups tend to respond in highly defensive and protective ways.

In the context provided by an understanding of this defence of dominant power, it is much easier to make sense of how monoculturalists have represented the racial dynamics of Western societies. Monoculturalists have been quite successful in their efforts to portray critical multiculturalists as the bad guys – authoritarian, anti-democratic, ideologues who want to impose an extremist agenda on Western societies. Such representations show up frequently in higher education in respect of those who have championed women's and various forms of ethnic and labour studies. Advocates of black studies, for example, have for almost three decades faced charges that they are purveyors of prejudice and bigotry who want to indoctrinate students with half-truths and unadulterated lies about the history of Africa and the African diaspora. Black studies has faced charges of contaminating the scholarship of higher education, in the process destroying the standards we (whites) had worked so hard to establish. Such accusations refuse to acknowledge the high quality, innovative scholarship that has emerged in black studies, chicano studies and indigenous studies departments. In the initial pages of Allan Bloom's monoculturalist *The Closing of the American Mind*, the author describes the development of a black studies programme at Cornell as if Western civilization had just been overrun by the Vandals. His work is typical of monoculturalist mourning over the multiculturalist barbarians sacking the gates of white male canonical privilege (Baker 1993; Perry and Fraser 1993; Macedo 1994; Taxel 1994).

The power dynamic implicit in the monoculturalist attack also involves who has the clout to shape the cultural imagination of the West. Critical multiculturalism has made it clear that it wants Western people to see their culture from the perspectives of a variety of groups who live both inside and outside its traditional boundaries. What does Western culture look like from the East; from Africa; from the perspectives of peoples of African descent living inside its borders; from indigenous peoples; from the poor? Questions concerning the cultural imagination cannot be separated from the cultural signifiers that inscribe popular cultural expression. The academic tradition in which we operate, critical pedagogy, is fervently concerned with questions of cultural pedagogy. Cultural pedagogy refers to the idea that education takes place and consciousness is constructed in a variety of social sites, including but not limited to schooling. Our work as cultural and educational scholars, we believe, demands that we examine both school and the cultural pedagogy that takes place outside of school if we are to make sense of race, class and gender and their relation to the socio-educational process at the end of the twentieth century. We will expand this discussion of cultural pedagogy in Chapter 2 as we begin a detailed analysis of critical multiculturalism.

In the context of monoculturalism it is important to note how important cultural pedagogy has become in the promotion of both conservative world views and understandings of self *vis-à-vis* other. Our delineation of a critical multiculturalism is extremely interested in uncovering the pedagogical dynamics of television shows, movies, video games, popular music etc. Not only, for example, did *Amos 'n' Andy* reflect popular views of African Americans, it also helped construct popular perspectives. Looking back we can see that in a 1950s sitcom such as *Amos 'n' Andy* or *The Jack Benny Show* the social world was depicted from a white perspective. Many white viewers experienced comforting reassurance in the reminders of black subservience and white supremacy included in the programmes. While such racial ideologies may be relatively easy to discern in popular cultural productions of a half century ago, viewers may encounter more difficulty reading the racial pedagogies in contemporary productions (Fiske 1993; Gray 1995; Grossberg 1995).

Since monoculturalists initiated their defence of Western traditions and white patriarchy, a variety of popular cultural products have appeared that implicitly or explicitly take up the cause of conservative multiculturalism. We can see this project in movies such as Jim Carrey's 1995 follow-up to his *Ace Ventura* film – *Ace Ventura: When Nature Calls*. Few observers even winced when Carrey portrayed Africans in a manner more primitive than in any 1930s Tarzan movie. Ace Ventura's Africans are superstitious, fat, grotesque objects of ridicule who take part in comical religious rituals. In pursuit of comedy, Carrey casually 'deflowers' the young African princess in a manner reminiscent of slavemaster forebears who had their way with their slave women. None of this seems to be problematic to American viewing audiences, who made it a giant revenue producer for Hollywood. As with *Amos 'n' Andy*, white audiences were comfortably reassured by the reminders of black subservience and white supremacy inscribed in the movie. Aaron Gresson (1996) insightfully describes such popular cultural productions as part of a larger 'call back to whiteness' or 'recovery of white supremacy'. Gresson's call back and recovery are inseparable from what we have referred to as the monoculturalist defence of Western cultures.

Using the movie *Forrest Gump* as a popular cultural manifestation of the rhetoric of the recovery of white supremacy, Gresson convincingly delineates the various racialized moments of the film, including: Gump's first human encounter taking place with a black woman wearing white shoes; the revelation that Gump is the namesake of Ku Klux Klan founder Nathan Bedford

Forrest; the depiction of Gump's black friend Bubba's female ancestors as a litany of dark-skinned Aunt Jemimas; the comedic use of Bubba's big lips, a central feature of traditional white caricatures of blacks. Under Gresson's critical eye *Forrest Gump* cannot claim to be race-free, a simple story of virtuous truths that induce individuals to aspire to greater moral heights – there is too much racial inscription to make such a claim.

The movie is also consistent with the monoculturalist effort to revise positive views of the Civil Rights, anti-war and women's movements of the 1960s and early 1970s. Forrest, the movie makes clear, may be slow but he definitely understands right and wrong. Thus, he is able to provide moral insight to the past forty years of American history as a supporter of the mainstream white male view of the 'kooky liberationist movements' that rocked the era. His true love, Jenny, takes the opposite tack, joining student protests against the war, racism, sexism and conventional middle-class behaviour. The point of the morality tale is obvious: Forrest shines as a sports star and becomes a wealthy businessman; Jenny is abused by her Berkeley protester boyfriend, becomes a prostitute and contracts AIDS. The political message is loud enough, but many fail to acknowledge its ideological dynamic even after it is spelled out for them. Cultural pedagogy accomplishes its work in complex and sometimes insidious ways. We will have more to say about monoculturalism or conservative multiculturalism throughout the book.

Liberal multiculturalism

The liberal version of multiculturalism believes that individuals from diverse race, class and gender groups share a natural equality and a common humanity. An intellectual sameness exists that allows different people to compete equally for resources in a capitalist economy (McLaren 1994b). Liberal multiculturalists often express this concern with sameness by way of the cliché: we are 'dedicated to working toward a world where there is only one race – the human race' (Franklin and Heath 1992: 2–3). This concern with sameness has led liberal multiculturalists to embrace the axiom of colour blindness in the pursuit of their race-related educational and socio-political goals. Liberal notions of feminism maintain that a woman is equal to a man in that she can do most anything he can do. When all is washed away, they believe that people's common humanity will illustrate that men and women and various races and ethnicities share more commonalities than differences. The reason for the inequality of position that exists across these groups involves the lack of social and educational opportunities to compete equally in the economy – not differences characterized by conservatives as deficiencies.

We see liberal notions of multiculturalism in a variety of places: schools, universities, workplaces, labour unions, the political sphere and popular culture. In the late 1950s, for example, when NBC produced *The Nat King Cole Show*, a liberal notion of multiculturalism moved this programme's presentation of blackness away from its more conservative portrayal of black subservience and comedic inferiority in *Amos 'n' Andy* and *The Jack Benny Show*. Cole was deemed to hold universal appeal as an entertainer and, as such an individual, he was racially 'sanitized' and distanced as much as possible from his own blackness. TV shows of the 1990s have for the most part remained within this liberal colour blindness/ideology of racial sameness motif. Indeed, black characters' acceptability has often been inversely related to their separation from everyday black life. Thus, in this cultural pedagogy of liberal multiculturalism, colour blindness was used to make blacks acceptable by portraying them as culturally invisible. *Amen, Homeroom, Snoops, Family Matters, True Colors* and other recent black TV shows depict safe representations of black middle-class family life in the USA, rarely presenting African American ways of seeing as different or challenging perspectives on the American social world. Characters in these shows are just regular people like all the rest of us, who rarely are affected by the fact that they are non-white. The problems they encounter are individual problems, not social or structural difficulties that involve questions of power (Gray 1995; Haymes 1995).

Such liberal ideological dynamics are grounded on an allegedly neutral and universal process of consciousness construction that is unaffected by racial, class and gender differences. These dynamics of difference are erased by the ideological appeal of consensus and similarity. Our critical critique of liberal multiculturalism is not meant to imply that we do not see connections between human beings that exist across lines of race, class, gender and other cultural features. Our worry is that an exclusive concern with similarity will undermine the democratic and justice-centred attempt to understand the ways that race, class and gender mediate and structure experiences for both the privileged and the oppressed. *The Cosby Show* offers an insightful example of a liberal cultural pedagogical repression of the ways race mediates and structures experience in pursuit of the larger goals of similarity and unity. Cosby erased the issues that concern/plague/oppress many African Americans in an effort to teach a warm and fuzzy, feel-good lesson on multicultural unity and racial accord. Even the basic idea that our racialized position shapes the way we see the world was out of bounds for *The Cosby Show* – the liberal producers were just not interested in presenting different (not to mention subjugated) ways of perceiving the culture. Thus, the unexamined sameness of liberal multiculturalism allows educators and cultural producers to speak the language of diversity but to normalize Eurocentric culture as the tacit norm everyone references. Like the conservatives, the liberal multicultural curriculum still assimilates to white male standards.

Liberal multiculturalism when all is said and done still positions multi-culturalism as a problem that must be solved. Yet at the same time it has been reluctant to address racism, sexism and class bias or to engage in a critical analysis of power asymmetries. Speaking a language of democracy and ethics but failing to ground such issues on the recognition that power is distributed unequally, liberal multiculturalism often neglects to focus on forces that undermine democratic goals. In the same way, liberal social analysts and educators fail to understand that power wielders – especially from the corporate world – have gained unprecedented access to the construction of individual consciousness and identity. At the end of the twentieth century, ideological and dominant cultural discursive power holds an exaggerated impact on the production of subjectivity. By ignoring the webs of power in which race, class and gender operate, liberal multiculturalism ends up touting a human relations curriculum that conflates white racism toward blacks with black racism toward whites. Such a stance fails to account for racial power relations that make white racism far more consequential than black racism. In late twentieth-century Western societies whites control far more resources and job hiring and promoting prerogatives than blacks. It makes little difference if blacks hate whites in this context – but when whites hate blacks, they can refuse to hire them or promote them (Giroux 1988, 1997a; Carlson 1991; Gergen 1991; Perry and Fraser 1993; McLaren 1994a; Alcoff 1995; Gray 1995).

Liberal political naiveté emanates from the modernist Cartesian-Newton-ian belief that social and educational analysis can be abstracted from every-day power relations. For example, Daniel Liston and Kenneth Zeichner in the name of critical pedagogy argue that the distinction between the teacher as educator and the teacher as political activist must be maintained. In the classroom, they argue, the teacher is first and foremost an educator. In the everyday common-sense conversation this is a persuasive argument, imply-ing as it does that teachers should not use the classroom to 'shove' their political opinions down their students' throats. Of course, Liston and Zeich-ner maintain that the world outside the classroom is the venue for political crusading. But like other liberal educators, Liston and Zeichner miss an important point: the attempt to separate education and politics is not so simple. How is a teacher to choose a textbook or how is he or she to decide what knowledge to teach? These are obvious political decisions that must be made on a daily basis in the classroom.

Liston and Zeichner call for educators to help students find their voices and identities, but voices and identities are constructed by incorporating and rejecting a multiplicity of competing ideological constructions. Which ones do teachers encourage? Which ones do they discourage? These are political decisions. Liston and Zeichner contend that teachers should enable students to acquire and critically examine moral beliefs. This must take place before students engage in politically transformative acts. Like weathervanes, such arguments play well to the popular winds with their glorification of neutrality. Political animals who believe that presidents appoint Supreme Court justices who are neutral, who will refrain from letting their political opinions 'taint' their judicial rulings, will accept the separation of moral belief from political action. Such a separation reflects a hyper-rationalization of politics that represents the political as a very narrow terrain which never overlaps the moral and ethical (Liston and Zeichner 1988). How can the moral and the political be separated? Wasn't the moral commitment to justice the basis of the political work of a Mohandas Gandhi or a Martin Luther King Jr, or a Susan B. Anthony?

As liberal multiculturalism engages in this pseudo-depoliticization, it allows itself to be co-opted for hegemonic objectives. The attempt of multicultural educators to understand and appreciate other societies can be used as a tool for the economic conquest of those societies. Godfrey Franklin and Inez Heath's words provide chilly insights into power's co-option of multicultural education:

Those who are resolved towards making multicultural education a political issue, are doing a great disservice to our nation in maintaining our place as a world leader. The military has led in this effort after its rude awakening during World War I. Never was this more evident than during the Vietnam War. Educators who are working in various levels and setting in public schools, realize the need for competent policy makers who have a well developed knowledge base in multiculturalism as it pertains to the schools for which the curriculum is being developed, and from which our future leaders will come.

(Franklin and Heath 1992: 3)

Such an attempt to depoliticize is obviously a smoke screen for a more acceptable political agenda – more acceptable to the powers that be. Such ideological camouflage can take place only in a social or educational venue where questions of democracy combined with race, class and gender are viewed in isolation from history. Such a decontextualized perspective insists that multicultural educators can bring about an unspecified positive change without either clarifying the nature of the change or understanding the historical, social and epistemological dimensions of all educational metamorphosis. Viewing liberal multicultural programmes and cultural production, one is struck by the fact that oppression and inequality are virtually invisible, that the assimilationist goal is unchallenged. When oppression, inequality and questions concerning assimilation present themselves, they seem to function at the level of individual circumstances – not as larger social issues. Returning briefly to *The Cosby Show* as an example of liberal multicultural cultural pedagogy, producers were stubbornly resistant to any mention of the socio-economic injustice faced by literally millions of African Americans.

These depoliticization/decontextualization impulses of liberal multi-culturalism can be understood only when we trace the modernist umbilical cord that connects it to the European Enlightenment, the Age of Reason. Liberalism has made a fetish of proper process, thus abstracting the lived worlds of individuals and the consequences of particular results from the realm of the political. Complex relations of power and human suffering get lost amidst the celebration of individualism and citizenship. As it focuses on the abstract concept of the fairness of the rules that govern a society, it emphasizes an education for rationality removed from time, place or the experience of individuals. In other words, as liberalism hyperrationalizes process, it disregards the social traditions that individuals and groups bring to schools, community organizations or labour unions. Liberalism's modernist faith that reason and reason alone will lead to a just society, Dennis Carlson (1991) carefully argues, squashes its attempt to connect itself with particular political movements and the ways individuals have framed their personal relationships to these movements. Such relationships have relied little on abstract principles and more on our emotional loyalties. Liberals have assumed that such emotional ties, related as they are to the highly subjective nature of consciousness, are not worthy investments. Thus, to liberals, the modes of thinking that emerge from our subjective lived experience, from the perspectives we gain from one particular position in the web of reality or from the values we develop through experience are too contingent, too tainted by feeling.

The failures of liberalism in general and liberal multiculturalism in particular involve liberal analysts' inability to identify the underside of its relationship to modernist hyperrationality. Indeed, the cult of the expert has grown in a liberal soil. Social engineering finds some of its most important historical roots in university departments of sociology, with their liberal visions of the good life. In the past thirty years this liberal vision has fallen into disrepute around the world. The brief challenge to professional authority of the late 1960s was as much anti-liberal as it was anti-conservative. One of the keys to understanding the success of right-wing movements of the 1970s, 1980s and 1990s was the right-wing co-option of the anti-authority rhetoric of the 1960s counterculture, translating it into the anti-government rhetoric of Reagan, Bush, Gingrich, Thatcher and Major and the anti-educational expert rhetoric of William Bennett and Keith Joseph. They were able to portray the domain of the expert as a liberal domain. If critical multi-culturalism is to be successful in its effort to challenge the various manifestations of white supremacy, class elitism and patriarchy, it will have to expose liberal multiculturalism's rationalistic blindness to the plethora of ways the non-white, the poor and women are dominated in contemporary

Western culture (Bourricaud 1979; Van den Berg and Nicholson 1987; Tripp 1988; Gray 1995).

Pluralist multiculturalism

More than any other of our forms of multiculturalism, pluralist multiculturalism has become the mainstream articulation of multiculturalism. When analysts speak of 'multiculturalism' and 'multicultural education' (with important exceptions), pluralist multiculturalism is often what they have in mind. While pluralist multiculturalism shares many features with liberal multiculturalism, the most significant difference between the two typologies involves pluralism's focus on difference as opposed to liberalism's focus on sameness. Still, however, the distinction between the two articulations is not as great as this opposition might imply; both forms still operate at times as forms of regulation, both tend to socio-cultural decontextualization of questions of race and gender, and both fail to problematize whiteness and the Eurocentric norm. Reflecting in the minds of many the evolution of multiculturalism, pluralism typically links race, gender, language, culture, disability and to a lesser degree sexual preference in the larger effort to celebrate human diversity and equal opportunity. In this context there is less emphasis on assimilation – although the relationship between pluralism and assimilation is ever fuzzy – as race and gender differences are explicitly recognized.

As race and gender differences are highlighted, pluralist multiculturalists operate on the assumption that such an emphasis does not disrupt the dominant Western narratives. In the context of the identity politics that have arisen in Western societies since the liberation movements of the 1960s, advocates of pluralism argue that democracy involves not merely the concern with the rights of all citizens but the history and culture of traditionally marginalized groups as well. Pluralism in such a construction becomes a supreme social virtue, especially in a postmodern landscape where globalization and fast and dynamically flexible (post-Fordist) capitalism are perceived as pushing the international community towards a uniform, one-world culture. Diversity becomes intrinsically valuable and is pursued for its own sake to the point that difference is exoticized and fetishized. The curriculum emerging from this position insists that in addition to teaching students that they should not hold prejudices against others, diversity education means learning about the knowledge, values, beliefs and patterns of behaviour that demarcate various groups. In the pluralist curriculum students read literature written by women, Jews, blacks, Latinos and indigenous peoples in addition to the traditional canon. Students also learn that social unfairness exists, as women, for example, who don't follow socially dominant sex roles are deemed to be too aggressive or man-like, or men who don't adopt macho ways of being are seen as wimps.

Pluralist multiculturalism in the name of diversity calls for students and other individuals to develop what might be called a 'multicultural literacy'. Such a literacy would allow men and women from mainstream, dominant culture the ability to operate successfully in subcultures and culturally differ-ent situations. At the same time, students from culturally different back-grounds would learn to operate in the mainstream culture – an ability, pluralist multiculturalists argue, that is essential in their effort to gain equal economic and educational opportunity. Another pluralist step in this attempt to help women and minority groups to gain equal opportunity involves building pride in one's heritage and cultural differences. Many teachers who operate in this multicultural context begin lessons with class-room discussions of where the families of students came from and which particular traditions they have maintained. In this context teachers help students to make recipe books with family dishes from different cultures or to construct coats of arms that highlight positive features about themselves and their families. Lessons are also designed around the study of particular groups – women, blacks, Latinos, indigenous peoples, Asians, etc. – and often focus on a litany of people from a specific group who have attained success and notoriety in one way or another. Slipping into the fallacy of socio-political decontextualization, pluralists often imply in such lessons that anyone can 'make it' by working hard. Pride in one's heritage, unfortu-nately, is not a panacea for the effects of years of oppression. In this way pluralist multiculturalism promises an emancipation that it can't deliver, as it confuses psychological affirmation with political empowerment (Collins and Sandell 1992; Sleeter 1993; Sleeter and Grant 1994; Gray 1995; Yudice 1995).

From a critical multicultural perspective this 'psychologization' process, this tendency for depoliticization, haunts pluralist multiculturalism. The spectre in question has absorbed such a generous dose of moral relativism that politically grounded action for social justice is subverted before it can begin. In this situation pluralist multiculturalism degenerates into an aca-demic position that may elicit intellectual respectability but leaves the unequal status quo intact. One important dynamic at work in this process involves the position's reluctance (as is the case with liberal multicultural-ism) to address socio-economic class. Indeed, pluralist multiculturalism has gained influence at the same time that poverty has been feminized, material circumstances for many blacks from the lower and lower-middle class have alarmingly deteriorated and the economic disparity between rich and poor has intensified. As these tragedies have occurred, pluralist multiculturalism has helped to generate the impression of upward mobility for women and non-whites. Inclusive representations of pluralism have increased to the extent that many white men (as we will discuss in Chapter 8) feel that they are now the victims of racial and gender discrimination.

The pluralist valorization of difference in combination with global capitalism's commodification of multicultural exotica works to increase the visibility of non-whites. 'Be like Mike', 'Shaq attacks', the modelling of Iman and Naomi Campbell, 'Oprah at Five', 'Wesley Snipes starring in Passenger 57', etc. have elicited unanticipated reactions from dominant cultural audiences. In this social configuration a new 'multicultural logic' is emerging where greater parity is being achieved in matters of symbolic representation while greater disparity grows in the distribution of wealth. Once again race and ethnicity are private matters with little connection to the structural dynamics of patriarchy, class elitism or white supremacy. Pluralist multicultural logic fails to see the power-grounded relationships among identity construction, cultural representations and struggles over resources. Only when this linkage is accomplished will schools and universities be able to transcend their historical role as the rationalizers for the behaviour of the privileged and the concealers of the ways hegemony operates to shape how the social order evolves (Collins and Sandell 1992; Yudice 1995).

Pluralist multiculturalism engages in its celebration of differences when the most important issues to those who fall outside the white, male and middle class norm often involve powerlessness, violence and poverty. Pluralism viewed outside of the power relations of the social structure becomes a vacuous exercise that fails to explore what difference issues of difference make in various individuals' lives. Issues of cultural diversity are reduced to points of 'cultural enrichment' that can be extolled without upsetting the power of dominant groups. TV shows such as *The Jeffersons, What's Happening!!, Sanford and Son* and *That's My Mama* embody a pluralist pedagogy in that they specifically delineate race (in these cases, blackness) as an important feature of US society. But as is typically the case in pluralist pedagogy, the social and historical contexts in which racial identity is expressed and made meaningful are avoided. More recent programmes, such as *A Different World*, have addressed important contemporary issues facing black people, but operating in a pluralist multicultural cosmos such shows failed to depict socio-economic and political inequality as anything more than a product of misunderstanding. In the case of *A Different World*, the show transcended pluralist boundaries only when it addressed gender issues such as sexual harassment, violence against women and the tragedy of AIDS.

Pluralist multicultural curricula, both institutional and cultural, have found it very difficult to escape the discursive boundaries of economic mobility, middle-class affluence, family values and, in the case of the USA, America as a nation of immigrants bound together by a common struggle of adversity and ultimate personal victory. In this pluralist racial context a neo-separate-but-equal dynamic develops that views blacks, Latinos, Asians and other racial/ethnic groups as operating in parallel universes to white people, with Western middle-class values intact. As in liberal multiculturalism, all groups are ideologically alike, except that in pluralist multiculturalism non-whites have a few unique and exotic customs and habits developed in their separate-but-equal experiences. In this post-colonial context – the era following the revolts of the various subjugated groups – pluralist multiculturalism like its liberal cousin can be hegemonically appropriated. Without a critical foundation pluralism's desire to understand the culturally different can help Westerners stay 'on top of things' – to understand the West Africans, for example, so 'we' can open new McDonald's franchises in Gambia.

The hidden hegemonic curriculum of pluralist multiculturalism involves the promotion of a form of cultural tourism that fails to address or understand the harsh realities of race, class and gender subjugation. Having worked on Indian reservations/reserves in both the USA and Canada, we have often witnessed this way of seeing by individuals from the dominant culture. It was not uncommon for white visitors to come to the reservation excited to see authentic Native American culture. After returning from sightseeing ventures, such visitors would be glum and disappointed, confiding that the Indian community they visited was littered with ramshackle houses and old cars on blocks in front yards. We didn't see any real Indian culture, they concluded. Such tourists, whether on the reservation or in the classroom, are unprepared to deal with contemporary problems resulting from racism, class bias and sexism. As they honour cultural difference outside of a historical, power-literate context, they trivialize the lived realities of exotic others and relegate them to a netherland of political isolation. A multiculturalism that operates within these pluralist boundaries will always serve the status quo as an unthreatening construction that consumes the cuisine, art, architecture and fashion of various subcultures. In many ways pluralist multiculturalism castrates difference, transforming it into a safe diversity.

Such a safe diversity still focuses on 'them', representing Africans, as does Disneyland's *It's a Small World After All*, in terms of loin cloths, tree swinging and wild animals. This ethnicity paradigm induces 'us' to understand how 'they' celebrate their holidays – 'Hanukkah, class, is the Jewish Christmas' – never problematizing the Eurocentric gaze. Such a multiculturalism consistently mistakes European ways of seeing for universal, neutral and objective methods of exploring reality. Such methods insidiously support the status quo, conveying in the process the deficiency of non-Western ways of producing knowledge. Make no mistake, the concept of difference is valorized in this context, but always from the position of whiteness. Whiteness as the unchallenged norm constitutes a neo-colonialism (a new improved postmodern colonialism) that constructs non-whiteness as lesser, deviant and pathological – but concurrently more interesting, more exotic, more natural and, therefore, more commodifiable than the 'white bread' norm.

These ostensibly contradictory dynamics of pluralist multiculturalism have precipitated cognitive dissonance among Westerners from various backgrounds. Yet, despite the contradictions, pluralist multiculturalism has emerged as a form of common sense that is believed to work in the best interests of the common good (Collins and Sandell 1992; Frankenberg 1993; Sleeter 1993; Gray 1995; Yudice 1995).

Left-essentialist multiculturalism

Essentialism is a complex concept that is commonly understood as the belief that a set of unchanging properties (essences) delineates the construction of a particular category. Of course, our concern here is to analyse essentialism as it relates to the articulation of multiculturalism. While we are critical of various aspects of what we label a left-essentialist multiculturalism, our purpose is not to expose vile examples of essentialism. Rather, we are more concerned with what happens when essentialism intersects with multiculturalism, and what we might learn from analysing the interaction. Our position is that a false binarism has been constructed between essentialism and social constructivism. We argue neither that (from a radical constructivist perspective) the use of race or gender as a category violently subverts the differences within such aggregations nor that (from a rigid essentialist perspective) race and gender are unchanging hereditary and biological categories. One additional caveat before we begin our analysis of left-essentialist multiculturalism: left-essentialist multiculturalism is not the only form of essentialist cultural politics identifiable on the contemporary landscape. A far more pervasive form involves a conservative, white, fundamentalist Christian variety that has often advocated an intolerant form of monoculturalism. Our focus on the problems of left-essentialism should not obscure this understanding (Fuss 1989; di Leonardo 1994).

Left-essentialist multiculturalism often fails to appreciate the historical situatedness of cultural differences. As we examine the concept of identity in this historical context, we come to understand that while extremely important, race and gender are not necessarily the most rudimentary categories of human experiences. Different historical periods produce diverse categories around which identity may be formed. In the nineteenth century, union membership was such a category, while in the 1960s membership in the 'counterculture' was central to identity formation. The salient point made by critical multiculturalists in this context is that since identity formation is socially constructed, it is constantly shifting in relation to unstable discursive and ideological formations. It is this dynamic that essentialist multiculturalists do not recognize – the poststructuralist notion that signifiers and signs and the material circumstances they help to construct can only be temporarily established.

In this context it will come as no surprise to students of a critical multiculturalism that a racially grounded identity is a recent phenomenon, that the meaning of the concept race has profoundly changed from time to time and place to place. At the end of the twentieth century, the meaning of race remains a highly contested question, as many scholars argue that no theory of race can escape complicity with the ideological and social contexts that helped to formulate it. While critical multiculturalists definitely don't want to relinquish the category of race, they do want to explore the 'border' concept that rejects some simple and static notion of ethnic/racial identity. Understanding the eclectic nature of border cultures, critical scholars fracture concretized racial categories, in the process forcing a more complex analysis of cultural identity. Studying those cultural spaces (borderlands) in an increasingly globalized society where cultures collide, analysts are better equipped to avoid the rigidity of essentialist multiculturalism and to explore the possibilities of new notions of identity formation. While in some ways it is problematic, some scholars have resisted essentialism by using the border concept of mestizaje. Mestizaje focuses on the mutually constructed and constantly evolving nature of all racial identities – unlike the dated concept of the melting pot that attempts to assimilate everyone into a white cultural norm, mestizaje emphasizes the way all cultures change in relation to one another (di Leonardo 1994).

The confrontation with essentialist multiculturalism forces us to examine how group members define themselves and their relationship to their groups. Essentialists tend to define themselves and their relation to their groups around their authenticity as a conservative Christian white American (in a right-wing sense) or individual of African heritage who advocates Afrocentrism (in a left-wing sense); left-essentialist multiculturalists often connect difference to a historical past of cultural authenticity where the essence of a particular identity was developed – an essence that transcends the forces of history, social context and power. Such essences can become quite authoritarian when constructed around a romanticized golden era, nationalistic pride and a positionality of purity that denies complications of competing axes of identity and power such as language, sexual preference, religion, gender, race and class. Such factors invariably create diverse modalities of experience for individuals within any essentialized category. After the Civil Rights movement of the 1960s, for example, black activists called for TV producers to present authentic images of blacks on their programmes. Many spokesmen argued that questions of gender, sexual preference and class simply should not be raised in the effort to present a united front to white people.

This essentialist tendency for romanticization produces a form of moral superiority among group members that sometimes translates into a form of knowledge production that streamlines the complexity of history. In some academic circumstances essentialist multiculturalism merely stands the traditional canon on its head, producing a dominant-culture-is-bad marginalized-culture-is-good inverse dualism. The essentialist search for authenticity in identity and history leads to the privileging of identity as the grounds for political and epistemological authority. Such a grounding inevitably leads to chaos in the group, as the multiple and ambiguous nature of any process of identity formation eventuates in fights over which articulation of identity is the truly authentic one. Before this struggle occurs, critical multiculturalists seek to inoculate themselves against such authoritarianism by opening to question what exactly constitutes a group or an aggregation. At the same time they attempt to maintain a space where a race, class or gender group can discuss multiple articulations of members' identities in relation to a decentred conception of the group itself. In this way romanticized essence is undermined and the authoritarianism that accompanies it is demobilized (Butler 1992; Young 1992; di Leonardo 1994; Gray 1995; Thompson 1995).

In this context Judith Butler (1992) argues that disagreements among women in feminist circles over the content of the term woman should be treasured and encouraged. Such a conversation, she maintains, might even be used as the 'ungrounded ground of feminist theory' (p. 16). Gone here is the official set of essential characteristics that make a group what it is. Herman Gray (1995) shares Butler's insights, and argues from a racial perspective that in his use of the term blackness he makes no claim to an 'authenticity or essence about black life' (p. 13). Black intellectuals in England, including Stuart Hall, Kobena Mercer, Paul Gilroy and Dick Hebdige, pushed inquiries into the nature of difference within the signifier of blackness, opening new vistas to black scholars around the world. In this context we can see *The Cosby Show* from an angle quite different from our previous views of it. In many ways the programme worked as a corrective to the essentialist call for authentic racial portrayals, opening a new terrain on diversity within blackness.

In their valuing of the power of authenticity, essentialist multiculturalists often assume that only authentically oppressed people can possess moral agency. This moral agency or 'oppression privilege' positions subordinated people with a particular set of 'natural' experiences as the only individuals who have the authority to make particular criticisms. In such a setting a white person would not have the moral authority to criticize a Latino or a man would be prohibited from criticizing a woman. In such an essentialized identity politics one would have to submit proper credentials before offering an opinion on a race or gender issue. This politics of location bases truth on identity, privileging an unexamined set of authentic experiences as the foundation of epistemological authority. In this context critical multiculturalists, while understanding the limitations of a politics of location, still appreciate the need for individuals from privileged groups to be sensitive to power differences when interacting with peoples from oppressed groups. For example, a male must be very careful in an interaction with a woman not to invoke his patriarchal privilege and speak down to her or speak *for* her. Operating on the basis of oppression privilege, many essentialist multiculturalist teachers simply transfer an unproblematized body of authentic data along to students, in the process moving perilously close to indoctrination. Critical multiculturalists maintain that merely transferring data from teacher to student is an inappropriate form of teaching in a democratic society, whether it comes from left-essentialist multiculturalists or from right-essentialist monoculturalists. In contemporary Western societies students are far more often subjugated to monocultural indoctrination than from the small group we are labelling left-essentialists. Critical multiculturalists contend that educational activity becomes critical only when students are granted the opportunity both to examine various perspectives and to reflect upon the contradictions they uncover among them.

The narrowness of essentialist multiculturalism is further exemplified by the tendency of its proponents to focus their attention on one form of oppression as elemental, as taking precedence over all other modes of subjugation. Certain radical feminists view gender as the essential form of oppression, certain ethnic-studies scholars privilege race, while orthodox Marxists have focused on class. The critical multiculturalist effort to study various forms of diversity and how the oppression that grows up around each one intersects with the others is viewed by left-essentialists as a diversion from what is most important in cultural analysis. Such a stance undermines the left-essentialist possibility of articulating a democratic vision that makes sense to a broad range of individuals and groups. Instead of struggling to articulate and act on the basis of a democratic politics, the various identity groups that constitute the ranks of essentialist multiculturalism have confronted one another over who can claim greater victimization and oppression privilege.

Thus, essentialist multiculturalism has concerned itself more with self-assertion than with the effort to build strategic democratic alliances for social justice. In making this argument we in no way mean to convey that there is no need for single-group coalitions and single group curriculums such as women's studies, African studies, gay and lesbian studies, chicano studies or indigenous studies. These are extremely important in any formulation of a critical multiculturalism, providing an opportunity for scholarship and teaching long neglected in academia. The salient point in this context involves the ability of single identity groups to promote their interests not in competition but in alliance with other identity groups and broader coalitions working for an inclusive political, cultural and economic democracy. From a critical multicultural perspective such democratic work would involve bringing class-consciousness into all identity-based work. When identity politics operates outside a critical concern with democratic solidarity, the danger arises that it will lapse into a fragmented essentialist group-centredness (di Leonardo 1994; McLaren 1994b; Sleeter and Grant 1994; Yudice 1995; Nieto 1996; Thompson 1996).

Such a group-centredness often induces essentialist multiculturalism to exclude friendly and morally committed outsiders or non-members. Most oppressed groups in Western societies simply do not possess the power to shape political, social and educational policy without help. At the same time, the politics of authenticity allows unsympathetic outsiders to go unchallenged in their anti-democratic or problematic race, sexual preference and gender-related beliefs and activities. Obviously, critical multiculturalism wants to move essentialistic identity groups to a more theoretically viable and pragmatic politics. In many cases, this has happened over the past couple of decades, as many white feminists have worked hard to transform their agendas in the light of what lesbians and non-white feminists have argued about essentialistic delineations of the feminine (Butler 1992; di Leonardo 1994; Yudice 1995). The same is true in other areas of identity, where many racial and ethnic alliances as well as homosexual and disability rights organizations have come to realize that identity alone, especially an essentialized notion of identity, may be insufficient as the grounding for democratic and justice-related movements.

Critical multiculturalism

All typologies reflect the values and assumptions of those who construct them – and ours is no different. Our classification of the forms of multiculturalism was formulated in order to highlight our delineation of critical multiculturalism – the form of multiculturalism we obviously find preferable to conservative, liberal, pluralist and left-essentialist varieties. In this context we will offer a few introductory statements about critical multiculturalism that will set up our detailed description of the position in Chapters 2, 3 and 4. The theoretical tradition that grounds our view of multicultural education comes from the critical theory emerging from the Frankfurt School of Social Research in Germany in the 1920s. Seeing the world from the vantage point of post-First World War Germany, with its economic depression, inflation and unemployment, the critical theorists (Max Horkheimer, Theodor Adorno, Walter Benjamin, Leo Lowenthal and Herbert Marcuse) focused on power and domination within an industrialized, modernist age. Critical theory is especially concerned with how domination takes place, the way human relations are shaped in the workplace, the schools and everyday life. Critical theorists want to promote an individual's consciousness of himself or herself as a social being. An individual who has gained such a consciousness understands how and why his or her political opinions, socio-economic class, role, religious beliefs, gender role and racial self-image are shaped by dominant perspectives.

Critical theory thus promotes self-reflection that results in changes of perspective. Men and women come to know themselves by bringing to consciousness the process by which their viewpoints were formed. Strategies that can be taken to confront individual and social pathologies can be negotiated once self-reflection takes place. Critical theory is quick to point out that such strategies do not take the form of rules and precise regulations. Instead, a framework of principles is developed around which possible actions can be discussed and analysed. Multiculturalists who are conversant with critical theory are never certain of the exact path of action they will take as a result of their analysis. This can be quite frustrating to those raised in the modernist tradition who are accustomed to a specific set of procedures designed to direct their actions. Critical pedagogy is the term used to describe what emerges when critical theory encounters education. Like critical theory in general, critical pedagogy refuses to delineate a specific set of teaching procedures. Critical pedagogies, Peter McLaren (1994a) maintains, confront the modernist/positivist ways of seeing that dominate traditional liberal and conservative critiques of schooling. Moving beyond these analytical forms, critical pedagogy helps students and teachers to understand how schools work by exposing student sorting processes and power involvement with the curriculum.

Advocates of a critical pedagogy of multiculturalism make no pretence of neutrality. Unlike with many theoretical approaches, critical theorists expose their values and openly work to achieve them. Critical multiculturalism, thus, is dedicated to the notion of egalitarianism and the elimination of human suffering. What is the relationship between social inequality and the suffering that accompanies it and the schooling process? The search for an answer to this question shapes the activities of the critical teacher. Working in solidarity with subordinate and marginalized groups, critical multiculturalists attempt to expose the subtle and often hidden educational processes that privilege the already affluent and undermine the efforts of the poor. When Western schooling is viewed from this perspective, the naive belief that such education provides consistent socio-economic mobility for working-class and non-white students disintegrates. Indeed, the notion that education simply provides a politically neutral set of skills and an objective body of knowledge also collapses. This appreciation that both cultural pedagogy and schooling don't operate as neutral, ideologically innocent activities is central to a critical theory grounded form of multiculturalism. When this historical critical theoretical base is submitted to an analysis by recent innovations in social theory shaped by feminists, critical race theorists, advocates of cultural studies and postmodern/poststructuralist scholars (a process we will detail in Chapters 2, 3 and 4) the grounding of our notion of how multiculturalism should be changed is revealed.

Changing multiculturalism, we argue, means moving beyond the conservative and liberal assumptions that racial, ethnic and gender groups live in relatively equal status to one another and that the social system is open to anyone who desires and is willing to work for mobility. Even though contemporary economic production in the West is grounded on unequal social divisions of race, class and gender, mainstream forms of multi-culturalism have been uncomfortable using the term oppression – critical multiculturalists are not, as they argue vehemently in the spirit of W. E. B. DuBois, for equality and democracy in the economic sphere of society. As Western cultures have begun to slide towards the hyperreality of post-modernity, with its fast capitalism, global markets and bombardment of electronic information, their ability/willingness to distribute their resources more equitably has substantially diminished. Class inequality is a central concern of our 'changed multiculturalism', although by no means should such an emphasis be taken as a privileging of class as the primary category of oppression. Class is a central concern of a critical multiculturalism as it interacts with race, gender and other axes of power.

Again, unlike other forms of multiculturalism, the critical articulation is concerned with the contextualization of what gives rise to race, class and gender inequalities. We are concerned throughout this book with the ways power has operated historically and contemporaneously to legitimate social categories and divisions. In this context we analyse and encourage further analysis of how in everyday, mundane, lived culture these dynamics of power play themselves out. Our friend Ladi Semali, who is a scholar of media and power, analyses 'innocent' everyday conversations for their revel-ations about the ways tacit racial politics operate. Along with Semali, we understand that it is at this unsuspected level that the power of patriarchy, white supremacy and class elitism accomplish their hurtful work. Critical multiculturalism appreciates both the hidden nature of these operations and the fact that most of the time they go unnoticed even by those who partici-pate in them. The subtlety of this process is at times disconcerting, as the cryptic nature of many forms of racism, sexism and class bias makes it diffi-cult to convince individuals from the dominant culture of their reality. Such subtlety is matched by the nuanced but vital cognizance of the fact that, con-trary to the representations of essentialists, there are as many differences within cultural groups as there are between them (DuBois 1973; Sleeter 1993; Macedo 1994; Yudice 1995; Semali 1997).

Another important theme of critical multiculturalism – also a central theme of our work (Kincheloe and Pinar 1991; Kincheloe 1991, 1993, 1995; Kincheloe and Steinberg 1995; Kincheloe, Steinberg and Gresson 1996; Steinberg and Kincheloe 1997) – involves the way power shapes conscious-ness. Such a process involves the processes by which ideological inscriptions are imprinted on subjectivity, the ways desire is mobilized by power forces for hegemonic outcomes, the means by which discursive powers shape thinking and behaviour through both the presences and absences of differ-ent words and concepts, and the methods by which individuals assert their agency and self-direction in relation to such power plays.

Critical multiculturalists also illustrate how individuals produce, revamp and reproduce meanings in a context constantly shaped and reshaped by power. Such cultural reproduction involves the way power in the multitude of forms it takes helps to construct collective experience in a way that operates in the interests of white supremacy, patriarchy, class elitism and other dominant forces. In this context schools often work in complicity with cultural reproduction, as teachers innocently operate as cultural gatekeepers who transmit dominant values and protect the common culture from the Vandals at the gates of the empire.

Critical multiculturalism draws upon the literature and analytical methods of cultural studies to gain a deeper understanding of how race, class and gender are represented in various social spheres. Not content with merely cataloguing such portrayals, criticalists make the next step of connecting representations with their material effects. Such material effects cannot be separated from issues of resource allocation as they relate to national and multinational capital. In this way the cultural, political and economic are viewed as parts of a larger power-related, hegemonic process that grants analysts insight into how claims to resources are legitimated and the disparity of wealth continues to escalate. In this context it becomes obvious that critical multiculturalism refuses to position the mere establishment of diversity as its final objective; instead, it seeks a diversity that understands the power of difference when it is conceptualized within a larger concern with social justice. Such a concern constitutes the grounding on which all critical multicultural work takes place (Macedo 1994; McLaren 1994a, b; Yudice 1995).

Outside of this emancipatory commitment to social justice and the egalitarian democracy that accompanies it, critical multiculturalism becomes nothing more than another apology for the status quo. As a politically transformative project, critical multiculturalism absolutely must appeal to diverse constituencies who have not traditionally supported movements for social justice. This is why critical multiculturalists are so committed to the development of a pedagogy of whiteness (see Chapter 8) that speaks to the concerns of a major portion of the population – the white working and middle classes – and the anxieties they face as education, employment and a plethora of other social and economic benefits fade from the late twentieth-century neoconservative political landscape (Yudice 1995). This is why class issues are so important to criticalists, who see themselves not merely as academic students of culture but as initiators of social movements. A multiculturalism dedicated to democracy that is unable to lead a social, political and educational transformation undermines the traditional critical notion that there is a moral emptiness to pedagogies that attempt to understand the world without concurrently attempting to change it.

two

CRITICAL MULTICULTURALISM: RETHINKING EDUCATIONAL PURPOSE

While we are excited by the pedagogical and political possibilities offered by critical multiculturalism, we would be duplicitous to argue that the concept is new. Throughout the twentieth century political activists and progressive educators have criticized the ways education and the culture at large privilege whites, males and individuals from the upper economic classes. These power asymmetries have traditionally had their critics and we are merely the latest in this lineage. We hope our analysis will sophisticate and update this critique, as it examines changing cultural and political contexts and their effect on the way power is deployed at the end of the millennium. We unabashedly work in the tradition of John Dewey, W. E. B. DuBois, Paulo Freire, Sylvia Ashton-Warner, Carter Woodson, Jo Anne Pagano, Raymond Williams, Stuart Hall, Sonia Nieto, Lois Weis, Peter McLaren, William Pinar, Henry Giroux, Steve Haymes, Christine Sleeter, Joyce King, Carl Grant, Mike Dyson, Cornel West, Donald Macedo, Mike Apple, Philip Wexler, Ivor Goodson, Deborah Britzman, Norm Denzin and Aaron Gresson. Their criticisms of injustice along the axes of white supremacy, patriarchy, class privilege and heterosexism have inspired our work here.

Critical multiculturalism: pedagogy, social change and justice

A critical multiculturalism concerns itself with issues of justice and social change and their relation to the pedagogical. As defined here, the pedagogical refers to the production of identity – the way we learn to see ourselves in relation to the world. While we will discuss pedagogy in more detail throughout this book, this simple notion of self-formation lays the groundwork for our analysis of race, class and gender and their relationship to questions of democracy, justice and community. How do we come to view race and racial difference? How do those outside our racial or ethnic group view us? How does our race, class and/or gender shape our access to socioeconomic and educational resources? How does our class position influence our personal style, our ways of seeing ourselves in the world? Do we understand how our gender roles position us along with individuals from the other gender? The same gender? And so on. The way we answer such questions influences the way we operate as human beings and as members of a society. In this context critical multiculturalists argue that any education worth its salt should address such issues as central features in its curriculum. The rest of this book is centred on this question: what are some of the central issues that need to be addressed by educators, social workers, politicians, artists, religious leaders, writers, union leaders, tradespeople, business people, city planners and other cultural workers in relation to issues of race, class and gender in a democratic society. Pedagogy in the sense we are employing it refers to learning no matter where it takes place – the school, the media, the street or the world of everyday life. The diverse sites where education, multicultural education in particular, takes place will concern us in every chapter.

Drawing upon the work of Raymond Williams, Henry Giroux (1997a) contends that the most fundamental impulse shaping critical multiculturalism involves the effort to make the pedagogical political; that is, to make 'learning a part of the learner's struggle for social justice. Such a struggle necessitates the attempt on the part of teachers and other cultural workers to take back power from those educational, political and economic groups who have for far too long been able to shape school policy and curriculum in ways that harm students from low status groups. In a critical multicultural school such students and their family members would study both how power shapes their lives and what they can do to resist its oppressive presence. In this context teachers, students, and community members analyse the nature of race, class and gender discrimination and oppression. Lessons might revolve around the infrequently appreciated concept that the decline in acts of discrimination between the late 1960s and the early 1980s (discrimination defined as a conscious, usually individual, act of exclusion and segregation) did little to reduce oppression (a structural dynamic that economically, politically and psychologically immobilizes a group). Oppression in contemporary democratic societies involves political, educational and social arrangements – for example, redlining in real estate, loan policies in banks, the use of standardized tests in education – that construct barriers to the ability of specific racial, ethnic, class, or gender groups to direct their own lives (Young 1992; Swartz 1993; Nieto 1996).

A key theme emerges at this point. Instead of focusing simply on the diverse cultural practices of different ethnic/racial groups as in a pluralist model of multiculturalism, critical multiculturalism focuses on how racism, sexism and class bias are economically, semiotically (pertaining to encoded and symbolic representations of particular groups), politically, educationally and institutionally produced. Aware of this dynamic, critical multicultural teachers become researchers of their students, the ways these cultural forces shape student behaviours and identities and place them in hierarchies of domination. Empowered by such understandings, teachers are able to help students to overcome these social barriers by engaging them in the exploration of different ways of reading the world, methods of resisting oppression and visions of progressive democratic communities. Students in this critical educational programme begin to see the 'self' as a site of political struggle in relation to oppressive and democratic forces. In so doing they gain consciousness of the pedagogical domain – a form of critical consciousness that moves them to a recognition of the forces that shape their identity, the various stages of reflective self-awareness and the strategies that personal empowerment demand.

In order for students to experience such a transformative process, teachers must have already experienced it themselves. Critical multicultural teachers and other cultural workers must understand where they are located in the web of reality – in relation to the various axes of race, class and gender power. Thus, the critical multicultural teacher is a scholar who spends a lifetime studying the pedagogical and its concern with the intersection of power, identity and knowledge. Indeed, such a teacher gains the ability to delineate the ways in which knowledge is produced and transmitted. Appreciating the complexity and subtlety of such a process, critical teachers and cultural workers trace the ways power is 'written' on the mind and body via the colonization of desire and pleasure. For example, Arnold Schwarzenegger movies produce pleasure for young viewers while at the same time constructing their view of masculinity, the role of women, problem-solving, etc. Without the production of pleasure and the engagement with the young viewers' desire, the gender lesson (the pedagogical dynamic) would be irrelevant. Critical teachers thus understand that their professional practice engages themselves, their students and the knowledge derived from the disciplines with the everyday experiences of real people struggling to live loving, just and democratic lives in both private and public domains.

Naming names: the pedagogy of critical multiculturalism

These are the pedagogical dimensions of a critical multiculturalism: racial, class and gender oppressions are implicit in the way knowledge, values and identities are constructed in a variety of social locales. For example, when the only fluorescent blond in Disney's *Hunchback of Notre Dame*, Phebus, wins the love of the dark-skinned gypsy, Ismarelda, the knowledge of Anglo (white) supremacy has again been inscribed at some level in our consciousness. We may react to this inscription in a variety of conscious and/or unconscious ways, but react we will. When tens of thousands of cultural inscriptions are added to this one, we find that power blocs within various race, class, gender, religious and geographic place structures produce diverse individual identities and human communities. In this pedagogical context teachers, students and cultural workers come to the dramatic realization that the knowledge produced in, say, popular culture is not objective – indeed, the fingerprints of power are quite visible. In this sense pedagogy is always engaged on some level with power in the human struggle over the scholarly, emotional and value-related investments people make in the living of our lives. How do we develop our belief structures? How do we adopt the values we employ to ground our romantic lives? What is the role of school in our lives? How do we identify ourselves when relating to other people? These are all pedagogical questions.

Understanding the importance of pedagogy, critical multiculturalism names the power wielders who contribute to the structuring of knowledge, values and identity – a trait, we might add, that makes the position quite unpopular in some circles. The power of white supremacy is an important target of critical multiculturalism, with its phenomenal ability to camouflage itself to the point it can deny its own existence. Whiteness presents itself not only as a cultural force or a norm by which all other cultures are measured, but as a positionality beyond history and culture, a non-ethnic space. Thus, in a culture where whiteness as an ethnicity is erased, critical multiculturalists receive strange looks when they refer to their analyses of white culture. Liberal and pluralist multiculturalists may include non-dominant cultural analyses in their curricula but generally do not examine the cultural dynamics of whiteness. In the same way references to people of colour, but not to white people, as 'ethnics' tacitly imply that ethnicity does not influence the identities and lifestyles of whites. In this way issues of race are seen as having little to do with white people; race concerns non-whites and ethnics and the problems caused by their difference – their difference from white people (Frankenberg 1993; Giroux 1997a).

Thus, critical multiculturalism examines whiteness, its privilege, normativity (its ability to designate itself as the standard) and erasure. It induces white people to rethink their understanding of their own ethnicity and the construction of their consciousness. It asks white people to reformulate whiteness in a critical multicultural context that values justice, egalitarianism and community. At the same time, critical multiculturalists analyse and rethink maleness in the same way they approach whiteness. How are male privilege, normativity and erasure accomplished within education and society? In the critical context the multicultural gender curriculum refuses to study only women's cultural production. Male supremacy/patriarchy, and the ways it subordinates women and renders them passive, creates a male-dominant knowledge base and promotes male ways of seeing as the norm, are central features of the critical gender curriculum. In many ways the critical multicultural socio-economic class curriculum performs the same type of function with upper-middle and upper-class privilege, normativity and erasure. An important feature of critical multiculturalism involves its ability to examine the domains of race and white supremacy, gender and patriarchy, and socio-economic class and upper-middle and upper-class privilege in relation to and as functions of one another (Sleeter 1993; Swartz 1993).

Important strides have been made over the past fifteen years to understand the ways in which race, class and gender interact to shape our education and our lives in general. In the everyday politics and interactions of schools and workplaces, however, such understanding is all too rare. Mainstream conservative, liberal and pluralist multicultural educators have been relatively uninterested in probing the connections that unite the spheres of politics, culture and the economy with education. Without such study multicultural educators and educational leaders view their task as merely addressing prejudicial attitudes towards women and minorities. Social life from these modernist perspectives is seen in fragmented segments – education here being isolated from politics, economics and culture. In this context conservative and liberal analysts see 'unattached individuals' unaffected by their membership in racial, gendered or class collectives or groupings. Critical multiculturalists maintain that such fragmentation distorts our view of how schools and society operate. When conservative and liberal scholars fail to account for power dynamics in schools, workplaces and the socio-economic context that shapes them, specific processes of domination and subordination of students and other individuals cannot be exposed. In the place of such specific exposés the individual behaviour of irrationality prejudiced men and women is embraced as the cause of unfair treatment. While such isolated irrational acts of prejudice certainly occur, they are not responsible for most of the oppression of racial, sexual and economic 'outsiders'. To get to the point where we can explain the particular processes of subordination, educators must understand not only the dynamics of race, class and gender but the ways their intersections in the lived world produce tensions, contradictions and discontinuities in everyday lives (McCarthy and Apple 1988; Amott and Matthaei 1991).

In this context Carol Gilligan (1981) was on the right track in her study of taxonomies of moral reasoning, and the ways they privilege male over female approaches. Subsequent analysis, however, has indicated that gender is just one of the plethora of social categories that shape the ways individuals engage in moral reasoning. When race and class (as well as geographic place,

national origin, religion and other categories) are added to the social caul-
dron, we discover that women from different social locations reason differently. In this circumstance gender analysis is insufficient; we must examine
the way gender interacts with other social categories to get a deeper and
richer picture of moral reasoning (Stack 1994). Such understandings are
important in our effort to understand why different individuals engage with
schooling in divergent ways. Such awareness can help us to distinguish
between being different or being deficient – a distinction that left unmade
can perpetuate forms of institutional racism, sexism and class bias.

Race, class and gender can be understood only in relation to one another

Our position is simple: racial, sexual and class forms of oppression can be
understood only in structural context. This means, for example, that gender
bias plays itself out on the terrain of economic and patriarchal macrostruc-
tures. An economic macrostructure might involve white male domination of
the highest salary brackets in American economic life. A patriarchal
macrostructure might involve the small percentage of upper level corporate
managers who are women or, in a domestic context, the high rate of spousal
abuse perpetrated by American males. Differences in men's and women's
lives in general and economic opportunities in particular revolve around
inequalities of power. For example, African American women, Latinas,
Asian American women and Native American women experience gender as
one aspect of a grander pattern of unequal social relations. Indeed, the way
one experiences race, class and gender is contingent on their intersection
with other hierarchies of inequality – other hierarchies in which the privileges of some individuals grow out of the oppression of others (Amott and
Matthaei 1991; Zinn 1994; Zinn and Dill 1994).

Let us focus for a moment on the ways in which gender intersects with
race and class. Some intersections create privilege. For example, if a woman
marries a man from the upper class, gender and class intersect to create
privileged opportunities for her. On the other hand, however, if a woman is
Haitian-American, forms of racial prejudice will exacerbate the ways in
which she experiences gender bias. Thus, whether it be through subordination or privilege, race, class and gender dynamics affect everyone – not
just those at the bottom of the status hierarchy. The problem is that those at
the top of the race, class and gender hierarchies often do not understand the
ways the intersections of the various axes affect them. The economic divisions of class serve to structure the ways race and gender manifest themselves. Though we understand that connections between race, class and
gender exist, we never know how to predict the effects of the interactions.

Racial and gender hostilities, of course, can subvert class solidarity. Class solidarity can undermine gender-grounded networks. Working-class women, for example, have rarely felt a close affinity to the middle and upper-middle class feminist movement (Amott 1993: 28; Zinn 1994: 309).

As these race, class and gender forces interact, sometimes in complementary and sometimes in contradictory ways, school experience cannot be viewed simply as an uncomplicated reflection of social power. The school experience is exceedingly complex, and while there are general patterns of subjugation that occur, such patterns play out in unpredictable ways with particular individuals. Cameron McCarthy and Michael Apple (1988) maintain that school mediates rather than imposes its power upon students. This means that students from lower socio-economic class backgrounds are not simply classified and relegated to low status classes and ultimately to low status jobs; instead, forces of race, class and gender create a multi-level playing field on which students gain a sense of their options and negotiate their educational and economic possibilities. Race, class and gender dynamics combine to create a larger playing field with more options for some and a smaller, more limited field for others. In these contexts students struggle to make sense of and deal with triple or more divisions of the social gridiron – here they wrestle with fractious social classes, genders and racial and ethnic groups.

As it integrates and connects the study of race, class and gender to the nature of consciousness construction, knowledge production and modes of oppression, critical multiculturalism embraces a social vision that moves beyond the particular concerns of specific social groups. While these concerns are important and must be addressed in a critical pedagogy, we ultimately embrace a democratic politics that emphasizes difference within unity. The unity among different racial, ethnic, class and gendered groups can be constructed around a well delineated notion of social justice and democratic community. Within this critical context the need for separatist, integrationist and pluralist moments are appreciated. Indeed, there is a time for African Americans to study Afrocentrism, women to study feminism and working people to study labour's continuing struggle for economic justice. Concurrently, there is a need for such groups to join together in the mutual struggle for democracy and empowerment. Critical scholars seek a multiculturalism that understands the specific nature of difference but appreciates our mutual embrace of principles of equality and justice. Another way of expressing this mutual embrace of equality and justice involves a commitment to the concept of solidarity (Collins and Sandell 1992; McLaren 1995).

European scholars have long maintained that the foundation of political and ethical thinking has rested on a close-knit community with a common set of precepts. Theologian Sharon Welch (1991) challenges such a perception, arguing from a postmodern perspective that heterogeneous communities with differing principles may better contribute to the cultivation of critical thinking and moral reasoning. A homogeneous community is often unable to criticize the injustice and exclusionary practices that afflict a social system. Criticism and reform of cultural pathology often come from the recognition of difference – from interaction with communities who do not suffer from the same injustices or who have dealt with them in different ways. We always profit in some way from a confrontation with another system of defining that which is important. Consciousness itself is spurred by difference, in that we gain our first awareness of who we are when we learn that we exist independent of another or another's ways.

Welch maintains that the concept of solidarity is more inclusive and transformative than the concept of consensus. Even if we perceive consensus to involve a common recognition of cultural pathology and the belief that we must work together to find a cure, we first have to accept the value of solidarity. Welch claims that solidarity has two main aspects: (a) the ethic of solidarity grants social groups enough respect to listen to their ideas and use them to consider existing social values; and (b) the ethic of solidarity realizes that the lives of individuals in different groups are interconnected to the point that everyone is accountable to everyone else. No assumption of uniformity exists here – just the commitment to work together to bring about mutually beneficial social change. In both schools and workplaces, this valuing of difference and its political and cognitive benefits exhibits itself in a dialogical sharing of perspective. In this process students, teachers and workers come to see their own points of view and the ways they undertake a task as merely one particular way of perceiving or working. As the classroom and the workplace develop, students and workers are exposed to more and more diverse voices, a process that engages them in other ways of seeing. Thus, their circle of understanding is widened as difference expands their social and educational imagination. As travellers have discovered, the attempt to understand the cultural schemata of peoples from other countries often allows for a recognition of belief systems and assumptions in oneself. When students and teachers widen their circles of understanding by exposure to non-Western perspectives, they gain understandings that become extremely valuable in the multicultural world. Such understandings may be on the surface very simple. In an American future, for example, which will be marked by far greater non-Anglo populations, the basic ability for different groups to live and work together in solidarity may be considered a survival skill. The critical multicultural ethic of appreciating and learning from diversity may be essential to the survival of the planet. In the multicultural curriculum of difference, students will learn about cultural differences revolving around perspectives on race, class and gender in light of larger questions of pedagogy, justice and power.

Postmodern dynamic of critical multiculturalism

Critical multiculturalism is inseparable from the paradigmatic analyses that have occurred over the past 25 years in academic circles. Understanding that culture is inseparable from ideology, critical multiculturalism argues that modernist Eurocentrism with its scientific epistemology and one-correct-answer ideology is not the only way to make meaning in the world. In this context we will briefly analyse the nature of Eurocentric modernism as it pertains to the emergence of the postmodern critique, and their relationship to issues of race, class and gender.

What is modernism?

During the European Middle Ages science was grounded on a Thomist–Aristotelian synthesis of faith and reason. The main goal of the synthesis was to understand the nature of natural phenomena. But when the Black Death swept across Europe, killing about one-quarter of the population, many realized that the mediaeval way of seeing was inadequate. Under the pressure of such catastrophic sickness, Western scholars began contemplating a new way of perceiving the natural world – a way that would enable them to understand and control the outside world (Leshan and Margenau 1982; Fosnot 1988; Kincheloe *et al.* 1992).

With the coming of the Scientific Revolution, or the Age of Reason, in the sixteenth and seventeenth centuries, nature was to be controlled, 'bound into service and made a slave' (Capra 1982: 56). The basis of this control was founded on the epistemological separation of knower and known. This bifurcation legitimates the assumption that the human perceiver occupies no space in the known cosmos; existing outside of history, the knower knows the world objectively. Thus, knowers are untainted by the world of opinions, perspectives or values. Operating objectively (without bias), the knower sets out on the neutral mission of science: the application of abstract reasoning to the understanding of the natural environment. Reason told the pioneers of science that complex phenomena of the world can be best understood by reducing them to their constituent parts and then piecing these elements back together according to laws of cause and effect (Mahoney and Lyddon 1988).

All of this took place within Rene Descartes's separation of mind and matter, his *cogito ergo sum*. This view led to a conception of the world as a mechanical system divided into two distinct realms: (a) an internal world of sensation; and (b) an objective world composed of natural phenomena. Building on the Cartesian dualism, scientists argued that laws of physical and social systems could be uncovered objectively by researchers operating in isolation from human perception, with no connection to the act of perceiving. The internal world of mind and the physical world, Descartes theorized, were forever separate and one could never be shown to be a form of the other (Lowe 1982; Lavine 1984; Kincheloe 1991). We understand now, but could not have understood then, that this division of mind and matter had profound and unfortunate consequences. The culture's ability to address problems like the plague undoubtedly improved, as our power to control the 'outside' world advanced. At the same time, however, Western society accomplished very little in the attempt to comprehend our own consciousness, our 'inner experience', the realm of the social and cultural.

Sir Isaac Newton extended Descartes's theories with his description of space and time as absolute regardless of context. Clarifying the concept of cause and effect, Newton established modernism's tenet that the future of any aspect of a system could be predicted with absolute certainty if its condition was understood in precise detail and the appropriate tools of measurement were employed. Thus, the Cartesian–Newtonian concept of scientific modernism was established, with its centralization, concentration, accumulation, efficiency and fragmentation. Bigger became better as the dualistic way of seeing reinforced a rationalistic patriarchal expansionist social and political order welded to the desire for power and conquest. Such a way of seeing served to despiritualize and dehumanize, as it focused attention on concerns other than the sanctity of humanity (Fosnot 1988).

Along with Sir Francis Bacon, who established the supremacy of reason over imagination, Descartes and Newton laid a foundation that allowed science and technology to change the world. Commerce increased, nationalism grew, human labour was measured in terms of productivity, nature was dominated and European civilization gained the power to conquer in a way previously unimagined. The rise of modernist science was closely followed by a decline in the importance of religion and spirituality. An obsession with progress supplied new objectives and values to fill the vacuum left by the loss of religious faith. Even familial ties were severed as the new order shifted its allegiance to the impersonal concerns of commerce, industry and bureaucracy (Bohm and Peat 1987; Aronowitz and Giroux 1991). Rationality was deified, and around the scientific pantheon the credo of modernity was developed: the world is rational (logocentric) and there is only one meaning of the term. All natural phenomena can be painted within the frame of this monolithic rationality whether we are studying gunpowder, engines, dreams or learning.

This modernist view of knowledge, this one-truth epistemology, affected all aspects of Western life, all institutions. Education was no exception. Since knowledge (like a child's conception of pre-Columbian North America) is predefined, waiting to be discovered 'out there', what use is it to teach speculative and interpretive strategies? Schools of the post-Enlightenment era emphasized not the *production* of knowledge but the learning of that which had already been defined as knowledge. Students of modernism's one-truth epistemology are treated like one-trick ponies, rewarded only for short-term retention of certified truths. Teachers learn in their 'educational science' courses that knowledge is acquired in a linear skill or subskill process. Pre-identified in the context of adult logic, the linear process is imposed on children in a manner that focuses teacher/parent attention away from the child's constructions of reality, away from the child's point of view. Thus, children's answers are often 'wrong', when, actually given their point of view, the wrong answer may indicate ingenuity (Brooks 1984). Indeed, a pattern begins to emerge: many of the children who get the wrong answers consistently fall outside the cultural norm of whiteness, maleness and middle- or upper-middle classness.

Even though it may blind us to various aspects of the social world and unfairly punish those who occupy the race, class and gender margins of Western society, this one-truth epistemology of modernism has held and still holds great appeal. Seduced by its claim to neutrality, scientists and educators employ Cartesian–Newtonian epistemology in their quest for the 'higher ground' of unbiased truth. The ideal modernist educator becomes the detached practitioner, an independent operator who rises above the values of 'special interests'. The detached practitioner occupies a secure position immune from critique – he or she has, after all, employed the correct methodology in reaching his or her position. If it is pursued 'correctly', there is no questioning the authority of the scientific method. Thus, the educational status quo is protected from critics, such as John Dewey, Paulo Freire or Maxine Greene, with their 'agenda' and value judgements. Their critiques are not scientific; they are 'mere opinions' (Codd 1984; Harris 1984).

The past 25 years of Western history has witnessed a retrenchment of dominant social groups' commitment to modernism. Reacting to threats of social change, calls for racial, class and gender justice, and the recognition of the failures of modernism, mainstream conservative and liberal educators, social critics and political operatives have sought educational and political solutions within Cartesian–Newtonian boundaries. Various individuals and groups have expressed discomfort with Eurocentric modernism and its 'solutions' to social, political and educational problems. Critical multiculturalists have argued that in its universalization of European male experience as a marker of normality, modernism operates in the defence of racism and sexism. In this context, critical multiculturalists have helped to develop and draw upon the development of a postmodernist critique of Eurocentric modernism.

What is the postmodernist critique?

Postmodern thought subjects to analysis social and education forms previously shielded by the modernist ethos. It admits to the cultural conversation previously forbidden evidence derived from new questions asked by those previously excluded along lines of race, class and gender. Postmodern thinkers challenge hierarchical structures of knowledge and power which promote 'experts' above the 'masses', as they seek new ways of knowing that transcend empirically verified facts and 'reasonable', linear arguments deployed in the quest for certainty (Greene 1988; Hebdige 1989). When postmodernism is grounded on a critical system of meaning that is concerned with questioning knowledge for the purpose of understanding more critically oneself and one's relation to society, naming and then changing social situations that impede the development of egalitarian, democratic communities marked by a commitment to economic and social justice, and contextualizing historically how world views and self-concepts come to be constructed, it becomes a powerful tool for progressive social change.

Please do not confuse what we have just described, postmodernism as critique, with postmodernism as social condition. Though the two are intimately connected, this is the point where many individuals become lost on the postmodern linguistic landscape. Jean-François Lyotard uses postmodernism to refer to the general condition of contemporary Western civilization. The 'grand narratives of legitimization' (i.e. all-encompassing explanations of history like the Enlightenment story of the inevitable victory of European reason and freedom) in the postmodern world are no longer believable. They fail to understand their own construction by social and historical forces. Reason is undermined because of its co-option by those in power who speak with the authority of a science not subjected to introspection, to self-analysis (Giroux 1991). Thus, the postmodern condition has arisen from a world created by modernism; the postmodern critique attempts to take us beyond the nihilism of the modern world, the deadening routine of the traditional school and the assignment of those who are not male or European to a marginalized role in society.

Critical multiculturalism employs the postmodern critique to help to construct a vision of a pedagogy of race, class and gender justice. For example, the analytical methodologies of postmodernism facilitate the critique of language as a reservoir of unexamined cultural and political assumptions. Indo-European languages, for example, confine us to particular ways of thinking. They often fragment experience by devaluing *relationship*. Because of their subject–predicate matrix, these languages induce us to consider the world in terms of linear cause and effect. Trapped in the view of language as a neutral medium of communication, modernist thinkers have found it hard to talk (or think) about subjects such as quantum physics, the nature of consciousness, higher orders of cognition or any other concept without identifiable boundaries, specified beginnings and ends, and a clear delineation of then and now. Postmodern critique attempts to denaturalize the modernist universalization of Indo-European linguistics. Pointing to the fact that events in nature often have simultaneous multiple causes, postmodernists argue that not all human languages have difficulty with non-linearity. Hopi and Chinese, for example, speak 'non-linearly'. Westerners from ancient Greece to modern America say 'the light flashed' even if the light and the flash are inseparable. If we spoke Hopi, we would simply say 'Reh-pi', meaning 'flash' (Ferguson 1980). No linearity, cause or effect is implied. Postmodernism offers an alternative to modernism, a starting place in our attempt to formulate new forms of analysis, of race, class and gender discourse that allow us to see beyond the modernist European gaze.

Critical multiculturalism makes use of the postmodern critique of Eurocentric modernism's tendency to decontextualize and fragment the world to the point that individuals are blinded to certain forms of human experience. Attempting to study the world in isolation, bit by bit, modernist educational scientists have separated education from society. For the purpose of simplifying the process of analysis, disciplines of study are divided arbitrarily, without regard for larger context. Educational reforms of recent years have been formulated outside of the wider cultural and political concerns for empathy. As the politicians mandate test-driven curricula, they create new forms of educational pathology and social injustice that once again punish those outside the mainstream. Thus, in a critical multiculturalism the postmodern critique empowers those marginalized by race, class and gender to take back their histories, epistemologies and ways of making sense of the world. By studying Eurocentric modernism and its virtues and limitations, a postmodern multiculturalism helps the oppressed to understand the ways power operates along the axes of race, class and gender and how they might respond to such power plays. In this way new identities and political strategies can be developed that work to reconstruct social relationships.

Critical multiculturalism: reconceptualizing curricular knowledge

One aspect of these reconstructed social relationships involves the acceptance of a pluralism that acknowledges the existence of many versions of reality. Such a critical postmodern pluralism insists that Western society act upon its knowledge of different cultural ways of seeing by opening to discussion traditional Eurocentric perspectives. Here, public discourse would focus on how specifically Eurocentrism dominates. What have racism, sexism and class-bias wrought? What forms of consciousness have they produced in both perpetrator and victim? What types of knowledge have such forces produced? One doesn't have to look far to notice that curricula existing at the end of the twentieth century don't contain knowledge produced about or by subjugated groups. Their stories have been deleted from the official curriculum for the purpose of maintaining the illusion of white male

Eurocentric and upper-middle and upper class domination. Critical multi-culturalist educators create a new cultural story, indeed a new culture, by resuscitating the histories, stories and cultural narratives of the oppressed so that they can be used to reshape official knowledge. We are not speaking here of the pluralist multiculturalist effort to add this cultural knowledge to the canon. Critical multiculturalism uses such knowledge to challenge the perspectives, the assumptions and the structuring metaphors of the traditional curriculum (Dion-Buffalo and Mohawk 1992; Perry and Fraser 1993; Swartz 1993).

A basic principle of pedagogy maintains that good teaching takes the lives of all students seriously. Critical multiculturalists affirm this principle, maintaining that it requires that they account for the race, class and gender diversity of student populations. In this context educators research and recover student experiences, analysing the process of their construction and the ways they shape identity. Critical multiculturalism insists that teachers learn to engage such experiences in a manner that respects them. In this situation respect does not imply some form of facile validation but a mode of pedagogical intervention that induces students to look beyond their own experiences wherever they might stand in the web of reality. Just because a student is African American or Native American doesn't mean that a critical multicultural teacher will romanticize his or her experiences. Most student experiences are contradictory, ambiguous and complex, and it is the role of the critical teacher to help students, other teachers and community members to understand them in relation to the forces of domination and hegemonic power. As they show students the ways their experiences shape their processing of information and reproduce their schooling, critical teachers also point out the ways that racist, sexist and class-biased curriculum materials may shape their self-image and social consciousness (Banfield 1991; Nieto 1996).

The power of difference

Like left-essentialist multiculturalism, critical multiculturalism values the power and importance of difference. While critical multiculturalism rejects essentialism's view of racial groups as possessing a specific set of romanticized fixed characteristics, the critical position works to make difference visible. In this process it seeks to open to those deemed culturally different a range of identities that allow them to move in and out of different cultural locations. In order to get to this point advocates of a critical multiculturalism must analyse the ways group differences are structured by power relations within the social and historical context. At first glance many individuals from the dominant culture view critical multiculturalism suspiciously because of their unfamiliarity with power relations and the role of power in everyday life. Thus, critical multiculturalism's effort to get beyond liberal or pluralist notions of positive interracial interactions and feel-good human relations may seem strange and hostile to on-lookers from mainstream culture. If democracy and justice do not already exist, then the goals of critical multiculturalism understandably involve participation in a larger struggle for social justice.

Participation in such a struggle would involve exposing the race, class and gender power relations embedded in disciplinary knowledge, the organization of schooling, popular culture and other cultural manifestations. Understanding difference in its social and historical context, critical multiculturalists engage the oppressed in the investigation of how mainstream institutions must be reformed so they can no longer assume the justice of unequal relations of power and privilege. This investigation is a central feature of critical multiculturalism. It can be viewed as a rigorous, innovative effort to contextualize difference historically, socially, economically and culturally. Without such an effort, race, class and gender difference can produce pathological effects, including everything from an 'otherizing the unfamiliar' process, a surrender to assimilation, to an acceptance of an identity politics (e.g. black, white, gay, female, Jewish) that operates outside of the dynamics of democracy and community and ultimately leads to a position of separatism. When critical multiculturalists contextualize and understand difference, such a process can move us beyond these problematic positions, as it reveals historically how race, class and gender make a difference in the lives of individuals and how racism, class bias and sexism have played a central role in shaping Western societies. It is in such a process that students, teachers and individuals from all walks of life begin to monitor the ways the culture shapes their identities and the nature of the social group with which they identify.

In a critical multiculturalism difference is connected to a democratic politics that understands schools as contested public spaces shaped by the forces of power. In this context attention to difference demands that teachers be aware of the specific histories and struggles of oppressed peoples in a variety of arenas. One of these arenas involves the school itself, as many scholars contend that the classroom is a central site for the legitimization of myths, lies and silences about non-white, lower socio-economic class and other marginalized individuals. If multicultural educators were actually to teach the specific histories and struggles of Latinos in America, for example, they would have to rethink the history of Anglos in America. When history books lie about the history of an oppressed group, they concurrently lie about all history – the entire curriculum is distorted by such duplicity. Critical multiculturalists understand these historical and curricular insights and use them to move the recognition of difference into a politically transformative form of education. Such a pedagogy does not accept the inevitability of social privilege and social inequality. Indeed, a pedagogy of critical multiculturalism understands Western societies as collectivities of difference where the potential exists for all men and women to be edified by interaction with the 'other' and the ways of knowing he or she brings to an encounter.

The benefits of a contextualized understanding of difference are multidimensional. In addition to moving beyond the 'difference-is-spice' curriculum theory to the use of difference to reformulate the basic concepts of a discipline, critical multiculturalism uses difference to debunk the myth perpetuated by conservative monoculturalists that Western societies are grounded on a social, political and cultural consensus. If the consensus myth is accepted, then critical multiculturalism can be positioned as a divisive discourse that tears the social fabric apart with charges of injustice. In this context critical multiculturalism is careful to situate different social groups *in relationship to* one another, not *in opposition to*. Contrary to conservative charges, the point is not to pit groups against one another but to emphasize the importance and specific nature of oppressed cultures. Such an emphasis helps to expose the specific nature and commitments of a dominant culture that often hides behind its proclamation of neutrality. Using difference in this way precludes Anglo, European, male and heterosexual culture from representing its norms as beyond history and culture. No longer can dominant culture celebrate its neutrality and universality while condemning the abnormality and deviancy of the marginalized (McCarthy and Apple 1988; Frankenberg 1993; Giroux 1993; McLaren 1993, 1994; Zinn and Dill 1994).

Combining Sharon Welch's notion of solidarity with the benefits of difference, critical multiculturalists work to extend democracy. Respecting the power of difference, critical scholars apply the concept to a variety of social locations. The workplace, unfortunately, is a social venue too often neglected by the interests of democracy. In this context critical multiculturalists reject economic and management theories and procedures where workers are used merely as a means towards the financial gain of management, where manipulation of employees is an unquestioned routine practice. Such an orientation extends solidarity, as it induces teachers, students, workers and other individuals to connect and empathize with each other in a manner that encourages risk taking in the name of social justice. Starting here, critical multiculturalism shapes a critical pedagogy of work that embraces a new economics. Such an approach understands the importance of cultivating human potential in a democratic context informed by the ethics of difference in solidarity. Such an economics would evaluate work and industrial production in terms of their contribution to the cultivation of human potential and the development of human intelligence.

Imagine for a moment what an understanding of a critical multiculturalism can empower teachers, students, workers and other political agents to accomplish in this economic context. Working together in solidarity they can develop a critique of the neo-classical economic theories that have deified the unbridled market and welcomed the return of Adam Smith's invisible hand. Such a critique exposes the free market's failure as the force that shapes the American economy's grand development strategy, guarantees the poor a minimum level of economic security, generates an equitable distribution of income, wealth and economic power, and watches over the deadly consequences of profit-seeking activity in the workplace and the ecosystem. The critical multicultural democratic ideal points to the necessity of the development of an economic policy that always considers profit making in relation to the total social framework. In other words, in a democratic economic system profit does not always take precedence over human needs and development. With a spirit of solidarity among teachers, students and working people, such humane proposals draw upon the diverse experiences of white and non-white peoples, men and women, individuals from middle and upper-middle class backgrounds and those from lower socio-economic class settings (Wirth 1983; Pollin and Cockburn 1991; Chesneaux 1992).

Learning from difference

If difference is more empowering than homogeneity, its power emanates from its ability to expand each person's horizon and social understanding. Students, workers and other individuals who belong to divergent socio-economic groups can learn much from one another if provided the space to exchange ideas and analyse mutual difficulties. As such a powerful force, difference must not simply be tolerated but cultivated as a spark to human creativity. Any description of critical thinking must include an understanding of difference that nurtures a critical sense of empathy. Cornel West (1993) argues that empathy involves the ability to appreciate the anxieties and frustrations of others, never to lose sight of the humanity of the marginalized no matter how wretched their condition. The point emerging here, of course, involves the ethical and cognitive benefits derived from the confrontation with diversity and the different vantage points it provides us for viewing the lived world. Taking a cue from liberation theologians in Latin America, critical multiculturalists often begin their analysis of an institution by listening to those who have suffered most as a result of its existence. These 'different' ways of seeing allow critical multiculturalists to tap into the cognitive power of empathy – a power that allows individuals access to deep patterns of racism, class bias and sexism and the way they structure oppression in everyday life.

With these understandings in mind, critical multiculturalists seek a dialogue between Eastern cultures and Western cultures, as well as a conversation between the relatively wealthy northern cultures and the impoverished southern cultures (Bohm and Peat 1987; Welch 1991). In such a context forms of knowing, such as the understandings of blue collar workers, that have traditionally been excluded by the modernist West move educators to new vantage points and unexplored planetary perspectives. Understanding derived from the perspective of the excluded or the culturally different allows for an appreciation of the nature of justice, the invisibility of the process of oppression and the difference that highlights our own social construction as individuals. In this spirit workers who appreciate the insights of critical multiculturalism begin to look at their work from the perspectives of their Asian, African, Latino and indigenous colleagues around the world. Such cognitive cross-fertilization often reveals the tacit assumptions that impede innovations. For example, home builders who study Native American, Japanese or African ways of building houses may gain creative insight into their craft. After studying the way Zuni pueblos addressed problems of living space, they might be empowered to tackle space problems creatively in ways conventional builders hadn't considered.

In the context of cognitive development Jean Piaget argued that conceptual change takes place when learners engage in the process of accommodation. He described accommodation as the restructuring of one's cognitive maps to take care of an unanticipated event – that is, to deal with difference. In order to accommodate, an individual must actively change his or her existing intellectual structure to understand the dissonance produced by the novel demand. Accommodation is a reflective, integrative behaviour that forces the realization that our present cognitive structure is insufficient to deal with the changing pressures of the environment (Kaufman 1978; Fosnot 1988). In a sense, accommodation becomes a subversive agent of change leading an individual to adjust whenever and wherever it might be necessary. When Piagetian accommodation is connected with Frankfurt School critical theory's concept of negation in a context that appreciates the critical multicultural notion of difference, interesting things begin to happen. Common to both critical theory and accommodation, negation involves the continuous criticism and reconstruction of what one thinks one knows. For example, critical theorist Max Horkheimer argued that through negation we develop a critical consciousness that allows us to get beyond old ossified world views and incorporate our new understandings into a new reflective attitude (Held 1980).

As critical multiculturalists recognize the potential of critical accommodation, they structure learning situations where individuals come to understand previously unrecognized aspects of the environment and expose the cognitive limitations that precluded insight in the past. Horkheimer maintained that through the awareness gained by way of critical negation (the philosophical analogue to the cognitive act of accommodation) an individual develops and becomes open to radical change. In this context critical accommodation can be described as a reshaping of consciousness consonant with a critical understanding of democracy and social justice. Thus critical educators see the diversity of classroom experiences as an opportunity for cognitive growth. An example from a critical multiculturalist classroom might help to ground this concept. A teacher exploring the meaning of intelligence would develop (assimilate in Piagetian theory) an understanding of the concept based on his or her personal experience and the coverage of cognition in his or her teacher education. The teacher would accommodate the concept as he or she began to examine students who were labelled unintelligent but displayed sophisticated abilities in the manual arts or in the practical understandings of the trades and crafts. At this point the teacher might take note of this contradiction and begin to integrate this recognition of exception (accommodation) into a reconceptualization of the prevailing definition of intelligence in the culture of school. The old definition of intelligence would have been negated; through exposure to diverse expressions of intelligence, new ways of seeing it would have been accommodated. Critical multiculturalism might have alerted teachers to the mainstream dismissal of the talents of students from the margins – non-white and economically disadvantaged young people. Picking up on these concerns, teachers would critically accommodate non-traditional expressions of intelligence that would free them from the privileged, racially and class-biased definitions that were used to exclude cognitive styles that transcended the official codes. In this and many other situations accommodation becomes the emancipatory feature of the thinking process. Critical educators recognize this and use it in the struggle for democratic economic, social and educational change (Hultgren 1987; Lather 1991).

Critical multiculturalism and subjugated knowledge

Derived from dangerous memories of history that have been suppressed and information that has been disqualified by social and academic gatekeepers, subjugated knowledge plays a central role in a critical multiculturalism. Through the conscious cultivation of these low ranking knowledges, alternative democratic and emancipatory visions of society, politics, education and cognition are possible. In a critical multicultural curriculum subjugated knowledge is not passed along as a new canon but becomes a living body of knowledge open to different interpretations. Viewed in its relationship to the traditional curriculum, subjugated knowledge is employed as a constellation of concepts that challenge the invisible cultural assumptions embedded in all aspects of schooling and knowledge production. The subjugated knowledges of African Americans, Native Americans, working class people, women and many other groups have contested the dominant culture's view of reality. Confronted with subjugated knowledge, individuals from white mainstream culture begin to appreciate the fact that there are multiple perspectives on all issues. Indeed, they begin to realize that textbooks discard data about unpopular viewpoints and information produced by marginalized groups. Curricula that include subjugated perspectives teach a lesson on the complexities of knowledge production and how this process shapes our view of ourselves and the world around us. The curriculum cannot stay the same if we take the knowledges of working class men and women seriously, if we get beyond the rosy, romanticized picture of immigration to North America and Britain and document the traumatic stories of the immigrants, if we seek out women's perspectives on the evolution of Western culture or if we study the culture enslaved Africans brought to the New World.

The white dominant cultural power blocs that dominate Western societies at the end of the twentieth century seem oblivious to the need to listen to marginalized people and take their knowledge seriously. Western power wielders are not good at listening to information that does not seem to contribute to hegemony, their ability to win the consent of the subjugated to their governance. Knowledge that emerges from and serves the purposes of the subjugated is often erased by making it appear dangerous and pathological to other citizens. Drawing up work within the discipline of cultural studies that seeks to reverse conditions of oppression, subjugated knowledge seeks new ways of validating the importance and relevance of divergent voices. Such voices are excluded not merely from schoolrooms and curriculum guides, but from other sites of knowledge production, such as popular culture. Having become a major pedagogical force in Western societies over the past few decades, the popular culture 'curriculum' is monitored for emancipatory expressions of subjugated knowledge. Though not always successful, power wielders attempt to neutralize the subjugated knowledges that find their way into TV, movies, popular music, the Internet and other popular cultural sites (Dion-Buffalo and Mohawk 1993; Fiske 1993; Mullings 1994; Nieto 1996; McLaren and Morris 1997).

Since the approval of subjugated knowledges is not contingent on the blessings of power wielders in the dominant culture, purveyors of subjugated knowledge can confront individuals from the white, upper-middle class cultural centre with the oppressed's view of them. Some of the pictures are quite disconcerting for mainstream individuals who have never given much thought to the way they are seen from the social margins. Individuals from dominant social formations have never developed their imagination about how they look to marginalized others. As a result, women often make sense of men's image of women better than men understand women's view of men, individuals with African heritages understand the motivations of whites better than the reverse and low-status workers figure out how they are seen by their managers more clearly than the managers understand how they appear to workers. Obviously, such insights provide us with a very different view of the world and the processes that shape it. Teachers who employ subjugated viewpoints become transformative agents who alert the community to its hidden features, its submerged memories, in the process helping individuals to name their oppression or possibly understand their complicity in oppression. Such a naming process helps students, teachers, workers and other community members to reflect on their construction of their lived worlds in such a way that they develop the ability to take control of their own lives.

Thus, critical multicultural teachers devoted to the value of subjugated knowledges uncover those dangerous memories that are involved in reconstructing the process through which the consciousness of various groups and individuals has come to be constructed. Such an awareness frees teachers, students and other individuals to claim an identity apart from the one forced upon them. Indeed, identity is constructed when submerged memories are aroused – in other words, confrontation with dangerous memory changes our perceptions of the forces that shape us, which in turn moves us to redefine our world views, our way of seeing. The oppressive forces that shape us have formed the identities of both the powerful and the exploited. Without an analysis of this process we will never understand why students succeed or fail in school; we will be forever blind to the tacit ideological forces that construct student perceptions of school and the impact such perceptions have on their school experiences. Such blindness restricts our view of our own and other people's perception of their place in history, in the web of reality. When history is erased and decontextualized, teachers, students, workers and other citizens are rendered vulnerable to the myths employed to perpetuate social domination.

Teaching that is committed to subjugated knowledge has 'friends in low places'. In a critical multiculturalism the view from above of the traditional Eurocentric upper-middle class male curriculum makes way for the inclusion of views from below. Emerging from an understanding of and respect for the perspective of the oppressed, such an epistemological position uses the voices of the subjugated to formulate a reconstruction of the dominant educational structure. It is a radical reconstruction in the sense that it attempts to empower those who are presently powerless and to validate oppressed ways of thinking that open new cognitive doors to everyone. As critical multiculturalists expose the way dominant power invalidates the cognitive styles of marginalized groups, we begin to examine testing procedures and their political effects. Eurocentric psychometricians devise tests to evaluate student performance, forgetting in the process that evaluation is based on unquestioned definitions of intelligence and performance. When well intentioned liberal multiculturalists attempt to develop curricula based on a recognition of the existence of marginalized experiences, they miss the lessons provided by an understanding of subjugated thinking. Liberal multiculturalism involves the inclusion of information on Africans, Latinos, Native Americans and women in a curriculum that has traditionally examined the contributions of famous white men. The power dynamics and cognitive orientation of the curriculum are not changed by such additions; they simply add a few new facts to be committed to memory. Such add-ons can be viewed as a tokenism that perpetuates the power relations of the status quo, that paves the way for a kinder, gentler oppression.

The advantage of subjugated perspectives, the view from below, involves what has been termed the 'double consciousness' of the oppressed. If they are to survive, subjugated groups develop an understanding of those who attempt to dominate them; at the same time they are cognizant of the everyday mechanisms of oppression and the effects of such 'technologies'. W. E. B. DuBois called this double consciousness of the oppressed a form of second sight, an ability to see oneself through the perception of others. A critical multicultural curriculum of second sight is grounded on the understanding that a critically educated person knows more than just the validated knowledge of the dominant culture. For example, to understand science from a critical perspective would involve analysis of its specific historical origins (the seventeenth and eighteenth centuries) and its cultural location (Western Europe). A critical multicultural science curriculum would appreciate that like other ways of understanding and studying reality Western science is a social construction of a particular culture at a particular time. Such a cognizance would not induce us to dismiss and discard the accomplishments of Western science – that would be silly. But it would induce us to study other ways of knowing, such as the scientific theories of Native Americans and other cultural groups.

Science as the term is typically used is, Vandama Shiva (1993) writes, a Euro-centred ideology with parochial origins in male-centredness and particular socio-economic classes. Such culturally specific roots of science have been hidden behind a claim of a transcultural, transhistorical universality. Only when we study subjugated histories and cultures such as those of women and non-Western societies are we able to expose the socially constructed nature of Western science and the logic implicit within it that accepts ecological destruction and the exploitation of nature. Science is not the only area where critical multiculturalists search for alternative subjugated knowledges, for such information exists around each axis of domination. In the domain of gender, for example, critical multiculturalists value ways of knowing that have traditionally been viewed as feminine. Such knowledges expose the hidden gender assumptions of male-centred mainstream perspectives, as they provide alternative ways of looking at the world. Ways of understanding and functioning in the world employed by disabled people, such as the use of sign language, are forms of subjugated knowledge that can be taught in a critical multicultural curriculum. Also important in this context is gay and lesbian subjugated knowledge that provides significant insight into the construction of sexual preference, sexual desire and the cultural dynamics of gender role production. Both homosexually oriented and heterosexually oriented individuals can gain insight into the production of their identities from a confrontation with such subjugated knowledges.

Because of their race, class and gender positions, many educational and scientific experts are insulated from the benefits of the double consciousness of the marginalized and are estranged from a visceral appreciation of suffering. Until I (Joe Kincheloe) was placed in a lower-track set of courses as a high school student – I was not viewed as a good student – I never understood what it felt like to be viewed as 'slow'. Such an experience alerted me to the pain of my fellow slow students and provided me with a second sight or a double consciousness of students in such a position. Such second sight has, in my opinion, served as one of the most important insights I have brought to my career as an educator. Such awareness is a subjugated knowledge, a way of seeing that has been ignored in too many educational situations. Contemporary social organization and its sanctioning of the suffering of various individuals and groups such as low-track students are often viewed as acceptable in the dominant curriculum. Educational leaders who often come from dominant groups don't typically challenge the ways of seeing that justify the prevailing social and educational system. What lived experiences would create a cognitive dissonance within the minds of the such leaders that would make them uncomfortable with the status quo? The oppressed – while often induced by the mechanisms of power to accept injustice and to deny their own oppression – often use their pain as a motivation to find out what is not right and to discover alternate ways of constructing social and educational reality. The following points illustrate the benefits of a reconceptualization of education in the light of an appreciation of subjugated knowledge (Ferguson 1984; Fiske 1993; West 1993; Sleeter and Grant 1994).

(1) *Subjugated knowledges help us to rethink the curriculum, the academic disciplines and our purposes as educators and cultural workers.* An understanding of subjugated knowledge alerts us to the fact that there are different ways of seeing the world. With this understanding in mind it becomes apparent that school and university curricula privilege particular views of the world. This can be illustrated by examining the discipline of mainstream educational psychology. If a foundational concept of the discipline involves the definition of intelligence as that which IQ measures, then what unstated cultural assumptions and values are embedded in such a

definition? Throughout the history of Western developmental psychology intelligence has been defined in a very *exclusive* manner. Interestingly, those excluded from the community designated as intelligent tend to cluster around categories based on race (the non-white), class (the poor) and gender (the feminine). The Western modernist tendency for logocentrism permeates definitions of intelligence. According to twentieth-century educational psychology and cognitive science, the way of knowing ascribed to 'rational man' constitutes the highest level of human thought. This rationality or logic is best exemplified in symbolic logic, mathematics and scientific reasoning. With the birth of modernity (the Age of Reason) and its scientific method in the seventeenth and eighteenth centuries, logocentrism was accompanied by a misogyny that associated feminine thinking with madness, witchcraft and Satanism. As a result, scientific knowledge became the only game in town. In this context individuals came to be represented in a dramatic new form – as abstracted entities standing outside the forces of history and culture. This abstract individualism eclipsed the Western understanding of how men and women are shaped by larger social forces that affect individuals from different social locations in different ways. Western society was caught in a web of patriarchy – a mode of perception that limited thinking to concepts that stay within white, androcentric boundaries, far away from the "No Trespassing" signs of the feminine domain.

As teachers and cultural workers begin to uncover these hidden values embedded in both prevailing definitions of intelligence and our scientific instruments that measure it, they embark on a journey into the excitement of critical multiculturalism. As they begin to search for forms of intelligence that fall outside traditional notions of abstract reasoning, they come to appreciate the multiple forms of intelligence that different individuals possess – especially those individuals who fall outside the racial, ethnic or economic mainstream. It is not uncommon for us to walk through the halls of an urban high school peeking in advanced placement (AP) or honours courses dominated by white faces – further down the hall the general education classes are filled with non-white, minority students and poor whites. Sensitive to the multiplicity of ways intelligence can be expressed, critical multicultural teachers begin to examine those students who have been labelled by mainstream educational science as unintelligent, slow learners who are at risk. Upon further examination, teachers often uncover abilities in these students that are unconventional but nevertheless sophisticated. Students who are raised in cultures that value active engagement with reality over abstract rationality are the first victims of the scientific definitions of intelligence. Forms of intelligence that emphasize doing over abstraction regularly reveal themselves if teachers are sensitive to the social, cultural and psychological dynamics discussed here. For example, a student's ability to draw, to build and to fix are all sophisticated forms of cognition that are not measured by a standardized test. Critical multicultural teachers can recognize, praise, cultivate and connect these abilities to other forms of knowing. This process is an extremely important aspect of a critical multicultural education. Once the values hidden in mainstream definitions are exposed, the possibilities opened for the education of the previously excluded are limitless. Valuing subjugated knowledge creates a new world for students condemned by the narrowness of traditional disciplinary ways of assessing them.

(2) *Subjugated knowledges contribute to the analysis of the ways knowledge is produced and legitimated.* In mainstream cultural and institutional pedagogies we are taught to believe that the knowledge we consider official and valid has been produced in a neutral, noble and altruistic manner. Such a view dismisses the cultural and power-related dimensions of knowledge production. Knowledge of any form will always confront other knowledge forms. When this happens a power struggle ensues (evolution versus creationism, Western history or world history, the new or the old maths, anthropological studies of non-Western cultures versus a traditional patriotic curriculum). The decisions made in these struggles over knowledge exert dramatic but often unseen consequences in schools, economic institutions, popular culture and the political sphere. For example, the role of the teacher as a neutral transmitter of prearranged facts is not understood as a politicized role accompanying knowledge production. If schools are to become places that promote teacher and student empowerment, then the notion of what constitutes politicization will have to be reconceptualized. Battle with texts as a form of research, Paulo Freire and Ira Shor exhort teachers. Resist the demand of the official curriculum for deference to texts, they argue in line with their larger critically grounded political vision. Can it be argued that capitulation to textual authority constitutes a political neutrality (Shor and Freire 1987)?

In their refusal to accept the authority of texts and the dictates of the official curriculum, critical multicultural teachers come to understand that they and their students are knowledge producers. This is one of the hardest lessons for teachers to learn, for most of their public school and university experience contradicts the concept. Research has been defined for them as finding information produced by experts. Many college students have become quite comfortable with the passive student role by the time they enter the university. They must only finish their assignments on time and pass exams that call on low-level cognitive abilities to memorize factual data. For those who have been influenced by such instruction, knowledge, at the least, is received – that is, it consists of isolated bits and pieces to be given back to instructors on tests. At the most, knowledge is something out there to be discovered via the application of proper procedures. Imagine students' cognitive and epistemological discomfort when confronted with the task of learning to become critical researchers, producers of knowledge. Before such students are immersed in such research activity, they must be conversant with the cognitive, political and epistemological issues that surround critical pedagogy in general and critical multiculturalism in particular.

Once they are cognizant of such issues and experienced in critical research, teachers' professional lives are changed forever. As knowledge producers, such teachers begin to construct curricula around student experience, promoting student understanding of the social, economic and cultural forces that have shaped their lives. Students are taught ethnographic, semiotic, phenomenological and historiographical forms of inquiry, in the process learning to deconstruct the ideological forces that shape their lives. In such a context, they explore their place in relation to race, class and gender hierarchies, their romantic relationships, their relationships with teachers and their definitions of success. Teacher understanding of why such critical research is positioned as an oppositional activity deepens, as they step back from the world as they have been conditioned to see it. In the process, they uncover the constructing forces: linguistic codes, cultural signs, power-driven representations and embedded ideologies. Here they are learning to research, to teach and to think. As critical multicultural educators study and engage in knowledge production, they remake their professional lives, rename their worlds and challenge white supremacy, patriarchy and rule by economic elites (Schön 1987; Slaughter 1989; Adler 1991; Noffke and Brennan 1991).

One of the great paradoxes of contemporary education involves the use of a language of empowerment in school talk coupled with pervasive ignorance of the way power operates to subvert the empowerment of teachers and students – racially and economically marginalized students in particular. Such a contradiction undermines the effort of teachers and students to gain new insights into the way power shapes consciousness (Giroux and McLaren 1988). Does it matter that we come from rich or poor homes, white or non-white families? These questions are not viewed as questions of power or knowledge production – indeed, they are often not recognized at all. In a postmodern era of information saturation, with its TV, movies, databases, Internet, CD-ROM and headsets such issues become even more important. In a mutating, globally expanding techno-capitalism that seeks to colonize everything from outer space to inner consciousness, questions of power and information become more important than ever before. As we move into the twenty-first century, postmodern power's control over information continues to expand – in book publishing, for example, 2 per cent of the publishers control 75 per cent of books published in the USA – as corporations continue to gain power. Advertising expenditures have increased dramatically since the 1960s. Corporate images have become more and more important, not simply for marketing purposes but also for capital raising, mergers, gaining the competitive edge in the production of knowledge, the effort to influence government policy and the advancement of particular cultural values.

Indeed, through the power of their money, postmodern corporations have transformed the role of the university from guardian of knowledge to knowledge producer for business and industrial needs (Harvey 1989).

In this context critical multicultural teachers, students and other cultural workers appreciate the need to analyse what they know, how they come to know it, why they believe or reject it and how they evaluate the credibility of the evidence. Starting at this point, they begin to understand the social construction of knowledge and truth. In school, for example, they recognize that the taken-for-granted knowledges that are taught do not find justification as such universal truth. Instead, critical multiculturalists appreciate the fact that the purveyors of such information have won a long series of historical and political struggles over whose knowledge and ways of producing knowledge is the best. Thus, critical multiculturalists are able to uncover the socially created hierarchies that travel incognito as truth. Though everyone knows their nature, these hierarchies mask their 'shady' backgrounds of political conflict. As truth, they are employed as rationales for cultural dominance and unequal power relations (McLaren 1991). With these dynamics in mind consider this example of knowledge production in mathematics.

Mathematics is typically taught as a deductively produced, pre-existing body of knowledge that is definitely European and androcentric. Study after study has indicated that prevailing maths pedagogies have alienated non-whites and women, preventing them from succeeding in the discipline. A form of Western elitism permeates maths teaching that considers mathematical discovery and knowledge production emerging only from a rigorous application of 'deductive axiomatic logic'. Western maths has traditionally dismissed African or certain Asian mathematical forms as 'childlike' and 'primitive'. Contemporary ethnomathematicians have successfully countered these ethnocentric arguments with empirical data pointing to the sophistication of these alternative, non-Western forms of maths knowledge – a subjugated knowledge of maths. In a critical multicultural curriculum maths students learn the different ways diverse cultural groups might define 'logic'.

A group of academic anthropologists were studying a group of African tribal people they had labelled primitive. Testing their intelligence in relation to set theory, the scientists asked them to sort twenty objects that fell into four categories: food, clothing, tools and cooking utensils. The researchers were checking to see if the people had the intelligence to group the objects 'properly'. Instead of making four groups, the Africans made ten. Basing their sorting on what they considered practical connections among the objects (e.g. grouping a knife with an orange because it cuts it), the 'primitive' people claimed that this was the way a wise person would group the articles. When researchers asked how a fool would do it, the people provided the 'correct' answer, making four neat piles with food in one, tools in another etc. Thus, one set of meanings, one form of knowledge, one path to cognitive sophistication is chosen as true. Studies of African mathematical thinking are not inserted into the curriculum, therefore, simply to study something (anything) non-European; they are added as a way of expanding not only the definition of rationality, intelligence and problem-solving, but as a means of understanding the effects of unexamined knowledge production. Without the addition and integration of such subjugated knowledge forms into the cultural and institutional curriculum, nothing challenges the mainstream Western assumption that tribal Africans are intellectually inferior. Indeed, using a bizarre set of psychometric manipulations, Richard Herrnstein and Charles Murray (authors of *The Bell Curve*) concluded that Africans who live in Africa possess an average IQ of 75 (Frankenstein and Powell 1994; Herrnstein and Murray 1994).

Studies such as the anthropology of African mathematics are important not simply because they illustrate quaint cultural differences, but because they expose the role of power of knowledge production in multicultural situations. Often misunderstood in educational circumstances, power refers not simply to the control of financial, institutional, political, ideological and communicative resources, but also to the control of representations of reality. By representations of reality we are referring to the ways in which particular ways of life are legitimated and delegitimated. In the case of the Western anthropologists' study of the Africans' notion of set theory, Western notions of mathematical knowledge were legitimated and the African notions were delegitimated. The colonial status of the Western anthropologists was expressed through the discourse of mathematics. Accompanying their colonial status was an attendant power – a power to control representations of whose knowledge was 'civilized' and whose was 'primitive'. Such studies rest at the core of the critical multiculturalist curriculum, as they facilitate public understanding of the way power works, the way it covertly shapes representations in both the school and cultural curricula, the way it constructs our view of self and world.

(3) *In the larger critical multicultural effort to construct more inclusive and just socio-political and educational spheres, subjugated knowledge must be justified in the academy.* Multicultural and subjugated knowledges should be included in the curriculum because it is more fair to include a variety of cultural expressions. We have emphasized issues of knowledge production and the construction of academic disciplines because these are the terrains on which the struggle for social justice can be won. Unless some form of cultural separatism prevails, we will have to work in existing academic structures. As critical multiculturalists we must raise questions about the weaknesses of these structures and how in the name of justice and academic excellence they must be reconceptualized in the new millennium. Thus, subjugated knowledge transcends status as a mere add-on that

operates in the academic margins in underfunded ethnic studies departments. While scholars of subjugated knowledges definitely support such departments, they are ultimately concerned with redefining and reshaping the colleges, universities and schools from the ground up.

Such reforms require that critical multicultural educators become critical hermeneuticists (scholars and teachers who structure their work and teaching around an effort to help students and other individuals to make sense of the world around them) and critical epistemologists (scholars and teachers who seek to expose how accepted knowledge came to be validated). Critical multiculturalists bring a new dimension to the academy, as they use subjugated knowledges to reconceptualize the practices of the academy, to uncover the etymology (origin) of its practices. This historical dynamic is extremely important in the context of subjugated knowledge. Antonio Gramsci (1988) noted that philosophy cannot be understood apart from the history of philosophy; nor can culture and education be grasped outside the history of culture. Our conception of self, world and education, therefore, can only become critical when we appreciate the historical nature of its formulation. We are never independent of the social and historical forces that surround us – we are all caught at a particular point in the web of reality. One of the most important aspects of subjugated knowledge is that it is a way of seeing that helps us to expose the fingerprints of power in existing academic knowledge. Subjugated knowledge by its mere existence proves to us that the ways in which academic knowledge is produced are riddled with assumptions of inferiority and supremacy. There are alternatives, it tells us, to knowledge produced within the boundaries of the positivist paradigm (Codd 1984; Fiske 1986; Daines 1987; Cherryholmes 1988; Greene 1988; Feinberg and Horowitz 1990).

If one of the basic features of a democratic education involves making use of student experiences in curriculum development, then a democratic and critical multiculturalism that gains credibility in the academy must involve connecting student experience with the themes of the classroom. If the democratic aspect of this type of education revolves around the provision of a meaningful education to those traditionally excluded from such an experience, then subjugated students and their marginalized cultural knowledge take on a new importance. In no way does mere reference to such knowledge constitute a critical multicultural education. The move to the critical involves making use of such ways of knowing in a manner that challenges the hegemony of a monolithic form of academic knowledge. Thus, in this context, student experience must be analysed and subtlely connected to larger sociopolitical and educational issues. Such a process is never easy, as it requires great skill and intellect on the part of the teacher. Critical multicultural teachers who are able to negotiate such an informed and nuanced process will render education meaningful in the lives of those who traditionally have discerned little connection between schooling and their lived realities. The success encountered by such teachers will help to legitimate the process in schools, universities and communities (Darder 1991; Ayers 1992; Pruyn 1994).

(4) *Subjugated knowledge helps to produce new levels of insight by making use of indigenous knowledge.* Indigenous knowledge is a specified form of subjugated knowledge that is local, life-experience based and non-Western science produced. Such knowledge is transmitted over time by individuals from a particular geographical or cultural locality. Indigenous ways of knowing help people to cope with their sociological and agricultural environments and are passed down from generation to generation. A critical multiculturalism that values subjugated knowledge realizes that indigenous knowledge is important not only for the culture that produced it but for people from different cultures. Only now at the end of the twentieth century are European peoples beginning to appreciate the value of indigenous knowledge about health, medicine, agriculture, philosophy, ecology and education. Traditionally, these were the very types of knowledge European education tried to discredit and eradicate. A critical multicultural education works hard to save such knowledges, which are, unfortunately, rapidly disappearing from the face of the earth.

Critical multicultural education sees a variety of purposes for the inclusion of indigenous knowledges in the school and university curriculum. Since indigenous knowledges do not correspond to Western notions of discrete bodies or packages of data: they must be approached with an understanding of their ambiguity and contextual embeddedness. Thus, any effort to understand or use such knowledges cannot be separated from the world views and epistemologies embraced by their producers. The confrontation with such non-Western ways of seeing moves the power of difference to a new level of utility, as it exposes the hidden world views and epistemologies of Westerners unaccustomed to viewing culture – their own and other cultural forms – at this level. In this context the critical multicultural encounter with indigenous knowledge raises epistemological questions relating to the production and consumption of knowledge, the subtle connections between culture and what is defined as successful learning, the contestation of all forms of knowledge production and the definition of education itself. An awareness of the intersection between subjugated ways of knowing and indigenous knowledge opens a conversation between the 'north' and the 'south', that is, between so-called developed and underdeveloped societies. Critical multiculturalists seek to use their awareness of this valuable intersection to produce new forms of global consciousness and inter-cultural solidarity.

(5) *If recognition and validation of subjugated and indigenous knowledges induce us to rethink academic disciplines and knowledge production, then educators and other cultural workers must all become adept researchers.*

Contrary to the pronouncements of many mainstream educators, critical multiculturalists believe that it is possible to create an education where many individuals no matter what their vocation can become researchers. By no means will this be easy – but it can be done. In critical democratic educational contexts teachers, labour leaders, cultural workers, critical psychologists and many other pedagogical agents can teach individuals to conduct *secondary* research (investigation of what other scholars have produced) by mastering the use of libraries, electronic databases, the Internet and other compilations of data. Critical multiculturalists also maintain that individuals from all walks of life can learn *primary* research (data collection taken directly from observations of the lived world). Indeed, critical multiculturalists contend that elementary, secondary and higher education as well as informal pedagogies that take place outside of an institutional context will be forever transformed when students learn skills of inquiry that allow them to collect, interpret and apply subjugated forms of knowledge.

Contrary to the accusations of conservative multiculturalists that critical forms of multicultural education are destroying the standards of education, the forms of pedagogy promoted here call for higher academic expectations. Students are too rarely challenged, we maintain. The schools we envision situate research skills and knowledge production abilities at the core of elementary, secondary and higher education curriculums. Thus, teachers – as Henry Giroux argued in the mid-1980s – become intellectuals who contextualize, interpret and create knowledge, all the while modelling such behaviour for their students. In this demanding context classrooms take on the appearance of 'think tanks' – institutions where important knowledge is produced that has value outside of the classroom. In modernist Eurocentric education teachers were instructed to say 'give me the truth and I will pass it along to students in the most efficient manner possible'. In the new critical paradigm teachers are encouraged to support themselves, to assert their freedom from all-knowing experts. Such critical multicultural teachers often say 'please support me as I explore the world of mathematics, sociology or whatever'. In this context teachers are intimately familiar with the Western canon but refuse to accept without question its status as universal, as the only body of cultural knowledge worth knowing. Thus, as scholars of Western knowledge, non-Western knowledge and subjugated and indigenous knowledges, such teachers are not content to operate in socio-educational frameworks often taken for granted. As critical multiculturalists, they seek to rethink and recontextualize questions that have been traditionally asked about schooling and knowledge production in general. While they respect earlier insight and are reverential in respect to the genius of past eras, such educators display their veneration by continuing to question the work of their intellectual ancestors.

three

CRITICAL MULTICULTURALISM: POWER AND DEMOCRACY

Our discussion of the birth of Western modernism in Chapter 2 lays the conceptual foundation for this chapter. The hyperrationality of regressive modernism, especially when combined with a *laissez-faire* view of economic theory, white supremacy and an authoritarian, unreflective patriarchy, reduced and fragmented Westerners' view of the world to the point that they were often blinded to particular aspects of human experience: feelings, emotions, spiritual concerns and the need for self-worth. In this context economists, for example, studied the world in isolation, bit by bit, in the process viewing financial and monetary issues separate from human concerns; as time passed, students of education studied pedagogy in a similar manner. In the context of economics this modernist fragmentation produced dire consequences that continue to undermine human dignity and the pursuit of democracy. We will begin this chapter with an analysis of the role of modernism in the economic sphere and the effects of such intersection on questions of social justice and the pursuit of a democratic education. In order to construct a critical multiculturalism we must understand these issues in nuanced detail.

Regressive modernism's legacy: *Homo economicus*

By removing humans from their social and moral context, modernist economists and other social and psychological scientists have positioned people as merely another variable, as *things*. In the economic sphere men and women come to be viewed as *Homo economicus* – a person whose humanity is subservient to economic needs and the demands of profit. *Homo economicus* is isolated from other humans, from nature and from larger social and economic goals. As merely isolated *things*, Westerners in the industrialized modernist state of the late nineteenth and twentieth centuries lost their right to be treated as sacred entities. The history of social, economic and educational organization from the late nineteenth century to the present must be viewed in the context of this scientific objectification of human beings. One of the best examples of this objectification was the efficiency movement of the early twentieth century. The further away from the middle and upper-middle class white male norm an individual fell, the more vulnerable he or she became to the efficiency movement's efforts to objectify and regulate. In this context, therefore, issues of race, class and gender are central to an understanding of the modernist regulatory project and, conversely, an appreciation of the social dynamics of modernism is necessary for an understanding of race, class and gender oppression in nineteenth- and twentieth-century Western societies.

Frederick W. Taylor, the father of the efficiency movement, published his influential *The Principles of Scientific Management* in 1911 – Western institutions have based their operations on it ever since. Human efficiency, Taylor argued, could be increased by replacing traditional work styles with scientifically validated rules for job completion. In this context workers would be taught the 'proper' set of procedures for carrying out any operation. Leaders of institutions found these ideas so compelling that factories, hospitals and schools soon built their organizations around them (Kohlberg and Smith 1992). The importance of Taylorism involved not simply developing new organizational strategies, but the redefinition of work in the process. Indeed, General Motors managers used to boast that every job task in their plants could be learned in fifteen minutes or less. The sacred goal of efficiency could be guaranteed by defining job tasks in such a way that any fool could perform them. If workmanship and morale were poor, then all managers had to do was to increase supervision and control (Wirth 1983). Such thinking leads economists, managers, educators, government bureaucrats and many modernist scholars into what many have labelled a 'technological fix error'. All problems, scientific managers argue, will give way to technical type solutions. Here the spectre of *Homo economicus* appears like a face outside a bedroom window, as managers ignore the fact that work is a social as well as a technical process. As a *social* process work involves the well-being of humans, their welfare, feelings and happiness.

Modernist degradation of the human: personnel management

The modernist mind-set that separates humanistic concerns with self-direction, empowerment and human dignity from the socio-economic realm embraces a profit-maximizing view of reality. Classical *laissez-faire* economic theory adopts this framework, as it excludes conceptions of humans as meaning makers, as beings who can replace regressive policies with life affirming ones. As modernist ways of seeing unhinged the economy from the social fabric, concepts such as economic growth became alienated from human concerns. The fragmentation of modernism is illustrated by the realization that economic growth has nothing to do with the growing poverty of women and African Americans, environmental disaster, the expanding disparity of wealth between rich and poor or the problems of the so-called Third World. The industrial transformation of Western societies from the integrity of crafts(man)ship to factory work precipitated a variety of nonmaterial consequences. As new factory work arrangements undermined creativity, self-expression, connection with the completed product and satisfaction with accomplishment, work grew to become a hated activity.

Workers were reduced to 'puttin' in time', and labour turnover increased so much that by the early twentieth century rates in many industries often exceeded the total number of employees. For example, the Ford Motor Company in 1913 reported a 370 per cent turnover. If the spiritual genocide of labour was not bad enough, the idea began to grow in industrial America that blue collar work represents a kind of social failure. Not everyone in this society can be a doctor, yet that seems to represent the mind-set of many parents. In the industrial workplace management's control has been maintained by portraying the error and inadequacy of the working class. In recent debates about falling business productivity, corporate and industrial leaders along with their right-wing allies have identified worker incompetence as the central problem. Such representations of the 'rank and file' create a new chapter in the history of socio-economic class bias and, as a result, are central features in a critical multiculturalist curriculum (Edson 1979; Bluestone and Brown 1983; Wirth 1983; Ferguson 1984; Block 1990; Copa and Tebbenhoff 1990; Jonathan 1996).

Viewing workers as human fragments, as *Homo economicus*, as incompetent production units, managers framed workers as the objects of social engineering and rationalist planning. Nothing within the scientific discourse of personnel management would allow for a humane analysis of the work process itself or for questions of worker empowerment. The very purpose of personnel management is, after all, to manage and control workers. Outside of their role as units of production, workers play very limited parts in the personnel management microcosm. When personnel management's salient role in the shaping of the concerns of educational leadership is analysed, the case can be made that in some ways twentieth-century American education is an extension of personnel management – indeed, educational institutions have often embraced the class bias, racism and sexism that have accompanied the management discourse. Goals of both personnel management/human relations and educational leadership have stressed adjusting manpower [*sic*] to the work process – in both a macro and a micro sense. The macro sense involves the larger social concern of fitting workers to the general needs of the economy; the micro sense involves the specific concern of fitting workers or students to the specific factory or the specific school. As incompetent objects to be controlled in jobs that anyone can do, is there any wonder that society has looked down at training programmes designed to mould 'these kinds' of workers? The status of educational programmes is determined by the socio-economic status of the jobs for which they are preparing students. This is why vocational education, for example, has been viewed with such condescension in Western societies.

The pathology of the socio-economic class bias of worker degradation in modernist Western culture finds expression at a variety of human levels. The health problems of low-status workers do not receive as much concern as those of managers and professionals. For example, the widely publicized concern for stress-related health problems of high-status workers is treated differently from the stress-related threats to the health of low-status workers. Few high-status workers ever experience the everyday work conditions of, say, an auto worker who works every day in the factory foundry. Faced with constant intense heat and an oil mist in the air, one's health inevitably declines after a few years of exposure. As one worker puts it, the company is 'paying me for five years off my life'. This worker accepted the choice to work in the foundry because the higher pay allowed him to avoid having to work two jobs (Ferguson 1984). Another human expression of the pathology involves the cultivation of self-hatred among low-status workers. Ben Hamper (1992: 13) writes of the lectures he and his friends received from their fathers, who were shoprats at General Motors. The factories weren't looking for competent and talented workers:

> They were dragging the lagoon for optionless bumpkins with brats to feed and livers to bathe. An educated man might hang on for a while, but was apt to flee at any given whistle. That wasn't any good for corporate continuity. GM wanted the salt of the earth, dung-heavers, flunkies and leeches – men who would grunt the day away void of self-betterment, numbed-out cyborgs willing to swap cerebellum loaf for patio furniture, a second jalopy and a tragic carpet ride deboarding curbside in front of some pseudo-Tudor dollhouse on the outskirts of town.

Hamper concludes his discussion with the observation that 'working the line for GM was something fathers did so that their offspring wouldn't have to.'

We all understand the degradation of work in the factories of the late nineteenth and early twentieth centuries. But we should not be fooled by contemporary arguments that such pathology is a relic of a distant past. In a contemporary era so unsure of its character or direction that analysts don't know what to call it – is it a post-industrial era or a postmodern era or a late modern period? – the impact of recent changes on the character of work is a topic of heated debate. Will the new forms of technology concentrate power in the hands of a few at the top or will workers be informed by that technology and gain the opportunity to exercise more autonomy in the workplace? Will the new workplaces allow them to escape the deskilling of the modernist factory with its attempt to limit how much workers know about their job and its relationship to the total process of production (Copa and Tebbenhoff 1990; Kohlberg and Smith 1992)? The past few years have provided little comfort, with an increase in the disparity of wealth between rich and poor and white and non-white. By the beginning of the 1990s the distribution of wealth in the United States significantly exceeded the level of inequality that existed in the mid-1800s when Marx was making his observations. Indeed, the chances of mobility are so remote for many poor children that American education is faced with the consequences of their hopelessness – apathy, crime, violence, suicide. The new service and information oriented economy has so far done little to upset these realities. Workers' wages are still absurdly low in relation to the budgets of transnational firms and the salaries of corporate leaders. As corporate profits have stagnated over the past two decades, policies have sought to cut costs not in executive salaries but in taxes and wages. Thus, socially harmful policies of capital mobility (moving plants to areas with lower taxes, less unionization and lower wages) and competitive advantage (placing labourers and governments in various locations throughout the world in competition to lure private corporate investment) have been implemented (MacLeod 1987; Lather 1991; Pollin and Cockburn 1991; Chesneaux 1992).

Critical multiculturalism, modernist fragmentation, corporate power and the conservative reaction: the struggle for democracy

True to its nature, critical multiculturalism names the names of those who undermine the struggle for race, class and gender justice and democracy. Modernist science, when combined with industrialization's creation of unprecedented economic and political power, pulled the rug out from under Western societies' attempts to create liberal democracies. The technological advances of the late twentieth century have been employed to catalyse the consolidation of corporate power, in the process moving democracy and social justice further out of reach. Indeed, the last three decades of the twentieth century have witnessed a conservative retrenchment – a call back to white supremacy, corporate power and patriarchy. The gains of the 1960s in areas of race, gender and the regulation of corporations signalled a threat to those who had traditionally held power. This right-wing consolidation of power on a number of fronts has shaped the status of the critical multicultural vision at the end of the twentieth century.

By 1980 academic conservatives intent on protecting Western civilization from attacks by feminists, African Americans and the political left joined with Republican business leaders and fundamentalist Christians to elect Ronald Reagan and scores of other conservative politicians. The new coalition accepted economic and political inequality as well as racial and gender discrimination as acceptable features of modern life. Once in power this conservative alliance undertook a massive redistribution of wealth in American society. In the 1980s low-income families lost US$23 billion in income and governmental benefits while high-income families gained $35 billion. The standard of living for middle class Americans declined during these years while a new underclass emerged, with homeless men and women living in the streets. Health care systems broke down, farm bankruptcies increased and the federal deficit grew at an unprecedented rate (Kellner 1989; Grossberg 1992). Conservative economists boasted of the massive job growth of the 1980s and early 1990s. Upon closer examination this job growth turned out to be primarily an increase in so-called secondary jobs. Such jobs require virtually no training and demand little commitment to the work itself. Workers 'put in time', viewing the job not as an end in itself but as a means to some other goal. Not only were many of the jobs secondary, but a large percentage were part-time. Part-time jobs are almost always of low status, as they deny individuals the possibility of promotion. Suffice it to say that the job expansion of the 1980s and early 1990s did little to help the poor and the working class (Falk and Lyson 1988; Block 1990).

The crisis of the workplace was exacerbated by the rise of the right wing and the accompanying consolidation of the power of business and industrial leaders. Exhibiting a radical version of modernism's tendency for fragmentation and decontextualization, conservative industrialists with the support of government adopted a human capital theory which placed the burden for economic development on changing the individual worker while de-emphasizing changes in workplace organization. Such individualism (albeit decontextualized) projects a humanistic ring; it fails, however, to account for the limitations on lower-level worker autonomy that characterize the modern workplace. Moreover, it assumes that a common good does not really exist, only a conglomeration of individual goods. In this postmodern world, however, this set of individual goods operating under the 'logic' of market forces produces a 'common bad' that undermines the connections between human beings.

Grounded on this individualist human capital theory, the conservative climate of the late twentieth century perpetuates the myth that anyone can make it in American society – as long as they have the ability and the perseverance. From this perspective education becomes the great opportunity provider that allows those with motivation to reach the American Dream. Schooling ensures that everyone has access to the ladder of socio-economic mobility. In the emerging postmodern era Horatio Alger mutates into Donald Trump, assuring all poor children that success awaits. If they fail, they have no one to blame but themselves. The power dynamic produced by such a picture of the world emerges from its ideological silence. Conveniently ignoring studies of actual socio-economic mobility in American society or the reality of racial and gender-related oppression, the conservative theory fails to consider the context of the social. In this way, questions of unequal power relations between rich and poor, white and non-white, and male and female are dismissed as the prattle of special interests (MacLeod 1987; Falk and Lyson 1988; Bellah 1991; Giroux 1993).

The erasure of inequality is merely one aspect of a larger right-wing redefinition of schooling and work and the relationship between them. The idea of equalizing the opportunities of school and access to better jobs was redefined in the 1980s and early 1990s as wasteful public spending. Instead of viewing social and economic justice as a principle for school organization and curriculum development in a democratic society, the right wing redefined schooling as a training ground for corporate needs. Schools in the 1980s and 1990s increasingly became places where students were adjusted to the needs of the workplace and the rest of the private sector. Indeed, the private sector was sanctified as that sphere of society which provides good things such as Christmas presents, new houses, shopping and holidays – the public sphere gives us only headaches, taxes, bureaucrats, red tape and critical multiculturalists.

The result of such a fragmentation of society manifests itself in social pathologies that undermine the quality of everyone's lives – especially the poor and non-white. Americans who live in urban areas, for example, are confronted by high-cost housing and traffic jams. Everyone who can afford it buys an upscale house with no concern for supplying low-cost housing to those who need it in the community. The cost of housing is thus inflated as the affluent become slaves of their mortgages and the poor become homeless. As urban commuters think only of driving private cars to work, they spend more hours on the congested highway breathing exhaust-filled air. The thought of working for better public transportation never crosses their mind. With the right-wing polarization of the public and private realms, the rich fashion private compounds, patrolled by private police, designed to remove them as far as possible from the decaying and ever more dangerous (read non-white and poor) public sphere (Horne 1986; Bellah 1991; Apple 1992; Giroux 1993).

Schools have played a special role in this right-wing redefinition of the private and public spheres. The public role of schooling as a training ground for democracy and democratic citizenship has been replaced by a private corporate view of the role of education. In addition to their role as supplier of 'adjusted labour' to the corporate machine, schools have come to be seen as commodities subject to the dictates of the market. Thus, we have witnessed the proliferation of private educational ventures in the USA, including the Edison Project and Channel One. In this milieu students are transformed from citizens into consumers, capable of being bought and sold – children are now relegated to the status of regressive modernism's *Homo economicus*. In this hyperreality of the private, we 'consume' our young. The conservative goals of Presidents Bush and Clinton's *America 2000* illustrated these trends, with calls for replacing government service agencies with private corporate services, redistributing wealth from the poor to the wealthy and building a private market system which promotes the values of isolated individualism, self help, corporate management and consumerism in lieu of public ethics and economic democracy. Thus, the sanctification of the private works to consolidate the power of the corporation and expand its freedom to redefine social and educational life in ways which help to maximize its profits (Apple 1992; Giroux 1993).

All of this talk of privatization is couched in the language of public improvement and democratic virtue. The public sphere has failed, the mystifiers argue. The private market is a much more effective mechanism in the attempt to achieve socio-economic improvement. This return to neo-classical economics holds serious consequences. Human destiny is couched in the imagery of a football game or an air raid over Baghdad. Market forces of competition govern the world, degrading those nations and those peoples who start with a economic disadvantage. These nations' and peoples' subsequent poor performance in 'the game' is chalked up to poor preparation or inferior ability. In other words, they failed for the same reasons that the Pittsburgh Steelers lost to the Miami Dolphins: bad planning, the inferiority of the offensive line. Be good sports, people; don't make excuses for your socio-economic failure (Block 1990; Chesneaux 1992).

The point here seems obvious. Reliance on the market for economic growth and social justice is not a realistic way of achieving such goals. Instead, it is nothing more than a disguised, undemocratic method for justifying the power interests of a particular group. It privileges a view of reality that sees market forces and competition collaborating to create a balance of supply and demand, wages and prices and goods and services when outside interference is minimized. In a postmodern, multinational economy, such neo-classicism is naive. The idea that freedom from outside interference in the market is possible in a world where multinational corporations control markets and pressure governments, where government expenditure on national defence is counted in trillions of dollars and where economic communities and oil cartels are common is absurd. Local economics are intimately tied to external realities in ways that upset free trade and fair competition. The market paradigm does not accommodate these realities, as it advocates free trade and competition as a panacea to problems of labour, production, equality and even the environment (Richmond 1986).

A prime objective of the conservative reaction in late twentieth-century America has been to co-opt the schools in the attempt to promote this market philosophy. Critical multiculturalists understand the ideological effects of schools shaped by the right-wing needs of business and industry. Indeed, they are often aware that their viewpoints are not welcome in most public and even private schools. In these corporate-influenced, modernist schools, teachers are often directed to teach to curriculum guides organized around the development of worker skills that business needs. Often devoid of concerns with contextualization and critical reflection, school programmes are designed to produce cooperative workers – employees capable of solving problems identified by employers. Of course, student response to these larger purposes of schooling is diverse and often unpredictable. Paul Willis (1977), Peter McLaren (1986) and Jay MacLeod (1987) have taught us that we can never be sure how the ideologies promoted by schools and businesses affect living and breathing students. Nevertheless, the power of business continues to shape the purposes of school, as well as the structural dynamics of the school.

Such structural dynamics have been moulded by modernist forms of vulgar efficiency and scientific management. In other words, schools in the twentieth century have taken on the structural dynamics of the factory. A simplistic production–process–product mentality that reflects Taylorism has shaped educational discourse. Such a way of thinking and talking about schools creates educational formats that have little to do with everyday life and the lived world. Questions of meaning, power and social justice are rarely asked or considered in such educational settings. Students are supposed to learn how to follow directions in this context, in the process becoming accustomed to the traditional production practices and to the control of managerial authority. Again, it must be emphasized that while industrial forms have influenced the structural dynamics of schooling as well as curriculum content and instructional style, individual students can respond very differently to such ideological structures. How these realities shape student consciousness is a very complex matter. As complex as it may be, we can argue with some confidence that much of what occurs in schools of this type does not empower African American, Latino and Native American students in their struggle to overcome the stranglehold of white supremacy, the poor to transcend class bias or women to escape the grasp of patriarchy. Such empowerment does sometimes take place in schools; but too often it is the result of the work of a brave teacher bucking the established curriculum, of community groups unwilling to allow the continuation of discrimination against particular students, or of poor or non-white students themselves to put their literacy and other academic skills to work in a process of self-empowerment.

Liberal reformers argue that at the end of the twentieth century, with the changing post-Fordist workplace and the lean, mean and flexible new Western economic systems that demand educated workers, a new more empowering education is emerging. Such an argument fails to account for the fact that most workplaces have not changed in a way that demands smarter, more highly skilled workers and that most job growth is taking place in low-status, deskilled jobs in the service industries. Indeed, corporations are cutting back on the hiring of highly educated, highly paid workers with health retirement benefits, focusing much of their energies on part-time, no benefits, low-paid 'secondary' workers. Indeed, if business and industry were so concerned with creating high-skill jobs and filling them with well compensated workers, why would they move so many of their factories to Mexico, Singapore or Malaysia and hire poor, *uneducated*, disempowered women for 75 cents an hour? High-tech industrial development and its alleged need for a rigorous, demanding education for the workers it hires offers false hope for more justice in both the workplace and the society at large. Technophiles of both liberal and conservative persuasions ignore the fact that even in high-tech industries managers still attempt to maximize their economic advantage over workers. The promise of high-tech as panacea, promoted by social leaders such as Speaker of the House Newt Gingrich, fades as we realize that a large percentage of the jobs within high-tech industries are low-paid, repetitive, low-skill positions offering little hope for socio-economic mobility (Lamphere 1985; DeYoung 1989; Grubb *et al.* 1991; Simon *et al.* 1991; Carnevale 1992).

Critical multiculturalists do *not* believe that Western democracy is a completed task

The purpose of this chapter is to expose the economic, political, cultural and educational forces that subvert the civic and democratic impulses within institutional (schooling) and cultural (TV, movies, music, video games, advertising etc.) pedagogy. Modernist science/epistemology is in our opinion a central culprit in the crime against democracy and social justice, with its masculinist subversion of human connection and caring. In this context critical multiculturalism draws upon the feminist reconceptualization of democracy and education. Such a rethinking involves far more than merely adding data on women to the content of courses. The feminist critique challenges the central concepts of academic disciplines. Feminist theorists contend that feeling should be united with reason in a way that strengthens our emotional identification with life and its preservation. All assumptions within a discipline must be re-examined in relation to this feminine emotional concern with life. Teaching can never be viewed in the same way after feminist theorists assert that experience does not take place in an isolated and autonomous self and that the individual is not the basic socio-political and psychological unit. Understanding these dynamics, feminist multiculturalists expose what appear to be individual idiosyncrasies as manifestations of larger power structures that undermine democratic and socially just relationships. For example, what passes as a self-policing of one's behaviour is often a product of a prevailing mode of domination shaping social action. For example, a young girl's refusal to join in an activity for fear of being labelled aggressive and unladylike; a male principal's authoritarian treatment of *his* women teachers; or lower socio-economic class girls' acceptance of middle and upper-middle class girls' control of the planning of Homecoming activities. The important point in each of the examples, critical feminists maintain, is that power is validated by its connection to a larger *social* structure (Fee 1982; Giddens 1986; Giroux 1988; Britzman 1991; Wertsch 1991).

In this same way, power produces systems of instruction, methods of evaluation, definitions of teacher and student success, and classification and tracking systems that arrange students into advanced, college-bound, general or vocational tracks. Such divisions provide the knowledge, social practices, cultural capital and skills required by the class-driven hierarchy of labour in the society's workplaces. The way in which power interacts with personal behaviour in this case is that school leaders induce students to believe that race, gender and class-based divisions of students and workers are natural and necessary. Students from outside the mainstream, the non-white and the poor, are convinced that they do not possess the ability to move into upper levels. They are captured by the entanglements of the myths of the cultural and academic inferiority of the outsiders. Many black students, for example, who are often very successful in college, report that by the time they were junior high students the culture of the school had convinced them that college was out of the question. Thus, students and their teachers come to accept the myths of inferiority. 'How can we expect these students to understand physics?', teachers and guidance counsellors ask as they channel the outsiders into non-academic vocational tracks (McLaren 1991). Thus, with the help of feminists and other agents of democracy, critical multiculturalists want to make sure that the public understands that democracy is not a completed task in Western society – a belief that shapes everything we do in the name of critical multiculturalism.

Democratic interventions: challenging the administration and purpose of education

How can critical multiculturalists act as a countervailing force against anti-democratic impulses in the educational arena? One of the most important ways involves challenging conceptually the administrative structures of schools. It is interesting that administration is taught only to people who serve at the head of the administrative structure and not to people who are to be administered. Ideas about democratic forms of management are not concepts that are typically discussed between principals and teachers or teachers and student. As Henry Giroux (1997a) argues, critical multiculturalists want to engage students and teachers in an analysis of what is involved in becoming a critical citizen capable of governing instead of merely being governed. Without the awareness produced by such discussion, the social ambiance of the school remains within an authoritarian frame. The ideological web formed by this authoritarianism produces a curriculum that teaches teachers and students how to think and act in the world. Both teachers and students are taught to conform, to adjust to their inequality and their particular rung of the status ladder and to submit to authority. Teachers and students are induced to develop an authority dependence, a view of citizenship that is passive, a view of learning that means listening. The predisposition to question the authority structure of the school and the curriculum it teaches or to reject the image of the future that the structure presents to teachers and students is out of bounds. The politics of authoritarianism rubs democratic impulses the wrong way (Shor 1992).

The authoritarianism that infects the modernist, anti-democratic school emerges from an androcentrism that is comfortable with hierarchical relationships. Critical multiculturalists ask if this androcentrism is compatible with more democratic forms of management – forms grounded on cooperation and independence. Efforts of critically grounded administrators to employ inclusive management styles are often perceived as weakness by teachers and community members. In the same context critical multicultural teachers who emphasize justice, self-discipline and democratic attitudes towards their students are perceived as lenient. In fact, when teachers throw off authoritarian constructions of their role, they are astonished to find that some students perceive that they have been given permission to ignore assignments and misbehave. Young teachers at this point often revert back to authoritarian forms of classroom control, assuming that democratization simply doesn't work. In the culture of the authoritarian school, democratic management and teaching styles are often equated with low quality standards. Quality education in this context is, after all, something done *to* students (Maher and Rathbone 1986; Torres 1993).

One of the hardest lessons we have to teach our teacher education students from mainstream cultural backgrounds concerns the fact that schools are not only academic sites but socio-political venues as well. The difficulty does not involve the specific nature of the social and political dynamics but the fact that education is a social and political act. Somehow this notion runs counter to the ideological countenance of their previous educational experiences. Critical multiculturalists seek to overcome this pre-vailing assumption of educational neutrality by exposing the historical and contemporary effects of school. Leaders and their political and corporate backers use schooling not as much to foster democracy as to provide for the social regulation of individuals (Kaufman 1978). In their effort to produce suitable citizens and safe workers, educational leaders have not questioned the justice of the existing socio-political order – indeed, they have rarely embraced efforts to contextualize the curriculum with a rigorous examin-ation of power inequities and divergent forms of oppression. Western democracies are presented to students as places where a legal equality of opportunity has been achieved. In such a context why would educators waste their time with the babblings of critical multiculturalists concerned with issues of power, democracy and race, class and gender relations? Of course, the answer to such a question is that they don't. If inequality does not exist, then why do we need to examine the ways it structures institutions and shapes the lives of individuals (Carlson 1991)?

Critical multiculturalism and the revitalization of democracy and democratic thinking

Critical multiculturalism sees the development of a democratic social and educational vision as one of its primary tasks. The reason such a task is so important involves the fragility of democracy and its vulnerability to the abuses of power and oppression. Without a democratic vision with an egali-tarian set of commitments, students must constantly resist modernist school-ing's effort to adapt them to the brutality of the neo-social Darwinist landscape. While not rejecting the need for students and other citizens to understand the nature of the world so that they can negotiate its dangers, critical multiculturalists maintain the importance of exposing individuals to alternatives, to visions of what can be. Without such visions we are doomed to the perpetuation of the structural inequalities and the political passivity of the status quo. This is why critical multiculturalists, operating in the spirit of Paulo Freire, seek to connect their democratic vision to a rewriting of the world. In such a pedagogical effort, teachers, writers, theologians and other cultural workers create a new history, as they work to revitalize democracy dissipated first by industrialization and next by the hyperreality produced by the communications revolution of the last half of the twentieth century. Analysing democratic issues historically, philosophically, pedagogically, in relation to hyperreality and as a benchmark for educational purpose, criti-cal multiculturalists construct a curriculum of democratic studies.

Such a curriculum is grounded on the assumption that self-directed edu-cation undertaken by self-organized community groups is the most powerful form of multicultural pedagogy. Critical multiculturalism in this context becomes a 'pro-democracy' movement that attempts to promote forms of thinking and action that retrieve the impetus for educational change from business and industrial elites. Grounded on a conception of solidarity with the oppressed and the excluded, this curriculum seeks to connect with democratic organizations dedicated to a cultural politics of emancipatory change. Here students can become part of social movements where they can employ their research and pedagogical skills to build new forms of democratic consciousness and counter-hegemonic action. Such work can revolutionize the view of knowledge as an entity produced by experts in remote locales. Critical multicultural knowledge becomes a product of democratic cooperation, a manifestation of what happens when experience is interrogated in the light of historical consciousness intercepting personal experience. As a pro-democracy movement critical multicultural teachers and cultural workers become engaged practitioners who expose forms of subordination that create inequities among racial, class and gendered groups. Such practitioners view learning in relation to civic courage and link education to the demands of the oppressed. Such activists understand the danger of their position, as it elicits the ire of those in charge. Despite these possibilities, they push on.

As a pro-democracy movement, critical multiculturalism recognizes the anti-democratic dynamics of modernism and the education it has spawned. In many ways the crisis of modernism can be viewed as a crisis of cognition – an inability to think democratically. Marked by a power-saturated mode of thinking that has become obsessed with the rational management of the lives of individuals, modernist education has found itself trapped within a prison of nihilism, a culture of manipulation. Education in the late twentieth century becomes a pawn of powerful groups who attempt to use it as a means of solving social problems in a way that serves their own interests. Pushed and pulled by such groups, schools are not moved by educational and political visions that value the human spirit but by self-serving and often cynical impulses that seek to control that very spirit. Thus schools, as most teachers would testify, are immersed in a crisis of motivation. Devoid of a meaningful justification for the pursuit of learning, teachers and students wander aimlessly within a maze of fragmented information. Classrooms often become spiritless places where rule-following teachers face a group of students who have no conception of any intrinsic value of the lessons being taught or their relation to democratic citizenship.

Is thinking to be shaped in accord with the perceived demands of economic production or is it to be nurtured by those who are interested in democratic personal and social development? The modernist concern with human development in terms of human capital and productivity allows for mass acceptance of Reagan–Bush–Clinton/Thatcher–Major educational reform as merely one step in a government-directed economic-technological competitive strategy. Like other aspects of the contemporary landscape, thinking has been commodified – its value measured only in terms of the logic of capital. The democratic and ethical dimensions of thinking in this context have grown increasingly irrelevant. Aware of the need to avoid oversimplification, it can be argued that much of contemporary cognitive education can be divided into one of two classifications: (a) education for cognition manipulation; or (b) education for cognitive growth and democratic emancipation. The one-truth epistemology of positivism dovetailed seductively with the scientific management orientations of the proponents of human capital development. Both viewpoints had overcome any moral qualms with the manipulation of human beings for desired ends. The controlled labour of the factory, with its 'team players' exercising their 'democratic' control of the workplace by making decisions about the most trivial dimensions of the operation (e.g. where to locate the water cooler), was similar to types of teachers desired by the 'schools of excellence' of modernist technicist reforms. Such teachers would follow top-down administrative edicts as they taught from their pre-packaged, teacher-proof materials and rewarded students for devotion to memory work that studiously avoided the encouragement of questioning attitudes about the entire process (Koetting 1988; Young 1990).

Conservatives have sought to employ a cognition of manipulation by appealing to the virtues of the Protestant work ethic to increase productivity in the factories and the schools. In addition to their appeal to traditional values, conservatives have perfected the science of management. Wrapping themselves in the banner of democracy, forces of the right have convinced many that forms of dissent are distasteful, are manifestations of a 'bad attitude' or are even unpatriotic. Liberals, on the other hand, have sought to provide a more equitable distribution of wealth, more equal educational opportunities. In this attempt, however, liberals have employed the same modernist forms of thinking, the same modernist bureaucratic mechanisms that led to the crisis of democracy and motivation in the first place.

Liberals have not challenged the manipulative strategies of advertising – one of the most important teachers in the cultural curriculum. Such strategies have revolutionized the nature of political campaigns in Western democracies. The corporate culture of marketing has dramatically altered the discourse of politics, relegating traditional forms of ethical and political thinking to the cloisters of academia far away from the public sphere. While the intent of the advertising-directed politics of the postmodern is manipulative, progressive impulses are salvaged by a myriad of contradictory readings. Many of those who view the ads fall victim to the manipulative intent of the producers; others, while recognizing the manipulation, become discouraged and turn off any involvement in a corrupt and degraded political system; and still others who recognize the manipulation are inspired to fight it by organizing community groups dedicated by authentic public conversation.

The manipulative intent of the new right of the late twentieth century is frightening and in no way should be minimized. When we are considering the politics of thinking, the impact of such an outlook must be carefully examined. The discourse of international competition constructs the framework for the right-wing justification of manipulation. If we are not to be economically surpassed by the developing economics of disciplined and authoritarian Asia, we must cultivate more social obedience and commonness of purpose and less democracy and liberty. As North American economies face more competition from the East, with its accompanying diminution of national profits, a disparity grows between the increasing claims made on government and its capacity to provide. The conservatives under Reagan and Bush attempted to reduce claims on government by deflecting them to the 'free market' and to volunteerism (Bush's thousand points of light). They attempted to discredit and gain control over voices of dissent such as intellectuals, school teachers and voices of the mass media. In addition, conservatives – in order to achieve greater steering power for the government – strengthened bureaucratic control of institutions such as education by injecting management strategies like cost–benefit analysis, detailed fiscal management and quantitative planning strategies.

The most important aspect of the Right's ongoing strategy of manipulation, however, involves a fundamental issue of cognition – the mobilization of consent. This process involves the way in which individuals come to see themselves and their role in society as a result of their identification with meanings produced in popular media and social institutions. For example, the conservatives have been able to draw upon male identification with the view of masculinity promoted by the films of Clint Eastwood, Sylvester Stallone and Arnold Schwarzenegger. While the identification is often subtle and subliminal, George Bush made the relationship explicit with his famous evocation of Clint Eastwood's 'read my lips'. What is especially important here for critical multicultural concerns with the relation of cognition to democracy involves the recognition of the way the consent of citizens is mobilized. In this context we come to appreciate the fact that ideological production, domination and even learning itself are processes that take place outside the boundaries of rational thinking. Feeling and desire are often more important in the individual quest for identity than is reason. Conservatives of our era have recognized this reality and have rather cynically used it for their political gain. Ronald Reagan did not attempt, for example, to convince the public logically of the need to return to traditional values; he mobilized the electorate's consent by appeal to the image of traditional values, by connecting them to the pleasure of a romanticized notion of a bygone golden era. We miss a major point when we assume that thinking is a rational process 'untainted' by feeling or cultural identification.

It is this aspect of thinking, its emotionality and symbolic identification, that allows the culture of manipulation to operate so effectively. At the same time, however, this aspect of thinking holds emancipatory possibilities as we come to understand the array of moral and ethical identifications that move individuals to perform courageously and heroically. With this understanding individuals can come to think in a manner that connects their logic to an ethical identification with a politics that rejects the manipulation of human beings and the subordination of people to external ends, while supporting an emancipatory politics of self-directed men and women working together in a democratic community.

Critical multiculturalism as democratic empowerment

Critical multiculturalism, buoyed by its concern with the socio-political factors that destroy democracy and democratic modes of thinking, provides a perspective on school reform usually missed by other perspectives. With its awareness of the multicultural context and its attention to race, class and gender oppression, it thinks in terms of educational alternatives that are equitable and responsive to the lived needs of marginalized students. As such, critical multicultural educational reform transcends simple modernist rationalistic attempts to raise test scores or transfer skills. Such democratically sensitive reforms are centred on a concept of student, teacher, worker and citizen empowerment. Critical multiculturalists, therefore, want to educate students who are ready, willing and able to take charge of their own worlds, as they seek to build communities of active citizens dedicated to universal education and social justice. They seek to emancipate students in the sense that young people are empowered to free themselves from dominant power's effort to shape their consciousness (Solorzano 1989; Nieto 1996).

The emancipatory confrontation with power allows us to glimpse who we want to be, as we struggle to understand how we have come to see the world. In our emancipatory journey towards self-direction, our interactions with critical multiculturalism alert us to the complexity of the task. Critical postmodern teachers come to understand that human identity is such a chaotic knot of intertwined forces that no social agent can ever completely disentangle it. Using Michel Foucault's concept of genealogy, we trace the formation of our subjectivities. We begin to see ourselves at various points in the web of reality, ever-confined by our placement, but liberated by our appreciation of our predicament. Thus, in the spirit of critical multiculturalism, we begin to understand and disengage ourselves from the power narratives that have laid the basis for the dominant way of seeing. Our ability to see from a variety of perspectives forms the basis of a long-running meta-dialogue with ourselves. This inner conversation leads to a perpetual redefinition of our images of both self and world. Emancipation/empowerment doesn't take place by merely wishing it so. The emancipatory process is long, difficult and too often unrewarded by those with whom one comes into contact. It takes courage, fortitude, analytical ability, time and rigorous research and study to exercise power over one's own life and to encourage such dedication in others.

In the process one comes to realize in ever more profound terms the fragility of democracy. Too often reduced to a mere set of formal measures of participation, democracy in a critical multicultural context involves the living of everyday life in an empowered way. Such a critical perspective transforms liberal notions of democratic education as equal access to schools and equal opportunity to a more power-conscious concern with emancipation of students from all walks of life. The flag of critical multiculturalism is an emblem of empowerment in both the personal and public spheres. Such empowerment is won by an ability to read the world differently from those who typically run educational and other social institutions. It is won by the ability to dream alternative democratic communities that connect race, class and gender differences to the needs of a democratic politics, education and economics. It is catalysed pedagogically by an understanding of Paulo Freire's problem-posing method of instruction that arranges classrooms around problems of democracy.

The instructional strategy, at once so simple yet profound, works in three phases: (a) naming the problem; (b) analysing the causes of the problem; and (c) finding solutions to the problem (Freire 1970). Each stage requires a knowledgeable and scholarly, power-literate educator to make the process work. Naming the problem involves a sensitivity to threats to democracy and an ability to see behind the curtain of ostensibly mundane everyday reality. It involves the ability to develop generative themes about the problem that can be represented to students visually, as in pictures, drawings and films, and narratively, as in stories, essays and socio-cognitive maps. In addition, the facilitator must be able to evoke passionate interest in the problem and then use the passion to engage students in the difficult processes of analysing and formulating solutions to it. Problem-posing teaching is no picnic, as students accustomed to more traditional methods of study, parents worried about basic skills, administrators concerned with curriculum guides and performance on standardized tests and community leaders protective of their power positions all present potential threats to the process. Critical multicultural teachers can protect themselves only by their own competence and political savvy and by making connections with historical traditions and community organizations that ideologically and personally support their educational purposes (Solorzano 1989; Giroux 1997a). Such connections are necessary in a society beset with anti-democratic forces.

What is power?

Although the nature and effects of power constitute the topic of contentious debate, rarely does anyone take time out to define the subject of the debate. In recent years a consensus seems to be emerging around the notion that power is a basic reality of human existence. Consensus, however, dissolves at this point, with various scholars running like quail in diverse theoretical directions. Critical multiculturalism contends that power is a fundamental constituent of human existence that works to shape the oppressive and the productive nature of the human condition. Scholars from the cultural studies tradition tend to accept the fundamental-constituent-of-reality thesis, as they contend that power is embedded in the social frameworks of race, class, gender, occupations and everyday interaction and communication. Poststructuralists such as Foucault agree, maintaining that power is present in all human relationships, be they the interactions of lovers, business partners or researchers and the researched. Indeed, Foucault concluded, after reading Nietzsche, that like the existence of capillaries in the circulatory system, power is inseparable from the social domain. As to the form of this ubiquitous social dynamic, Foucault never offered a definition more specific than that the exercise of power is a way in which particular actions modify others or guide their possible conduct. Since power is everywhere, therefore, it is not something that can easily be dispensed with or overthrown. Simplistic politics or pedagogies that propose to put an end to power relations, do not understand its relation to the web of reality (McCarthy 1992; Musolf 1992; Cooper 1994).

Critical multiculturalists understand that there is nothing simple about the workings of power, that power is not simply the unchanging exercise of a binary relationship: A exercises its power over B and B responds by formulating acts of resistance against A. In its complexity and ambiguity power is deployed by both dominant and subordinate individuals and groups; it is not the province of one group and not the other. Indeed, we are all empowered and we are all unempowered, in that we all possess abilities and we are all limited in the attempt to use our abilities. Thus, conceptions of power that depict it as a one-directional, unified force with standardized outcomes miss important aspects of its nature. For example, when advocates of free market capitalism argue that the market works to satisfy consumer needs – i.e. that consumer power flows in one direction toward the producers of goods to shape their production decisions – they fail to understand the two-way (and more) flow of power in the circumstance. Consumer power is not sufficient to thwart producer ability to hide information concerning safety, environmental aspects of production, exploitation of labour in the production of particular goods etc. that would drastically change the behaviour of many consumers. Thus, power flows in a variety of directions often behind the curtain of surface appearances (Bizzell 1991; Rorty 1992; Cooper 1994; Keat 1994). Thus, power is nothing if not complex, ambiguous and perplexing – indeed, that is part of its power. In hyperreality, with its information saturation and global media networks, power wielders are invisible. As remote social actors, power forces are absent from everyday interactions; in this context the ambiguity of power becomes even more pronounced, thus enhancing power's power.

John Fiske (1993) uses the term power bloc to describe the social formations around which power politics operate in Western societies in the late twentieth century. Employing the term as used by Antonio Gramsci, the Italian political theorist and Stuart Hall, the British cultural studies scholar, Fiske argues that power wielders do not constitute a particular class or well defined social category. The power bloc, he contends, is more like an ever-shifting set of strategic and tactical social alliances. Such alliances are arranged unsystematically whenever social situations arise that threaten the interests of the 'allies'. Power blocs are historically, socially and issue(s) specific as they come and go in relation to changing cultural arrangements. Power blocs are often formed around social formations involving race, class, gender or ethnicity in the pursuit of privileged access to particular rights or resources. For Fiske, power 'is a systematic set of operations upon people that works to ensure the maintenance of the social order . . . and ensure its smooth running' (Fiske 1993: 11). It stands to reason that those individuals and groups who benefit the most from the maintenance of this social order align their interests with those of the dominant power system and work to keep it running smoothly. In this context, Fiske concludes that the power bloc can be described better by 'what it *does* than what it *is*'. In this configuration the notion of 'the people' includes those who fall outside the power bloc and are 'disciplined' by it. Falling outside the power bloc does not mean that such an individual has no power. The power such outsiders hold is a weaker power (Fiske labels it a localizing power) than that of the power bloc. Indeed, it is a power that can be cultivated, strengthened and sometimes successfully deployed.

Along lines of race, class and gender, individuals can simultaneously fall within the boundaries of one power bloc and outside another. While no essential explanation can explain the way an individual will relate to power blocs *vis-à-vis* his or her race, class or gender, such dimensions do affect people's relationship to power-related social formations. In most cases individuals are fragmented in relation to power. An African American male may be disempowered in relation to the racial category of white supremacy yet may enjoy the political benefits of being a male in a patriarchal power bloc or an upper-middle class male in the economic power bloc. Thus, individuals move in and out of empowered and disempowered positions. In our critical multiculturalist perspective such fragmented power-related understandings are central, yet at the same time we maintain a keen sense of awareness of the human suffering that is caused by life outside of particular power alignments. Critical multiculturalists understand that there is little ambiguity in relation to the pain, degradation and horror that women experience from the batterings of men acting in complicity with the patriarchal power bloc or that the poor experience as the result of the economic power bloc's insensitive fiscal politics, or that African Americans experience as a result of the white supremacist power bloc's racism.

In these painful examples a basic aspect of power is starkly illustrated: power produces inequities in the ability of human beings to delineate and realize their material and emotional needs. Teachers and other cultural workers who do not recognize this political dynamic will always be limited in their attempts to understand, provide for and help to empower their marginalized students and clients. The power bloc works consistently to obscure such appreciations; indeed, it labours to fix any violation of its borders by localizing powers. Such violations of the boundaries of power blocs have become common fare in later twentieth-century Western societies. Public debates over affirmative action, minimum wage legislation, universal health care, sex and violence in TV and movies and multicultural curriculums all constitute skirmishes at the doorstep of the power bloc. The reaction of the power bloc as expressed in the forceful pronouncements of the conservative monoculturalists indicates a sense of threat; from a racial perspective it reveals white perception of challenge to racial supremacy. Conservative multiculturalism, with its monoculturalism, singularity of standards of excellence and one-truth epistemology, is a quintessential representation of a power bloc resisting challenges to its previously unquestioned authority.

In the late 1990s one formation of the contemporary power bloc unites several groups: (a) dominant economic and political elites concerned with building good business climates to enhance corporate profits; (b) white working class and middle class groups who sense their white privilege under attack by minority groups and who are uncomfortable with what conservative leaders refer to as an attack on traditional values like the family (such threats are perceived as coming from immoral African American welfare recipients, homosexuals and feminists); (c) Social Darwinist conservatives with free-market economic perspectives and guardians of Western cultural values who advocate a return to 'standards of excellence' and discipline in schools; and (d) upwardly mobile members of the new middle class who may not be comfortable with the other groups represented in this power bloc but who join the alliance because of their desire for professional advancement – such advancement is possible only if they buy into the corporate management procedures and non-controversial conformist identities. While such a power bloc constantly aligns and dealigns itself depending on the issue in question, some groups are obviously more predisposed to alliance than others (Fiske 1993; Macedo 1994; Apple 1996).

Productive power

A critical multiculturalist view of power understands that power is both oppressive and productive – as previously delineated, power does not flow one way from oppressor to oppressed. Productive power creates knowledge, meanings and values, and must be cultivated wherever it is uncovered. In this context critical multicultural educators and other cultural workers can use productive power in the struggle to establish a critical democracy, to engage the marginalized in a rethinking of the role of education in their lives. Subordinated groups can cultivate their power to rewrite the too often formulaic stories of their lives – narratives that relegate them to lives of pain and desperation. Such rewriting uses power to construct alternative story lines which transcend preordained outcomes. These productive uses of power move educators beyond the immobilizing cynicism that often accompanies the monolithic view of power as oppressive. As a constitutive element in our lives, power takes on an educational purpose that must be studied and understood by all teachers. For example, critical multiculturalists understand the intersection of power and language, as they engage students in linguistically creative and generative activities. These activities might include examining the hidden assumptions embedded in language, extending word meanings, creating new words, twisting common word usages through metaphor and reinterpreting accepted linguistic connotations. Such productive activities operate pedagogically to expose the way words and grammar work to sustain and undermine our connection(s) to the world. This understanding of productive power helps critical multiculturalists to create a social imagination that reshapes their relationship to power and, accordingly, their views of self in relation to society (Thompson 1987; Giroux 1997a).

Operating with these understandings of productive power, critical multiculturalists such as Theresa Perry and Jim Fraser (1993) argue that school should ground itself around a vision of the society we want rather than simply reinforcing the social arrangements of the status quo. Such a critical social vision positions schools, of course, as multiracial, multi-ethnic, class inclusive and multigendered democracies. W. E. B. DuBois recognized these dynamics decades ago, as he argued that African American education should aim to develop the latent *power* of students. Such students will become, he continued, people of 'power, of thought – who know whither civilization is tending and what it means' (DuBois 1973: 14). Thus empowered, such black students – no matter how dramatic their disempowerment – gain the ability to resist politically, socially and economically by acting in solidarity with one another. African American scholar Cornel West (1993) picks up on DuBois's theme, maintaining that educators must develop the *power* of discernment among oppressed students. A powerful analytic moment is produced when minority (and all) students gain a deep grasp of their present condition in the light of the past. Such a moment highlights the ability of productive power to mitigate the effects of oppressive social structures by subjugated individuals' capacity to make meaning, interpret and produce knowledge (Murray and Ozanne 1991). In this context we can appreciate the need for a critical multiculturalist education to be as rigorous as possible. Such rigour is demanded by the strategic role the ability to analyse, refute and reconstruct plays in any effort for social justice and the creation of a participant political and economic democracy.

Standing in the shadows: the invisibility of power

Power is clandestine in its stance of plausible deniability – a term used by CIA operatives who set up a covert operation in such a way that, if it becomes unpopular or fails, they can deny their involvement in it. 'Power? What power?', power wielders innocently ask when caught in an act of oppression. Confronted with examples of power-generated subjugation, many scholars mouth the power bloc's party line – power asymmetry and oppression don't exist in the USA, Canada, Britain and other Western industrialized democracies. In a pedagogical context, critical multiculturalists point out that many educational scholars view school from a privileged perspective, never sensing the raw power covered by 'objective' curricula, bulletin boards and pronouncements of love for the children. When students emerge after the final bell, their identity has been affected by their location in this web of power. While students always have the ability to produce their own power and use it to resist, they must deal with power-produced socio-educational formations that work to align students with the interests of dominant power blocs. Coercers hide their authority while social and educational researchers identify power as the political province of the king, the state, or the legislature (Thiele 1986; Airaksinen 1992; Rorty 1992; Fiske 1994). Because power is everywhere, it can pass itself off as being nowhere. Thus, meanings are produced covertly – cloak and dagger hermeneutics (the art of interpretation). Liberal and conservative multiculturalists produce knowledge and curricula unwilling or unable to penetrate the facade constructed by power; thus, power is portrayed as a peripheral player in their version of the political and educational socio-drama.

The discussion of power in the public conversation about politics and education is taboo in the USA at the end of the twentieth century. A form of socially situated power supported by particular cultural alignments or relationships presents individuals and/or groups of individuals with limited sets of options from which to choose in particular situations. Recognition of such social alignments, critical multiculturalists argue, is an important aspect of any attempt to understand the way the social and educational world operates. Liberal multiculturalists' attempts to understand, say, the relationship between workers and corporate managers will be undermined by a lack of focus on the social alignment that supports the nature of their interaction. Such an alignment limits the worker's options, as he or she attempts to escape the low wages and degrading conditions of a particular workplace. The limited options the worker faces are a direct reflection of the social power alignments in question. Such analysis is ignored in much contemporary scholarship, leaving students of society, pedagogy and politics with little understanding of the impediments to a democratic society and egalitarian institutions.

Such culturally situated power with its complex social alignments is so well hidden, so far removed from everyday consciousness, that even those who benefit from it are sometimes unaware of its existence. Despite the fact, for example, that many men are cognizant of the patriarchal domination of women, they often deny their complicity in such a power dynamic. In this particular case they are unable to perceive the culturally situated, pervasive nature of patriarchal domination characterized by a social structure in which women have more trouble gaining access to goods, services and opportunities than do men. In such a circumstance many wives must often depend upon their husbands to help them meet their material needs. Thus, wives need husbands in ways that husbands don't need wives – a need that creates power asymmetries in their relationships. The asymmetries express themselves in a variety of ways, economically in particular: women find fewer financial opportunities than men; they earn only 60 per cent of what men earn; and they experience greater difficulty achieving economic mobility than men. Thus, even though a husband's intentions might involve the establishment of a loving and equal relationship with his wife, he still retains power over her in this social situation. Many husbands, of course, use these circumstances to enhance their position in the family. Even husbands who refuse to engage in such power plays cannot deny the existence of this gender-related power asymmetry. Such inequality can only be understood contextually, as individuals negotiate social relations on a terrain marked by historical, structural and ideological restrictions. An analysis of social, political or educational dynamics, of course, outside of this field distorts our understanding of the world.

The clandestine social alignment of culturally situated power by no means presents some definitive statement on power. Ever frustrating in its complexity and ambiguity, power is a chameleon as it takes on the colour of its context. Indeed, situated power can be subverted and quite often is. In our example of the disempowerment of women in the patriarchal social alignment, the entrance of an indecently wealthy woman dramatically changes the power context. In the new context created, the woman's wealth works to negate the disempowering effect of the patriarchal social alignment. On another level the limitations of the oppressive potential of culturally situated power is expressed at the level of consciousness construction. The larger concept of patriarchal domination of the social field does not explain the ways women see themselves, their aspirations, the nature of their male relationships or their perceptions of their role in the home. Such microphysics takes place at a more particularistic level that, while not entirely disconnected from the cultural situation of power, does not linearly follow a predictable pathway. All expressions of power are contextually specific.

Critical multiculturalists do not seek the capacity to predict and control manifestations of power. They hope only to anticipate better the way power works, so as to make their critical interventions as conducive to democratic egalitarianism as possible. Students of cultural studies, for example, understand the constant shifting of power contexts. Such an understanding leads them to the realization that no one theory of the workings of power can be developed for all times. All theories, thus, are contingent – ever shifting with the sands of time. Foucault often made this point, arguing that no permanent and consistent grids illustrating the effects of power upon humans will ever be found. No structured path always taken by power will be discovered by some lucky social analyst. Since human beings have no transhistorical, inimitable nature, no ultimate structure of the impact of power on humans exists. Such contextual contingency and confusion, he argued, cannot be solved by attempting to explain power, as did Marx, as the result of structured and fixed historical processes. If an analysis of power reveals a pattern of domination, Foucault contended, the analyst should not conclude that it is a permanent structure, a manifestation of a historical dynamic that could have developed in no other way (Thiele 1986; Wartenberg 1992b).

four

CRITICAL MULTICULTURALISM: HEGEMONY, REPRESENTATION AND THE STRUGGLE FOR JUSTICE

Power erasure – which often is accompanied by racial/colour evasion – exerts a reactionary and oppressive influence in late twentieth-century Western societies. Such erasure often leads individuals from dominant race, class and gender groups into an uncritical complicity with socio-political structural power asymmetries and cultural manifestations of inequality. Indeed, liberal and pluralist multiculturalists can embrace particular aspects of cultural diversity and at the same time leave power hierarchies invisible and hence intact. The liberal notion of sameness – the we-all-bleed-red mind-set – serves as an excellent form of power and racial erasure. In the larger context shaped by liberalism the view of schools as neutral sites that reflect the Western principles of equal opportunity extends the illusion of power's invisibility and irrelevance.

The curriculum of erasure: power as cultural imperialism

In elementary and secondary social studies curriculum, for example, erasure takes the form of the exclusion of knowledge that fails to justify dominant institutional arrangements and white middle and upper-middle class modes of conduct and deportment. In curriculum guides, textbooks and other social studies materials one is hard pressed to find reference to social conflict, social injustice or oppression structured along lines of race, class or gender. Dominant themes in these materials often emphasize social harmony and cultural consensus – everyone gets along, decisions are made for the good of all and no one dissents. Even social studies texts that reference 'controversial issues' erase social conflict and the unequal power relations that construct them. No curricular domain is exempt from such dynamics. In vocational education questions concerning the power and status aspects of particular jobs are not addressed. For example, the reasons why particular jobs merit low pay, thus reflecting the low worth dominant society relegates to the people who perform them, are not discussed. In this way dominant power's capacity to denigrate particular workers – no matter how adeptly they perform their tasks – is naturalized.

Thus, in these examples we see the efforts of the power bloc to make light of perceptions of socio-economic, cultural and political differences and to emphasize consensus. Issues of socio-economic, cultural and political difference involve disparities of material, discursive and knowledge-related resources and, of course, power. Therefore, difference becomes a register of conflict that when broadcast reminds individuals outside the power bloc of their place in the world. The interests of power blocs are not served by the marginalized's consciousness of their marginalization. At the same time, interestingly, such silence about power and conflict also enculturates members of groups that fall within the parameters of particular power blocs (middle and upper-middle class white people, for example) to be blind to their own privilege. By ignoring the relation of difference to power, institutions, such as schools, media, churches and many others, pass whiteness, middle-classness and maleness off as normal. Typically (but not always in the 1990s) depicting such ways of being as *normal* and not superior, the dominant culture achieves status as common-sensical, safe and non-threatening. Members of the dominant culture are protected from the subjugated knowledge of whiteness, for example, as a power force that often terrorizes the non-white (Simon *et al.* 1991; hooks 1992; Frankenberg 1993).

The traditional dominant cultural tactic of blaming the victim is another manifestation of the power bloc's erasure of power. In the public political conversation carried by the media, victim blaming constitutes a major theme, as commentators consistently ascribe the cause of African American poverty to teenage pregnancy, to middle class black flight and to black male immorality. Such a strategy has successfully served to erase the role of power by diverting analysis of hidden forms of racism and white supremacy that shape institutions and deny blacks equal participation in all realms of the society. Modernist educational psychology lends a scientific stamp of approval to this victim-blaming process by relegating the poor and non-whites' lowly state and even alleged criminal tendencies to genetic causes not to the discriminatory dispositions of institutional centres of power. In the economic realm students and the public at large are taught by schools and the media that capitalist societies offer forms of freedom unknown in other societies. Workers have the freedom, the narrative contends, to contract or not contract with employers, and anyone at any time can choose to open a business in our free enterprise system. With such universal economic freedom, there is no possibility in Western democracies of economic domination. Those who are poor simply have not worked hard enough or taken advantage of the endless opportunities that exist. Indeed, it is their own fault – no reference to power structures or oppressive social conditions is necessary in the curriculum of erasure (McLaren 1994a; Fraser 1995).

This erasure of power is one feature of what is often labelled cultural imperialism. Cultural imperialism involves the employment of one social group's experience as the norm for everyone. In this context, the power bloc consolidates its ability to regulate subordinate groups by framing their differences as deficiencies. Working most efficiently when members of oppressed groups internalize the dominant group's view of them, cultural imperialism renders invisible the perspectives of the marginalized while concurrently stereotyping them and designating them as 'other'. Such a process highlights the culturally imperialistic power bloc's capacity for making meaning for the society at large. Such power is a form of hermeneutic domination that privileges the experiences, values, cultural capital and viewpoints of the dominant group. As it invisibly exerts its effects, cultural imperialism shapes the social role of the disempowered. In such a context, for example, family values become whatever best reflects the preferred familial structure of the dominant group; marginalized family structures, no matter how well they might work for those living within them, are deemed pathological by the power bloc. In the process the culturally different are further dehumanized, creating a vicious circle that justifies even more inhumane treatment of them (Young 1992; McLaren 1994a). Critical multiculturalism induces the power bloc to see the invisible, to confront its cultural imperialism. As it monitors the dominant culture from below, critical multiculturalism provides a picture of power from the perspective of the oppressed – a subjugated knowledge of power (Fiske 1993).

Cultural studies and critical multiculturalism: new insights into power and democracy

Cultural studies is an interdisciplinary, transdisciplinary and sometimes counter-disciplinary field that functions within the dynamics of competing definitions of culture. Unlike anthropology, for example, cultural studies has emerged via the analysis of contemporary industrial societies. Cornel West (1993) argues that cultural studies involves (or at least should) the analysis of lived experience of various groups and individuals in late twentieth-century capitalist societies. Dedicated to this notion of diversity, cultural studies refuses the equation of culture with high culture; instead, cultural studies asserts that myriad expressions of cultural production should be analysed in relation to other cultural dynamics and social and historical structures. Such a position commits cultural studies to a pot pourri of artistic, religious, political, economic, racial, gender and communicative activities. In this context, it is important to note that while cultural studies is associated with the study of popular culture, it is not primarily *about* popular culture. Cultural studies interests are much broader and tend generally to involve the production and nature of the rules of inclusivity and exclusivity that guide academic inquiry and evaluation – in particular, the way these rules shape and are shaped by relations of *power*. Because of this concern with power and the political, cultural studies offers critical multiculturalists not only a new perspective on cultural dynamics but a moral and political vision in a world of pain, suffering and a loss of hope.

Advocates of cultural studies believe that the study of culture is fragmented among a variety of disciplines (e.g. sociology, anthropology, history, literary studies, communications) to the point that communication between scholars is undermined. Scholarship has become so isolated that scholars work in private, focusing on narrow areas and rarely analysing the way this isolated work fits into a larger whole. Producing knowledge that is so specialized, scholars often have little concern with how such knowledge articulates with broader discursive and institutional contexts. Cultural studies attempts to overcome this fragmentation by highlighting culture as a living process that shapes the way we live, view ourselves and understand the world around us. By adopting cultural studies' overtly multidisciplinary approach, scholars can study larger social issues such as race, class, gender, sexuality, ethnicity, immigration and pedagogy from unique perspectives and theoretical positions. As students of cultural studies question the dominant ways of seeing that evolve around the 'normal science' of disciplines, they free themselves from the self-validating redundancies that limit insight and chain them to familiar explanations. Indeed, they liberate themselves from the power bloc's complicity with the protocols of education and academic work in general.

Cultural studies advocates argue that the power bloc's development of the electronic mass media has changed the old rules of how culture operates. Media have become sufficiently powerful to produce both new ways of seeing the world and new meanings for lives and work. Media produce and validate those data described as knowledge. Thus, media shape identities and self-images. The last quarter of the twentieth century has witnessed a major transformation in how knowledge is produced. If this is true, cultural studies proponents argue, then we should expand the types of issues we study in the academic domain of education. For example, while we should, of course, continue to study books and print as academic artifacts, we should also begin to study the values that aural and visual media produce, market and distribute in TV, film, CDs, computer networks, advertising images etc. A major transformation has taken place in cultural epistemologies and as of yet academic disciplines have not been sufficiently equipped to account for such change. Cultural studies has positioned itself as a social force determined to confront these systemic changes and their implications for the purposes of scholarly activity and cultural work.

While critical multiculturalists who are involved with the work of cultural studies are undoubtedly committed to the academic domain of schools and universities, such educators are also concerned with cultural pedagogy. As we briefly referenced in Chapter 2, cultural pedagogy involves education and acculturation that takes place at a variety of cultural locations, including but not limited to formal educational institutions. Cultural studies scholars extend our notion of cultural pedagogy, focusing their attention on the complex interactions of power, knowledge, identity and politics. Issues of cultural pedagogy that arise in a cultural studies context would include:

1 The complex relationship between power and knowledge.
2 The ways knowledge is produced, accepted and rejected.
3 What individuals claim to know and the process by which they come to know it.
4 The nature of cultural/political authority and its relation to the dialectic of empowerment and domination.
5 The ways individuals receive dominant representations and encodings of the world – are they assimilated, internalized, resisted or transformed?
6 The manner in which individuals negotiate their relationship with the 'official story', the legitimate canon.
7 The means by which the official and legitimated narrative positions students and citizens to make sense of their personal experience.
8 The process by which pleasure is derived from engagement with the dominant culture – an investment that produces meaning and formulates affect.
9 The methods by which cultural differences along lines of race, class, gender, national origin, religion and geographical place are encoded in consciousness and processed by individuals.
10 The ways scientific rationality shapes consciousness in schools and the culture at large.

The implications of such issues for a critical multiculturalism are profound. Operating with such understandings, the possibility of critical multicultural education and cultural work is greatly extended. Indeed, the analytical and meaning-making abilities created by the intersection of cultural studies and cultural pedagogy produce an empowering conversation with critical multiculturalists about what they are doing and its impact on the lives of individuals included in their pedagogical orbit.

Such a conversation moves critical multiculturalists to use cultural studies to facilitate their struggle for social justice and democracy. Critical scholars maintain that the project of cultural studies is to address the most urgent social questions of the day in the most rigorous intellectual manner available. Thus, the everyday concerns of cultural studies are contextually bound – indeed, the work of the interdisciplinary 'discipline' is constantly being articulated and rearticulated around new social, cultural and political conditions. Its engagement with the ever-evolving historical context subverts any tendency on the part of cultural studies scholars to become complacent about the field's contributions both inside and outside the academy. So important is this notion of context that some scholars label the work of cultural studies as radical contextualism. To conceive cultural studies as radical contextualism or a theory of context making speaks directly to the field's contribution to the reconceptualization of analysis.

Radical contextualism implies that the knowledge produced and transmitted by scholars can never stand alone or be complete in and of itself. When one abstracts, one takes something away from its context. Of course, such reductionism is necessary in everyday life because there is too much information out there to be understood in detail by the mind. If an object of thinking cannot be abstracted, it will be lost in a larger pattern. Radical contextualism is certainly capable of abstraction, but at the same time it refuses to lose sight of the conceptual field, the context that provides separate entities with meaning. For example, traditional education has often concentrated on teaching students the 'what' of the scholarly disciplines. Life and job experience has traditionally taught us 'how' and 'why'. Data (the 'what') are best learned in the context of the 'how' and 'why'. Thus, academic knowledge may best be learned in a situated context – as the information connects to the social dynamics of the present. If deeper levels of understanding are desired, tasks must be learned in the context in which they fit. In the light of such a pronouncement critical multiculturalists can begin to see that the immature scholar is one who possesses no specific knowledge of a particular socio-cultural setting even though he or she may come to the situation with rigorous academic information. Such scholars become seasoned veterans only after they gain familiarity with specific social, symbolic, encoded, technical and other types of analytical resources, i.e. the context of the lived world.

From an analytical perspective, therefore, cultural studies motivates scholars to push beyond the limits of what we already know. For example, we already understand that particular cultural practices reproduce forms of racism and sexism – an important but insufficient social understanding. Cultural studies scholars insist that such understandings provide only a starting place for academic analysis. How does, for example, this production of racism and sexism engage in particular contexts with specific individuals to shape political struggles, individual identities and the role that education plays in the lives of students. It is engagement with this form of specific analysis that motivates cultural studies' encounter with the popular, the everyday and the particularistic. These domains do not merely produce unusual texts to be analysed; but constitute the stage on which political struggle is played out in the late twentieth century.

If critical multiculturalism is serious about the radical contextualism of cultural studies, then innovation in educational analysis looms on the horizon. Educators have not yet come to appreciate the diverse ways in which technological innovation, electronic communications and the globalization that accompanies them have changed the social, economic and power-related context in which education takes place. For example, globalization in this context involves not only the integration of financial systems, the mobilization of planetary communication networks and the reconfiguration of labour/management systems, it also entails confrontation with new constellations of racial and cultural diversity. While developments such as virtual reality and digital technologies will raise ethical issues unimaginable in the present, issues of diversity will demand attention to questions of social justice that have been repressed in the last two decades of the twentieth century. Globalization creates a social context where Western culture can no longer simply be positioned as the paragon of civilization. Non-Western cultures and other marginalized groups have revolted against this exclusionary practice, demanding that their voices and histories be acknowledged. The growth of visual and print media and their impact on all phases of intellectual and artistic life has shifted attention from the traditional study of Western culture to global concerns such as ecology, technology, colonialism and their manifestations in the omnipresent popular culture. Attention to such a changing context informs us that neither the world in general nor education in particular will ever be the same again.

Power, hegemony and representation: the pursuit of race, class and gender justice

One cannot talk of securing race, class and gender justice without understanding and challenging the way power operates on the contemporary cultural landscape. Here specifically is where the contextual analysis of cultural studies informs critical multiculturalism. The cultural realm has become a more and more important location in the shaping of both historical and everyday experience. Dominant power is no longer exercised simply by physical force but through social psychological attempts to win men and women's consent to domination through cultural institutions such as the schools, the media, the family and the church. This notion of hegemony developed by Antonio Gramsci in Mussolini's Italian prisons of the 1920s and 1930s recognizes that the winning of popular consent is a very complex process. The power bloc wins popular consent by way of a pedagogical process, a form of learning that engages people's conceptions of the world in such a way that transforms (not displaces) them with perspectives more compatible with the elite. The existence and nature of hegemony is one of the most important and least understood features of the late twentieth century. Students of power, educators, sociologists, researchers, all of us are hegemonized, as our field of knowledge and understanding is structured by limited exposure to competing definitions of the socio-political world. The hegemonic field with its bounded socio-psychological horizon garners consent to an inequitable power matrix – a set of social relations that are legitimated by their depiction as natural and inevitable (Goldman 1992; West 1993; McLaren 1994a; Giroux 1997a).

The technologies of hegemony (the methods by which social consent is garnered) move social domination from condition yellow to condition red. Critical multiculturalists find themselves in a state of full alert in regard to the exacerbation of domination in the postmodern condition of the late twentieth century. This reality, termed hyperreality by postmodernist theorist Jean Baudrillard (1983), is marked by a blurring of the distinction between the real and the unreal. Such a blurring produces a social vertigo precipitated by a loss of touch with traditional notions of time, community, self and history. New structures of cultural space and time generated by bombarding electronic images from local, national and international venues shake our personal sense of place (Aronowitz and Giroux 1991; Gergen 1991; Kincheloe 1995). This proliferation of signs and images characteristic of media information-soaked hyperreality functions as a mechanism of control in contemporary Western societies. The key to a successful counter-hegemonic critical multicultural pedagogy hinges on: (a) its ability to link the production of the representations, images and signs of hyperreality to power blocs in the political economy; and (b) its capacity, once this linkage is exposed and described, to delineate the highly complex and ambiguous effects of the reception of these images and signs on individuals located at various race, class and gender coordinates in the web of reality. No easy task, this effort – but to avoid it is to turn our backs on the democratic experiment and the possibility of social justice. This is why the effort to trace the effects of power in the ways the power bloc represents reality is so important.

We must be very specific about the nature of domination in contemporary life. Power in hyperreality in its obscured yet ubiquitous guise is amplified by corporate control of the means of simulation and representation. By determining what is important (worthy, for example, of time on TV) and what is not, corporate-owned media can set agendas, mould loyalties, depict conflicts and undermine challenges to the existing power bloc without a modicum of public notice. The question of power/domination that confronts critical multiculturalists cannot be too important an issue, for it is not a topic addressed on the mediascape. CBS will not present a two minute story on domination in hyperreality on tomorrow night's evening news – neither will a single 'local affiliate' on any of its news programming in the foreseeable future. Electronic media will make programming decisions on the basis of issues of commodity exchange; that is, cultural codes will be conveyed to the viewing audience on the basis of their capacity to engage men and women in their *duty* to consume (Luke 1991). The constituency of hyperreality serves the needs of the power bloc with honour and civic reverence – its 'patriotic' acts of consumption constitute the life-affirming productive energy (*élan vital*) of late twentieth-century capitalism.

Obviously, the conditions under which knowledge is produced and hegemonic consent is won have dramatically changed over the past couple of decades. Power is now produced and exercised in a way that allows it to penetrate national and global boundaries. Western corporations transmit hegemonic power to Third World countries through advertising images sent by satellites, experts sent to speed 'development' in agriculture, education and the physical sciences and cultural representations plastered on billboards throughout the countryside. Critical multiculturalists understand that hegemonic power wins consent through the production of pleasure, as popular culture in the form of advertisements, TV shows, popular music, movies and computer games induces individuals from both Third World and Western cultures to make emotional investments that tie them to such cultural productions. Such investments produce meaning as they shape identity and an individual's view of the world. Men and women always view power, no matter how or where it is produced, through their own histories and race, class and gender filters. Understanding contemporary power production and the individualistic filters everyone possesses, critical multiculturalists appreciate the need for more nuanced understandings of the way hegemonic messages are received, incorporated and resisted. Such understandings provide important insights into the effects of power, the ways the individual interfaces with socio-political structures and the way meaning is made on power-produced terrains of representations and dominant cultural formations. Concern with the phenomenological experience of the individual through the influence of social power allows scholars to focus on the moment of self-creation, the way belief structures are formed and, in a hegemonic context, the way consent is elicited. In their analysis of this process critical multiculturalists want to know the way in which power leaves its hegemonic imprint on individual consciousness. The better such a process is understood the more we are empowered to understand what white supremacy, patriarchy and rule by class elite have done to individuals from all cultural spheres (Giroux 1997a).

Unlike more essentialist forms of multiculturalism, criticalists do not buy into the concept of a unitary self. Drawing up postmodern analyses of identity, critical multiculturalists understand human identity or subjectivity as a fragmented, non-unitary, contextually contingent entity. As a terrain of conflict and political struggle, identity formation is seen as a process of both emancipation and oppression. In this context the way power represents particular social formations, including, in particular, manifestations of race, class and gender, exerts a profound impact on white and non-white, rich and poor, and male and female struggles for self-determination and their efforts to make sense of their relationship to the world and its people. Such struggles shape everything from one's political beliefs, school performance and life expectations, to one's capacity for self-determination. With these ideas in mind, critical multicultural educators and cultural workers focus on cultural pedagogy and the informal (non-school-based) cultural curriculum of hyperreality. We can develop as many wonderful multicultural school curriculums as we like, but as important and influential as they may be, such lessons often don't address the cultural curriculum being taught by TV, movies, popular music, video games and the Internet. Popular cultural consumption shaped by TV and movie corporations and other entertainment industries positions power-wielding commercial institutions as the *teachers* of the new millennium. Corporate cultural pedagogy has devised pristine lesson plans, constructing educational forms that are wildly successful when judged on the basis of their bottom-line 'behavioural objectives'. Replacing traditional classroom lectures with more pedagogically effective animated fantasies, youth movies, TV and an entire array of entertainment forms produced ostensibly for adults but voraciously consumed by young people, corporate pedagogy has 'educated' youth. Such a pedagogical revolution has not taken place in some crass manner with Lenin-like corporate wizards checking off a list of institutions that have been captured; instead, the revolution has been brought to you in Cinemascope, Technicolor and Sensaround. Deploying fantasy, corporate entertainment has created a new utopia with visions of freedom and pleasure unimagined by previous generations.

Power, representation and the cultural curriculum

In this sobering context it is the duty of critical multiculturalists to develop methods of studying the cultural pedagogy of hyperreality and the corporate curriculum, carefully monitoring and documenting their social and political effects. Teachers, educational researchers, political leaders, parents and students must be empowered to expose the corporate curriculum and to hold corporate decision-makers accountable for the pedagogy they produce. As we develop methods of analysing the ideologies of corporate pedagogy as encountered in movies and other media, we must use them to produce a body of information that activists can draw upon. As we gain a more sophisticated view of the ways cultural pedagogy operates, we are better able to expose race, class and gender oppression and even rewrite popular texts when the opportunity presents itself. Our analyses can be used to ground strategies of resistance that understand the relationship among cultural pedagogy, knowledge production and subjectivity. For example, consider Disney films in the context of the critical multiculturalist concern with cultural pedagogy, power, representation and hegemony. Disney films are not the innocent, non-political texts they are assumed to be by liberals and conservatives, with their implications for economic policy, ecological politics, race, class and gender relations and US domestic and foreign policy. Henry Giroux (1997b) focuses on the gender curriculum of *The Little Mermaid* and *The Lion King*. In both movies female characters are depicted within very traditional gender roles, lead lives subservient to men and identify themselves within the parameters of men's positive or negative perceptions of them. In *The Little Mermaid*, Ariel (the woman mermaid) in the early portion of the movie appears to be enveloped in a rebellion against the control of her father in her efforts to pursue a life out of the sea in the world of humans. Soon, however, the audience learns that Ariel trades one form of patriarchal submission for another, as she makes a pact with Ursula, the sea witch, to give up her voice for a pair of legs. The purpose of the deal involves Ariel's desire to engage in a romantic relationship with the handsome Prince Eric. The cultural curriculum of *The Little Mermaid* teaches profound hegemonic lessons in gender relations: women gain their identity only through the validation of males; and within our patriarchal society women always submit to male authority whether it be that of one's father or husband.

Representations can be used by the power bloc to expand their influence, Norm Denzin argues, by posing as objective depictions of reality. Thus, power wielders use film, TV and other mechanisms to transmit particular representations. Critical multiculturalists understand that there is a direct link between cultural representation and hegemonic patriarchal, white supremist and elite socio-economic class domination. Corporate and business leaders buttress their economic power by using their media access to represent prestige and connect it to the ownership of their products – wouldn't you rather drink Beck's Beer, drive an Infiniti, dress in Versace and carry a Gucci bag? The power bloc has the resources to present positive representations of itself to the world. Of course, such representations have little if anything to do with reality, as evidenced by oil and chemical companies representing themselves as champions of environmental protection or automobile companies representing themselves as the home of happy, contented and empowered line workers turning out products shaped by their highly respected viewpoints. The neo-imperialism or contemporary colonization that the USA inflicts on Asian, African and Latin American societies involves economic and cultural occupation rather than military occupation and is accomplished by Hollywood and Madison Avenue's ability to represent the world to and for American economic interests (Luke 1991; Musolf 1992; Brown 1993).

Through its control of representation, therefore, the contemporary power bloc gains the unprecedented ability to create, organize, articulate and dis-articulate the affective sensibilities and cognitive perceptions that motivate individuals to identify with particular socio-political and educational pos-itions. In contemporary Western societies the effort to understand the politi-cal realm and the domain of educational politics cannot be accomplished outside of a knowledge of the power of representation in previously dis-missed cultural and 'mere entertainment' venues such as TV, film, popular music, video games, computers and the Internet. For example, the way whiteness is subtly represented in these cultural domains exerts a major impact on the racial distribution of power. In addition, the way TV erases class relations by portraying contemporary society as classless helps to shape the way wealth is distributed. One is far more likely to see explicit torture and rape scenes and hear the screams of victims than to see representations of the class struggle or hear the word 'class'. TV news also removes class from contemporary affairs, at most showing brief shots of workers on a picket line during a strike. Doug Kellner (1990) points out that TV news often portrays the strike as a conflict between strikers and consumers, as it focuses its report on how the strike will hurt consumers. Little coverage is given to the unfair corporate policies that motivated workers to take action (Frankenberg 1993; Gray 1995).

Obviously, in late twentieth-century hyperreality, media representations revolving around the axes of race, class and gender play an important role in shaping the nature of Western cultural development. The ways in which dominant commercial institutions represent blackness are one of the most important stories of the last two decades. These representations and their effects constitute a major concern of critical multiculturalism. Young black males, for example, have been demonized by conservative and liberal rep-resentations in the last years of the century. They have been used as symbols in the attack on welfare, educational funding, civil rights legislation and job training. Represented in the media as violent and pathological criminals, black youth have been used to rally white racial solidarity and support for racist, right-wing social and educational policies. Using racialized code words to prey upon white fear of young black males, both conservative and liberal politicians have tied black males to the erosion of standards in edu-cation and the decline of morality in the public sphere in general.

Black youth and their radical supporters, the story goes, are waging an attack on Western values, the traditional family, well defined gender roles and the 'common culture'. Such racialized coding can be heard in all sectors of society, education in particular. School administrators and educational leaders in predominantly white schools often speak of their desire to send black students back to their own neighbourhoods – such a statement can be read as a code for a resegregation policy that sends black students 'back where they belong *away from whites*'. Critical multiculturalists are painfully aware of the ways in which such codes and representations are used to perpetuate and intensify inequitable power relations in contemporary societies. Ellen Swartz (1993) extends our understanding of critical multiculturalist goals in this context, maintaining that representations of black youth and other subordinated race, class and gender groupings must be 'unfixed'. Such a process, she concludes, involves challenging the way this representational process has implanted white supremacy, patriarchy and class elitism into the consciousness, cultural productions and imaginations of members of the dominant group.

The effectiveness of power inequality: the nature of powerlessness

Critical multiculturalists believe that too many individuals from the dominant culture fail to understand the effects of power inequality. A central aspect of a critical multicultural curriculum involves acquainting mainstream individuals with the pain of oppression. Iris Marion Young (1992) is helpful in the initial effort to define oppression in clear and precise terms. While Young delineates five 'faces' of oppression (exploitation, marginality, powerlessness, cultural imperialism and violence), we will focus for the moment only on powerlessness. Such a category, Peter McLaren (1994a) reminds us, typically affects groups such as women, blacks, chicanos/Latinos, Puerto Ricans, most Spanish-speaking peoples, West Indians, Native Americans, Jews, Appalachians, lesbians, gay men, Arabs, Asians, the elderly, working class people, the poor and physically and mentally disabled people. Contrary to the assertions of essentialist multiculturalists, no one group's oppression can be designated as the causal foundation of all other oppressions or be deemed more important than all others. Indeed, Young argues in the same way we did in earlier chapters that group differences interact with individuals in a manner that can induce both privilege and oppression for the same person along different axes of power.

Powerlessness involves structures of social, political and economic division, and often entails issues of status. Powerless people in contemporary Western societies possess little control over their work lives, are deskilled in jobs that rarely involve their input or creativity, hold little knowledge recognized or valued by dominant culture, express themselves in ways viewed condescendingly by the power bloc, are unfamiliar with the workings of institutions and bureaucracies and are considered unwelcomed outsiders by those in privileged settings. Such individuals fail to meet the norms of respectability constructed by dominant society and prove their failure by way of their manners, dress, speech, deportment, personal style and taste. Such norms and powerless individuals' shortcomings in relation to them cannot be separated from the dynamics of race, class and gender. Young also uses the vocational category 'professional/non-professional' to designate this status difference between individuals – a category also inscribed by race, class and gender. Powerless individuals don't have the status professionals possess. Three examples illustrate what is missing in the lives of the power-less: (a) little opportunity to develop one's talents throughout one's life; (b) little autonomy to act on one's own prerogative outside the authority of pro-fessionals; and (c) little hope of being taken seriously, of being listened to with respect, of being treated with dignity. In this context powerless people must attempt to prove their respectability in every new social encounter.

Unfortunately, affluent white people are often blind to the suffering of the powerless. Young extends our ability to render the powerless visible through a description of oppressed people, whom she describes as marginalized. Marginalized people are men and women who possess so little power they cannot escape the underclass. Western labour systems will not employ the marginalized, whose ranks include large numbers of old people, people who have lost industrial jobs that have moved to Third World locales, black or Latino young people who cannot procure a first job and have lost hope and American Indians living on reservations. The effects of marginalization are tragic, as capable individuals are denied useful social and economic partici-pation. While the material deprivation that accompanies marginalization is intolerable, the punitive treatment marginalized peoples must endure from the government agencies that administer them is as bad. In this bureaucratic context marginalized men and women lose their rights to privacy, dignity and individual self-direction. Unfortunately, in late twentieth-century West-ern societies the numbers of the powerless and marginalized are growing and efforts to provide dignified assistance to them are being abandoned.

At the same time that attempts to assist the oppressed are waning, obstacles to what Young labels exploitation are falling. Western societies are increasingly becoming democracies ruled by business priorities, nations where less than 1 per cent of the population owns nearly one-third of the wealth. Thus, as wealth becomes more and more maldistributed, conserva-tive and some liberal leaders argue that all efforts to help the powerless are counterproductive – they make life worse for everyone. W. E. B. DuBois (1973) understood the folly of such arguments when he advocated a democ-ratization of industry. Critical multiculturalists pick up on DuBois's democ-ratization of industry, as they call for an economic democracy. Keenly aware of the suffering of the powerless, such a concept maintains that a political democracy cannot exist without a concurrent economic democracy. An economic democracy is grounded on the belief that every worker deserves to work in a dignified and reasonably well paying workplace with an opportunity for personal development. Unlike the right-wing market viewpoint, an economic democracy maintains that corporations, workers and consumers hold citizenship in the economic sphere of society. Economic policy should be formulated with the common good in mind, for few economic decisions are private in their repercussions. A critical multicultural education must help students and citizens to understand the indirect outcomes of so-called private economic actions. Such actions must ultimately be regulated in a way that tempers their negative consequences. An economic democracy refuses to trust the short-term logic of economic growth or technical management by 'experts' of large corporations and government. In this context many citizens have begun to understand that the old ways of doing business are working poorly. The struggle proponents of economic democracy now face revolves around the effort to free men and women from the familiarity of the old patterns that inhibit the adoption of a new, more humane economic paradigm (Wirth 1983; Bellah *et al.* 1991; West 1993).

When the goals of business are viewed in the light of critical multiculturalists' concern with power, interesting things begin to happen. Unusual questions, such as what are the basic goals of an economic enterprise or what is the public responsibility of a private firm, begin to be asked. Western societies had just begun to ask such questions in the 1960s when the conservative reaction exploded. As a result of such inquiries, many people decided that private businesses did have goals that transcended profit making. For example, affirmative action was grounded on a logic that assumed that private firms had an obligation to reduce racial and gender inequality. In a critical multicultural democracy this idea could be expanded to include social goals such as the provision of interesting work, the protection of the environment or the reformation of public health and safety (Block 1990). Such goals do not demand the growth of bureaucracy and an army of government regulators swarming around private firms. As the notion of economic democracy becomes more and more a part of the economic landscape and employees become participants in the administration of firms, they can become watchdogs who monitor the consistency between the firm's action and larger social goals. While regulatory agencies could not be dismissed, the accent would be on inducing firms to embrace critical democratic goals as part of their *raison d'être*. Such a consciousness can be created – it is not merely a pipe dream. The words of the Swedish president of Volvo raise our hopes: 'The purpose of business is to help achieve and maintain the public good and the logical extension is the obligation to administer the resources with which the company is entrusted and use them to create economic growth' (Wirth 1983: 27).

At the end of the twentieth century, however, we must be realistic in our understanding that economic democracy is a project we work on now for future realization. Young reminds us that the present workplace is exploitative in nature. Western workplaces are locales where the fruits of the labour of workers are transferred to managers and wealthy owners. Indeed, the difference between the earnings of workers and business executives continues to grow at alarming rates. Along the axes of race and gender economic exploitation takes shape. Low-status, low-paid jobs – bell hops, porters, chamber maids, bus boys etc. – are often filled by blacks and Latinos. Women are still used as exploited labour, as one aspect of women's oppression involves the transfer of power from women to men. Indeed, the power, status and freedom, Young argues, that men enjoy is made possible by women's work for them. Not only do women often see the benefits of their labour transferred to men, but men also receive the reward of women's tendency for nurturing and emotional care. The gender enculturation women still experience induces many of them to provide empathy and support for other people's feelings – often they receive little reciprocation for their own needs. As women have left home to go to work over the past few decades they have often suffered a double exploitation. The jobs women have procured often involve 'feminine' tasks such as nurturing, caring for another person's body and peace-making in interpersonal conflicts – waitressing, clerical work, nursing, etc. (Young 1992). Critical multiculturalists understand that their pedagogy demands an understanding of powerlessness, marginalization and exploitation in many cultural locations. Critical multicultural educators know that oppression in school is intimately connected to oppression in the society at large.

Schools as disciplinary sites: the complexity of educational oppression

The oppression that occurs in the workplace, the media and the home helps to shape the oppression that occurs in schools. In the middle of the nineteenth century schools began to develop as state-supported institutions used in the attempt to discipline future workers and citizens in general. As envisioned by many socio-economic and political leaders, schools would normalize students so they would fit into the existing socio-economic structure. Such efforts, of course, collided head on with the efforts of democratic reformers who saw the school as a site for the empowerment of democratic citizens. The conflict between the regulatory and democratic purposes of school constitutes a main theme in both historical and contemporary schooling. Locating the cause of school failure in the individual pathology of the student, the disciplinary/regulatory educational impulse has assumed that there are right and wrong ways of doing things – and poor and non-white children's ways of operating are usually wrong. This is only one of countless ways a Eurocentric hegemonic norm structures the lived experience of students and the everyday life of school. Such a norm invisibly establishes a school culture that subtly validates white supremacy, patriarchy and class elitism.

The way these dynamics work is always within a common-sense framework and is, therefore, missed by teachers, educational leaders and educational scholars. For example, many educators assume – falsely, Jeanne Oakes (1985) argues in *Keeping Track* – that the presence of lower performing students in a classroom will hold back smarter students. Thus, a tracking system is justified on the assumption that higher-order scholarship can take place only in a cognitively segregated classroom. Such cognitive segregation almost always takes place in a racially and class-oriented manner. Such 'common sense' eventuates in a situation where privileged predominantly white students from middle and upper-middle class homes receive privileged educational experiences. When such unfair practices are combined with the curricular content discussed previously, which validates existing inequality and suppresses conflict and dissent, we find that the power bloc often uses schools as a part of a larger strategy to defend its interests against the social discord its policies have produced. Hegemony is never a simple process where power wielders merely force their subjects to comply. Instead, it works via negotiation, compromise and struggle to elicit the compliance of the oppressed to the structures that oppress them. By convincing non-white and lower socio-economic class students that they don't meet the standards required by schooling, the power bloc induces such students to consent to their own degradation. 'I'm not good in academics,' we hear scores of brilliant workers in the trades and the clerical domain tell us, reflecting the pronouncements of school personnel who had no idea other than standardized test scores of what such individuals can do. Hegemony is an unequal struggle between groups and individuals with disparate power and authority. What power did our friends in the trades and in clerical work have to fight the authority of the school, with its experts anointed with the mantle of science? Experts too often carry with them the interests of the power bloc, for the knowledge they possess typically comes from a Eurocentric, white, class elitist, male academic domain. Draped with authority, their pronouncements are difficult to oppose (Denzin 1987; Fiske 1993, 1994; Swartz 1993; Christian-Smith and Erdman 1997; Jipson and Reynolds 1997).

Mainstream schools structure the hegemonic terrain on which students operate by validating and invalidating competing definitions of reality. The world view of poor students is often viewed by schools as an absence of 'class' and proper breeding. When students resist and assert their world views, they may act on particular values that further disenfranchise them in the classroom. Clinton Allison (1995) reminds resistant students that their silence, disruption, non-performance, lateness and absence may 'cost them the possibility of using school for their own liberation' (p. 36). Paul Willis (1977) taught us in his study of the 'working-class lads' in Birmingham, England, that their resistance to the class inequities helped to reinforce the class structure by locking them into their working class status. Marginalized student resistance to mainstream norms often expresses itself in terms of a cultivated ignorance of information deemed important by the so-called 'cultured'. It is, of course, the dominant culture, not the students, who benefit from this cultivated unawareness, as young people lose the ability to critique, to make sense of the world around them. Such resistance leaves them no escape, no way out. Many times in the last years of the twentieth century they have been unable to enjoy a sense of solidarity with their fellow resisters because of race, ethnic or gender antagonism. Their disempowerment and isolation in this context is complete (West 1993; McLaren 1994a).

Teachers often inadvertently operate as cultural brokers for the power bloc, and in the name of following the curriculum guide transmit dominant cultural expectations and modes of evaluation. Amazingly, in the 1990s this process may take place under the flag of multiculturalism – albeit conservative, liberal or pluralist versions. In the name of progressive school administration, hegemonic notions of management as a technical process replace attention to power relations, student empowerment and issues of justice. Educational leadership in this context becomes little more than the scientific management of inequality – an organizational approach that rationalizes the disciplinary role of schooling while subverting the democratic impulse. The demand for student conformity to managerial dictates is promoted as a politically neutral quest for order – the suggestion of patriarchal, white supremist or class elitist assumptions within the discourse is viewed as an absurdity, the babbling of radicals. Critical multiculturalists in their understanding of the complexity of these multiple hegemonic educational dynamics reject macro-social and political, determinist and reductionist descriptions of the domination of schooling. Drawing upon the insights of critical pedagogy and cultural studies, critical multiculturalism avoids reductionism by focusing on the interaction between structuring sociopolitical forces and the everyday experiences that individuals construct within the context created by those forces. One theme of the work of Henry Giroux (1997a) has involved the criticism of reproduction theory that posits that schools mechanistically reflect and reinforce the oppressive power relations of the larger society. Such relationships between schools, students and macro-social formations are very subtle, as a myriad of forces interrupt an ordered correspondence between power and oppression at school. Richard Brosio (1994) explains this relationship between oppressive forces and students and other individuals as a mediated interaction, a 'soft version of correspondence'. The playing field of lived experience is shaped by forces of power and human beings create their lived realities on this power-saturated terrain. No outcome is predetermined, no effects are guaranteed; but patriarchy, white supremacy and class elitism may be the most influential players in town (Ferguson 1984; Fiske 1994; Macedo 1994).

Power, struggle and resistance in critical multiculturalism

Obviously, critical multiculturalists believe that the decentring of race, class and gender power is one of the most important needs of Western societies. In this context critical multiculturalism seeks to increase the localizing power of non-whites, women and individuals from lower socio-economic backgrounds. Such a goal requires an ability to recognize and a will to contest imperializing power as expressed in Eurocentric and white ways of understanding the world. White people must learn to listen to non-whites' and indigenous people's criticism of them and the cultural norms they have established and imposed on non-European and lower socio-economic class peoples. The struggle for empowerment of marginalized and exploited people must include everything from engaging such individuals in an empowering education to a more equitable distribution of wealth. Indeed, as Western societies have moved to the right, traditional concerns about the welfare of the working class have faded. Too often in the contemporary global economy we find unemployed and underemployed individuals with insecure temporary, part-time and low-paying jobs. The exploitation of working people has intensified in the contemporary era, as the working class has been fragmented and disorganized.

At the end of the twentieth century corporate and business leaders are free to specify the size of the workforce in relation to the demands of global economic productivity. If international competition necessitates it, post-modern Western economies justify lower wages. The corporate vanguard is rarely contained in its relations with labour; it can employ or dismiss workers at the whim of the market (MacLeod 1987; Kellner 1989; Borgmann 1992; Smart 1992). In their cultural work and pedagogy, critical multiculturalists deem it essential to explain that this is a time of decreasing labour power and increasing labour control. Indeed, labour control as a social strategy invades all aspects of contemporary life and cuts across the race, class and gender axes of power. Workers, Jean Baudrillard (1983: 134) writes, 'must be *positioned* at all times'. The system of socialization is expanded, labour is shaped to specifications. In the name of worker empowerment, business and industrial leaders apply Japanese management techniques to increase worker responsibility for parts of the production process. Yet at the same time that this flexible team concept moves workers closer to the decision-making traditionally controlled by management, they are excluded from the status and power of the corporate power bloc.

Nothing illustrates this exclusion as much as the disparity of pay between workers and managers. The emerging postmodernist economy of the 1980s simply transferred money from the poor to the rich in the name of trickle down and supply-side economics – the poor losing US$23 billion in income and federal benefits, while the rich gained $35 billion (Grossberg 1992). Former Chrysler chairman Lee Iacocca made over $38 million in 1986 and 1987 from his salary, bonuses and stock options. A worker toiling at minimum wage for forty hours per week since the birth of Christ would not have earned this much. Managers defend salaries such as Iacocca's, arguing that corporate executives face great stress in the contemporary economy and must be rewarded for steering businesses through troubled economic waters. In the period that Iacocca earned more than $38 million, Chrysler profits fell by 7 per cent.

Executive salaries rose dramatically in the 1980s despite the performance of their companies. Texaco chief executive James W. Kinnear's salary went up 14 per cent at the same time the company was dealing with bankruptcy proceedings and a record $4.4 billion loss. The median cash compensation for chief executives in the nation's largest companies passed the $1 million mark in 1987. Executive salary increases of 113 per cent in one year are not uncommon. In the same year that Iacocca made over $20 million, workers at Chrysler were being exhorted to cut waste in the light of the company's falling profits. As Iacocca said in response to questions about his salary, 'That's the American way. If little kids don't aspire to make money like I did, what the hell good is this country?' (DeYoung 1989: 152–3).

Critical multiculturalism, unlike liberal and pluralist forms of multiculturalism, focuses on these class dynamics as well as race and gender. Indeed, we cannot understand race and gender oppression outside the context of socio-economic class. Mainstream Western education teaches students to accept the class inequities – all in the name of a neutral curriculum, all in the attempt to take politics out of education. Critical multiculturalism induces students, workers and citizens to question the hidden political assumptions and race, class and gender bias of school and media education. As members of Western societies, we see such overtly political pronouncements as somehow inappropriate and out of place in public institutions such as schools. Teachers should remain neutral, many students argue, not understanding the covert political implications of almost everything that presents itself as objective information, disinterested science and balanced curricula. Of course, we understand where such students are coming from: they are making a case for fairness, for delineation of both sides of a question. They have been taught to believe that objectivity is an attainable virtue that should be practised by everyone involved with education. They have never been exposed to the argument that education is never neutral, that when we attempt to remain neutral, like many churches in Nazi Germany, we support the prevailing power structure. They are unfamiliar with the critical multicultural perspective that teachers, writers and cultural workers cannot help but take political positions; they only have the choice of being conscious or unconscious of the political positions they broadcast. Indeed, teachers in particular can learn that their political commitments do not grant them the right to impose these positions on their students. But to hold a position and to force a student to accept that position are two different things entirely.

In a postmodern hyperreality where global corporations are armed with a storehouse of technological innovations that provide them with unprecedented power to shape opinions and regulate more and more aspects of our lives, critical multiculturalists' concern with power and hegemony takes on even more importance. The neglected realm of politics, of political literacy as it relates to everyday life, the workplace and the economic domain and to race and gender, becomes more important than ever. Any critical multiculturalist education or cultural work must take on the responsibility of making sure that students and citizens are politically literate. Any attempt to study the nature of social justice must be grounded on a familiarity with the political, that domain of social study that analyses the way power is produced and distributed. Mainstream education and its conservative, liberal and pluralist multicultural perspectives in the name of democracy actually subvert democracy with their whitewash of social antagonisms and conflicts. Mainstream media take the same evasive action with their reduction of social conflict in the USA to electoral politics among Democrats, Republicans and the Perot-financed Reform Party, and sometimes liberals and conservatives. Such battles are often little more than cat fights within the power bloc and have relatively little to do with questions of social justice and the egalitarian distribution of power. Critical multiculturalism makes sure that students understand as a part of the curriculum of political literacy that Western societies are terrains of socio-political struggle involving diverse economic, gender and racial groups (Kellner 1990).

The critical multiculturalist curriculum of power and political literacy asserts that it is never sufficient to speak in general terms about race, class and gender oppression. Indeed, such a curriculum 'names', focusing attention on, for example, corporate power wielders and the specific ways race, class and gender groups suffer in historic and contemporary Western societies. While names are named and conscious oppressors are delineated, critical multiculturalists also appreciate the fact that many aspects of race, class and gender oppression are not intentional and often take place in the name of good intentions. In Chapters 5, 6 and 7, we will specify in detail various aspects of such oppression. Without an understanding of these specific dynamics, teachers are too often unable – even with love in their hearts and the best intentions – to protect students from the radioactive fall-out of hidden structures of racism, patriarchy and class bias. Teacher education reform has traditionally ignored such issues, focusing instead on classroom rearrangement, curricular format, lesson planning and attention to clearly (and behaviourally) stated objectives. Too often such matters served only, in Donald Macedo's (1994) term, to stupidify those who took them seriously, as they pushed questions of how both school purpose and teacher/student identities are shaped *vis-à-vis* larger socio-political and cultural formations off the table.

In the context of these questions of power, oppression and struggle, critical multiculturalists understand, even as they document the insidious tectonics of racism, sexism and gender bias, that such structures are porous with numerous tunnels for escape. Even when educational purposes are consciously oppressive, Clint Allison (1995) reminds us, purposes and outcomes are not the same thing. Even though they have operated as tools of the power bloc, schools are places that often teach literacy – an essential skill in the process of empowerment. Many students use those portions of education they find applicable to their lives, concurrently identifying and rejecting hegemonic attempts to win their consent to stupidifying perspectives. Of course, these are students who are often deemed to have a bad attitude, who may be labelled surly and unteachable; but they may also be the students who are sufficiently empowered to lead critical pro-democracy movements in Western societies. Thus, critical multiculturalists recognize the possibility for resistance, even successful resistance to the forces of imperializing power. Because patriarchal, white supremacist and class elitist oppression is not deterministic, because it is mediated by countless factors, the power bloc's intentions may mutate in the kaleidoscope of everyday school life. When the advances in social theory over the past two decades are brought into the study of the hegemonic efforts of the power bloc, we gain new insights into the nature of power and domination. Much of our work involves the analysis of power in hyperreality's mediascape, the changing nature of corporations and businesses in the global age and the effects of these dynamics on education and the formation of identity (see, for example, Kincheloe 1995; Steinberg and Kincheloe 1997).

The conditions under which knowledge is produced have changed dramatically over the past twenty years. With the construction of the global network of communications, science and technology and its effect on the generation of information, power and hegemony will take on new forms and guises. Teachers interested in social justice will have to understand these changes in such a way that they can connect them to the lives, histories, cultures and everyday experience of students from historically subjugated groups. What is the effect of the corporate commodification of black culture? How does such commodification shape and reshape black students' identities? White students' identities? How do such corporate and media depictions reconfigure the struggle for social justice? Where are the openings they create for positive resistance to oppression? How do teachers incorporate these issues into the curriculum and lived world of the classroom for positive effect? As racial demographics change in Western societies, relegating white people to a smaller percentage of the total population, those social groups once viewed as living on the margins of society become more and more important. Such news does not rest well with many Westerners – especially those from traditional centres of race, class and gender power. Like it or not, they will have to listen to marginalized, angry voices more and more frequently in the twenty-first century (Fiske 1993; Perry and Fraser 1993; Brosio 1994). If the social order is not to be torn apart with racial and class wars, Western peoples had better begin listening not only to the marginalized but to the benevolent voices of those advocating a critical political and economic democracy. We passionately believe that the issues that surround multiculturalism will shape the future of the West. Peaceful change can only take place through an embrace of democratic principles and a critically defined notion of social justice. As the new century dawns, we stand at a dangerous crossroads.

five

THE IMPORTANCE OF CLASS IN MULTICULTURALISM

Most forms of multiculturalism ignore questions of class and the ways they intersect with issues of race and gender. Critical multiculturalists appreciate the centrality of class in any effort to understand the nature of social diversity in America and the racism, gender bias and power inequalities that accompany it. The concept of class is extremely ambiguous and complex, and must be used very carefully in any multicultural analysis. We assume that economic and occupational location in a social order is one of many factors that help to construct consciousness, perception of others and relation to power. In this context socio-economic class is defined in relation to the labour process, which is always changing as it interacts with social and cultural dynamics. Thus, all institutions (including work but not limited to it) are structured as hierarchies of inclusion and exclusion that shape individual and group power relations. Undoubtedly, class inequality is intensifying in Western societies – a fact that makes the inclusion of class in the study of multiculturalism more important than ever.

Our conception of class is intimately tied to our understanding of the power bloc described in previous chapters. Expanding that understanding, we see the power bloc not as a social class *per se* – such a definition would inscribe it with a fixity and permanence that distorts the concept. The power bloc is an ever shifting alignment that seeks to maintain dominant power relations in regard to particular issues. As John Fiske (1993) puts it, the power bloc is better conceived in relation to what it does rather than what it is. Like the power bloc, socio-economic classes are always in process, taking shape and disintegrating around particular axes of power and specific contextual dynamics. Unlike previous notions, our concept of class does not involve empirically defined social groups with a shared monolithic view of the world. Thus, traditional depictions of ruling class and proletariat give way to descriptions of shifting power blocs and disempowered peoples who are class-inscribed by their relationship to practices of inclusion and exclusion and their respective access to socio-political and economic mechanisms to promote their interests (Young 1992; Fiske 1993; Aronowitz and DiFazio 1994; House and Haug 1995).

Both/and: the importance of studying both the inseparability and the specific dynamics of race, class and gender

As we have argued, race, class and gender issues cannot be understood outside an appreciation of the complex and contradictory ways these forces interact with one another. Since such interactions are so ambiguous, social experience cannot be viewed simply as an uncomplicated reflection of social power. In education, for example, Cameron McCarthy and Michael Apple (1988) maintain that students from lower socio-economic class backgrounds are not simply classified and regulated to low-status classes and low-status jobs; instead, forces of race, class and gender create a multi-level playing field on which students gain a sense of their options and negotiate their occupational possibilities.

Race, class and gender dynamics combine to create a larger playing field with more options for some and a smaller, more limited field for others. In these contexts students struggle to make sense of and deal with triple or more divisions of the social gridiron – here they wrestle with fractious social classes, genders and racial and ethnic groups. Star Trekkies understand the three-tier gridiron in terms of Mr Spock's three-dimensional chessboard – all three dimensions are in play at the same time. In this conceptual context educators and policy-makers have not achieved the understanding that America has a high level of unemployment among specific population groups and that among those groups there exists an inordinately high number of female-headed families. Avoiding the connections between these class and gender realities, such professionals fail to discern that the causes of poverty and class inequality among women are fundamentally different from the causes of poverty among men. Thus, the same remedies, the same educational experiences for women and men will not address these gender-related class differences. Gender expectations define different locations in both the cultural terrain and the occupational area. Women's lives are intimately involved with caring for others. Most people understand that women devote much time to child care, but the effort they devote to taking care of men, aged parents, grandchildren, friends and distant relatives is less frequently acknowledged. As weavers of the fabric that connects us, women have less time and energy to devote to making a living. When their domestic work in housekeeping and child rearing is added to the mix, time for paid work decreases even further. Gender expectations once again intersect with class to produce a socio-economic context hostile to contemporary women (Sidel 1992).

When these dynamics are traced in the high-tech postmodern economic terrain, with its hopeful promise of good work, interesting revelations appear. Silicon Valley, located in California's Santa Clara County, is widely recognized for its high-tech microelectronics industry and the economic revolution it catalysed. As the home of the nation's most celebrated computer jocks and financial whiz kids, Silicon Valley hides a labour force that is more heavily stratified by race, class, gender and nationality than any economic segment in the USA. It doesn't take a genius to figure out that the celebrated, multi-millionaire Silicon Valley executives are almost all white males, while the vast majority of low-paid manufacturing workers are minority women. The tendency of Silicon Valley managers to hire minority women – primarily Third World Asian and Latina women – is not limited to Santa Clara County but is typical of high-tech glamour industries around the world. Thus, race, class and gender hierarchies structure the most high-tech industries of the late twentieth century and the news is not good for those who are small, poor, foreign and female. Employers argue that women can work for less, even though they possess little if any specific knowledge about their women employee's family circumstances. Postmodernist micro-electronics company managers generally assume that their female workers are married to men who are earning a 'livable' salary. In actuality, over four out of five women employees in the industry are the main money makers in their families.

Karen Hossfeld (1994) contends that when employers assume that women, non-whites and/or immigrants accept low-paying work because they are content with it or because they are unprepared for and/or undeserving of better work, they are complicit with forces that keep the marginalized in their place. She labels these managerial assumptions racial, immigrant and gender 'logics'. In the high-tech microelectronics industry there is no conflict between these logics and 'capital logic' – business strategies that contribute to profit maximization while increasing class stratification and the control of labour. Obviously, white employers' use of racism and sexism to construct an exploitive division of workers is nothing new and is not limited to the microelectronics industry. We can find the same social dynamics in the international textile industry, with its racial and gendered labour hierarchy. In many industries managers justify their use of Third World women in assembly line repetitive tasks because of such workers' allegedly superior hand–eye coordination and patience. White male managers frequently report that the tiny size of many Asian and Mexican women allows them to sit still for hours at a time performing detailed work that would push larger white people beyond the limits of sanity. When workers were asked to respond to this manager's comments about them, they agree that he preferred to employ small female workers so he could feel superior and appear more intimidating around the plant. Here the intersection of race, class and gender can easily be seen on a variety of levels, including the masculinist anxieties of industrial supervisors.

Although we know that race, class and gender are intertwined, we also appreciate the need to focus on each axis separately. Critical multiculturalists believe that in addition to intersective studies, we need to focus on single group studies for the purpose of appreciating the specific forces involved with a group's disempowerment. In this way strategies for empowerment can be devised, as group members and non-group members understand group identity and history as well as the political, economic and cultural forces shaping the group. Such intellectual experiences are vitally important for group members, as individuals need to understand the social construction of their own experiences before they can understand others. Critical multiculturalists believe that such single group studies can work as a catalyst for the empowerment of marginalized groups and develop leadership that facilitates the escape from social and psychological subjugation. In this context students can discern why the group holds less than its share of power and resources. They begin to figure out that the conservative and liberal notions of civic participation require the acceptance of a social structure shaped by patriarchy, class elitism and white supremacy. Such insights expose once and for all the myth that social institutions and the knowledge they produce is neutral, that all social groups have equal access to resources and opportunity. The study of class as an important social force in Western society has never been more important than it is at the end of the twentieth century, with the massive redistribution of wealth from the poor to the wealthy. In 1980, for example, the average corporate chief executive officer (CEO) in the USA earned 38 times the salary of the average factory worker. By 1990 the average CEO earned 72 times as much as a teacher and 93 times as much as a factory worker (Coontz 1992; West 1993; Sleeter and Grant 1994).

The intensification of class inequality

When such unequal realities exist and continue to grow, the importance of the study of class and the need for class analysis in a critical multiculturalism expands. When the specific dynamics of the polarization of wealth in the USA are analysed in further detail, new insights into mobility are uncovered. Americans have always placed great value on hard work. People who work hard should be rewarded for their effort – indeed, Americans believe that the backbone of society rests upon hard work. Most Americans would be surprised to find out, therefore, that the redistribution of wealth of the past fifteen years has been accomplished inversely in relation to hard work. Much of the new wealth created in the 1980s and 1990s did not come from inventing a better mousetrap or long hours of study or working overtime. Most new wealth befell those with enormous assets who were able to reap 'instant wealth' from rapidly fluctuating return rates on their speculative investments. Dividends, tax shelters, interest and capital gains were at the centre of the action – not hard work (Coontz 1992). The connection between class position and one's willingness to work hard may be less direct than many Americans have assumed. The attempt to dismiss class as an American issue must be exposed for what it is – an instrumental fiction designed to facilitate the perpetuation of the status quo by pointing to the poor's laziness and incompetence as the causes of their poverty.

After the 1980s and the policies of Reaganomics in the USA and Thatcherism in the UK, it became harder and harder to dismiss class as an important feature in Western societies – although more and more people did dismiss its role in everyday affairs. Calls to abolish welfare, exact more severe punishments for crime, end social programmes, cut educational funding, destroy affirmative action – policies steadily being implemented in the 1990s – threw gasoline on the fire of growing inequality and class stratification. Blacks and Latinos were more severely affected by these politics than whites, families headed by women grew poorer than those headed by men and after a divorce women's income plunged while men's rose. Indeed, the intensification of class inequality was fuelled by race and gender and the patterns of oppression that accompanied them. According to supply-side, trickle-down economic theory, the substantial increase in the wealth of the upper socio-economic class in the USA and Britain was supposed to provide a corresponding increase in wealth for the poor. Of course, no such process occurred, as the poor become poorer than they had previously been. Still, at the end of the century right-wing politicians continue to promote trickle down economics in spite of its impact on the poor (House and Haug 1995; Apple 1996).

Such policies are developed not on the basis of empirical evidence of the success of trickle down economics, as much as they are grounded on a romantic right-wing belief in Forrest Gumpism – that everyone, no matter how inadequate, has a place in a nineteenth-century view of community. 'Darkies' had their place on the plantation, women in the home and the town Jew his peddler's cart. White males from the economic elite might feel quite good about such a social arrangement, for it would remind everyone that such men deserve their close connection to the power bloc because of their innate superiority. Keith Joseph, the former minister of education for Margaret Thatcher, argued in the 1980s that socio-economic inequality is a good thing. Inequality, the argument goes, allows the gifted and energetic (the rich) to create enough wealth to pull up the less able poor to a new material well-being. In such convoluted conservative formulations it becomes morally acceptable to have winners and losers in the economic and social sphere. With such profound qualitative differences in the abilities of the white and non-white and the rich and the poor, the argument concludes, how could we not have winners and losers? Democratic impulses in this context upset the social apple cart, as the poor and the marginalized begin to get the idea that they can gain social mobility. Indeed, the desire for social mobility actually oppresses the inept poor because they really don't have the ability to do better. We can talk about opportunity all we want, but our relegation of the poor and non-white to low-ability tracks in school reveals society's true feelings about such losers (Berger 1995; Wieseltier 1995; Willis 1995; Apple 1996).

It is in this context that anti-affirmation action arguments can be better understood. Right-wing opponents of such policies maintain that Western societies must learn to live with the reality of inequality. Affirmative action, Richard Herrnstein and Charles Murray (1994) argued in *The Bell Curve*, is injecting a poison directly into our social soul. The poison they are referring to involves a nasty democratic belief in equal opportunity, a chance for oppressed peoples to gain a taste of the advantages privileged white upper-middle class males have enjoyed precisely because of their race, class and gender positions. Such a poison must be neutralized before marginalized peoples gain a sense of entitlement – indeed, right-wing policy-makers fear, it may already be too late. In this context conservative monoculturalist schools and other institutions must reorder the society. They must convince Western peoples that when a truly meritocratic social order is created the talented will prosper and the inept will stay where they are. By ending affirmative action and other forms of social meddling with the natural order, such a meritocracy can be re-established. Such a right-wing utopia will produce a Natural New World Order that will reward the worthy and punish the unworthy – the *justice of inequality* will rule the society like an invisible hand (Gould 1995; Wolfe 1995).

Justifying inequality: power and ideology

The process by which inequality and class stratification is justified is quite complex and requires some clarification. Whenever reality is defined in a way that works to maintain the existing power structures, the process of ideology is probably involved. Dominant ideology reifies (makes appear natural) inequality as the inevitable outcome of the power bloc's superior talent and effort. Even though the term ideology is used in a variety of ways, two categories of use prevail. The first usage involves ideology as political beliefs – as in the ideology of a political party, the basic ideas that are traditionally associated with the party and are drawn upon by party operatives in the tailoring of policies and platforms. Under this definition ideologies come to be thought of as 'isms' – Marxism, liberalism, conservatism etc. Conceptualizing ideology in this manner causes problems, as it conveys two misconceptions in the study of power: (a) if ideology exists as a system of beliefs held by politically oriented groups and individuals, then our analysis of the ways ideology operates in everyday life in the schools, media, interpersonal relations and so on is clouded; (b) ideology conceived as belief systems presents us with a view of the concept as a static phenomenon removed from the cultural context in which it always operates.

The way beliefs are acted upon (many use the term mobilized) is central to a critical understanding of ideology. Certain ways of seeing the world may work to sustain existing power relations in one context but undermine them in another. In order to understand these continually shifting contextual dynamics we need to move beyond the definition of ideology as a coherent system of beliefs and develop a more complex, process-oriented, culturally sensitive approach. In this context the definition of the concept involves ideology in its dominant guise as part of a larger process of protecting unequal power relations, of maintaining domination. Specifically, a dominant cultural form of ideology involves sustaining these power asymmetries through the process of making meaning, producing a common sense that justifies prevailing systems of domination. Ideology theory was invented in the first place to explain why in industrialized societies individuals from the lower socio-economic class continued to support the political and economic systems that exploited them or, later, why many women seemed to accept patriarchal domination. A critical multiculturalist conception of ideology finds its grounding in this traditional democratic concern with the maintenance of power disparity, taking very seriously the contextually sensitive aspects of meaning making that accompany it. When such contextual dynamics are viewed as a cardinal aspect of ideology, then we can begin to appreciate the insidious ways power operates in the culture at large and in institutions. With these dynamics in mind we can extend and sophisticate the effort to explore the role of the social in the process of identity production (Thompson 1987; Fiske 1993).

Of course, ideology cannot be separated from our understanding of Gramscian hegemony. As previously delineated, hegemony involves the maintenance of domination not through force but through the winning of the consent of those individuals being dominated. If hegemony is the larger effort of the powerful to win the consent of their 'subordinates', then dominant, or better, hegemonic ideology involves the cultural forms, the meanings, the rituals and the representations that produce consent to the status quo and individuals' particular places within it. Hegemonic consent is never completely established, as it is always contested by various groups with differing agendas. Ideology *vis-à-vis* hegemony moves us beyond simplistic explanations that have used terms such as propaganda to describe the way media, education and other cultural productions coercively manipulate citizens to adopt oppressive patterns of meaning. The proponents of what could be labelled hegemonic ideology understand a much more subtle and ambiguous form of domination that refuses the propaganda model's assumption that its subjects are passive, manipulable victims. Students of hegemonic consent understand that dominant ideological practices and discourses socially construct our vision of reality. Thus, a social theory of hegemonic ideology is a form of epistemological constructivism buoyed by a nuanced understanding of power's complicity in the constructions people make of the world and their role in it (Kellner 1990; McLaren 1994a).

Such understandings of complexity correct earlier delineations of ideology as a monolithic, unidirectional entity that was imposed on individuals by a secret cohort of ruling class tsars. Understanding domination in the context of concurrent struggles among different classes, racial and gender groups and sectors of capital, students of hegemonic ideology analyse the ways such competition engages differing visions, interests and agendas in a variety of social locales – venues previously thought to be outside the domain of ideological struggle. This emerging more nuanced view of ideology also understands that ideology does not produce a depiction of the socio-political world that is mechanically inserted into the mind of the subject; instead, hegemonic ideology produces representations of reality that influence people's personal relationships to the socio-political world. Such a process can be referred to as a construction of the social imagination, the affective and emotional dynamics of individuals' interactions with the world that operates in conjunction with their rational understandings of it. Thus, the consent hegemonic ideology wins is nothing if not fragile and, accordingly, has to be constantly won and rewon. In this precarious context the power bloc must accept compromises with hegemonized groups. Thus, in the spirit of total quality management (TQM) forms of workplace administration, power wielders may agree to allow subordinates more prerogative in determining certain aspects of their everyday lives. Like TQM, however, essential interests are still controlled by those with the power (Mumby 1989; Walsh 1993).

This critical multiculturalist view of ideology, while understanding the perplexing complexity of domination, does not allow such ambiguity to conceal the ways that power works to oppress and regulate the lives of the poor and non-white. Various ideologies come out of and sustain the power interests of dominant groups in relation to the axes of race, class and gender. Understanding that ideology reflects the presence of power and that the world can only be known through ideologically mediated perception, any study of the social must acquaint itself with such dynamics. Conservative, liberal and pluralist multiculturalism have consistently ignored these power-saturated ideological dynamics, portraying business and corporate leaders as operating in the society's best interests. Not including class issues or labour history in their agenda, such multiculturalists uncritically accept the pronouncements of business leaders about their social and environmental concerns. Indeed, as business and corporations have used technological advances to extend their power in the late twentieth century, issues of ideology and hegemony become more important than ever. Drawing upon technology, corporate and business leaders have developed a postmodern 'techno-power' that increases their ability to maximize profits and control workers. Many argue that the corporate growth of the last two decades of the twentieth century has been grounded on managers' ability to widen the gap between worker compensation and worker production (Harvey 1989; Kellner 1989; Sleeter and Grant 1994).

Class exploitation in hyperreality: deploying techno-power

In the late twentieth-century public conversation about education, we frequently hear that the interests of business and education are beginning to merge. Such a statement ignores the fact that business still operates on the basis of their private interests even when they conflict with public needs. With corporate public relations people leading the crusade, Americans have retreated from their commitment to the maintenance of a 'public space'. The needs of low-salaried workers, the poor, the environment – needs of the public space – have diminished in importance to Americans. Freedom has been redefined as the right of corporations to desecrate this public space in the effort to pursue private gain. Technological development has undoubtedly changed what democratic citizens must know, but the dynamics of techno-power are rarely considered a part of that knowledge. Despite conservative politicians and fundamentalist ministers' claims to the contrary, American commitments to the 'private space' of family remain very strong. What have diminished over the last quarter of the century are commitments to the 'public space' – community activities, political organizations, volunteer agencies etc. Most high school seniors, for example, say that they do not think that a company going out of business has any moral obligation to pay its outstanding debts.

In the name of profit maximization American companies have shut down thousands of factories, moved entire operations to Third World locations and migrated from state to state in search of cheaper labour and lower taxes. In 1991 in Tarrytown, New York, General Motors (GM) embarked on a campaign to lower its taxes by one million dollars a year. Announcing that it would close the Tarrytown plant unless workers made benefit and wage concessions and the city lowered its corporate taxes, GM held the city hostage. Because of the subsequent decline of tax revenues, the Tarrytown schools were forced to lay off personnel, eliminate new orders for books and school supplies and delay needed repairs of school buildings. Given techno-logical advances enabling them to move operations quickly from one state or country, corporations have found themselves endowed with new power. This is the nature of techno-power (Borgmann 1992; Carnevale 1992; Coontz 1992).

Corporate techno-power comes in many sizes and colours – it is the heart and soul of what is often called the dynamic flexibility of the post-Fordist (post-mass production and assembly line) arrangement of business and industry. Since the early 1970s, techno-power has steadily expanded, as technology plays a more and more important role in organizing and regu-lating both economic production and our everyday lives. Indeed, with a few exceptions technology has been deployed as a tool of corporate leadership in its attempt to maximize profits, to extend its power. Data banks, radio and TV transmissions and transnational communications systems all con-tribute to a global network that allows corporate leaders to regulate markets all over the world. As these communications systems filter into cities, villages and rural areas throughout the world, corporations present an ideological view that promotes their interests. The process takes place in a quiet and subtle way, as values such as competitive individualism, the superiority of an unregulated market economy (a neo-classical economics) and the necessity of consumption are implicitly promoted. People's identities, their sense of who they are, begin to be formed not in their communities but by their radios and televisions. The popularity of video compilations of old 1950s and 1960s TV commercials and the emotions they trigger within those of us who grew up in that era is evidence of this media-based identity formation (Kellner 1989; Giroux 1992; Smart 1992; Brosio 1994; McLaren *et al.* 1995).

This corporate control of the media and the knowledge that accompanies it dramatically affects Western societies' perception of the world in general, the nature of work and the way socio-economic classes are produced. With their access to media, corporations can portray workers as lazy and unpro-ductive in ways that dramatically affect the politics of labour–management relations. Using their techno-power for ideological purposes, corporate leaders can rally the public to support their denial of higher wages and more power in the shopfloor to workers – after all, they don't deserve such rewards. These understandings of techno-power are essential to the edu-cation of citizens in a democratic society. Empowerment of these citizens to challenge race, class and gender ideologies can only take place when they are able to see through the myth that technological developments in media have served to produce a better informed community. Indeed, students in a critical multicultural educational context begin to understand that private interests are building information monopolies; the public nature of information is quickly mutating into information as a private commodity. As fewer and fewer large corporations control the flow of information, public access to counter-hegemonic information is reduced. In the process techno-power expands.

It is important to understand that this shaping of public opinion by way of media control is never simplistic. Often efforts to manipulate opinion backfire, as men and women perceive what is happening to them and rebel. Futhermore, technologies such as computer links and information highways can be used to convey alternative messages that challenge corporate control. Still, however, most Americans are unable to comprehend the degree of influence corporate leaders attain as they control TV and other media that by-pass reason and focus directly on the management of human feelings and emotions. Media presentations that are not obviously political play to our emotions on a level that shapes our political perspectives. Images of children exuberant as they open gifts on Christmas morning have no overt political message. At a deeper level, however, such images may be influential, as they tell us that such happiness in our children can be evoked only by the consumption of goods and services. If we truly love our children and want to see them happy, then we must support the interests of the corporations who produce these valuable products. The process of political opinion formation is not a linear, rational procedure, but is grounded on our emotional hopes and fears. Thus, when Mattel Inc. calls for lower corporate taxes and a better business climate in which to produce its toys, we accede to its wishes. After all, this is the company that allows us to make our children happy (Harvey 1989; McLaren *et al.* 1995). The better the business climate corporations are able to create, the greater the disparity of wealth between management and workers.

In this context critical multiculturalists argue that the development of late twentieth-century information technology has not served to promote more honest communication, democratic values or empowerment of the marginalized. On the contrary, the primary use of these technological innovations has been to sell and to create consumer markets for particular goods and services. Techno-power becomes a medieval alchemist that instead of turning base metals into gold transforms 'truth' into 'what sells'. Valuable information in this context becomes not that which explains or empowers but that which creates a cooperative community, a culture of consumption. Communication media do not exist to help ordinary citizens improve their lives or understand the demands of democratic citizenship. The need to capture the attention and the emotions of consumers transcends all other uses.

In the process of improving ratings, TV reduces everything to the same level – everything that happens must be reconstituted to capture viewer interest. In terms of traditional notions of importance all events and messages are equally trivial – death, destruction, war, famine, unemployment, better feminine hygiene, weight loss programmes, acne medications etc. CNN presents "War in the Gulf", brought to you by Depends Undergarments.

Techno-power has allowed corporations a form of mobility, a nomadic predisposition, that allows them to be everywhere simultaneously. Like the Catholic Church after the Counter-reformation with its grand architecture, the ideologically inscribed crucifix, and its worldwide presence, contemporary corporations like McDonald's have their standardized architecture (replete with arches) and their rituals of consumption that provide familiarity, comfort and security to customers. Such multinational firms employ media to disseminate and legitimate their corporate signifiers and logos. When TV advertisements sell for over $100,000 (sometimes over $300,000) per minute only the most wealthy members of the society can afford media validation. The study of socio-economic class at the end of the twentieth century can no longer ignore techno-power and its ability to produce persuasive images and representations of the world. In a culture of images, 'reality' is displaced by simulations of reality that can be understood only as they relate to the larger socio-economic goals of corporations. The ways corporations employ media to legitimate social practices that enhance their power to create 'good business climates' concurrently work to undermine principles of democracy. The corporate elite uses its media-saturated techno-power to discredit labour movements by connecting them to anti-American signifiers. If they are not discredited by this form of representation, labour and working class people are erased by techno-power's media. Questions of economic justice are simply not raised by corporate-financed TV. Corporate-owned networks and TV stations in their pursuit of high ratings and profitability cut back on political news and investigative journalism, focusing instead on 'politically neutral' human interest stories. Thus, the logic of capital and profit turns TV into a servant of the power bloc – the interests that own and control it (Kellner 1990; Critical Art Ensemble 1994).

The ideology of classlessness: power and myth-making

Four class myths perpetuated by class elites lay the ideological foundation for dismissal of class in economic, political and educational life.

(1) *Myth of equal opportunity.*Western capitalist societies produce success in a way that is open to everyone. Some analyses refer to this myth as the 'just world phenomenon' – the tendency to blame the victim rather than the victimizer in unjust situations. Economic elites employ the just world

phenomenon to justify their privilege to both themselves and others. It also can be used to support elite individuals' refusal to help oppressed individuals and groups to escape their situation. Anyone who wants good work can get it in an industrial capitalist society that accurately mirrors a state of nature where the strong survive and the weak perish, the story goes. The myth conveniently ignores the fact that in the everyday world people get ahead more on insiderism and inherited privilege than on any notion of merit (Merleman 1986; Appiah 1995; Staples 1995; Apple 1996; McLaren 1996).

(2) *Myth of meritocracy.* Elite advocates argue that those who succeed in schools and society deserve the spoils of victory. This myth is often expressed by the cliché: cream rises to the top. Richard J. Herrnstein and Charles Murray, authors of *The Bell Curve* (1994), support the myth of meritocracy when they argue that poor people in America tend to be the least intelligent members of the culture. In this context conservatives can easily make the argument that biological factors form the infrastructure for class divisions – that the poor and non-white will never successfully compete with the white middle class because of the qualitative differences in their gene pools. Here Herrnstein and Murray make the classic error that has plagued psychologists and educators for decades – they confuse intelligence with socio-economic advantage. Right-wing politicians and analysts buy into such mythology, explaining intensifying inequality as the product of the poor's growing lack of initiative and ability. The development of unprecedented homelessness and the growth of the underclass is not complex – it is merely the manifestation of genetic justice (Fraser 1995; Muwakkil 1995; Raspberry 1995).

(3) *Myth of equality as conformity.* Right-wing ideologues assert that when democratic progressives advocate social and educational policies grounded on the goal of equal access to upward mobility, they envision a communist Chinese-like society characterized by zombie-like conformity. Such an argument is absurd, as advocates of a critical multiculturalism value individual differences and the need for individuals to fight demands for conformity. The degree of this myth's absurdity is illustrated by the fact that it is a critical multiculturalism that understands the concept of ideology and hegemony with their explanations of how popular conformity is sometimes engineered by the power bloc. The effort to deploy this myth is a cheap attempt to connect calls for an egalitarian democracy to some authoritarian and totalitarian form of communism or socialism long used to frighten Westerners into the support of a class-stratified status quo.

(4) *Myth of power neutrality.* In a just world where the meritorious rise to power, the elite economic, political and social groups they constitute work for the best interests of society – or so the story goes. Power elites are benign, and because of the merit and wisdom of their members, such groups provide the best leadership, the most disinterested (objective) social management

available. Such a mythology sounds suspiciously like the benevolent invisible hand of Adam Smith's free market, that benevolently bestows rewards to those most worthy. Economic power in this theory – a conception of economics amazingly popular at the end of the twentieth century – is neutral and plays no favourites. Critical multiculturalists understand that the invisible hand is actually a sleight of hand ideology of an economic elite designed to hide the free market's tendency to bestow its greatest benefits on those already in possession of wealth and power. Free-market capitalism creates a climate that justifies the privileged few's view of reality. Market forces and competition are presented in this construction of the world as cherubs and angels who joyously but silently work to create a harmony between supply and demand, wages and prices, and goods and services. The free market never worked this way, even in the nineteenth century. It certainly doesn't work this way in the last years of the twentieth century, with the power of multinational corporations to sway governments and control markets, the obsession of government with military spending and the maintenance of the 'defence sector' of the economy and the formation of economic communities and oil cartels. No local economy is free from larger influences that undermine free trade and equal competition. The free market model does not account for these less-than-neutral intervening factors. Despite all appearances to the contrary, neo-classicists operate in a simple universe – a fantasy land that exists only at Disneyland (Richmond 1986).

The ideological function of the four myths works to inhibit the growth of a class consciousness that would move the 'have nots' to protest the maldistribution of wealth in society. In the USA the development of a class consciousness has always been impeded by a racially and ethnically diverse lower socio-economic class. Traditionally, ethnicity not only meant more to poor individuals than class but ethnic consciousness often undermined class consciousness. Thus, the American poor were more socially diverse than the European poor, subverting the efforts of American labour movements to challenge the economic injustice of the workplace. This diversity expresses itself in the late 1990s as a reluctance even to talk about class. Indeed, when candidates for office mention poverty, they are often silenced by charges of class baiting, of attempting to pit classes against each other. Thus, the attempt to write and speak about class issues is a dangerous enterprise that leaves one open to severe criticism. In the conservative 1980s and 1990s such criticism is more frequent and more strident than ever. The myths have worked effectively to erase the moral and ethical component attached to the critique of the disparity of wealth – if everyone has an equal chance on an equal opportunity playing field, what is there to be morally upset about when some win and some lose? In an amazing rhetorical reversal moral indignation in Western societies has been transferred to any attempts to facilitate poor people's attempts to escape their poverty. The poor and their advocates are the bad guys. Little outrage is left for those sons and nephews of the wealthy who gain their managerial positions and six-figure earnings not by way of diligence and merit but by the accident of their birth (Fiske 1993; Fraser 1995; Staples 1995).

In the discourse of multiculturalism over recent years, even when proponents spoke of race and gender issues, class was sidestepped. When Herrnstein and Murray's *The Bell Curve* appeared in 1994 with a class-specific theme and subtitle – *Intelligence and Class Structure in American Life* – all journalists could see were the racial dynamics of the work. It was as if no public language existed that would allow for a public discussion and debate about socio-economic class. Such realities make it extremely difficult to form alliances of the marginalized to counter the ideology of the elusive power bloc. When the ideology of abstract individualism is added to the four myths new forms of domination emerge. There is no need for social support for poor people, as the doctrine of abstract individualism relegates all success and all failure to the volition and ability of the individual. Any concern with justice or socio-economic mobility involves merely the ability of a man or a woman to compete in a competitive market place. The idea that social, cultural and political factors such as white supremacy, class elitism or patriarchy might interfere with one's ability to compete is offensive to those who promote this dominant ideology. Critical multiculturalists understand that abstract individualism is the servant of the power bloc, as it undermines recognition of the social, political and economic forces that undermine awareness of injustice. Such an absence of recognition subverts efforts to develop a sense of solidarity among individuals oppressed along different axes of power (Giroux 1988; Willis 1995).

Yvonna Lincoln (1996) expresses concern about the poor's lack of awareness of the ways hegemonic ideology is deployed against their interests, and their lack of access to the writings and ideas of analysts that expose such dynamics. Too often, individuals from lower socio-economic class backgrounds (as well as individuals from other classes) only see the political world from the perspective of implicit popular cultural representations and explicit manifestations of power-saturated political news. Power wielders have become increasingly adept at the use of the media over the past forty years. For example, Ronald Reagan's handlers in the 1980s set new standards for governmental manipulation of the electorate via TV and other technologies. In order to win mass consent these media experts had constantly to provide TV with a 'positive spin' on daily events; that is, they had to present a version of reality that portrayed Reagan and his policies positively. Over and over, like TV commercials, the administration fed the media this reconstituted and pasteurized version of events. Because news is a commodity that seeks to increase ratings just like the entertainment sector of TV, networks never have enough information on political leaders. Knowing this the handlers provided sound-bites and visuals of Reagan that carefully presented the desired picture of reality. The corporate-driven world-view of the Reagan administration fitted quite neatly with the corporate-run media – it was one of many manifestations of the ideology of the power bloc.

Many analysts of power, ideology and media are amused by the common question: does big business control the media? Critical multiculturalists maintain that the only response to such an inquiry is that the media *are* big business. The corporate owners of the four US commercial networks, General Electric (NBC), Disney (ABC), Rupert Murdoch (Fox) and Westinghouse (CBS) are corporate media monopolies. Squashing or absorbing any competition that might appear, these corporate conglomerates are above public accountability. The prospect of any serious competition in the future is undermined by the prohibitively high cost of establishing a media enterprise. The Reagan administration was extremely cosy with corporate leaders, so cosy in fact that General Electric made $10 billion in profits during the first Reagan term (1981–5) and paid not one cent in taxes. In these circumstances the idea of democracy and the power of democratic institutions fade under the domination of the hegemonic ideology of corporate techno-power. Accountable to no one, such power continues to shape the nature of material and ideological production and consumption (Brosio 1994; McLaren *et al.* 1995).

Not just blaming but vilifying the poor: there's gold in them there negative representations

As we have maintained, right-wing analysts and political leaders have attempted to win popular consent to the notion that anyone who has the ability and exerts the effort can make it in Western capitalist societies. Those who don't, they argue, are held back by their lack of morals, their lack of family values (Ellwood 1988). Such talk ignores thousands of poor people who embrace the work ethic, labour year upon year with hardly a break and still remain at the bottom rung of the economic ladder. Those who make this 'character' argument often refuse to address the social context with its political and economic structures that work to privilege the privileged and punish the poor. Concurrently, they refuse to discuss the nature of white racism, sexism and class bias – such talk, they confide, induces the poor to see themselves as victims not agents. While the purpose of empowerment involves the ability to move beyond victimization and to take charge of one's own destiny, the way to do it does not involve the denial of history (Jennings 1992; West 1992). Social, political and historical analysis grounds our understanding of the forces that overtly and covertly undermine socio-economic mobility. Such knowledge is essential in a critical multiculturalism that is dedicated to the empowerment of the poor.

The right-wing vilification of the poor is grounded on the notion that the poor are not only dumb but socially pathological as well. A major cause and effect of this pathological behaviour, the argument goes, involves the absence of strong family values – middle class family norms in particular. The model middle class family existed at one point in our golden past, the narrative reads, but progressives in their rejection of American values undermined the institution through welfare and giveaway programmes. Such actions, by providing something for nothing, so reduced self-initiative that the poor have subsequently refused to work. In this 'golden past' mothers were totally available to their children and intensely intimate with their husbands – a construction that placed so much pressure on women in the 1950s that thousands of them were driven to therapy, tranquillizers and alcohol. Ignoring these mid-century problems, conservatives of the 1990s ascribe a large part of the blame for deteriorating family values on women's embrace of feminism. The feminist ethic, they argue, undermined women's dedication to the family and began the process of family breakdown (Coontz 1992; Stafford 1992). Decontextualizing the rise of feminism, conservatives speak of that time when women were peaceful, happy, traditional and dedicated to their families. The feminazis, as Rush Limbaugh puts it, destroyed that wonderful world.

The argument that poverty is caused by the lack of family values is not new to America. In the last quarter of the nineteenth century white essayists made the family values argument in reference to newly freed African Americans. The problems of blacks, they wrote, are not the result of racism and poverty but of their family values and personal behaviour. Black parents were commonly believed by whites to raise their children without discipline or morality. Such inferior rearing produced boys born to roam and sexually promiscuous girls who frequently gave birth to illegitimate babies. Some commentators were more vitriolic, declaring that African Americans knew no more about fidelity in a marriage than a bull or heifer. Throughout the first half of the twentieth century black families were described by adjectives such as vicious and depraved. One disturbing aspect of the family values argument in the late twentieth century is that both conservatives and a sizable number of liberals have ascribed poverty to family breakdown. A middle and upper-middle class consensus has developed that attempts to repress understandings of context and structure and their role in shaping poverty.

This new consensus speaks of its anger towards the poor and non-white and their 'incessant whining' about their victimization. Liberal politicians scramble to realign themselves with the anger, arguing that in the 1960s the cause of poverty was the lack of opportunity caused by class bias and racism; in the 1990s, they contend, the problem involves not class bias and racism but pathological patterns of behaviour on the part of the poor themselves.

Thus, all we can do is cut social services, education, job training, college aid and welfare support for the poor – Murray and Herrnstein (1994) argue that since the poor are less intelligent such programmes are not likely to help them anyway. In a time when such arguments occupy a central position in public policy, critical multiculturalists have an important role to play. Concerned with social justice and economic opportunity, they must claim a voice in the conversation (Coontz 1992). They must be able to speak to moral problems inherent in the attempt to vilify the poor and articulate a vision of economic democracy and social justice.

If the power bloc is able to maintain the notion that the poor are debasing our society, then few will be able to challenge its domination. We are amazed with the right wing's success in portraying the poor as dangerous welfare cheats who must be disciplined and punished for their transgressions. Contemporary observers rarely, if ever, witness explanations on network or cable TV or in the mainstream printed press of why most poor people turn to welfare. Research, Maria Vidal (1996) writes, indicates that the consequences of low pay for low-skilled work and the absence of affordable childcare and health care pushes many people on to public assistance. Having nothing to do with the effort to vilify the poor, such realities are rarely referenced in the public conversation about poverty at the end of the century. Also absent is information on the market forces that are shaping class divisions in contemporary society (Lincoln 1996). Flagrant efforts to redistribute wealth began to take place in the Reagan and Thatcher eras in the USA and Britain – from poor to rich, like anti-matter Robin Hoods. Accompanying such redistribution policies have been offensives against labour unions, adoption of exploitative labour practices such as the utilization of part-time and Third World labour (usually women and minorities), the re-establishment of patriarchal sweat shops and domestic piece work, and the extensive use of subcontracting. Such policies have undermined the stability of the middle class, as an ever-increasing percentage of new jobs are low-wage. A growing number of people are marginal to the workforce, as they accept 'contingent employment' in jobs with few benefits and no assurance of security (Block 1990; Grossberg 1992). As post-Fordist changes moved workers from industrial and agricultural jobs to service and information employment, many men and women watched their middle class status disappear. Workers with jobs in the industrial sector were displaced by new technologies, computerization and automation. These 'deindustrialization' strategies affected middle-level and semi-skilled jobs ($9–12 an hour jobs in particular), resulting in further economic bi-polarization (Rumberger 1984; Kellner 1989).

When employers deindustrialize, not only do they automate but they also close plants in one location and move them to another – either to a more 'favourable business climate' domestically or to one in the Third World. A more favourable business climate is characterized by lower labour costs, less unionization, or reduced governmental regulation. Throughout the 1980s, wage levels declined while skill levels remained virtually the same. As intermediate skill level jobs declined in number, corporations whose bargaining position had been strengthened by deindustrialization and pro-management government policies paid intermediate skill workers lower wages. The case can be made that all of these management policies are part of a larger corporate strategy to disentangle themselves from the remnants of New Deal and Labour Party compromises between unions, management and government. No longer do Western corporations need to give in to labour demands for high wages and highly unionized workforces – in the favourable business climate of the 1990s, they don't have to. Thus, the ability of corporations to maximize profits by lowering wages and benefits and firing low-status workers has reached new heights at the end of the century.

One of the most important of the new corporate strategies involves the use of part-time workers. As part of their post-Fordist dynamic flexibility, businesses have begun to cover inconsistencies in demand with employees hired from temporary agencies. Making up a large percentage of the new jobs created, such positions are filled by workers with little bargaining power. This situation dramatically separates core from peripheral labour, in the process exacerbating divisions between white and non-white and men and women. For example, many of the part-time jobs are held by women. The flexible corporate structures have allowed managers to substitute lower-paid female labour for that of core male workers who make higher wages. The resurgence of subcontracting and family labour systems has further damaged women's status in the workplace, as they are often relegated to low-status roles in patriarchal workplaces and in homeworking. Unfortunately, when mass production jobs are moved to Third World locales in Mexico or Malaysia, factories employing extremely low paid women become the norm. Indeed, women have suffered disproportionately in the postmodern upheavals (Harvey 1989; Murray 1992). Young people constitute yet another increasingly marginalized group in the post-Fordist arrangement. Many young people cannot entertain even a glimmer of hope concerning their economic futures – a reality little understood by the economically well-to-do. These kids are ignored, concealed and forgotten; they are an embarrassment to a system that sees the presence of a permanent underclass as an embarrassment, as bad PR, as a dangerous contradiction to the individualist ethic (MacLeod 1987). Young urban dwellers carry a hopelessness so great that they embrace an anti-work ethic as a defence against the psychic scars of unemployment. Urban youth communities are built around their exclusion; their lived worlds are marked not by protest or passivity but by hostile, angry and aggressive despair.

The more vile the power bloc's portrayal of the poor, the more corporate profits increase – who cares about the rights and needs of such sociopaths? After all, the ideological narrative reads, the incompetent poor have caused our social ills; only bleeding heart fools would want to help these people. The new conservative cultural war carries the battle against immigration, genetic inferiority and issues of reproduction within poor communities. How dare, the right wing asks, these inferior poor people seek equality when what they need is to be more effectively controlled. Democracy just may not work with these types of people. Indeed, the democratic effort to bring them into schools, many conservatives argue, has been a tragic failure. Their presence has undermined educational standards – dumbed schools down – in the process spoiling education for the educable. In this context schools need more efficient testing practices that allow educators to track bright children into advanced classes and remove those deemed to be unable. Perhaps they could be funnelled into expanded special education programmes that taught discipline and low expectations. The poor in such circumstances could learn their place in a meritocratic society. After graduation perhaps they could be corralled, as Herrnstein and Murray suggest, in a high-tech Indian reservation (Marsh 1993; Brimelow 1995; Jones 1995; Pearson 1995; Reed 1995).

The smokescreen of family values

Individuals from the middle and upper-middle class often know very little about poor and non-white people. Indeed, much of the prevailing wisdom about the underclass is simply not true. For example, the folk wisdom of the 1990s asserts that the poor, black women in particular, have been producing 'exploding' numbers of babies out of wedlock. The truth is that birth rates of single black women have fallen by 13 per cent in the past 25 years. During the same period, birth rates for unmarried white women increased by 27 per cent. Such information might induce some right-wing politicians to temper their descriptions of poor black mothers as 'brood mares' and 'welfare queens'. As wealth began to polarize in the 1970s and 1980s, new problems emerged in poor communities, especially poor urban black communities, that cause concern for all of us. Levels of violence have worried everyone, though the poor suffer the effects disproportionately. The attempt, however, to ascribe the cause of such problems simply to the pathology of the poor is both logically simplistic and emotionally unempathetic. The causes of the urban crisis have been reduced to a few basic factors: broken families, high divorce rates, unwed pregnancies, family violence and drug/alcohol abuse. The same problems confront families whose members serve as police officers or in the military, yet most Americans refrain from blaming them for their dysfunctionality. Typically, we have little trouble understanding that the context in which police officers and soldiers operate is in part responsible for such pathologies. Work stress from danger and conflict can produce devastating results. With this in mind it is not difficult to imagine the stress that accompanies living for just one week in an inner-city war zone – now imagine living there with no hope of getting out.

In this context the argument can be made that the strong family values that the socially and economically marginalized possess actually serve to impede economic mobility in some cases. Imagine that an elderly poor couple living in rural West Virginia inherit $5,000 from a deceased uncle. For years they have tried to save enough money to buy a new house with indoor plumbing, a heating system that worked consistently and a location closer to the grocery store and the doctor's office. The money is just enough for a down payment on a modest two bedroom home on the outskirts of town. Right at the time that they were closing the deal on the new house, a cousin who had lost his job in the coal mines tells them he is being evicted from his house. He owes $1,200 in delinquent rent. Another relative, the wife's sister who was recently widowed, needs money to pay a long-distance phone bill she accumulated talking to her husband's four brothers, who live in various parts of the country, about her husband's medical condition, his death and the funeral arrangements. Another relative had a car repair bill of $1,000 she was unable to pay. If she was going to keep her job, she had to get her car fixed – she didn't have the money. The house deal fell through – within a month the inheritance was gone. It had not been spent on a Cadillac, drugs, booze or fancy clothes; it was not lost because of the poor couple's inability to defer gratification or plan for the future – a charge frequently levelled at poor people. Because of the couple's commitment to their extended family, their socio-economic mobility was subverted. Strong family values alone cannot solve the polarity of wealth in America.

Many analysts contend that if all poor people who don't now possess traditional family values were miraculously to develop them by next week, very little would change in relation to the widening disparity of wealth. Even if poor families are together, few will advance economically if jobs are not available. No matter how hard conservatives might try to prove that individual pathology causes poverty, they will not succeed. Indeed, it may even be possible to establish a link between deviant social behaviour and high income. Obviously, many make the observation that a larger number of the most well-to-do young people in inner-city neighbourhoods have made money through violent and pathological crimes – the reward of pathological behaviour.

Social analysts make the point that one feature that separates the poor from the middle class is the pathological inability of the poor to delay gratification. When corporate behaviour in America is examined over the past quarter century, one is struck by the emphasis on short-term quarterly profits at the expense of long-term development. The credit card debt compiled by middle and upper-middle class consumers in the 1980s and 1990s points to the possibility that the pathology of the poor is not all that different from that of other Americans. This ascription of pathology and individualistic blame to the poor is not based on some objective body of facts pointing to their complicity. Rather, it is an example of power at work: the maintenance of the existing polarization of wealth is a condition that is imposed on the poor by the powerful guardians of the status quo (Coontz 1992; Jennings 1992).

This does not mean that there is some secret conspiracy operating behind the social curtain. However, it does mean that conditions are perpetuated that benefit those who hold power at the expense of those who don't. When North Carolina Senator Jesse Helms, for example, airs TV campaign ads that pit the black and white poor against one another in the scramble for the working class jobs that still exist, the status quo is defended. By dividing the poor people into competing racial groups, the possibility of them uniting to fight for social justice and economic democracy is negated. So much of the contemporary right-wing conversation, whether it be Rush Limbaugh on the TV, Oliver North on the radio, William Bennett on the lecture circuit or Bob Dole on the campaign trail, is focused on distinguishing between 'us/we' and 'them/they'. We are positioned as family loving, hard working, values-promoting decent people; they are represented as violent, immoral, intimidating and family-neglecting individuals. They are often non-white, gay/lesbian, feminists and poor – and always undeserving. If we don't stop supporting them, they will destroy our standards, our way of life. Such characterizations, believed by millions of people, use love of family, country and sometimes even God to construct an ideology of social regulation (Gardner 1995; Apple 1996).

Education for demoralization: the curriculum of class elitism

The power bloc has always promoted conservative goals, especially for the education of the young. Maintaining social order and social regulation have typically been viewed as educational purposes superior in importance to the promotion of social mobility. Learning to obey the rules and defer to authority is often more important than academic learning. Social regulation usually refers to the control of the poor. Researchers have discovered that classroom management strategies differ significantly between classrooms composed primarily of poor students and those composed primarily of middle and upper-middle class students. But control of the poor is never achieved easily – if it is achieved at all. The dynamics of social control always involve contestation and conflict; students who perfect an oppositional identity do not lend themselves to being controlled by the school or anyone else. The identities that students wear are directly affected by the dynamics of this struggle for control – critical multicultural educators study these everyday power struggles very carefully.

How does it affect young men or women from poor families once they gain the understanding that most of the resources of the school are devoted to the more 'promising' (read middle class) students? What happens to poor students when they learn that they can expect little from the school? How long does it take them to understand the often subtle and sometimes not so subtle procedures to persuade them into the lower ability classes? Many of the young people we've talked to have been livid when they finally appreciated (often years later) the ways in which their opportunities were undermined by their high school experience. Once they have gained some wisdom in the workaday world and some insight via self-education or perhaps a return to school, these students explode with anger when they recall the ways standardized intelligence tests rationalized their relegation to the low-ability groups. They are flooded with emotion as they recognize that the knowledge they acquired in their education had little exchange value in the open market place (Giroux 1988).

In such circumstances how could marginalized students be motivated to learn, to be excited about school? Educational sociologists have for decades reported the cold, impersonal ways teachers often treat their lower socio-economic class students. Rarely are teachers empathetic with the painful existential choices poor students have to make between acceptance by their peers and school success (Banfield 1991). School is sometimes like a jealous lover who demands that marginalized students must choose between their peers or school – if school is chosen then one must give up one's culture and adopt the identity of a school achiever. So hard are these choices for marginalized kids that students from poor backgrounds who remain in school and are at least moderately successful in their classes are, when compared to school dropouts, more depressed, less politically conscious, more passive in the life of the classroom and more prone to conform. The price of success in the modernist school for marginalized students may be a form of coerced cultural hara-kiri.

Under such circumstances it is not surprising when schools that should exist to empower lower socio-economic class students actually serve to demoralize them and strip them of a desire for self-determination. Indeed, studies indicate that the school does a good job of convincing the poor of their inferiority. Since they often fail in school, individuals from the lower socio-economic classes often feel that they have no right to help to make political and economic policy – that is, to help to govern. There is little that could be done that would better maintain existing power relations, keeping the poor in poverty. Poor people in this failure mode should not even attempt to voice their concerns and fight the injustice that chains them to their dead end jobs – after all, they are incompetent, resting as they do at the base of Murray and Herrnstein's bell curve. This psychology of inadequacy supplements more obvious forms of domination, such as factory ownership, control of information and expertise, the power to represent the world and its people, placement in governmental positions and lobbyist access to political officials. All of these dynamics work synergistically to maintain the polarization of power and wealth (Zweigenhaft and Domhoff 1991)

Marginalized students often believe the equal opportunity fable propagated repeatedly in their classrooms. Caught in the psychology of inadequacy, they internalize the psycho-babble and the labels it ascribes to them – we're problem children, emotionally distributed and learning impaired, they tell us. On one level they understand the absurdities of some of the labels and laugh uproariously at the irony of their usage; but on another level, a very personal one, they accept the classifications as transcendental truths about themselves (MacLeod 1987). A critical multicultural education intervenes in this context, assuring mislabelled students of their intrinsic worth and helping them to understand the social dynamics that contextualize their bizarre position in the culture of American schooling. Clint Allison (1995) writes in *Present and Past* that social and political power wielders have traditionally feared the poor and the non-white, arguing in the middle of the nineteenth century that something had to be done about them. Their 'inferior cultures and dangerous ideas' must be addressed by the schools, they maintained and students from these groups must be taught order and self-control. What better way to accomplish this holy mission than by convincing marginalized students that they are failures and that they have no one to blame but themselves? The system cannot work until the poor accept the ideology of their inferiority that justifies their lowly place in hierarchy.

In this context who wouldn't lose their self-esteem and desire to speak? Imagine that you have been taught for eight years that you are abnormal, unable to think and understand like the more well-to-do and popular students in your class, who typically look at you with disdain. You are conspicuously removed from the classroom each day and taken on a Bataan death-march to the 'resource room' for kids with special needs. You are mercilessly forced to drill and repeat arithmetic and grammatical lessons on division and verbs. In your 'abnormality' you are taught that you are helpless and in need of expert help; you have no input or control over anything that is done to you. All you can wish is that this day-by-day, hour-by-hour humiliation would end. To escape it you would do almost anything, no matter how dangerous or foolish it might be. This is just one of many ways in which the macro-social structure of class bias might be internalized by poor children. Such consistent daily and hourly reminders keep pushing one to accept a dominant–subordinate set of relationships. Such acceptance involves the lower socio-economic class student taking on the role of the 'other'. Such a process of ideological internalization is often referred to as reflexive legitimation – a key concept in the larger effort to understand how power in the form of ideology shapes the educational/pedagogical process. In this context ideology as an idea or set of ideas transmogrifies into a material force – a force that actively thwarts the ability of the poor to escape their poverty. Teachers who are unaware of these invisible but deadly forces at work in their classrooms allow individual tragedies to play out daily while they teach their multicultural curriculum with its piñatas, tortillas and celebrations of Cinco de Mayo (Musolf 1992; Marsh 1993; Jones 1995).

Critical multiculturalists want poor students to understand how this class-biased social regulatory process works. Through our own teaching experiences and the work of many others, including Paulo Freire and Myles Horton, we know that such consciousness-raising pedagogy can take place. As they begin to see beyond the horizon of their poverty and the reflexive legitimation of their lowly status, students often gain an unprecedented sense of excitement about school and the power of ideas. Many of them gain a new sense of efficacy, an empowerment that induces them to join the fray – for both personal development and social justice. They are awestruck by truth-telling, motivated by the desire to get the whole story and moved by the vision of what education can be. Here critical multiculturalists engage marginalized students in the meaning of social justice and democratic civics in their everyday lives. In this lived context students come to understand that democracy cannot survive in a society that assumes the incompetence and pathology of poor people. Such a belief is not grounded on some sterile notion that everyone has the same ability and volition – although we do believe that human abilities are not nearly as disparate as some psychometricians and right-wing politicians say they are. Rather, the belief that democracy cannot survive intense class bias is based on an ethical imperative: an individual or a group's difference, actual or imaginary, provides no justification for subordination. By nature of their humanity, people from the lower socio-economic class have the right to live in a society with educational and political institutions that are not organized on the basis of eugenics, class elitism, white supremacy and patriarchy (Ryan 1995; Willis 1995; Britzman and Pitt 1996; Giroux and Searles 1996).

A critical multicultural pedagogy of empowerment for the poor

In the light of these understandings critical multiculturalists advocate a politically informed, socially contextualized, ethically grounded, power sensitive pedagogy for students from poor backgrounds. Such a cultural and institutional education would possess several features.

(1) *The recognition of class bias within education.* Teachers, students,

cultural critics and political leaders must understand the subtle and hidden ways in which class bias filters into educational policy, schooling and the cultural curriculum. Schools, media, religious groups and politicians often maintain that Western capitalist societies are lands of wealth and opportunity open to all who are willing to work. Lessons are taught daily that former communist nations in Eastern Europe and Third World societies in Africa, Asia and Latin America are stricken by poverty and its concurrent social problems, but that Western societies are above such pathology. Indeed, countries like the USA, Britain, Canada, Australia and New Zealand constantly use their expertise to repair the problems of other, less developed nations. Implicitly embedded in such a curriculum is the notion that Western societies are at their essence white and middle class nations. They are populated by upwardly mobile white men who are the smartest, most industrious people in the world. Their main concern is to make a prosperous life for themselves and their families – an objective that operates in the best interests of everyone on the planet.

In the school curriculum the poor are rarely studied. In elementary and secondary social studies curricula the contributions of workers are erased, as textbooks and curriculum guides depict a world where factory and business owners and politicians do all the work. At an implicit, subtextual level such teaching inscribes irrelevancy on the lives of the working classes. The study of the past is an examination of 'the lives of the rich and famous'. One can almost hear Robin Leach's grating voice uncritically enshrining and ennobling the behaviours of the privileged, especially when they are engaged in morally reprehensible practices such as slavery, conquest of indigenous peoples, political and economic colonization and urbanization. Such activities are often presented unambiguously as heroic acts of 'progress' that brought honour and wealth to the motherland. The brutal, often genocidal, features of these practices are too often ignored. Students and citizens involved in a pedagogy of empowerment gain the ability to expose features of the class-biased curriculum that operate daily in their lives (Swartz 1993; Sleeter and Grant 1994).

(2) *The appreciation of the nature and effects of the polarization of wealth*. Again, everyone benefits, the poor in particular, from an understanding of the way power works and poverty develops. Such knowledge empowers the poor not only to escape such forces themselves but to initiate public, institutional and private conversations about the relationship between poverty and wealth. Such knowledge empowers the poor to 'call' media commentators and political leaders on the superficial and misleading pronouncements that pass for an analysis of the causes of poverty (Jones 1992). Western peoples – Americans in particular – have yet to discuss the social, political and economic aspects of privilege *vis-à-vis* deprivation. In this context students and citizens will learn that the polarization of wealth

and the economic perspectives that allowed it to happen have created a situation where our society's economic machine no longer needs young inexperienced people. Adolescence as a preparatory stage for adulthood is obsolete. In the 1990s it has become a corral for unneeded young people drifting in a socio-economic purgatory (for more information on these changing conditions of youth in the late twentieth century see Steinberg and Kincheloe 1997). Demographers report that elderly men have the highest suicide rate. Perceived by society and themselves as socially superfluous, old men are removed from the workforce, stripped of a future and left to wait for death. Over the past quarter century the group that witnessed the fastest growing suicide rate was males aged fifteen to nineteen (Gaines 1990). Stripped of their hopes for socio-economic mobility and burdened with the masculine expectation for self-sufficiency, these young men reflect the Western social dilemma in the 1990s. Critical multiculturalism must provide a voice of hope, an avenue of participation for students and citizens victimized by contemporary economic strategies and youth policies.

(3) *The articulation of a political vision.* Any pedagogy of empowerment that fails to produce a political vision that grounds the political organization of the economically marginalized will fail. The poor must gain the political savvy to uncover hegemonic ideological attempts to disempower them. In this context they will turn such political knowledge into the political clout to resist those who attempt to undermine their solidarity by appealing to their racial, gender, ethnic or religious prejudices (Jennings 1992). A critical multicultural political vision understands that the traditional route to socio-economic mobility has, contrary to the prevailing wisdom, involved first achieving income stability and then investing in education (Coontz 1992). In the light of this understanding the basis of an economic empowerment policy should revolve around job creation/full employment policies that provide child care for workers and reward and punish businesses on the basis of their contributions to the creation of good jobs and democratic workplaces in poor areas. The critical multicultural political vision calls for an increase in wages and a commitment to end welfare by providing jobs to welfare recipients. In two-parent families where one or two of the parents is a full-time worker or in single-parent families where the parent works either full-time or part-time, work should be rewarded. Health care for such workers should be guaranteed and tax burdens should be reduced (Ellwood 1988; West 1992; Nightingale 1993). Obviously, such a political vision is not popular in Western societies at the end of the century. Thus, it will take a monumental effort on the part of the poor and their allies to generate support for the policies demanded by the vision.

(4) *The development of the knowledge and skills required to escape poverty.* The core of the critical multicultural pedagogy of empowerment revolves around an understanding of the impediments to social and economic

mobility and the specifics of how one gets around such social, cultural and educational roadblocks. As a rigorous multidimensional course of study, the empowerment curriculum views men and women in more than simply egoistic, self-centred and rationalist terms. Individuals, especially poor ones, need help making meaning in their lives, developing sense of purpose, constructing a positive identity and cultivating self-worth. Unlike previous forms of conservative and liberal education, the pedagogy of empowerment would address these issues, using the categories covered in this book as the programme's theoretical basis. Understanding socio-economic class in the larger context of historical power relations, students would understand that poverty is not simply a reflection of bad character or incompetence. In this context students would appreciate the organizational dynamics necessary to the effort to 'pull oneself up by one's bootstraps' – an undertaking often referenced but infrequently explained. The empowerment curriculum would help poor individuals to develop strategies to take control of schools, social agencies, health organizations and economic organizations. Understanding how these organizations work to undermine the interests of the poor, with their narrow and often scientifically produced definitions of normality, intelligence, family stability etc., the curriculum helps students to devise strategies to resist the imposition of policies grounded on such definitions (Ellwood 1988; Jennings 1992; West 1992).

The curriculum begins with the personal experiences of working class students but moves to understandings far beyond them; teachers constantly relate what is being learned back to student experience. Concepts and information about the world are integrated into what students already know. Such data are then analysed in the light of questions of economic justice, environmental/ecological connections to class bias, an understanding of Western modernist ways of seeing the world and the needs of democracy. Such understandings help to create a critical consciousness grounded on an appreciation of both the way ideology works to convince the marginalized of their own inferiority and how empowered people are capable of generating democratic change. Students with a critical consciousness are able to point out the ways the power bloc enforces its dominance and how in the electronic world of postmodernity the process takes on new degrees of impact and complexity. Empowered students who possess a critical multicultural consciousness draw upon the reality of everyday conflict in their lives, their recognition of the gap between the promise of democracy and the despair they have experienced as members of the low socio-economic class to illustrate to all the reality of injustice. In this emotional connection of lived experience to larger conceptual understanding, students and teachers begin to get in touch with their passion, the lived impact of their encounter with critical multiculturalism (Sleeter and Grant 1994; Britzman and Pitt 1996; Giroux 1997a).

In the light of the engagement with this passionate new consciousness, all forms of knowledge are opened to question. Here, an important skill for poor students involves the ability to reveal the power interests hidden within allegedly neutral knowledge forms. Thus, a central feature of any critical multicultural curriculum involves an analysis of existing literary works, important philosophical, political and religious texts and particular accounts of history that shape a curriculum – the Eurocentric canon, for example. In this analysis students explore where such knowledge comes from, why particular knowledge forms have not been included and the strengths and limitations of the ways of knowing that accompany the canonical discourse. What we are describing here is rigorous scholarly activity that refuses to dispense information to students dispassionately, but insists on engaging students in the discovery of personal meanings within knowledge and in the production of knowledge. As subjugated groups begin to make sense of their histories and their personal worlds, critical multiculturalists display their respect for the intellect of members of such groups by not simply accepting any meaning they make or knowledge they produce as authentic. Critical multicultural teachers and cultural workers engage the knowledge production of particular individuals, inducing them to become more and more aware of the socio-political, cultural and moral dynamics embedded within their constructions. It is not uncommon to find racist and sexist undercurrents that undermine the dignity of non-whites and women. In this context critical multiculturalists have no problem challenging the assumptions behind such knowledge. Such engagements with canon, meaning making and critiques provide not only empowerment and cognitive development, but also a form of cultural capital that emerges from an understanding of the discourse of education. Education can be thought of as a discourse community with its own rules of knowledge, decorum and success. In the process of engaging students with the issues discussed here, critical multicultural teachers from elementary school to college are consciously involved in introducing students to this educational discourse community. Students from subjugated groups typically feel that they are not a part of the school community, that they don't possess the secret knowledge that will let them into the club. The type of critical education discussed here provides students from lower socio-economic class backgrounds with a sense of belonging that holds implications not only for their lives in school but for vocational, spiritual and interpersonal domains as well (Darder 1991; Harred 1991; Hauser 1991).

(5) *Awareness of the liabilities and possibilities of resistance.* When marginalized students come to the conclusion – and most of them eventually do – that education is set up to reward the values of the already successful, those whose culture most accurately reflects the mainstream, they have to negotiate how they react to this realization. Most lower socio-economic

class students are, understandably, confused and dislocated because of this reality. Critical multiculturalism is devoted to helping marginalized students make sense of this reality and facilitating the formulation of the resistance to it. A central lesson for angry marginalized students involves developing an awareness of the costs of various forms of resistance. Rejection of middle class propriety often expresses itself as an abrasive classroom behaviour antithetical to mutual respect and focused analysis. Critical multiculturalists believe that the outcome of marginalized student resistance does not have to be disempowerment. To formulate an emancipatory form of resistance we draw upon the world of cultural analyst John Fiske (1993). Fiske argues that marginalized peoples comprise localized power groups who typically produce popular forms of knowledge. Such knowledge forms are powerful and can be drawn upon for psychic protection from the ideological teachings of the power bloc. Marginalized knowledge forms or, as we described them earlier, subjugated knowledge allow the oppressed to make sense of their social and educational experiences from a unique vantage point and in the process to reconstruct their identities. Critical multiculturalists both study these knowledge forms and encourage their students to explore their origins and effects. Without such understanding and encouragement, we fear that lower socio-economic class anger over the unfairness and oppression they encounter will turn violent.

Obviously, it already has in many places, but what we have observed so far may simply represent the tip of the iceberg. Marginalized peoples become violent when they are not heard. Obviously racial and class violence has a plethora of causes, but one of the most important involves the fact that the power bloc often does not listen to non-white or poor people. In this context studies indicate that while violence can be observed at all socio-economic levels, it is concentrated among males from poor backgrounds. As the disparity of wealth increases, the impulse for violence also grows. We can see such an impulse quite clearly in a variety of popular cultural forms consumed by working class men and women, young males in particular, including heavy metal music, violent movies and professional wrestling (Gaines 1990; Fiske 1993). To avoid the escalation of violence among the oppressed, issues of social and economic justice will have to be taken seriously by individuals from various social sectors. Without dramatic action, Western societies face a violent opening of the new millennium. Constructive, nonviolent strategies of resistance must be carefully studied in the coming years.

(6) *Emphasis on the ability to organize the poor.* Many observers consistently underestimate the localizing power of the poor to assert themselves. The localizing power of the poor is a social resource typically misunderstood by the power bloc that helps to define the parameters of what the power bloc can or cannot do. When thoughtfully organized, the poor can extend the influence of such power and move it in an emancipatory direction. Such

organization increases the odds that the poor will be able to draw upon the subversive power of their localized or subjugated knowledge. An empowering aspect of such knowledge involves the insight it can provide into the connections between the actions of various power blocs – consistencies in the ways such power wielders attempt to maintain the status quo. One of the roles of critical multiculturalists – indeed, one of the central purposes of this book – involves pointing out and conceptually extending such subjugated understandings. For example, an organized group of poor people would understand the class elitism at work both in a school curriculum that focused on the 'great contributions' of business, industrial and political leaders and in newspapers and TV reports that provide business news and not labour news. Though they occur in different social venues, these realities work to undermine the power and importance of the poor and working class. Such an understanding leads to the possibility of an informed resistance.

Any organizational efforts for the empowerment of the marginalized must understand that power does not flow in some unidirectional hierarchy from the powerful to the oppressed. Though their power is weak in relation to the power bloc, the oppressed possess a variety of means of eluding the control of oppressors – in many historical cases this bottom-up power has led to the overthrow of the power bloc. Organizational efforts to mobilize the disempowered must always be mindful of this potential and appreciate the marginalized individual's capacity to use his or her creativity and localized knowledge to question dominant ideologies and the hegemonic purposes of its institutions. The very lower socio-economic class students who are saddled with the disempowering burden of a low IQ, for example, are the students who because of their social location are empowered to recognize the foibles and naiveté of privileged individuals with high IQs. On many occasions we have heard the oppressed laugh at the incompetence of high-status individuals whom they had encountered at some point during their lives. Such a subjugated knowledge can serve as a conceptual basis for rejecting the cognitive essentialism of intelligence tests and the psychic scars and socio-economic disempowerment that accompany them. Such understandings can be used as a foundation for the development of a counter-hegemonic and empowered consciousness. They can experientially ground the development of counter-organizations that produce counter-histories and counter-knowledges of the relationships between the marginalized and the privileged. New forms of political organizations and pedagogical interventions must be formulated that draw upon both subjugated understandings of the privileged and critical multicultural understandings of how power works (Wartenberg 1992; Fiske 1993; West 1993; Britzman and Pitt 1996; Carspecken 1996).

six

THE IMPORTANCE OF GENDER IN MULTICULTURALISM

Obviously, one of the most important features of a critical multiculturalism involves its attention to questions of gender and its respect for feminist theory. Critical multiculturalism does not simply embrace issues of gender equity – though it finds them extremely important – but also rethinks the very basis of how we see the world and ourselves via the reconstructive philosophy of feminist theories. One of the most fundamental features of ways of seeing that fall on different sides of the postmodern divide involves one's relation to feminist scholarship. Critical multiculturalism, as delineated here, is so influenced by feminist critique that it can never return to the old kingdom of modernism. In this context new epistemologies and reconstructed identities come together in a larger effort to rethink not only categories of gender but questions of justice, knowledge production and democracy. In this sense postmodern articulations of feminist theory rest at the heart of critical multiculturalism. As in all of our descriptions of critical multicultural critique and analysis, our focus on the importance of gender in multiculturalism begins with an analysis of existing power relations.

What is patriarchy?

Patriarchy is the gender arrangement in which men form the dominant social group. In a patriarchal society the male role is granted a higher status than the female role. While originally the term patriarchy was used to mean control by the father, critical multiculturalism employs the term in a more expansive sense to involve the power men gain by birthright to define reality and enjoy the rewards of privilege by way of their domination of subordinates

(Balsamo 1985; Ferguson 1991). Patriarchal power, as with most power, constantly interacts with the axes of race and class, finding itself either undermined or enhanced by the interaction. Patriarchal power's capacity to define reality, for example, is more pervasive when it is combined with the power of socio-economic class privilege and the racial privilege of white people. The male definition of reality in this privileged context is inseparable from the tenets of Cartesian–Newtonian modernism's point central to the understanding of Western patriarchy. This view sees the world constructed by physically, socially and biologically disembodied 'things', ruled by predictable laws that can be rationally perceived and deployed by 'men of science'. Thus, the world can be viewed objectively and disinterestedly in this patriarchal cosmos. In such a context scientific work is deemed a high-status enterprise that seeks to predict and control those of lower status. Such activity has been called 'bad science' by some individuals – bad in the sense that it places research 'purity' and rigour above the needs of people and the problems of the community. These critics urge us to rebel against the rules of patriarchal ways of seeing and re-establish our connections with one another and the natural world (Ferguson 1984; Williams 1992).

Many men, especially Anglo men from well-to-do backgrounds, form their male self-identity through the denial of their connections with other people. Late twentieth-century American patriarchal culture defines manhood in terms of separation and self-sufficiency – Clint Eastwood in *High Plains Drifter* comes to mind. Here was a man who was such a loner he didn't even need a name. Some critics claimed that Eastwood is acting style consisted of 'squinting and not-squinting', a humorous reference to his low-affect style of acting. Male self-identity in patriarchal societies is grounded on the repression of affect, the disruption of connection. Eastwood in the man-with-no-name westerns and later in the Dirty Harry movies set the standard for male disconnection, for man as self-sufficient loner. He repressed his hurt feelings and learned to hide and disguise them from the world. Indeed, in a traditional patriarchal culture the only approved techniques of dealing with one's emotion involve evasiveness, bravado, boasting, bluster, lying and various forms of aggression. In the attempt to master such techniques young boys in our culture begin to cultivate a 'cool male pose' around the time they enter the fifth or sixth grade. Such a pose negates public emotional display – obviously crying is forbidden and even smiling and displays of enthusiasm are restricted (Nightingale 1993).

The emotional repression and lack of interpersonal connection that patriarchy breeds create severe social dysfunctionality, especially in the areas of family, child care and women's issues. Men who are unable to deal with emotional conflict and the interpersonal dynamics of marriage and familial relationships have left their wives and families in ever-increasing numbers over the last third of the century. Such fathers are unable to deal with the 'breadwinner-loser' male character who forfeits his patriarchal power (his 'male energy') in his domestication and subsequent acceptance of fidelity in marriage, dedication to job and devotion to children. This 'domesticated loser' has been the subject of male ridicule in post-Second World War America: to the beatniks he was square; to *Playboy* devotees he was sexually timid; to hippies he was tediously straight. The search for a hip male identity in a patriarchal culture of disconnection has devastated the stability and nurture of the family. Indeed, to connect with one's family and to develop a faithful and communicative relationship with one's wife is to lose status among one's fellow men in a patriarchal culture.

In this context the male's escape from commitment has become the order of the era, with its panoply of negative consequences for women. The majority of men who flee the family refuse to offer any assistance to the wife and children left behind. Child support has become an important women's issue in the last decades of the twentieth century because of the dramatic increase in women-headed families. When men's failure of commitment is combined with women's inability to earn high wages, women-headed families too often fall below the poverty line. When the courts mandate child support, more than one out of four women never receive a penny of the money awarded – less than half ever receive the full amount. A more telling statistic reveals the average *annual* child-support payment for white, Hispanic and black women: white women, $2,180; Hispanic women, $2,070; and black women, $1,640 (Sidel 1992).

In patriarchal societies men's claim to knowledge, its production and validation, carries more weight than women's. While different classes and racial groups of women hold different perspectives on this social dynamic – white working class women, for example, seem to defer to it more than other groups of women – men's knowledge about work and other activities garners the most status in this society. This power dimension is illustrated daily on the individual level with men in board meetings, union meetings, shopfloor meetings' or teachers meetings interrupting and speaking over women or appropriating authority over what women have said; for example, 'What Cindy meant was that . . .' The same pattern is discernible on TV, when an advertisement promotes a household product for women (dishwashing detergent). While the video depicts a woman using and enjoying the product ('my hands are softer after washing the dishes'), a male voice-over provides technical information ('three out of four dermatologists conclude that new, improved Bongo Liquid . . .') and the trappings of authority. The woman alone with her 'inferior' form of knowledge is an inadequate authority in a patriarchal society. Bring in the man with the deep voice (Meissner 1988; Luttrell 1993).

This power differential between men and women in the patriarchal society is also seen in other forms of media. In many movies women are marginalized as parents, as, for example, in *Boyz N the Hood* where director John Singleton drives home the point that boys who don't have fathers fail, mothers are irrelevant. Both *Boyz N the Hood* and *Jungle Fever*, two brilliantly written, powerful and appealing movies, designate female sexuality as a threat to male (in these movies, black male) heterosexual identity. Indeed, Singleton and Spike Lee are so seductive as movie makers that women can actually enjoy their own symbolic denigration. Similarly, network news accounts of economic issues such as unemployment also reflect patriarchal structures in their verbal and visual focus on unemployment in the male-dominated industrial sector. Stories on the dramatic increase in lay-offs and permanent unemployment in service sector, predominantly female positions such as secretaries, information processors and government workers constitute only 1 per cent of TV news stories on such matters (Apple 1992; Wallace 1992). It is no secret that TV producers, scholars, researchers in education and teachers devote less attention to women than men (McLaren 1994b). Critical multiculturalists are aware of this situation and are working to change it.

Such a patriarchal context induces some women, especially working class women, to devalue their own knowledge and abilities. Instead of understanding what they know as valuable forms of knowledge about the world, working class women have been conditioned to view it as '*just* common sense'. When women view their knowledge as affective not cognitive and as feelings not thoughts, their subservient role is perpetuated and their power is diminished. Women scholars have argued that such working class female forms of understanding make it impossible to distinguish emotional from objective/rational thinking. Such a cognitive form, they conclude, is important for women to study and analyse, in that it challenges the false dichotomy patriarchy constructs between feminine emotionalism and masculine rationality. In the economic sphere this false dichotomy produces lower-status emotional and intuitive feminine care-giving work and higher-status masculine 'skilled' labour. The false dichotomy perpetuates an unjust system that exempts men from nurturing, service types of work while holding women responsible for such unpaid forms of domestic toil. It is essential for educators and cultural workers to understand these patriarchal dynamics, for it is these forces that work to hide a young woman's abilities from her teachers, her potential employers and, most importantly, herself (Luttrell 1993).

Critical multiculturalists are keenly aware of patriarchy and its effects on both females *and* males. Such analysts know that: two-thirds of all poor people over the age of 65 are women; four of five single-parent families are headed by women and a substantial majority of them are poor; one in six wives is beaten by her husband; and one in six women is sexually assaulted. In almost all of these situations, from poverty to abuse to assault, women tend to hold themselves responsible:

If your life does not fit the middle class, or even better, the upper middle class, image that appears on TV, something is wrong with you. For, if you are poor in America, you are an outsider and it's your own fault. If you are blind, disabled, or old, there is some excuse; you are one of the worthy poor. But if you are a welfare mother, you must be doing something drastically wrong.

(Sidel 1992: 8)

In this context it is not difficult to understand that a variety of patriarchal discourses from several social domains, science, philosophy, religion, economics – work together to discipline women. Thus disciplined, women's options are limited and their ability to shape and control their own lives is reduced (Beck 1992). Any democratic project, critical multiculturalism in particular, must work to expose and dismantle this patriarchal network and its material consequences.

The power bloc and masculinity have an interesting way of aligning their interests, as even in ostensibly oppositional texts and social practices patriarchal undercurrents emerge. Bombarding individuals from various sociopolitical and pedagogical locales, different manifestations of patriarchy distort the production of subjectivity. Viewed by many as an oppositional TV show designed to call white racism into question, *In Living Color*, for example, constructed a gender curriculum grounded on a traditional patriarchal view of women. Black women in particular found their bodies positioned as objects of satire and denigration. While most skits in the show were performed by and about men, those involving women typically marginalized them, with frequent reference to 'bitches', overweight black women, 'ugly' women unable to procure a man and other racialized gender stereotypes. The Fly Girls who danced during transitional moments of the show were positioned by the camera's consistent focus on their breasts and thighs. Such women were viewed through the traditional patriarchal gaze that engages them not as much for what they do but what they look like (Gray 1995). Positioned in this way in countless TV shows and movies, women are trivialized and marginalized. In this pedagogical context the patriarchal cultural curriculum teaches the society that self-assertion and self-sufficiency are masculine values. Indeed, women's weakness is grounded on their lack of such powerful traits. When such a cultural curriculum is combined with male-centred modernist science and its representation of women, one begins to gain a sense of the patriarchal infrastructure of Western societies.

The rational man

Critical multiculturalists understand that the rise of Western science in the Enlightenment and the Age of Reason cannot be separated from the political dynamics of gender relations. As Western society moved away from the interdependent perspective on reality of the Middle Ages to the logocentric, mechanistic view of modernity, there came to exist an accompanying misogyny that associated feminist thinking with madness, witchcraft and satanism. Intuition and emotion were incompatible with androcentric logic and reason and, as a result, scientific knowledge became the 'only game in town' – we will refer to this in Chapter 8 as 'white reason'. The masculinization of thinking was a cardinal tenet of Western social evolution. Individuals came to be represented in a dramatic new form – as abstracted entities, individuals standing outside the forces of history and culture. Society was caught in the cognition of patriarchy – a matrix of perception that limited our imagination to concepts that stayed within the androcentric boundaries, far away from the No Trespassing signs of the feminine domain.

Standing outside the forces of history and culture involved observing at a distance. Valid knowledge was produced exclusively by personally detached, objective observers. Knowers were separated from the known. Masculinist autonomy, abstraction and distance denies the spatial and temporal location of the knower in the world and thus results in the estrangement of human beings from the rhythms of life, the natural world (White 1978; Lowe 1982; Anderson 1987; Mahoney and Lyddon 1988; Bowers and Flinders 1990). Feminist theory has asserted that the autonomy and isolation of the logical, masculine individual have necessitated a mechanistic perspective on the universe. Such a perspective guards against the ascendance of more feminine forms of meaning and identity based on connecting, caring, empathy, inclusivity and responsibility. Devoid of such characteristics, masculinist modernism created a behavioural science which set out to manipulate individuals and an educational system that utilized the behavioural sciences to mould students and their consciousness in a way that would foster efficiency and economic productivity, often at the expense of social justice and creativity.

Feminist theory has taught critical multiculturalists that Enlightenment science – as a traditional masculine way of knowing – has denigrated the importance of context, thus allowing for a decontextualized science that produces a dissociated and fragmented body of knowledge about the social, psychological and educational world. Such a decontextualized science produces a 'quick and dirty' analysis of human behaviour and social interaction. The study of gender itself provides an excellent example of the problematic nature of such ways of seeing, as gender is viewed as a causative factor, not taking into account the existence of other variables in a social situation. When positivistic research ignores the wider context and the multitude of other variables which attend it, the conclusions drawn from such studies typically suggest innate differences (often hierarchical) between the sexes. Studies, for instance, that look only at gender differences in maths achievement might discover (accurately) that boys do better than girls on particular standardized maths tests. By not examining the results contextually, not pursuing explanatory factors, positivistic researchers fail to consider the panoply of reasons for the different scores. Appealing to the accuracy of their statistics as authority, researchers fail to confront the quick and dirty simplicity of their research design. Thus, 'what is' appears to be only what has to be; the public is provided with further 'proof' that boys are naturally better than girls in maths (Jayaratne 1982). Scientific 'proof' of the superiority of 'rational' man has been mobilized. Gender differences have been essentialized.

Feminist-informed critical multicultural researchers might describe their approach to social inquiry as methodological humility. As opposed to the quick and dirty positivist who seeks concrete structures and validated data which can be used to make predictions, the humble researcher practises a form of inquiry which is humble in the sense that it respects the complexity of the socio-cultural world. Humility in this context is not self-deprecating and does not involve the silencing of one's voice; humility implies a sense of the unpredictability of the social microcosm and the capriciousness of the consequences of one's inquiry. Methodological humility is an inescapable characteristic of a postmodern world marked by a loss of faith in scientific salvation and the possibility of a single frame of reference, a common vantage point from which we might all view the world. Methodological humility eschews the patriarchal positivistic impulse to dominate the world through a knowledge of it. Though it was on the lam for a long time, patriarchal science can no longer escape the creeping scepticism that dominates our postmodern conversations about almost everything else (Ruddick 1980; Aronowitz 1993).

Feminist scholar Schulamit Reinharz (1979, 1982, 1992) is always helpful in analysing the failure of patriarchal positivism in social research. The use of questionnaires, she contends, which force a 'yes', or 'no' opinion, is an example of the positivistic distortion of the lived world. Using such instruments positivistic researchers substitute a controlled reality, a social situation with its own conventions and rules for the ambiguity of the world of schools. They make a serious conceptual error when they correlate respondents' answers to questionnaires (responses peculiar to the controlled situation of being questioned about their attitudes) to their attitudes in another, completely different, social situation, the lived world of their workplace, their educational situation. Reinharz appreciated the limitations of such questionnaires when she tried to answer the questions herself. She could not answer the questions seriously for her feelings and thoughts were not capable of being translated into simple, codable responses. Like the lived world itself, her attitudes were subtle, often ill-defined and capable of being discovered and articulated only in dialogue with friends or during silent introspection (Reinharz 1979).

Patriarchal positivistic science, then, can be very misleading for practitioner fields such as education or social work, for example, because it fails to produce insights germane to the professional lives of the teacher or social worker. Positivistic educational research is limited in the sense that its language, the language of propositions, does not speak to the practitioner. Propositional language is concerned with the specification of the criteria by which statements about the world can be verified or refuted. The needs of the teacher transcend the language of propositions for they revolve around the particularity of certain entities; the creativity of one child, the 'feel' of a child's anger or affection, the ambiance of a classroom full of students captivated by a lesson. This is the stuff of teacher knowledge; and this is precisely the type of thing that androcentric positivistic propositional language cannot address. It is irrelevant in such contexts for it cannot capture the subtleties of interpersonal emotion – the subtleties that, feminist educators maintain, move us to the heart of the teaching act. Simply put, patriarchal positivistic measurements or frequency studies cannot convey a nuanced understanding or feeling for the individuals and social contexts under observation. In its quest for propositional generalization positivistic research misses an essential point: for the practitioner it is often the infrequent behaviours, the deviations from the general tendency, that are most important to pedagogy (Doyle 1977; Mies 1982; Eisner 1984).

The patriarchal paradigm, with its rules of rationality and positivistic research, is also of limited usefulness in educational contexts, since teachers do not 'own' such inquiry. The positivistic impulse renders research inaccessible to teachers, in that it prevents teachers from conducting their own research. The practicalities of school life preclude teachers from collecting the number of samples that the method requires, not to mention the time it takes to process the copious data demanded. Only trained professional researchers have the time or interest to engage in such research. Because of their status-superiority relative to the practitioner, professional researchers set the research agenda, formulating questions primarily of interest to them. Thus, the practitioner is excluded; the professional researcher is the real proprietor of the inquiry – indeed, the professional researcher becomes both producer and consumer of the knowledge gleaned. Practitioners are the passive objects that are acted upon; they are invalidated as reflective teachers (Tripp 1988; Van den Berg and Nicholson 1989). In such situations patriarchal power of male experts over female practitioners is re-established and justified by a science that is ideological in its effect.

Schooling is an excellent venue for the study of rational man and patriarchal forms of analysis and knowledge production – and their lived consequences. Few institutions reflect the patriarchal nature of modernist ways of seeing more than the school. Bastions of male supremacy and dominant cultural power, schools have been shaped by what patriarchy has viewed as

acceptable behaviour and appropriate ways of being. Sophisticated thinking, indeed humanness itself, has equated with maleness. Because of this
male-centred nature of schooling, white male students from middle class
homes are imbued with a confidence that allows them to see failure as more
a reflection of the teacher's inadequacies than their own. Because female cognitive development proceeds along a different path, women's interpersonal
and connected qualities are sometimes viewed as inferior to the androcentric
notion of intellectual autonomy. Women find it risky to 'go with their intuitions' in school, in that such cognitive styles are so seldom recognized as
valuable. Over the years many women students begin to lose confidence,
often coming to feel that their failure is a result of their own inadequacy
(Maher and Rathbone 1986).

   Critical multiculturalists gain tremendous insight into the subtlety of
oppression from the feminist critique of rational man and patriarchal science. Contrary to more liberal forms of multiculturalism, they do not
assume that the recognition of the patriarchal infrastructure mandates that
we teach women to think more logocentrically – more like men. Instead,
critical multiculturalists infer from the feminist critique that we need to
reconceptualize the prevailing definition of inquiry and social analysis.
Utilizing a critically reconstructed concept of analysis, critical multiculturalists use feminist theory to reformulate what constitutes sophisticated cognitive activity. As they appreciate the feminist notion that serious analysis
comes in a variety of shapes and sizes, critical observers understand that
abstract maths and science skills (traditionally associated with males) are
important ways of knowing – but in a patriarchal culture, many encultur-
ated into the ways of patriarchal science do not appreciate analytical and
inquiry styles that fall outside the domain of such abilities. In this context
males see themselves apart from others, as independent entities. Such perspectives hold powerful political implications, as they shape social policy on
everything from the social role of government to economic theory to the
vision of community that guides us. For example, is the role of government
to be a caregiver, a provider of social services to those in need? Or is it to be
the guardian of 'fair' competition? Recent political leaders have opted for
the latter role, emphasizing androcentric autonomy and separateness.

Positioning and disempowering women: stand by your man

In the light of our assertion that patriarchal power emanates from many
directions, it is important to note that the patriarchal power of science is
extended by other ideological forms of meaning making. The ideology of
domesticity and the culture of romance refer to women's responsibility for
unpaid work at home and their acquisition of status by way of their male

relationships. Home and family in this context become central concerns for working class female students, while their interest in wage labour is secondary. Such a perspective sets them up for failure in a patriarchal society – they become in a sense patriarchy's women. Because of their identification with the domestic sphere, they become especially vulnerable to the whims and moods of their male partners. If a man leaves a domestically identified woman as the sole supporter and caretaker of the family, she has little experience to draw upon in her attempt to find wage labour outside the home. This is not an isolated scenario in the late twentieth-century feminization of poverty, as women face the patriarchal reality that devalues their talents and abilities. Indeed, the domestic code dictates that women's work in the economic market place is worth about 60 per cent of men's work and does not provide single mothers with sufficient resources to support their families by themselves (Valli 1987; Weis 1987).

Lois Weis (1987) contends that women are caught in a double bind: they define themselves around themes of home and family but are forced by economic realities to work outside the home. When declining Western economies forced married women into the workforce, little change took place in the social dynamics and work responsibilities within the home. Women found themselves bound by a double workday – full shifts in both the home and the workplace. Recent studies indicate that employed, married women perform three hours of housework for every one performed by their husbands. In addition to their jobs outside the home, married employed women perform an average of five hours a day. If a married woman's domestic work was monetarily compensated, her family's income would be increased by more than 60 per cent. Critical educators understand the negative impact of the domestic ideology and romance culture on women – working class women in particular. In so doing they appreciate the reality that has been created by society's refusal to provide special support for women in these circumstances. Therefore, critical multicultural educators prepare their female students to deal with the social dynamics surrounding these gender issues, while engaging them in a larger struggle to help to increase public awareness of the need to redistribute some of women's caring functions. Such a redistribution can relieve women of their mind- and body-numbing double workday. It is hoped that the critical consciousness that surrounds such an understanding can be used to help the public to employ these caring qualities traditionally relegated to women to humanize society, schools and workplaces (Wolff 1977; Sidel 1992).

This so-called feminine ethic of caring holds great potential when applied to the reconceptualization of education and other social institutions. At the same time, it can undermine women's best interests when it is employed without a cognizance of power relations between women and men. When working class women operating out of an ethic of caring place their own concerns and own needs last, they inadvertently reinforce patriarchal power relations between themselves and their husbands. Indeed, many working class women can justify their educational pursuits only in terms of their commitment to husbands and families – 'I'm doing this for them,' they often tell their teachers. Such a nurturance ideology, such a way of making sense of woman's role in the world, reached the level of social obsession in the years immediately following the Second World War. The ideology of domesticity and the culture of romance expressed themselves in TV's June and Ward Cleaver, Alice and Ralph Kramden and Lucy and Ricky Ricardo – visions of mother in the kitchen and father at work. The roots of late twentieth-century feminism can be traced to the emotional toll this view of womanhood exacted on the 'loving housewife' of the 1950s and early 1960s. Housewife depression, increasing divorce rates and a general discomfort with family life characterized this era of hyper-domesticity (Luttrell 1993; Rubin 1994).

Women caught in the patriarchal trap who fail to understand the underside of the ideology of domesticity and the culture of romance are less able to protect themselves from the social forces that oppress them. Self-sacrifice and passivity, common features of traditional notions of femininity, should come with the Surgeon General's health warning in the 1990s. Young women who embrace such traditionalism, Michele Fine (1993) reports, are far more likely to find themselves with unwanted pregnancies and child care than more assertive teenagers. In a study of girls in a public high school in New York City, Fine noticed that a large number of the students who got pregnant were quiet and passive – not those girls whose dress and manner signified sexuality and experience. Such an observation should not be interpreted to mean that teenage mothers are always a certain type of female – obviously the issue is far more complex than this. What it does mean is that the traditional practices of femininity often subvert the economic, social and educational development of young women (Fine 1993).

Some of our students often assume that this ideology of domesticity and culture of romance are now behind us, a relic of an era past. Such is not the case, we tell them, focusing their attention on the second curriculum, the 'girl curriculum' that operates covertly in American schools. Researchers have found that schools offer more career choices to boys, white, upper-middle class boys in particular and fewer for girls, lower economic class, non-white girls in particular. Career education booklets often list four career options for boys for every one listed for girls. Thus, career counselling often directs female students to career choices that dramatically undermine their wage earning possibilities and lead them towards a life of poverty (Johnson 1991). Even in the newest job programmes these gender dynamics are still at work. Analysis of the fifteen federal school-to-work demonstration programmes developed in the 1990s indicates that three of the programmes enrolled no girls and four enrolled three girls or fewer. The types of programmes attended by students conformed to traditional gender stereotypes: girls were guided into office, allied health and clerical programmes; boys enrolled in electronics, metal working and automotive programmes (Pullin 1994).

Socialization of women for subjugation

Like all forms of oppression, the most powerful forms of the subjugation of women are the hardest to expose. Employers, for example, don't often reveal the fact that the reason why a woman wasn't hired or promoted was that she was a woman (Shrubsall 1994). Even men who engage in oppressive acts towards women will deny their guilt, often expressing genuine surprise that their actions could be perceived as patriarchal. Western societies after 25 years of attempts to raise gender consciousness are still caught in a web of patriarchal oppression – men are still socialized for gender dominance and women are still psychologically inducted into a culture of passivity and acceptance of patriarchal subjugation. Women who have drawn upon feminist theory to gain a new consciousness of patriarchy and its effects on their own consciousness construction often experience emotional conflict when they find themselves in professional roles. In this context women come to the discomforting realization that the democratic process and emancipatory thinking run head-on into the values promoted by the hierarchically structured technicist organization. They begin to discover that the processes of emancipation that have played such an important role in their lives – the questioning of their belief system, their attempt to disembody themselves from the validated culture and their efforts to transcend procedural forms of thinking – are sometimes considered inappropriate if not pathological behaviours in their institutions (Maher and Rathbone 1986; Shor 1992; Torres 1993).

The cultural gender curriculum, despite proclamations to the contrary, still produces male-identified girls and women. While such individuals may still have friendships with females, patriarchy demands that male perceptions determine their sense of femininity and ways of defining themselves. Such an oppressive context induces competition between women for male attention – a situation that illustrates the pathology that patriarchy causes. Girls are socialized to let boys dominate them so that harmonious relationships can be sustained. Such feminine passivity and cooperativeness is rewarded at all social levels. Hillary Rodham Clinton evoked the wrath of a nation when she stated that she would not submit to the culture of feminine passivity and would not always be cooperative when particular ethical principles were at stake. Such a stance is still not tolerated at the end of the twentieth century. The gender message emerging from Hillary Clinton's reception is clear: women, to be successful, must be unassertive and accommodating. Thus, a paradoxical situation is created, as unassertive and accommodating women will be viewed as incapable of leadership – patriarchy's Catch-22.

Like other students who fall outside the white, middle/upper-middle class mainstream, many women are socialized to abandon the subjugated forms of knowledge they bring to the classroom and the workplace. Women are often taught to give up their bent towards concern with process and connectedness, to 'repackage themselves' to achieve a more 'power look'. 'Professional behaviour' is continuously defined in white male terms, relegating more feminine ways of operating to the realm of inferiority and inappropriateness. Humane values based on cooperation, solidarity with peers, sharing and compassion are often represented as values that will cause one to be left behind the organizational hierarchy. In the web of patriarchy such values and the behaviours that are based on them are perceived as manifestations of weakness. In the patriarchal context, unfortunately, people and personal relations must be devalued if one wants to succeed. Women who are able to maintain values of connectedness and caring will often find such orientations co-opted for the service of patriarchal power. The profound links many women experience with other people as care-givers are transformed by male-dominated power into women's subjugation. Feminine connectedness and caring embraced outside of an understanding of patriarchal domination can be used to relegate women to the margins (Ferguson 1984; Banfield 1991; Jacques 1992).

How-to-succeed self-help books admonish their female readers to disguise their femininity and conform their behaviours to the norms of the office – unspoken here is the *white male* norms of the organizational culture. The ideology of patriarchy induces a form of reflexive legitimation among women, as they internalize the ideological notion that they as females should not expect to occupy the same positions and receive the same rewards as men in professional, organizational and workplace situations. When women have internalized such concepts, no political work that mandates equality of pay, expanded opportunity for promotion or preparation for leadership will neutralize patriarchal domination. Of course, this to not to argue that these political dynamics are not important – they are. But such changes alone will not provide for gender equality. Women who have reflexively legitimated their own oppression will choose to be dental hygienists not dentists, and para-legals not lawyers, even when the opportunity for professional mobility is available. Such a reality raises an important realization in the critical multicultural struggle for gender justice – gender discrimination that results in the exclusion of women is not perpetrated simply by individual action but by a 'social field' – some might call it a situated power – that is constructed by a society-wide set of beliefs and behaviours. Of course, this dispersion of patriarchal power is another factor that makes it difficult to resist (Wolff 1977; Palmer and Spalter-Roth 1991).

Viewing patriarchal power as socially dispersed or situated helps critical multiculturalists to understand how two ostensibly contradictory claims can both be true: (a) late twentieth-century Western societies are male dominated; and (b) even so, many men do not see themselves as oppressors of women. Take, for example, a relationship between spouses in which the husband argues that he does not dominate his wife. Even if he desires not to do so, the husband may still dominate his wife because of the couple's relationship to the situated power of patriarchy. In Western societies women who are unmarried do not have the same degree of access to material items that are typically seen as important. For example, single women have greater trouble procuring loans from financial agencies – rules for loans are more strict for single women and such women do not have a husband to employ as a reference. When numerous other structural features are added to these discriminatory practices a patriarchal power bloc is mobilized that makes use of a woman's gender and marital status as a marker determining the way she is treated. Such situated patriarchal power, even though it is not overtly recognized or acknowledged by the husband and wife, permeates the relationship, providing power to the husband. When the wife examines the advantages of the marital relationship, she cannot help but note the life she would encounter without being married to him.

Within the material context, it is easy to see how the power bloc will position her without him. Thus, the wife gains advantages from the relationship that go beyond any romantic notion of love or commitment. Regardless of the husband's intentions or particular actions, he is granted a power that the wife doesn't have (Wartenberg 1992). Because of his social role, his relationship to the patriarchal power bloc, the husband can make demands on the wife that are inscribed with the threatening observation: 'Where would you be if I left you? I know where I would be.' Critical multiculturalists, promoting a critical literacy of power, maintain that it is important for women and men to understand these dynamics for a variety of reasons. One reason in particular might involve the attempt of marriage partners to negotiate a truly democratic and egalitarian relationship in which an informed husband would neither consciously nor unconsciously resort to the use of his situated patriarchal power to hold his wife emotional hostage. Without such awareness and open negotiation of its meaning, wives are often tacitly socialized to submerge their feelings and needs in fear of male deployment of their patriarchal power advantage.

The patriarchal curriculum

Until these issues of gender and power are seriously examined by educational policy-makers, knowledge producers and teacher educators, elementary schools, secondary schools and colleges and universities will continue to teach a patriarchal curriculum that reinforces an inferior social role for women and distorted notions of masculinity for men. Without critical multicultural reassessment, women will continue to be situated in a dependent relationship to men and when socio-economic class intersects with gender poor women will continue to be prepared for low-status, low-paid labour. While such preparation occurs in a variety of covert ways, a particularly important method involves the formal curriculum's historical and literary depiction of passive women. As the curriculum displays male success, women are reduced to the status of passive observers. Liberal reforms of the past couple of decades have 'added on' a cadre of 'acceptable' women such as Susan B. Anthony, Marie Curie and Sally Ride, but the achievements of such women are decontextualized as sexism, gender bias and the existence of patriarchal power is erased. Girls learn an important lesson in such curricular experiences – men are the measure of human normality. Critical multiculturalism insists that such an assumption be challenged in schooling, that both male and female students be provided with an alternative way of viewing gender relations (Maher 1992; Swartz 1993; McLaren 1994a).

Carol Gilligan's brilliant feminist critique of Lawrence Kohlberg's abstract, legalistic and decontextualized theory of moral development is an example of the information that an alternative gender curriculum might embrace. Kohlberg, like other liberal modernists, operated too much within a patriarchal behavioural science to realize that the ways of knowing (the epistemologies) and the values that sometimes come out of women's subjective lived experiences are not inferior because they are too contingent, too tainted by feeling and emotion. Because of these subjective ways of making sense of the world, girls' development of moral reasoning is often different from boys'. Girls' moral reasoning often involves the consideration of personal experience, caring and connectedness, negotiation over absolute judgements, responsibilities over rights and contextual and narrative-based thinking over cognition that is formal and abstract. Delineating these points, Gilligan posed a challenge to Kohlberg that took both him and patriarchal behavioural science to task for relegating women to an inferior place on the hierarchy of moral reasoning (Gilligan 1981; Carlson 1991). Most importantly for our interests as critical multiculturalists, Gilligan exposed one of the ways patriarchal science oppresses women by producing knowledge documenting their inferiority to men. When alternatives to the dominant gender curriculum are not included in the everyday life of schooling, we find that the self-esteem of school girls declines every year they remain in school. The patriarchal curriculum teaches girls helplessness and self-doubt concerning their academic abilities. So powerful is the gender curriculum that girls learn to blame their academic failures on their personal inadequacies. The low self-esteem internalized by adolescent girls finds tragic expression in the fact that they attempt to kill themselves four or five times more often than boys (Allison 1995).

Simply put, boys receive a lot more attention and validation in schools than girls. Male students are involved in far more interactions with teachers than girls regardless of the instructor's race or gender. Teacher feedback to males tends to be more precise in its praise, criticism and suggestions for improvement. Boys are more likely to receive specific information that enables them to succeed in the classroom than girls – an extremely important dynamic in the effort to make use of school for purposes of personal empowerment and economic mobility. Since the classroom deportment of girls has traditionally been less disruptive, less at odds with their academic performance, teachers have held different expectations for girls. Such expectations involve the assumption that girls will accept their socially constructed role of passivity. Indeed, when teachers say that a girl is doing well in school, the tacit message may involve the girl's willingness to be an observer not an active agent, to follow the teacher's directives and always to be cooperative, i.e. 'ladylike'. Being a 'good girl' in this context involves accepting patriarchal power (Sadker and Sadker 1991; Swartz 1993).

This expectation of feminine passivity can be observed throughout the curriculum. For example, in many high school maths departments, courses in computer science are offered that are designed to teach students how to write programs and to analyse the social impact of computers and the opening of cyberspace, and to produce computer experts who can recognize glitches and develop new applications and uses for hardware and software. Many business education teachers who prepare girls for office work see no reason for their students to take such courses. Justifying their decision on the basis that office workers don't need the skills such courses teach, teachers once again relegate girls to the margins, to passive roles. In this way female business education graduates are removed from the possibility of obtaining higher-status, higher-skill, or higher-paid jobs. Their business education degree is a badge advertising their placement as a low-skill worker. It is merely one more manifestation of patriarchy's power to regulate women. The patriarchal curriculum is taught not only in schools and universities but in the media curriculum as well. In her study of sixth grade girls' formation of self, Michelle Maher (1992) analysed a series of milk commercials made for TV touting its nutritional value. In the first commercial a young male in a football uniform holding a VCR remote control in his hand shows the audience a tape of himself as a younger boy being physically pushed into a school locker by a group of larger and stronger classmates. Motivated by the incident to drink milk, the boy plays a tape of himself now. In this cut he is standing strong, tall and proud, as attractive girls gather around him – he never looks at the girls but stares arrogantly into the camera, lifting his chin in self-confidence. He is a model male, successful now because he is strong, a failure before because he was weak. The message is clear: boys, drink your milk so you can grow up strong and macho and have lots of sex with women.

The next commercial Maher uses is another milk ad structured in the same manner as the first one, but this time with a girl. Her tape of herself 'before milk' depicts a scene at a school dance where she was unable to attract a boy to dance with her. Alone she stood on the gym floor wearing no make-up and a collared shirt buttoned to the top covering her neck. Not surprisingly, she begins to drink milk and plays the tape of her 'new self'. In the video she is wearing heavy make-up and a low-cut sexy dress and is surrounded by adoring men. She looks at the men to her right and then her left; switching back to her viewing position, she tells the viewers that she wants to see that clip again and proceeds to rewind and play it over. She is extremely proud of the way the men are looking her up and down. Their objectification of her is presented as proof of her 'womanly success'. Both her early inferiority and her later success are defined in relation to males. The football player was successful because he became physically strong and therefore was able to attract women, not simply because he attracted women. In this context the commercials teach a series of the traditional lessons of the patriarchal curriculum: male attention is more important than female attention; maleness is the benchmark of normality; and women are valued for how they look, while men are admired for their accomplishments (Weiler 1988).

When socio-economic class intersects with gender the teaching of the patriarchal curriculum becomes even more repressive. School tends to teach working class women that their 'common sense' does not really count as 'intelligence'. Thus, such women are socialized to buy into an ideology of a just world where people rise to the level of their intelligence and industriousness. The reason, they are taught to believe, that they have remained poor involves their own lack of real intelligence. Such ideological influence validates the meritocratic notions that people get what they deserve and equal opportunity exists. When race intersects with gender another set of oppressive lessons in the patriarchal curriculum is produced. Black girls, for example, are often situated in public schools as helpers and nurturing service providers. In this context intellectual skill development is negated and black girls are set up to enter low-skill, low-paid occupational roles in which they are presently over-represented; for example, practical nurses, teacher aides, home care-givers. Some studies indicate that black females, more than males or white females, are socialized at home to take care of their peers. The patriarchal curriculum reinforces this tendency when nurturing tasks first performed spontaneously come to be expected. Such a predisposition to care-giving need not lead to low-status service jobs for black women when critically informed teachers are aware of the tendency. Refusing to give into stereotypes of black women, critical multicultural teachers often induce black female students to pursue careers as doctors, teachers/professors and social workers instead of nurses, teacher aides and home care-givers (Luttrell 1993; Grant 1994).

The job curriculum: the patriarchal workplace

The on-the-job curriculum of patriarchy is formed around one central concept: the subjugation of women is profitable. Knowing this, critical multiculturalists understand that there will always be opposition to a curriculum of empowerment that seeks to undermine this structural dynamic. Many analysts have made the argument that the very foundation of industrial society is based on patriarchal domination. If male and female socio-economic rules are separated, then a hierarchical commercialization of human labour power can be developed where 'well socialized' women can be hired at low wages. As profit margins rise with these lower labour costs, corporate and business leaders work to protect such a social arrangement from democratic groups, such as feminists or critical multiculturalists, who call such exploitation into question. The hiring of cheap female labour in both Western societies and Third World cultures has been a central corporate strategy in returning profit margins to pre-1960 levels. Employers know that women are less likely than men to be union members and more likely to accept temporary work with no benefits. Such realities have led to the feminization of labour forces, as women migrated into positions previously held by men – jobs that were already populated by women became even more feminized.

As the number of employed women increased in the 1980s and 1990s, corporate profits increased. Such gender exploitation can be understood as one of many contradictions of industrialized societies. The free market fails to realize its movement of women from the domestic role of compulsory housework under the protection of a husband to an increasingly vulnerable second shift in the workforce. In the vacuous family values conversation of the late twentieth century few pause to reflect on the role of the market in family troubles. If the labour market demands geographical mobility regardless of personal circumstance, committed marital relationship and stable families require the opposite. Meeting the demands of the market would be a lot easier if no one had families and children. Indeed, children are impediments in the labour process, as they impede both male and female workers in their freedom of movement. The child's needs undermine worker flexibility, especially for women, who remain the primary child caretakers at the end of the twentieth century. The damage has been done. Western societies cannot return to a 1950s style domestic patriarchy even if it was desirable.

Such contradictory realities place women and children in a negative social space in a patriarchal and narcissistic society that worships upward mobility and material success. In such a pathological social arrangement males often come to see women and children as the obstructions that held them back from career success. Such a positioning reveals itself in a plethora of problematic ways, including everything from divorce to abuse. Much scholarly work remains to be undertaken on the social dynamics of the feminization of a patriarchal economic system (Hacker 1989; Beck 1992; Amott 1993).

'Beating the bitch' – patriarchy's workplace culture/curriculum

If the macro-foundations of postmodern industrial society are grounded on the oppression of women, so are the micro-dynamics of the patriarchal workplace culture. 'It's a man's world', James Brown sang in the 1960s in reference to the patriarchal control of the workplace. The workplace's continued existence as a male domain has taken a heavy toll on the career aspirations of the millions of women who have had to enter it in the economically troubled 1980s and 1990s. As with all of our critical analyses of the workplace and the school, an understanding of the patriarchal control of the workplace demands an appreciation of the power dynamics between women and men. In the conversation about work the male workplace has been designated as the normal state of a workplace. Women's entry into the workplace in the context of this dominant conversation comes to be viewed as deviant, abnormal – thus the ability of dominant power to classify and name. In this case many women's orientation to connectedness and cooperation comes directly into conflict with many men's notions of self-sufficiency and isolation. These larger social issues involving unequal power relations, critical multiculturalists argue, are not esoteric theoretical notions – they shape the material realities of the workplaces we enter daily (Jacques 1992).

It does not take a long time to uncover the effects of unequal power relations in the gender dynamics of the workplace. The subordinate status of male factory workers, for example, has produced generations of men who have been forced to forfeit their dignity on sometimes a daily basis. The impact of this reality on male self-esteem and sense of worth is dramatic – indeed, it is one of the most tragic effects of both the industrialization process and market-driven capitalism. One of the few domains of male workers' lives over which they can exert power and exercise control involves their relationships with women. It is this social dynamic that creates the context where working class women find exaggerated assertions of patriarchal power by their husbands. Scarred by the indignity of the workplace, many such husbands seek to re-establish their dignity through the domination of their wives in the domestic sphere. In the workplace these male workers may hang pictures of sexually available women in submissive erotic positions. Such pictures grant men a symbolic position of power over women that substitutes for the lack of power they possess in the daily affairs of the firm (Weis 1987; Livingstone and Luxton 1988).

In the context of their powerlessness, working class men search for hidden passages to dignity. The danger and brutality of many industrial workplaces are not typically viewed as employer-imposed hazards by male workers, but as tests of masculinity. Male dissatisfaction with unsafe or uncomfortable work is not formulated as a form of political resistance to insensitive bosses but is expressed in terms of sexual aggression through language and sado-masochistic play among workers. Difficult work is characterized as something feminine to be conquered: 'We'll beat this bitch.' Exploitation by managers is described by terms for rape: 'We're getting screwed by the boss.' Women bosses or workers are separated from the male group and placed into a separate category by name-calling: 'bitches', 'whores' or 'sluts'. Such categorization of women serves to justify different treatment of them, to relegate them to a less powerful position in the workplace. These male power plays are central to many men's self-definition in their reassurance that they (the male workers) are the only ones 'man enough' to accomplish dangerous and dirty work (Livingstone and Luxton 1988; Rubin 1994).

In addition to these direct attempts by males to dominate women in the workplace, a set of inadvertent gender practices serves to marginalize women workers. Men's conversational practices, aggressive and characterized by shared experiences, military and sports metaphors, tend to silence women and make them invisible in an organization or a workplace. The conversation community established by male communication is exclusive and tends not to be open to women workers. Studies indicate that many women workers experience feelings of loneliness and isolation in the workplace. Social isolation at work strips women of the informal connections needed by individuals who want to rise in the workplace hierarchy – thus, men continue to occupy positions of power at work. These institutional impediments to women's success in the workplace illustrate cultural conflicts between particular forms of masculine and feminine identity patterns. When women view their work more as a process than a specific outcome, they introduce an alien culture into the masculinist job site (Ferguson 1984; Bhatnagar 1988; Meissner 1988). Young women workers who are able to ape the male culture and communication patterns at a job site are much more likely to develop practical forms of resistance to the exclusionary practices that accompany them. Young men workers who recognize the dynamics are empowered to model more just ways of operating in a gender-integrated venue.

The male workplace culture is a curriculum grounded upon a patriarchal discourse that shapes worker identity and action. Such a discourse separates individuals from one another, tying them to workplace roles and regulations rather than to each other. The patriarchal discourse constantly reinforces the negative effects of women's difference from men, positioning them outside job networks and the male culture of the workplace. 'That girl just won't fit in here,' male managers remark daily, making informal reference to the conflict between women job applicants and the male culture of the workplace. The male-dominated workplace discourses structure forms of communications that employ metaphors from and references to sports, the military and pornography. The knowledge assumed in this discourses excludes women, whose life experiences often fall outside these domains. When the language of a male-centred workplace or a male-dominated managerial staff is researched, analysts typically uncover what outsiders perceive as secret codes, double meanings and esoteric slang. When individuals understand that the factor most important to success at work involves not as much competence on the job as access to these informal networks and comfort in these workplace cultures, empathy for the difficulties experienced by women and other marginalized groups will expand. Right-wing moulders of opinion have been so successful in the 1980s and 1990s that empathy of this type is lacking. One of the main tasks of critical multiculturalists involves the effort to promote empathetic understandings of race, class and gender dynamics in the workplace. Such awareness can help to lay the foundation for the support of policies promoting inclusivity and social justice.

In a political cosmos that does not understand the ways in which women are structurally and discursively excluded from the informal networks of workplaces and professional cultures, women find themselves increasingly vulnerable. Standing outside the informal patriarchal networks, women are unable to gain access to grapevine data through which alliances are formed and salient organizational resources are exchanged. Such dynamics are inseparable from the larger analysis of women's difficulty in achieving upward mobility in various types of organizations – the ability to break through the 'glass ceiling'. The glass-ceiling metaphor is used to delineate the impediments to female mobility that are, like glass, transparent and difficult to see, yet substantial enough to preclude women's climb to the top of the hierarchy. In this context women understand that the higher the status of a workplace, organizational, professional or academic position, the lower the percentage of women who occupy it (Evetts 1994; Pascall 1994). Kathy Ferguson (1984) argues that the relationship between many women employees and their bosses can still be classified as feudal. In office work, for example, despite the alleged advances of the women's movement, male bosses still can exercise patriarchal authority over women subordinates – the same feudal relationship still often exists in elementary schools, with their male principals and female teachers (the educational harem). Women workers still perceive that they must feign demeanours of self-effacement and mousiness to remain in good favour. Contrary to the pronouncements of conservative commentators, gender oppression in the workplace is alive and well.

Many people are surprised to learn that women with three years of college earn less than a man who finishes only the eighth grade. In the early decades of industrialization in the nineteenth century, women worked alongside men in vocations as widely diverse as mining, manufacturing and printing. In the first decades of the twentieth century, however, a new form of patriarchy began to arise that associated 'heavy' labour in the industrial sector with manliness and male strength. The 'gender wisdom' that developed in tandem motivated legislators to pass laws 'protecting' women from industrial work and crafts. Such perspectives have helped to shape the domestic ideology and romance culture that have limited women's job opportunities throughout the twentieth century. The Second World War, of course, interrupted such viewpoints, but the system struggled to reassert itself when the men came home from the war. The cultural debate about women's 'proper' place has waged ever since (Johnson 1991; Coontz 1992; Aronowitz and DiFazio 1994).

An important thread in this debate has involved the equation of paid work with masculinity. Skill is a male discourse. If women pushed their way into a workplace where a particular skill was performed, then the skill was devalued. Thus, the male attempt to exclude women from the workplace was not simply a matter of men thinking women were not capable of performing a job skilfully – it was more an attempt to protect their craft's integrity from the devaluation caused by women's involvement with the work skills in question (Aronowitz and DiFazio 1994). 'I think a lot of the men were threatened,' women steelworkers reported after encountering extensive male resistance to their presence in the mills. 'Here was a woman coming along who said she could do it just as well as they could"(Livingstone and Luxton 1988: 31). In addition, male steelworkers were embarrassed to disclose their shopfloor behaviour to women. As one female steelworker put it:

> For them it's like having two personalities. Like Jekyl and Hyde sort of thing . . . At work they swear, they throw their garbage on the floor. I'm sure they don't do that at home . . . They're like kids at work . . . and I could just see them go home and be, you know, straight and narrow, very serious with their wives and as soon as they get to work it's crazy . . . Some of them just cannot handle women being in their line of work.
>
> (Livingstone and Luxton 1988: 32)

Thus, the gender oppression of the workplace curriculum never works in some simple way. It can be understood as a constellation of social, cultural, economic, political and psychological forces in relationship to the patriarchal power bloc that intersects at various points in the social web of reality.

This workplace gender bias expresses itself in a variety of ways and on a number of levels. For example, the double workday problem that working women face with their paid 'day shift' at work and their unpaid 'graveyard shift' at home is rarely addressed by individuals in leadership positions. In addition to the two shifts, many women have been forced to take a second job because of the low pay of many 'feminine' jobs. When race and ethnicity are added to this reality, researchers find that African American and Latina women moonlight even more than white women. In the 1970s and 1980s many women double shifters who worked in low-status, low-paid jobs saw nothing within the women's movement with relevance for their lives. Because of the hardships of their lives and the growing understanding of the role gender plays in structuring such hardships, women in similar situations in the 1990s take seriously the issues of gender inequality that feminists have highlighted. If men had to face the difficulties of the double shift, corporate, governmental and educational organizations would scramble to solve them. As long as the double shift is a women's problem, little action will be taken because women are expected to take care of domestic tasks no matter what their circumstance. In the political climate of the 1990s many elected officials have ridiculed the idea that society should provide assistance for women who are both mothers and workers. The most obvious form of assistance, public child care, would provide a wider range of choices to working class mothers seeking employment. Despite women's increasing participation in the workplace, public policy has continued to be based on the assumption that outside-family child care should be reserved for children with inadequate parental care (Amott 1993; Rubin 1994).

As these socio-economic gender dynamics have pushed women into worse and worse lived circumstances, an undercurrent of misogyny connected to a cultural backlash against the women's movement, men's resentment of having to deal with women as equals and the effects of women's reduced time for traditional domestic, wifely and child care functions has been detected. Women, poor mothers in particular, have been blamed for everything from the decline in young people's educational performance, teenage pregnancy, violence and child abuse to the moral decline of society in general. Of course, in the political climate of the 1980s and 1990s black women experience the greatest vilification, as they are connected to images of promiscuous sexuality and failure to run households successfully. Such images deflect society's focus from the fact that the social and economic policies of recent years have closed employment and educational opportunities for black women, thus causing the numbers of such women who head households to rise dramatically. A vicious circle of gender bias/racism is created that facilitates the re-creation of the socio-economic conditions from which the gender/racial stereotypes evolve. In this context the injustice of the vilification of doubly disadvantaged black women becomes painfully obvious – a classic case of blaming the victim. Critical multiculturalists understand that unless this vilification of women is addressed, the neo-misogyny that emerges from it holds frightening possibilities for the future of women in Western societies (McCarthy and Apple 1988; Mullings 1994; Jones 1995).

The expression of misogyny: the sexual harassment of women

The resentment of women and the development of this neo-misogyny expresses itself in a variety of pathological ways. Perhaps the most visible aspect of it involves sexual harassment. Sexual harassment is a form of domination that reproduces patriarchal domination in general. The form sexual harassment may take depends on the context that surrounds it. Vice-presidents of corporations corner file clerks between filing cabinets and massage their backs while telling them how good they look. At the same time, however, a group of maintenance workers may make catcalls and other sexual sounds each time a female co-worker walks by them. While those who engage in harassment may come from diverse points in the status hierarchy of the workplace, they all share a view of women that emphasizes their sexuality rather than their skill and work abilities. When women attempt to extend kindness and care to these traditional male colleagues, the men often interpret such acts as manifestations of the women's sexual desire for them or as evidence of their subordination as servants or quasi-servants (Meissner 1989).

Job training programmes for women often fail to examine the power relations and patriarchal context in which sexual harassment thrives. Indeed, some programmes actually contribute to the maintenance of the context, as they promote an ideology of the 'glamorous young women'. Such an orientation induces women to prepare for job interviews not by presenting their work knowledge but by highlighting their bodily image (Valli 1987). In such a context women are reduced to frills, to window dressing in the workplace. Ray Kroc, the founder of McDonald's Hamburgers, illustrated this view of women as frills when in his autobiography he wrote about June Martino – one of the most brilliant of the early core of McDonald's business people who made the fast food restaurant one of the most successful corporations in history.

I thought it was good to have a lucky person around, maybe some of it would rub off on me. Maybe it did. After we got McDonald's going and built a larger staff, they all called her 'mother Martino.' She kept track of everyone's family fortunes, whose wife was having a baby, who was having marital difficulties, or whose birthday it was. She helped make the office a happy place.

(Kroc 1977: 66–7)

From this description the reader would not have known whether or not June Martino knew anything about business.

June Martino's business acumen was not recognized by Kroc because she was a woman. Had she been a man Kroc would not have written of her ability to keep up with everyone's birthday – a man would have been insulted by such a trivialization of his serious work. Like June Martino's work, secretarial labour has been devalued simply because it is performed by women. The complexity of the work secretaries are assigned has to be constantly denied in offices where male managers make ten times the wages of their female secretaries. It is no secret that secretaries daily perform the same functions as managers – the only difference is that they receive fewer rewards, less compensation and only token recognition. Women clerical workers remain the lowest status group in a firm not because of the lack of complexity of their job skills but because of the low status of their gender role. Definitions of the complexity of particular job skills are not innocent descriptions of the nature of work but are socially constructed labels that justify the socio-economic advantage of some jobs and the disadvantage of others. Typically, such skill definitions are used to maintain existing power relationships in the workplace by privileging those abilities usually associated with masculinity (Gaskell 1987; Block 1990). Respect for ability and upward mobility aside, the power and status differential between women and men in workplaces, organizations and academic institutions provides many men with a perceived licence to 'handle' women in ways that are degrading and hurtful. Such harassment continues despite the social conversation about gender dynamics that has taken place over the past three decades.

Even after all this conversation, violence against women continues, economic injustice persists. In vocational education and job training programmes the preparation of women for clerical jobs is still totally separate from the world of management education – the status differential is so great that a student is not allowed to enrol in one programme and take a set of courses from another (Gaskell 1987). Many how-to-get-ahead-in-the-workplace books for women reflect mainstream education's goal of adjusting women to the reality of the patriarchal workplace. Use your feminine attributes, the books exhort their women readers. The same manipulative skills women learn in dealing with men in romantic and domestic relations, the success authors argue, can be utilized to get ahead at work. These manipulative skills are described by the authors as 'an unlimited repertoire of manipulative, two-faced, guileful tricks' (Ferguson 1984).

Such reprehensible advice is derived from the same patriarchal mind-set that encourages sexual harassment and violence against women. You can almost hear such language ('manipulative, two-faced, guileful') being used to justify misogyny and workplace abuse of women. General Motors line-worker turned author Ben Hamper provides a realistic but sobering picture of the mind-set:

> It wasn't easy for a woman on the Rivet Line. They [*sic*] were under constant siege by legions of moronic suitors. Almost every guy down there perceived himself as some kind of rodent Romeo. A woman working in the midst of so many men was looked upon as willing prey. Personality, looks, martial status hardly mattered. If it had tits and ass and jiggled along, it was fair game. Being that she was young and attractive, Jan was swarmed nightly. She deflected them nicely, defusing their advances with talk about her husband and snapshots of her little boy. Sooner or later, the vultures would hang it up and drag their libidos toward the next shapely bottom.
>
> (Hamper 1991: 146)

The polarization of wealth along lines of gender

Many individuals in Western societies since the late 1960s and early 1970s have maintained that since the Civil Rights movement blacks have achieved equality and that since the women's movement there is no more gender discrimination. Such 'conventional wisdom' could not be further from reality. While changes have occurred in law and legal statutes, at the end of the twentieth century the observation has to be made that the more we have talked about gender equality, the more material inequality exists. When a new consciousness of gender equality is combined with a neo-misogyny and a feminization of poverty, the possibility for social conflict increases. In this context men have too often engaged in a rhetoric of equality without connecting language with action. It is true that the lives of millions of women have been transformed since 1970, as they entered the workforce in massive numbers: in 1950 about one in three women worked outside the home; by 1990 seven out of ten did. It is also true that since the early 1970s women have entered professions such as law, medicine, business, banking, film directing and publishing. In the same time period they have broken blue-collar taboos and have found partial acceptance in the male provinces of police work, fire fighting and, in limited roles, the military.

As their lives were transformed, socio-economic changes created a climate of vulnerability that women had not previously experienced. After the conservative victories in the 1980 elections in the USA, social and economic policy changed in such a way that poverty rates among women and children began to grow. Cuts in human services such as Medicaid, maternal and child-health programmes, community health centres, family planning and child nutrition programmes placed poorer and minority women especially in precarious economic situations. All training and employment programmes under the Comprehensive Employment and Training Act (CETA) were eliminated in the 1980s, 80 per cent of Youth Employment Demonstration Projects' funds were cut and Employment Demonstration Projects' funds were significantly reduced. The desire to cut and eliminate such programmes has intensified throughout the 1990s. Over a decade and a half of such cuts have affected all poor people – no group has been more adversely affected than female-headed families. Reductions in socio-economic government programmes have more than doubled the percentage of working mothers living below the poverty line – and their numbers are still growing (Beck 1992; Malveaux 1992; Sidel 1992; Apple 1996).

In the mid-1990s women have higher unemployment rates than men, women college graduates earn less than men with an eighth grade education, minority women make less money than any other demographic grouping of workers, pregnancy is the leading cause of dropping out of high school and 60 per cent of women living in poverty dropped out of high school. Two-thirds of women who work outside the home are the sole or primary source of support for themselves and their families (Sidel 1992; McLaren 1994a). Obviously, not all women are in imminent danger of falling into poverty. Gender intersects with class in such a way that excuses most upper and upper-middle class women from such anxieties. Such women typically have the financial resources, the cultural capital, the education and the skills to control their own lives even if they are left without a man. Still, the socio-economic and political changes of the last third of the twentieth century have left all women more financially fragile than their male counterparts. Far too many women at the end of the twentieth century are members of the new poor – women who were not born into poverty but have been pushed into it by the social, economic and personal dynamics that shape their lives. When the globalization of the economy, with its corresponding depletion of good jobs, is combined with governmental budget cuts in education and social programmes for the poor, women are placed in a precarious position. All it takes for them to fall through the cracks of economic stability is a job loss, a divorce, a sickness or a childbirth.

Wealth polarization correlates significantly with high teenage birth rates. The poverty rate among children born to teenage mothers is extremely high. The lack of options experienced by poor women holds devastating consequences for both their children and society at large. With poverty just a divorce away for millions of women, educators must understand the great importance of career counselling and economics education for young women in high school (Fine 1993). Citizens in Western societies must appreciate the need for a humane environment in which women can work and raise their children. Critical multiculturalists understand the type of political action that must be taken to ensure the interests of women. Women need a form of political action that is cognizant of the connection between their role as caretakers of children and the feminization of poverty. While men may impregnate and run, women are faced with a twenty year commitment. Young women must understand that they cannot count on a man taking care of them and, as a result, they must make preparations for economic self-sufficiency. This belief in men as caretakers is a cultural dinosaur from a previous era. The culture of feminine dependency, however, is still cultivated by social, political and educational institutions, thus rendering transcendence of traditional gender role very difficult. When such cultural realities are viewed in relation to the intolerable neglect of prenatal and well-baby care, accessible day care and after-school care, and the lack of an adequate child welfare system, the harsh reality of patriarchal negligence is exposed. Such a reality undermines the dignity of women and the sacredness of children. When childcare for working mothers, for example, is closely examined, the human results of the logic of capital once again display themselves in cage-like cribs, dog leashes used to restrain children and minimum numbers of caretakers for maximum profits (Sidel 1992; Aronowitz and DeFazio 1994). A coherent, democratic, mother-friendly, child-oriented family policy is the victim of fatuous moralizing about family values. Until political action is taken, poor working women will continue to be victimized.

Identifying and employing women's subjugated knowledge in the struggle against the oppression of women

Once again the critical multiculturalist conception of subjugated knowledges emerges – this time in the context of gender. Drawing upon W. E. B. DuBois's notion of subjugated consciousness, women's subjugated knowledge is a second sight that provides a theoretical basis for making sense of how women react to the oppression they face. Rejecting liberal notions of diversity as 'spice' – the inclusion of differences in the social tossed salad – critical multiculturalists fighting for gender equality use women's subjugated knowledge as a base for formulating a cultural and institutional pedagogy for social change. Subjugated insight into the workings of patriarchy empowers women to fight male domination on a variety of levels, exposing power relations as they go. In this context it helps young women to devise skills and analytical abilities that help them in their struggle to participate equally in the workplace and the society at large. In an era of misogyny, where women's attempts to achieve justice at work earn them the labels of 'aggressive bitches' and 'feminazis', women's economic self-sufficiency becomes a serious issue. Based on the statistics, a large percentage of women will be forced to lead independent lives despite their individual preferences (Ferguson 1984; Sidel 1992).

In addition to the exposé of patriarchal power relations in the workplace, women's subjugated knowledges provide an alternative to patriarchy's hierarchical and bureaucratic conception of the organization of work. Women's subjugated knowledges often cultivate the understanding that the struggle for social justice is as much a matter of emotion as factual data, of human empathy and connectedness as analysis. Those who have struggled for justice in the past were often men who didn't appreciate the power of such feelings and who, as a result, failed to link their social analyses to the domain of the visceral. Women's subjugated knowledges operating at this affective level provide an anti-hierarchical orientation that sutures the fissure between private and public life. Such an orientation provides a social vision around which critical multiculturalists can reinvent social organizations. Relying on personal relationships rather than formal rules, a spirit of egalitarianism, information as an asset shared by everyone and process rather than outcome, feminists and critical multiculturalists move organizations beyond the scientific and patriarchal rationality of scientific modernism. The economic workplace, for example, becomes a place not simply to make profit but also to develop ourselves and to transform the outside world. Labour is divided in a way that charges each individual with responsibility for both creative and routine features of a job. As creativity is emphasized, workers come to remember that work is the most fundamental way human beings express their humanity. Such a memory is inherently dangerous, as it turns all imaginative workers into subversives whose lives are dedicated to the transformation of the old order (Bluestone and Harrison 1982; Ferguson 1984; DeYoung 1989).

Women's subjugated knowledge: developing social visions, new ways of seeing

The growth of Western science was profoundly shaped by a variety of gender dynamics. Specifically, the development of medicine and psychiatry involved the insertion of patriarchal power into spheres traditionally viewed as the domain of women. The creation of the male medical expert, the doctor, destroyed the traditional passage of medical knowledge from mother to daughter. The male doctor usurped the female midwife and sexology and psychiatry provided men with power over women's bodies and emotions that women had previously controlled themselves. The development of modernist science, therefore, was an overt attempt to squash women's knowledge of their own bodies. In the process of this scientization the public world was masculinized, forcing feminine knowledges to retreat to the domain of the domestic. Simply stated, science became a imperializing power of patriarchy that worked to relegate feminine knowledges to the realm of the unreal, the delusionary. In this way science became a masculinist voyeur that objectified women in the sense that they became the *passive* objects of the controlling scientific gaze. In this voyeuristic usurping role one can quickly grasp the feminist contention that Western science held little commitment to social or ethical responsibility (Ulmer 1989; Fiske 1993).

Intuition derived from what in modernity quickly became women's subjugated knowledge told women that scientific objectivity was a signifier for women's ideological passivity and their acceptance of the privileged social position of males. Thus, scientific objectivity came to demand separation of thought and feeling, the devaluation of any perspective maintained with emotional conviction. Feeling is designated as an inferior form of human consciousness – those who rely on thought or logic operating within this framework can justify their repression of those associated with emotion or feeling. Feminist theorists have pointed out that the thought–feeling hierarchy is one of the structures historically used by men to oppress women. In intimate heterosexual relationships if a man is able to present his position in an argument as the rational viewpoint and the women's position as an emotional perspective, then he has won the argument – his is the voice worth hearing.

Patriarchal science, with its emphasis on the rational production of abstract disinterested generalizations, feminists inform us, has moved us away from the domain of specific human beings with their passions, feelings and intuitions. We must become more familiar, they continue, with the traditional concerns of feminine subjugated knowledge – the domain of the living, the interpersonal, the communal. In this context the connected consciousness we have discussed initiates an attempt both to understand and to empathize with those who surround us. Present economic conditions, with the growing disparity of wealth and the feminization of poverty remind us of what horrors await if we don't take women's subjugated knowledge of passion and connectedness seriously. Antonio Gramsci well understood such concepts as he wrote from Mussolini's prisons in the late 1920s and 1930s. The intellectual's error, he wrote, consists of believing that one can know without 'feeling and being impassioned' (Gramsci 1988: 349). The role of intellectuals from Gramsci's perspective revolved around their attempt to connect logic and emotion in order for them to 'feel' the elementary passions of the people. Such an emotional connection would allow the inquirer to facilitate the struggle of men and women to locate their lived worlds in history. Finding themselves in history, they would be empowered by a consciousness constructed by a critically distanced view of the ways that the structural forces of history shape lives. One cannot make history without this passion, without this connection of feeling and knowing, since without it the relationships between the people and intellectuals are reduced to a hierarchical formality. The logic of bureaucracy prevails, as intellectuals move to the higher rungs of the organizational ladder, assuming the privileges of a superior caste, a modern Egyptian priesthood.

These subjugated understandings provided by women help us to make sense of a variety of lived realities. Peter McLaren (1994a) grounds this analysis of feminist passionate knowing educationally with an insightful analysis of the difference between the ways of knowing in the street-corner world of Toronto's Jane-Finch Corridor and the world of classroom knowledge. In the streets students gained a 'felt' knowledge which made use of the body, organic symbols and intuition. Classroom knowledge was abstracted from the lived world, objectified and corrupted by a Cartesian rationalism. To the students the abstracted knowledge of the classroom was light years away from their everyday experience. Students resisted what seemed to them to be useless ways of knowing in a variety of creative and often disconcerting ways. They struggled for creative control of knowledge production, viewing experience as open to question rather than something simply to be taken for granted. In other words, McLaren argues that street-corner epistemology challenged the school's tendency to present knowledge as unproblematic, not open to emotional negotiation. Students from such subjugated cultures questioned the school view of them as passive recipients of concrete facts. Teachers themselves have assumed the same passive position in relation to expert educational researchers. Teachers are the passive recipients of the objectified, abstracted knowledge handed down to them. Even though they formulate their own understanding of classroom life and teaching on both an emotional and logical base, they are induced to sophisticate their understandings of the educational process by consuming and incorporating the scientific knowledge of the experts into their professional labours.

What McLaren observed was a group of students operating outside the confines of Western modernist ways of viewing knowledge – outside the epistemology of dominant culture. Women's subjugated knowledges share much in common with Afrocentric, Native American and other indigenous ways of knowing that refuse to privilege rationalism as the one true way. Such epistemologies seek to make sense of everyday life, to produce cultures of practice, to develop ways of living that attempt to shape only those particular ways of living, not to control the world. Students who enter Western schools with such a perspective typically do not do well in rationalistic schools if they cannot quickly discard such epistemologies. Such epistemological dynamics tacitly saturate Western goals, definitions of success and intelligence and school performance. Stages of human development are constructed on such notions, as Jean Piaget argued, for example, that the optimum educational course was to move students' development away from the emotions so that rationality could dominate the progress of the mind. Stages were thus constructed around this logocentrism – stages that would become key supports in the common-sense, unquestioned knowledge about intelligence. Feminist theory would challenge this meta-narrative, arguing that cognizance of the social construction of individuals and the inseparability of rationality and emotion causes us to question essential categories of human development.

The feminists asked us to examine the difference between masculine and feminine ways of knowing. The masculine, of course, represents the 'proper' path for human cognitive development. Proposing that intelligence be reconceptualized in a manner that makes use of various ways of thinking, feminist theorists taught us that intelligence is not an innate quality of a particular individual but something related to the interrelationship among ideas, behaviours, contexts and outcomes (Lawler 1975; Walkerdine 1984; Bozik 1987; Fiske 1993). Such feminist insights open new realms of possibility that allow us to break the chains of Western patriarchy and the variety of damages it inflicts. In addition to direct socio-political interventions into the political and economic realms of Western societies to correct the patriarchal domination of women's work and other aspects of their lives, critical multiculturalists advocate longer-term strategies to rethink patriarchal ways of seeing the world. Such patriarchal frames of reality produce forms of consciousness that allow concrete and material malformations to exist without challenge. Such challenges to the power bloc's construction of consciousness rest at the heart of critical multiculturalism.

With these understandings in mind it is apparent that a critical mulitic-culturalist cultural and institutional curriculum involves more than merely adding information about women to pedagogies of gender. The feminist critique of Western patriarchal modernism along with its subjugated women's knowledge has challenged the very foundations of academic disciplines and organizational hierarchies. As feminist theories unite feeling with reason in a way that strengthens our emotional identification with life and its preservation, previously unchallenged assumptions about the social world are called into question (Fee 1982; Bowers and Flinders 1990; Wertsch 1991; Reinharz 1992). The universality of social, educational and psychological theories that privilege male experience as the norm are included in the feminist challenge. Such an essentialized form of analysis leaves women to be defined as innately inferior, as they exhibit less competitive spirit, rationality and 'objective' standards of judgement. Indeed, it often views feminine/maternal thinking and sensitivity to the needs of others not as ethical virtues but as exploitable female characteristics (Maher and Rathbone 1986). Understanding the ways that patriarchy operates, critical multiculturalists informed by feminist theory work to develop creative means of empowering those vulnerable to patriarchal power.

seven

MULTICULTURALISM AND THE IMPORTANCE OF RACE

At a time when half the anthropologists in the world maintain that there is no such thing as race, it is ironic that racism in Western societies is on the rise. As we argued in Chapter 1, there are no essential categories of race – no fixed notions of whiteness, blackness, Hispanicness or Asianness. The number of US citizens who label themselves 'Native American', for example, rose by 72 per cent between 1970 and 1980 and by another 38 per cent between 1980 and 1990. Thus, no stable category of American Indianness exists, as constructions of a society's view of Native Americans contribute to who claims such a position. Romantic perceptions of Indians coming out of the 1960s and reborn Indian pride undoubtedly contributed to the dramatic increase in the number of Native Americans – not an increase in Indian pregnancies. Important here is the idea that no one is any longer sure of what constitutes race, as attempts to divide human beings into four or five distinct racial categories are completely arbitrary. At this point in the discussion many people bring up skin colour; can't humans be divided into discrete races by the criterion of colour? Skin colour does not provide a means of separating sub-Saharan Africans, the inhabitants of Southern India and the Australian aborigines. In traditional typologies, of course, these three groups with similar skin colours have been consigned to three different races.

Thus, critical multiculturalists see race as an ever-shifting, unstable social construction with no essential biological justification. Nevertheless, the white supremist power bloc continues to lump individuals into arbitrary categories, as political commentators speak of the sociopathic characteristics of some categories and psychologists point to the cognitive abilities of others. While critical multiculturalists understand the arbitrariness of biological categories of race, they also appreciate the importance of race as a factor that shapes human experience. Critical multiculturalists find race an extremely important category for study and social action precisely because human beings have *made* race such an important factor in our lives. Thus, an understanding of the social construction of race and especially racism becomes a central feature of the larger critical multicultural project. Critical multiculturalism fails if it is unable to bring pressure on the power bloc through understanding, mobilization and organization in the name of racial justice. Such cultural work involves the identification of the power structures that help to construct the racialization of Western societies.

At the end of the twentieth century, unfortunately, new arguments are being made in support of eugenics (although not using the word) and a custodial state for minorities and the poor. Since blacks and Latinos are not as smart as whites, are much more prone to crime than whites and reproduce more quickly than whites, the growth of their numbers will bring down average IQs and intensify social problems. Such dysgenic pressure can be alleviated only by eliminating services for poor non-white women who have babies, establishing strict birth control measures for such women and closing national borders to such people who want to come in. Just because particular groups of individuals who advocate such policies deny their complicity with eugenics (the science dealing with factors that influence the hereditary qualities of a race and ways of improving the race) doesn't exonerate them. The racist ghosts stalking the landscape at the end of the millennium are frightening – their ability to hide their poison behind cleverly constructed facades is especially scary. The critical multiculturalist fight against racism at this point in human history is an uphill battle (Carby 1992; West 1993; Fraser 1995; Hitchens 1995; Holmes 1995; Judis 1995; Kamin 1995).

Grounding cultural traits in biology: essentialist racism

Racism must be understood as a historically specific, constantly mutating phenomenon. The most common historic expression of white racism is known as essentialist racism – the belief that there are *essential* qualitative, biological differences between different races. From the beginnings of European exploration, white people viewed the 'savages' they encountered in new lands as primitive and inferior. African 'natives', it was assumed, could never achieve the heights of civilization attained by Europeans. Today, when racism is discussed in the public culture, most Westerners see essentialist racism as the *only* form of racism; that is, to be racist is to exhibit an essentialist racism. Many individuals who identify with right-wing politics ascribe to an essentialist form of racism, though they often express it only in the company of like-minded white people. Manifestations of essentialist racism reveal themselves in schools when black or Latino students are placed in lower educational tracks because of their 'cognitive deficits' or 'cultural deprivations'. Non-white youth are assumed in these contexts to lack qualities necessary for educational success – *academic* educational success in particular. Essentialist racism reveals itself in social policy when white voters assume that blacks and Latinos are unequipped to 'do their jobs right' and therefore take advantage of employment policies that favour them over whites. This is *our* country, essentialist white racists proclaim, not *theirs* (Banfield 1991; Hacker 1992; Frankenberg 1993; Rubin 1994).

Essentialist racism works to shape the way its adherents see the world and their role in it. A few examples of essentialist racism in education may clarify the concept. Teaching materials thought by many to be wholesome and totally innocent have been some of the most flagrant perpetrators of essentialist racism. One of the most popular and long-lasting children's book series, the Bobbsey Twins, entertained hundreds of thousands of students with Dinah, the family cook. As the ultimate stereotype of an African American happy servant/slave, Dinah told the children outlandish stories reflecting her laughable superstitions, ate watermelon whenever she could get it and was not above stealing from the family. Hugh Lofting's 'innocent' Dr Doolittle taught generations of children about ignorant Africans. With his superior knowledge, Doolittle fulfilled the 'white man's burden' by ministering to the needs of these 'grotesque and uncivilized' peoples. Laura Ingalls Wilder's *Little House on the Prairie* and Walter D. Edmonds's popular *The Matchlock Gun* portrayed Native Americans as hated and feared 'savages' and Claire Huchet Bishop garnered great praise for her *The Five Chinese Brothers* – a book that depicted Chinese as yellow, disturbingly similar in appearance, slant-eyed and morally suspect.

Textbooks, often, were even more blatant in their essentialist racism than tradebooks. Well into the last quarter of the twentieth century some American educational textbooks have continued to represent Native Americans as a bellicose, war-like people, African Americans as incompetent and violent, Asian Americans as passive and duplicitous and Puerto Rican Americans as violence-prone and dangerous when living together in urban areas. A few quotations illustrate these stereotypes from textbooks published in 1975: from Harcourt, Brace and Jovanovich's *America: Its People and Values*, 'The Iroquois were a fierce and warlike people'; from Allyn and Bacon's *The Pageant of American History*, 'Many slaves did not know how to live without their former masters'; from Addison-Wesley's *The American Experience*, 'In San Francisco, the historically compliant Chinese aggressively resisted attempts to bus their children to schools outside of Chinatown' and 'groups such as the Puerto Ricans in New York City . . . form additional suburban populations which keep the nation's cities seething with discontent and conflict' (Banfield 1991: 79–80). To many observers, given the nature of the pictures of non-whites presented throughout our nation's history, it is not surprising that essentialist racism lurks in our cultural shadows. White people are never too far away from expressions of essentialist racism – expressions that privilege white genes over those of non-whites, white intellectual capacities over those of racial 'others'.

Employing the logic of essentialist racism, non-white economic failure is not the fault of our unjust system, it is a problem of non-white inferiority. Indeed, in this mind-set slavery was not a moral and political problem of whiteness, it was the result of the 'slavishness' of African Americans. Prejudice, discrimination and institutionalized racism are concepts irrelevant in the American experience. The belief structures of white supremacy not only discount such sociological concepts, but are poised to deny quickly the existence of white privilege in educational and economic institutions. The common belief that African Americans or Latinos are unemployed because they are lazy and incompetent merely reflects this way of making sense of the world.

Obviously, all white people don't buy into white supremacy – many white people have courageously fought such an ideology at great risk to their lives and financial well-being. Many white cultural workers have risked job security to expose essentialist racism, white supremacy and other forms of racial injustice. Tragically, nevertheless, the 1980s and 1990s have witnessed a regrowth of racisms of all types, even a resurgence (albeit in new guises) of essentialist racism. Radio talk show hosts, right-wing politicians, super-patriots and many traditional educators fan the fires of the essentialist racist resurgence, arguing that minority groups must 'get with the programme', change their attitudes and conduct and get to work. Such views are often self-contradictory, as they argue that non-whites should start applying themselves but at the same time question their talents to 'make it' even if they exert the effort. In a society historically shaped by essentialist racism, minority groups have had nowhere to turn, no way out; such an ideology structures their failures no matter what avenues to mobility they choose.

It is unfortunate that at the end of the twentieth century the point has to be made, but, alas, it must: the essentialist racist charge that non-whites (blacks in particular) are unwilling to work hard for a living is a ludicrous assertion. When a new hotel publicizes openings for porters and chambermaids, lines of predominantly black men and women snake around the block. Military recruiters know their best prospects are often black youths unable to find a career-type job anywhere else (Hacker 1992). Clint Allison (1995) describes in his history of American education, *The Present and the Past*, the fervent desire of African American ex-slaves to attend school. Where schools existed, young and old aspiring black students lined up at their doors; where there were no schools black communities pooled their resources and built them. One of the most tragic stories in American educational history, of course, is that the African American faith in schooling fell far short of its promise. One of the most pernicious fables of essentialist racism is the welfare mother stereotype with its depiction of multiple child-bearing, stupid and lazy black women. Contrary to the stereotype, young non-white women on welfare want good work. Often welfare mothers seeking socio-economic mobility run into pathological hostility from welfare functionaries who remind them that welfare won't pay them a penny for their college degree. It is often emotionally easier for such women to sit home watching TV than to make the sacrifices demanded by the attempt to better themselves (hooks 1993).

This damned-if-you-do/don't position blacks, Latinos and many Asians experience in situations structured by essentialist racism induces non-whites to ask just what it is that white people want. If black students and black communities, for example, ask schools to teach more about black culture, they are shocked when whites demand in response that schools teach more about white culture to keep things equal. 'What do whites think their sons and daughters have been learning about in school for the past few centuries', black observers want to know. Schooling, they contend, has been the story of white people, their lives and accomplishments. To protect the 'white story' many white people in the last two decades of the twentieth century have staged what some scholars label a 'white counter-revolution'. The postmodern economic reorganization has been accompanied by a white-dominated movement to decrease social spending for non-white citizens. The movement seeks to undermine or revoke affirmative action, subvert the enforcement of civil rights laws, slash grants and loans for minority higher education and cut funding for minority-oriented vocational education programmes. It is apparent that what many white Americans want is a return to a pre-Civil Rights movement, pre-1960s America – a country that was much too comfortable with economic injustice, unemployment and bad work for non-white men and women (Zweigenhaft and Domhoff 1991; Hacker 1992; Rubin 1994).

Institutional/structural racism

As compared to essentialist racism, institutional or structural racism tends to be far more subtle and difficult to identify. In separating institutional/structuralist racism as a distinct category from essentialist racism, there is no intent to imply that the two practices operate in isolation from one another. Essentialist assumptions held by individuals in institutions, for example, cannot be separated from the structural discrimination institutions exhibit towards non-whites. The distinction is made in order to facilitate an understanding of the ways racism operates. Most white people do not identify what is defined here as institutional/structural racism as a form of racism at all. Most institutions develop informal cultural practices that are internalized by their members (and vice versa). Such institutional cultures are diverse in their expression and specific to particular organizations; but they do tend to be white. Historically in the USA, most of the individuals who work in the upper and middle management of General Electric, teach at the University of Virginia or serve in the FBI have been white. This reality has created the public image of such institutions as well as their *modus operandi*. The organization 'thinks' and carries on its business in a white manner. White people via their cultural experiences are perceived to be better suited for inclusion in these cultures, although class and gender issues obviously affect dimensions of 'suitability' as well. As we have already discussed, the dynamics of cultural capital exert dramatic influences on social relations between job applicant/employee and organizational culture.

Policies that produce racially discriminatory effects do not have to be conscious or intentional – though in expressions of institutional/structural racism consciousness and intentionality are difficult to determine. Setting aside questions of consciousness and intent for the moment, institutional/structural racism is judged on the terms of its effects – do the institutional structures reinforce and extend racial exclusions and subordinations? When business people make hiring decisions, the logic of profit induces them to ask how customers will respond to, for example, non-white salespeople, or non-white technicians creating complex equipment. Upper-level managers often express concerns about the effect on promoting non-whites to supervisory roles in the firm: will white subordinates work for them without resentment or resistance? Obviously, expressions of racism are present in these issues, but everyone denies personal culpability. Managers squirm uncomfortably when asked about such dynamics and assert that racism is simply not involved. When outside observers leave, however, white-only coteries of supervisors and managers may express how hard they find it to work with Puerto Ricans or blacks, citing instances of non-white individuals with chips on their shoulders. Too infrequently do they question why interpersonal difficulties between races develop. Their response, in this context, is to avoid the problem by hiring and promoting as few non-whites as possible, finding 'safe' tokens to deflect outside criticism (Anthias and Yuval-Davis 1992; Hacker 1992).

Such situations do not typically evoke the self- and institutional-reflection needed to expose and remedy structurally embedded racism in the economic sphere. Thus, cultural practices develop that encode the racist practices into the formal structures of the organization. For example, the on-the-surface innocent use of the term quality can develop into one of these cultural practices of encoding. No one is against standards of quality. When questions of admission into a law school or hiring in a service industry arise, 'quality-based' decisions can become the organizational code word for whites-only policies. Criteria for hiring and admission decisions are narrowed – suggestions for alternative guidelines that might culturally widen the pool of applicants are often characterized as attacks on the integrity of the institution. Codes proliferate, taking on a fascinating character: 'defending the Western tradition'; 'cultural literacy'; 'transitional or good neighbourhoods'; 'at-risk students'; 'dressed for success'; 'welfare mother'; 'inner city'; 'safe schools'; 'traditional values' etc. The racial decoding process is an important dimension of the work of critical multiculturalists and all people who value social justice. Contrary to the belief of some, individuals can confront institutional/structural racist practices, expose them and change them. No matter what its form, racism can be overcome.

Strange mutations: the evolutionary, context-specific nature of postmodern racism

In multicultural education a debate has developed between those who focus on essentialist racism and those who emphasize the institutional/structural form. Those who focus on the essentialist dimension tend to believe that the purpose of multicultural education involves addressing problems of individual prejudice; those who emphasize the institutional/structural form tend to believe that multicultural education's greatest contribution involves exposing social, economic and political impediments to racial equality – structural dynamics that shape patterns of distribution of social goods and power. There is no doubt that simply addressing racism as a form of individual prejudice does little to undermine white racism. Appeals to the rationality of racist individuals through curricula that seek to expose the irrationality of racism are not very successful. At the same time, however, multicultural approaches that privilege institutional/structural dynamics often assume that institutions possess a generic nature that is separate from the perspectives and practices of individuals. Separate from the actions of living human beings, institutional racism seems beyond reproach. Such a positioning leaves individuals powerless to change these generic structures – the possibility of democratic reformulations of the educational and corporate domains is negated. Educators and workers interested in social justice are left in the lurch with no ideas about where to begin the struggle for economic justice and race, class and gender equality.

The key concepts that help critical multiculturalists to get beyond this dualism involve the notions that: (a) social institutions are and have always been constructed by individuals; and (b) individual racial prejudice and essentialist racism help to shape racist structures and institutions. As we will discuss in more detail later, critical multiculturalists must understand that racism is virus-like. While we can identify particular prototypes of racism and come to understand the ways they interact in the lived world, it is more difficult to appreciate that a virus-like racism is always mutating, taking on new forms and posing new dangers. New contexts, such as the dawning of postmodernity and the advent of technological innovations that have created an era of corporate techno-power, have helped to shape new forms of racism. While general features of racism persist (it is important, for example, that we should understand essentialist and institutional/structural prototypes), racism is context-specific (McCarthy and Apple 1993; Rizvi 1993; Sleeter 1993). In an era where innovation and technological change alter contexts so quickly, racist forms mutate in frightening sci-fi rapidity. The task, admittedly, is exceedingly difficult, but critical multiculturalists must make the effort to comprehend the mutating nature of racism and the ways it distorts various social spheres.

As recessions and stagflation and corporate migrations and downsizing intensified the perception of scarcity among Westerners, minority-preference college admissions and workplace hiring policies allowed a few non-whites to make small but *visible* intrusions on to what had been an all-white terrain – the combination of the two trends was electric. Throughout the seventies, eighties and nineties the economy kept faltering, local, state and federal governments continued to cut services, the quality of life of the middle and lower socio-economic classes continued to deteriorate and the passion of the debate over who gets what was left accelerated. Indeed, as power concentrated in the hands of the predominately white, richest segment of the society, social discord between everyone else intensified (Rubin 1994). This social dissonance has taken many forms. One of its most important and influential manifestations involves the claim made by many conservative whites that racism is a thing of the past – we live in a 'post-racist era'. We live in a land of opportunity, the white narrative reads and since everyone is granted access to material well-being, those who don't achieve it have no one to blame but themselves. The re-encoding of black and Latino inferiority is connected to a social-Darwinist survival-of-the-fittest social theory – '*those people* who keep bitching and moaning about discrimination would be better served to shut up and get their lazy butts to work'. The mobility experienced by a small portion of middle class blacks over the past thirty years and the high visibility this successful group receives has been misinterpreted by many from the struggling white working class as evidence of black economic success as a group. A closer examination does not support such an interpretation. Indeed, such black middle class success has intensified fiscal inequality in the black community, as tens of thousands of them have fallen into poverty and the underclass. Thus, the very groups that have been victimized by the inequitable distribution of wealth – blacks and working class whites – have found little solidarity in their similar plight. Instead, they are political enemies reduced to fighting for an ever-decreasing slice of the economic pie (Cotton 1992; Jones 1992; Stafford 1992; Rubin 1994).

Turning back the clock: neo-racist mutations – whites as victims

Postmodern economics and the social dissonance that follows it can be and *is* nasty. Cultural workers and educators operating in the 1990s do not have to be told of the racial tensions they witness in their everyday professional lives – they observe the distrust and suspicion engendered by inter-racial competition for limited opportunities. Such a context places racial inter-action in a pressure cooker, exacerbating the racism mutation process. New forms of racism emerge that call for new understandings and approaches on the part of critical cultural workers. The corporate use (commodification) of non-whites and the superficial celebration of diversity in media cannot be confused with genuine democratic movements to decentralize wealth and more equitably distribute political power in America (Fusco 1992). Critical multiculturalists must stand ready to point out that such movements have not taken place in the USA. They must gain the language to tell their students that this commodification of 'ethnicity', expressed in terms of 'Shaq attacks', 'Be like Mike', and 'Oprah at 5:00', cannot be equated with a per-vasive non-white access to economic mobility. Such misconceptions distort both the public conversation about and individual perceptions of the relationship among hard work, schooling and financial success.

The postmodern era has been hard on most Americans – only the upper-middle class and the wealthy have been spared. We empathize with the white working class and poor white people, as they have watched their financial security and opportunities for economic success pulled out from under them over the last quarter of the twentieth century. We appreciate their frustra-tions and anger as they work hard and struggle daily to make ends meet. It is difficult to write about these racial issues that surround education and politics – difficult because they evoke such passion and fury on the part of everyone. Critical multiculturalists must appeal to the best instincts of their students, colleagues and communities; that is, they must appeal to their com-passion, sense of justice and empathy. Black people must empathize with working class whites and their frustrations concerning their lack of mobility and crushed aspirations. At the same time whites must empathize with non-whites and their continuing frustrations with their inability to gain access to the promise of upward mobility. Until such empathy is engendered, the possibility of dialogue and unity among individuals victimized by viral forms of racism, sexism and class bias cannot be realized. Such empathy will lead to dialogue and unity; and such unity will form the basis of a pro-democracy movement – an inter-racial, inter-ethnic struggle for political and economic justice.

Such words may sound idealistic, and they are; but we must retain the ability to envision a better day, to dream social dreams. This book, of course, is itself a social dream that lays out a sense of possibility for Western societies. This chapter focuses attention on one of the most important impediments to hope: racism, its context, effects and mutating expression. Awareness of this phenomenon takes on more importance than simply the phenomenon of racism itself. The awareness of the ways our consciousness is socially constructed around issues of race (not to mention class and gender) grants us insight into the way the world works. Power relations in a society work ambiguously to induce us to adopt identities and perspectives that undermine our self-interests and our collective interests as a culture or a nation. In this context Aaron Gresson's description of 'racial recovery' and its social divisiveness becomes very important.

Hegemony, as we have previously discussed, makes the world seem natural, as if it can be explained by a dominant cultural story. Certain stories become privileged at particular historical junctures because they fit so well with the maintenance of existing power relations. Gresson calls to our attention the emergence of a *new dominant story* over the past couple of decades: – the narrative of the recovery of white supremacy. In many ways the new story is a white story that inverts a traditional black story. The new story rejects essentialist racist descriptions of non-white inferiority, substituting in their place a narrative of non-white *privilege*. Because of the media appearance of black and other minority group success, the story contends that non-whites have greater power and opportunity than whites (Gresson 1995). Thus, non-white privilege has been gained *at the expense of white Americans – especially white males.* The story is portrayed at a variety of levels and in a multitude of ways, but always with the same effect: the production of *white anger* directed at blacks, Latinos, Asians, Native Americans and sometimes women. Such anger works, of course, to divide poor and working class people of all races and genders, and to support the interests of privileged power wielders.

Such a story induces whites to see themselves as a people under threat. Sociologists have long maintained that individuals and groups under threat often react with an attempt to reassess their power and regain their former social position – the social phenomenon of status anxiety. This reassertion, of course, takes many forms and many degrees. Manifestations may include modest efforts to reassert one's self-worth by way of private expression of racial disdain ('I hate the way Deion Sanders struts around the end zone like a rooster every time he scores a touchdown') or racial superiority ('Many of the people who work in my office don't make a very good impression – with their loud "street talk" and everything'). Another example of white reassertion in the USA may work more at the level of group recovery with the passing of 'English only' legislation in heavily Latino areas such as Florida, California and Arizona, or battles over 'multicultural curricula' as evidenced throughout the nation (Frankenberg 1993). More extreme expressions involve the dramatic growth of white supremist organizations in the 1980s and 1990s and the terrorist activity associated with some of them – for example, the April 1995 bombing of the Oklahoma City federal building. The vast majority of Americans are dismayed by this level of angry white reassertions, yet the perception of whites as victims becomes more and more deeply embedded into white collective consciousness as the century comes to an end.

Re-deploying the folklore of white supremacy

The racial recovery with its white victimization narrative draws on a nostalgia for a pre-Civil Rights movement 'simpler and more natural time' characterized by the legal, social and economic subordination of non-white peoples. The regime of 'Jim Crow' in the 'newly recovered' South of the post-reconstruction era – a time that also saw the return of white supremacy – is represented as a romantic era when a true meritocracy provided 'authentic' opportunity. During this 'wonderful period' from around 1890 to 1915, government rigged a new order of white supremacy based around the racial segregation of public places and organizations. As industrialization and urbanization efficiently marched into the future, African Americans held jobs such as porters, bell*boys*, maids, domestic servants and farm workers. Black southerners lived in the fear that Judge Lynch would condemn them to an execution ordered by angry white mobs with vivid imaginations when it came to black crime. There was no agency, public or private, to protect black citizens from capricious lynchings, as 'local control' was the order of the day. Local control during this period came to be a code phrase that would be used throughout the Civil Rights movement, all the way to contemporary efforts by right-wing politicians to dismantle federal governmental protections for non-whites.

Travelling even further back historically in their racial recovery time machine, right-wing politicos invoked the late eighteenth-century racial rhetoric of the Founding Fathers of the American republic. Ignoring these men's language of democracy and human rights, the white supremist politicians appropriated their *Zeitgeist*-reflecting treatises on the inequality of human beings. The democrat Jefferson was remembered for his concept of a natural aristocracy, other leaders were invoked for their suspicions about the vulgar levelling influences of democracy. The lesson that contemporary right-wing leaders take away from their encounter with the American Revolution, the Constitutional Convention and the Early National Period involves the recognition that the political philosophy of equality might have been beneficial in some instances but many of its effects have been nothing but harmful. Such a reading signals a dramatic shift in America's view of itself.

While the Civil Rights movement failed on a variety of levels, it did produce a public facade of civility on matters of race and a genuine effort on the part of many whites to rethink their racial consciousness. The architects of the recovery of white supremacy had to reshape the cultural representation of blackness in a way that would elicit white fear while not exposing the architects themselves as racists. With these guiding concerns, right-wingers rhetorically positioned blackness as the opposite of family values, morality, nostalgia, authority, safeness and prosperity. Facilitating their efforts to avoid the racist label, the politicos embraced upper-middle/upper class blacks with 'cultivated tastes', 'class' and 'pedigree'. The Republican Party's enthusiastic celebration of Colin Powell and George Bush's embrace of Clarence Thomas are excellent examples of this aspect of recovery politics. Since racism no longer played a role on the contemporary political landscape, as recovery proponents including Dinesh D'Souza maintained, no reason existed for structural adjustments to take care of the disadvantages of racism and social inequality. Whether in America or Britain the recovery rhetoric worked its magic. The rise of the Conservatives in British politics was very much grounded on 'discourses of racial and ethnic difference' that connected being 'truly British' to tradition, conservatism and whiteness. Prime Minister Thatcher and her allies positioned non-whites as responsible for an erosion of standards in British culture. Immigrants, outsiders, black people were used in the production of images and signifiers to shape the persuasive power of what came to be labelled 'Thatcherism' (Gray 1995; Jones 1995).

In America the recovery project was championed by a new breed of talk radio hosts – Rush Limbaugh, G. Gordon Liddy, Oliver North and many others – who successfully worked to make racism respectable. As they played to their audience's racial fears, they fanned fires of white supremacy to the degree that many of the political policies they advocated subverted the fundamental assumptions of democracy and egalitarianism (Giroux and Searls 1996). The recovery rhetoric struck a resonant chord with white American and British audiences, as the narrative was deftly articulated by individuals who appeared neither confrontational nor bitter. How could jovial, self-effacing Ronald Reagan be peddling a politics of hate, whites wondered, when he's such a wonderful man. Like Reagan, they too could express their racial anger and antagonism without thinking of themselves as intolerant bigots. In this context the medium of television worked in tandem with the recovery project, with its magical ability to represent and disseminate morally repugnant messages without appearing to be mean-spirited or intolerant. As reporters presented the words and messages of racial hate, they conveyed them with such low affect, calm and media congeniality that the sting of its hurtfulness was airbrushed away.

Right-wing, corporate-driven, twenty-first century hegemony, Joyce King (1996) argues, depends on a folklore (ideology) of white supremacy that moves white people to accept the degradation of the poor non-white as a natural process. Indeed, the rhetorical abilities of neo-racists rose to the challenge of the recovery project, employing phrases such as a 'new species' to describe poor ghetto-raised blacks of the late twentieth century. Racial scapegoating was raised to a new aesthetic form, as right-wing commentators on TV claimed that racial integration's infusion of non-white students and the multiculturalist programmes devised to accommodate them have 'dumbed down' schools. Using declining SAT (Scholastic Aptitude Test) scores as their empirical proof, analysts painted a picture of schooling run amok, with unqualified teachers teaching silly multiculturalist curriculums. Employing a pretzel logic, *The Bell Curve* authors Richard Herrnstein and Charles Murray did their part for the recovery, maintaining the party line about non-whites' role in undermining quality education and causing SAT scores to fall. Interestingly, such an argument contradicted their previous assertion that cognitive ability is innate and cannot be raised by educational intervention. Apparently black and Latino students possess the uncanny ability to make everyone dumber by their mere presence.

The right-wing redeployment of white supremist rhetoric has successfully uncovered feelings deeply buried in white consciousness about blacks, Latinos and indigenous peoples. Right-wing politicians feasted upon this racial unconsciousness, framing blackness as a signifier for threat and irresponsibility. TV news played its part with its nightly portrayal of menacing black rappers, gang members, Willie Horton-like killers, welfare scammers, crack pushers etc. In these ways conservatives stripped blacks of the moral authority they had gained in the Civil Rights movement of the 1960s. Thus, many whites came to view non-whites as the lazy and immoral poor – a group of people who were after something for nothing. The moral economy was changing, moving the focus of concern away from poor minorities and re-establishing it around the needs of taxpayers, white upwardly mobile suburbanites and white people concerned with the alleged 'attack on family values'. The rhetoric of race was reversed, as Aaron Gresson (1995) has termed it, and blame for social pathology was placed directly on the backs of the non-white poor (Fraser 1995; Gray 1995; House and Haug 1995; Staples 1995; King 1996). Conservatives in the UK and North America understood that in an era of a struggling economy and individual economic frustration, appeals to white superiority and racial self-justification would 'play' well to white audiences.

Yet another mutation: neo-scientific racism

Social analysts have recognized a pattern in Western societies that involves white reactions to social reform. Whenever reforms have been widely recognized as failures, a set of theories emerge claiming that movements for social justice are doomed because some groups of people (always the poor and non-white) are inferior to individuals from the white middle class. From this perspective the reformer is positioned as a busybody sticking his or her nose into nature's process of sorting people into their proper social slots. As the pattern unfolds, genetic explanations become more widely accepted and inferior traits of particular racial, ethnic or class groupings are deemed to be causes of indignant social situations, not contextual factors such as discrimination. Such a pattern has reared its ugly head in Western societies in the last two decades of the twentieth century and can be clearly identified in relation to the recovery of white supremacy. The claim that genetic inferiority precludes the success of social reform has moved from the fringes of society to the mainstream. Again, such movement fits the pattern, as conservative forces in the seats of power use the genetic argument to thwart reform efforts for an economic justice that would more fairly distribute wealth. Compare, for example, the similarities between the social Darwinists of the late nineteenth century and right-wing perspectives at the end of the twentieth century.

In both cases the science of genetic biology supports a politics of disdain for the 'other'. If biology determines ability and success then we are simply wasting our time and money supporting Head Start, minority student loans for college, Upward Bound, free breakfasts and lunches at school and pre-natal care for the poor. In making such an argument it is essential to prove the congenital inferiority of non-whites and make it attractive to whites, who have not always bought into such racism. In the USA in the 1860s, the non-whites in question were not blacks or Latinos but Irishmen, who were reported to make the streets of New York unsafe. The Irish were designated as a unredeemable race apart who bred like rabbits and could be identified by their 'simian brow and saddle nose'. Like blacks and Latinos in contemporary societies, the Irish were positioned as the source of social instability and, as a result, had to be controlled by whatever means necessary. Whether in the nineteenth or the twentieth century, the pattern is consistent – neutral science was used to prove racial inferiority in a world where discrimination, oppression and other social forces were literally erased from consideration. Racism? What racism? Racism is the product of a distant past (Merleman 1986; Dionne 1995; Sautman 1995; Tucker 1995; Gilman 1996; McCarthy *et al.* 1996).

How low will they go? Neo-scientific racism and the subverting of multiculturalism

In 1996 we published a book with Aaron Gresson entitled *Measured Lies: The Bell Curve Examined*, about Richard Herrnstein and Charles Murray's book *The Bell Curve: Intelligence and Class Structure in American Life*. What we and our assemblage of authors attempted was to expose the fraudulent nature, in our opinion, of this vicious attack on African Americans, Latinos, Native Americans and poor people of all types. We deemed such a task important, for we read the book as a justification for an array of political and educational policies designed to undermine opportunity and hope for marginalized men, women and children. Even though our book consisted of 454 pages, we were unable to say all we wanted. Because Herrnstein and Murray so faithfully represent a large segment of the population and its political leaders, we feel that it is important to document how far some advocates of a new-scientific racism are willing to go to fight against a critical multiculturalism grounded on notions of egalitarianism and human dignity. Any book that has shaped the debate about racial and class differences to such a degree must be addressed in any analysis of race and racism.

The Bell Curve represents the coalescence of the agendas of the political right with white supremist heriditarianism. In the nineteenth-century racist dystopian vision that drives Herrnstein, Murray and their fellow travellers, images of poor houses, Brave New surveillance tactics for the poor and non-white and other sugar plum fairies dance through the thick fascist air. Herrnstein and Murray, however, present themselves as good guys who care about injustice, who can't bear to see the upper class partition itself from the rest of society. Upon careful reading one finds that such a partition is precisely what the authors are advocating. Such fake-outs and misrepresentations saturate a book so filled with inaccuracies that a good editor would have quickly put an end to this vengeful nonsense. When IQ correlates with an undesirable psychological or moral trait, Herrnstein and Murray scream causation; for example, low IQ causes, they argue, poor job performance or criminal behaviour. Other factors and competing explanations are eliminated in such an absolute way that few scholarly journals would publish such work. It quickly becomes apparent that Herrnstein and Murray are willing to pull out all stops in the effort to forestall the coming of a political and educational system grounded on the tenets of a critical multiculturalism. Using science as their guide, they lead the charge for a recovery of white supremacy.

Contradictions fill the pages of *The Bell Curve*. After vehemently denying the viability of race as a category that can stand up to scholarly examination and arguing that it is also a typology that misleads and hurts (points with which we strongly agree), Herrnstein and Murray spend the next 800 pages of their book 'documenting' the vast difference a loosely constructed, ill-defined conception of race makes in terms of human worth. At the same time, a book-long contradiction shakes the conceptual foundation of the book, as the authors argue repeatedly that IQ accurately measures cognitive ability and is unchangeable; if such is the case then why do they spend so many pages explaining major changes in test scores over the past couple of decades? When Herrnstein and Murray's politico-educational agenda demands that genetic endowment of cognitive ability cannot be changed – as in the futility of programmes designed to make the culturally marginalized smarter – *it can't*. When the agenda demands that they 'prove' that liberal schools have 'dumbed down' kids via an inadequate education then genetic endowment *can* be changed.

Another contradiction also revolves around Herrnstein and Murray's insistence on the intractability of intelligence, their belief in the futility of environmental intervention in the lives of low achievers. Even if heredity played no role in shaping intelligence, the authors hyperbolically contend, no programme or policy could be devised to change cognitive ability. If this is true then why has Murray maintained that a simple governmental programmatic change – ending welfare – would signal a new day for black students? Without the 'tyranny' of welfare to drag them down such young people would become more productive, better parents, less criminal and better students. How ironic: low performance and sociopathic behaviour are intractably determined by intelligence and nothing can change such a harsh reality – that is, except for the miracle of abolishing welfare. In the same context, the authors lament the increasing reliance of the affluent on private services (e.g. private schools) rather than public services. Of course, the slashing of funds for public projects and institutions such as public education is exactly what they advocate throughout the book (Genovese 1995; House and Haug 1995; Muwakkil 1995; Carspecken 1996).

This tendency permeates the book – the authors present crude biological evidence supporting genetic determinism of white superiority and then follow such presentations with recommendations for conservative changes in public policy. The key to their strategy involves their pretence that there is an authoritative scientific association between the 'proof' of white superiority they provide and the policies they advocate. Such logical misconduct coupled with statistical misconduct adds up to *disinformation*, right-wing propaganda. Take, for example, Herrnstein and Murray's analysis of the well documented narrowing of the IQ gap between black and white students over the past two decades. Every study the authors cite describes the gap as being reduced by anywhere between a high of 8 points and a low of 4.2 points – the median estimation is 6 points. Yet inexplicably Herrnstein and Murray cite the reduction as 2 to 3 points. In a book that documents the serious cognitive differences between blacks and whites this question of IQ convergence would seem to be an important matter of careful analysis, but the authors dismiss most studies of the phenomenon. Indeed, their central strategy in dealing with the convergence involves the effort to explain away reasons for the rise in African American scores. Much of the increase in SAT scores, for example, comes from black students at the low end of the range, they argue. This is simply not true. Few blacks had high SAT scores fifteen years ago, Herrnstein and Murray posit, so any gains they have made are not very significant. What? Such non-sequiturs are not uncommon in the book. Not to be unrelenting but, again, what happened to genetic intractability? IQs, SATs and other test scores are quite malleable. For examples, SATs – which the authors call 'an intelligence test' – can be improved by over 60 points with a few days of studying. Herrnstein and Murray fail to mention that IQ scores can be raised by a dozen points by placing poor children in affluent homes. The Abecedarian Project raised poor student IQs by an aver-age of almost 8 points by placing them in day care programmes for five years. Genetic cognitive intractability – we don't think so.

One of the most important distortions of *The Bell Curve* involves the author's analysis of the Minnesota Transracial Adoption Study, in which 100 children from varying ethnic backgrounds were adopted by white par-ents. By the age of seven the non-white adoptees scored an average of 106 on intelligence tests – scores that were higher than the US average for non-white children, almost the average for white children. By the time the adoptees were sixteen, researchers Sandra Scarr and Richard Weinberg dis-covered that the non-white children's IQ scores had dropped an average of 17 points to 89. After analysing the situation, Scarr and Weinberg concluded that racial prejudice and discrimination at school had effected the 17-point decline. Other researchers agreed. William Cross (1996) sees transracial adoption studies as relatively easy to interpret: when non-white children are raised in poor, slum-like conditions their IQ scores will be significantly lower than those of non-white children adopted by middle class black or white homes. Despite such evidence and generally agreed upon interpretations, Herrnstein and Murray maintain that the Minnesota Transracial Adoption study revealed little environmental impact on cognitive ability. Racial hered-ity, they maintain, determines a rank ordering of IQ that will become more pronounced as the adoptees grow older.

Cross explains that part of the duplicity of Herrnstein and Murray's interpretation involves their concealment of the pre-placement history of the children. Not only do the authors ignore racial prejudice and institutional racism in school, but they fail to acknowledge the problematic placement histories of many of the non-white adoptees. Problematic placement his-tories have proven to interrupt a healthy developmental process. Weinberg *et al.* (1992) maintain that the average IQ difference between early placed and late placed black children is 11.7 points. If Herrnstein and Murray were searching for fair analysis of the adoption study, they would have to compare IQs of children who were early placed with few pre-placement problems with similar children of a different race. When such a comparison is made, researchers find that there is no difference between the first testing of non-white and white adopted children with optimal pre-placement histories. Cross also points out that in the context of transracial adoption Herrnstein and Murray avoided reporting a study on the topic produced by Elsie Moore in 1986. Moore's study maintained that adopted black children placed in middle class black and white homes achieve higher IQ scores in white than in black homes *because* African American parents are unable to translate their 'middle classness' into the same cultural capital as whites. Thus, Moore concluded that environmental not hereditary factors explain the racial IQ gap even after African Americans move into the middle class. Herrnstein and Murray conveniently ignored this study. Contrary to *The Bell Curve*, William Cross and many others argue that instead of abandoning racially and economically marginalized students because they are genetically incapable, we should search for practical ways to assist them. To argue against environmental intervention as do Murray and Herrnstein is to interpret questions of performance and ability in a way that is dictated by an ideology of recapturing white supremacy (Beardsley 1995; Kamin 1995; Kaus 1995; Nisbett 1995; Cross 1996).

More attention to Herrnstein and Murray's inability to distinguish between correlation and cause is needed. As the authors present a plethora of studies sanctioned by the National Longitudinal Survey of Labour Market Experience of Youth, they maintain that there is a connection among IQ scores, race and socio-economic class. No problem, they are correct. But Herrnstein and Murray are not content to stop at this point. Instead, they push forward with an unsubstantiated inferential leap that low IQ *causes* low socio-economic status. Social scientists are far from developing a definitive empirically verifiable account of the specific causes of human performance – we believe that the question is so complex that such verifiable accounts will *never* be developed. Yet the unabashed Herrnstein and Murray keep on pushing, contending that they understand that low IQ *causes* not only poor school and work performance but low *moral behaviour* as well. The most vulgar Marxists in the Stalinist USSR could not have been more deterministic, more contemptuous of the human ability to overcome the constraints of environmental circumstances. Herrnstein and Murray's social and educational vision is an overt denial of human potential on the part of the poor and non-white. With the understanding of causality so limited one would think that responsible social researchers would think long and hard before announcing with certainty what humans can and cannot achieve.

Low socio-economic status is no more caused by IQ than it is by a high fat diet, though both factors do correlate with such a situation. We have understood for decades that socio-economic circumstance can roughly indicate what type of environment a child might experience. It is not controversial to point out that the son of a wealthy brain surgeon is more likely to be exposed to academic language experiences, reading and books, and arguments supporting the centrality of education in one's life than the son of a migrant worker. Such exposure will undoubtedly affect these boys' IQ scores. But where in this mix do we gain a sense of certainty about the causality of genetic inferiority? As Yvonna Lincoln (1996) recounts from her beginning logic class: '1) polio outbreaks occur when the highest per capita consumption of Coca-Cola takes place, therefore 2) Coke causes polio'. Lincoln's point is well taken; such a spurious logic of causality permeates *The Bell Curve* to the point that only an ideological agenda could have shaped such a reading. Based on a careful analysis of their work, it is our opinion that Herrnstein and Murray set out to prove regardless of the evidence the cognitive inferiority of non-white and poor people (Kamin 1995; Loury 1995).

Without questioning it, Herrnstein and Murray use the Minnesota twins study to support the genetic inheritability of intelligence and to validate the twin research of Cyril Burt earlier in the twentieth century. The white supremist crowd has invested heavily in the Minnesota Twins study despite the persistent chorus of researchers who see it as invalid because of methodological manipulations. Though many statisticians believe that Cyril Burt made up his research on twins, Herrnstein and Murray defend him and almost anyone else who argued that intelligence was genetic. Such blind defence includes from our perspective such charlatans as Richard Lynn and his descriptions of 'Negroid intelligence'. A Lynn article written in 1991, and used by Herrnstein and Murray, positively employed the work by Ken Owen to calculate the mean IQ of 'pure Negroids' as 70 – if such a figure is accepted then about 50 per cent of all Africans are mentally retarded. Using eleven studies of African intelligence, Herrnstein and Murray generously raised Lynn's estimate by five points, to 75. Leon Kamin (1995) figures that Herrnstein and Murray arbitrarily added five IQ points to Lynn's figure because an average IQ of 70 was pushing the bounds of credibility.

Herrnstein and Murray also fail to mention that Richard Lynn is the associate editor of *Mankind Quarterly*, a vulgarly racist publication devoted to proving the genetic superiority of white people and a major recipient of grant money from the Pioneer Fund, a eugenicist organization. Herrnstein and Murray use twenty-three of Lynn's publications to support their case for white cognitive superiority in *The Bell Curve*. When psychologists examine Lynn's work and methodology, they are often repulsed by the inferential leaps and statistical prestidigitations that permeate it. At the same time that they accept without qualification the work of Lynn, they refer to Howard Gardner (the eminent Harvard theoretician of multiple intelligences) as a radical who does not believe in the 'now accepted' validity of IQ tests. These same authors are unembarrassed in their use of 'welfare Cadillac' type stories about black students who receive $100,000 grants for student tuition, travel and research. The purpose of such stories is to incite white outrage at flagrant preferential treatment of non-whites. What is more irritating about Herrnstein and Murray's work is their assertion that this whole bill of goods is the mainstream position among psychological and educational scholars. Everyone knows, they imply, that we're right; everyone (read, white people) knows that blacks, Latinos and Native Americans are inferior (Chidley 1995; Easterbrook 1995; Kamin 1995; Staples 1995).

The Bell Curve justifies the social and educational abandonment of the poor and non-white

One of the most important (and frightening) aspects of *The Bell Curve* is that its assertion of non-white genetic inferiority is deployed to justify a neofascist political vision. What can we do about the 'reality' of inequality, Herrnstein and Murray ask. Couching their socio-political vision in pastoral and comforting terms, the authors construct a return to simpler times where societies find a place for everyone, with rewards for virtue and punishments of vice, and the police are everyone's (read, white people's) friends. When men and women know their place and accept their biological limitations, we will all enter the 'promised land'. In this neo-feudal society a ruling elite runs things in a way the cognitively inferior can understand. No equality of opportunity exists here; such a reality is too disruptive, too much a threat to the established order. Herrnstein and Murray's cognitive utopia is a land of close-knit neighbourhoods, where those with low IQs come to accept and even love their place in the hierarchy. The authors give absolutely no attention to how this Forrest Gump-friendly world could be established or how Forrest and his low-IQ peers would gain their self-esteem. By following Herrnstein and Murray's lead, the psychotopian society simply ignores the fact that a large percentage of the population, especially the non-white segment, is mentally inept.

The Bell Curve's everyone-knows-and-accepts-their-place psychotopia is not presented gratuitously. The authors carefully build their cognitive argument to justify a political vision that assumes that, since the cognitive dregs of society are beyond help, the best thing government can do is allow the laws of nature and Adam Smith's invisible hand to shape the social order. Such a bold stroke signals the return of social Darwinism and its dogma that any help of the marginalized constitutes a breach of the natural order, the *natural* (read bell curve) distribution of talent. Thus, in the name of the natural order Herrnstein and Murray provide an academic justification for the various neo-nationalist movements: E. D. Hirsch and Allan Bloom's cultural literacy defence of the European school curriculum; the anti-immigration defence of America as a northern European Anglo-Teutonic nation; the patriotic white separatist defence of white rights etc. Indeed, Herrnstein and Murray justify the inequality of present society via intractable biological realities about which we can do absolutely nothing. In this context the powerful can bash blacks and Latinos because we can finally repeat something that the Civil Rights movement and the alleged tyrants of political correctness took away from us: the reality of white supremacy. Finally, the unspeakable can be uttered: the great threat to America is not socio-economic inequality but non-whites with bad attitudes and criminal tendencies who resent the inequality they have to face on a daily basis.

Thus, a neo-essentialist racism is developed that is overt in its talk of racial inferiority and white supremacy but is still covert in its acknowledgment of its own mean-spiritedness and viciousness. Herrnstein and Murray's racism, unlike other essentialist racisms, is wrapped in a language of democracy and social meliorism – we say these things, they argue, because we want to protect the social order and promote the social good. That which is actually protected is the privilege of the predominantly white professional middle class and corporate elite. A power bloc that believes it deserves its privileged position because of its superiority is both dangerous and repugnant. If Herrnstein and Murray's ideology is taken seriously, it will exaggerate the smugness and complacency of the elite while catalysing the despair and hopelessness of the marginalized. In such a social scenario there is a need for controls on those who have lost hope – a need of which Herrnstein and Murray are well aware. To address this need Herrnstein and Murray turn to fascism for help. Stephen Haymes (1996) maintains that fascist social policy demands that groups who need to be controlled must be constructed as an internal threat, an inferior breed that is incapable of competent behaviour. Using this process of pathologization against non-whites, blacks and Latinos are inscribed with a criminality that justifies their repression and the denial of their civil liberties. To protect the social order we must conform to a white norm. Those who are incapable of or refuse such normalization are open game in the world of Herrnstein and Murray (Brimelow 1995; Gardner 1995; Gould 1995; Jones 1995; Kennedy 1995; Ryan 1995; Willis 1995; Apple 1996; Britzman and Pitt 1996; Freire and Macedo 1996; McCarthy *et al.* 1996).

Such inferior individuals are definitely open game in Herrnstein and Murray's educational system. They are the ones who have been allowed by the multiculturalists to precipitate the dumbing down of American education. As the multiculturalists lowered the standards, the group most adversely affected included those unfortunate elite and gifted students who deserve a better education. Genetically inferior poor and non-white students must not be allowed to wreck our educational system, the authors maintain. Advocates of school vouchers and parental choice are naive if they believe that moving inferior students to better schools will improve their education. One imagines Herrnstein and Murray slapping their audience and screaming 'Don't you get it? Nothing is going to change the IQs of such students; the best thing we can do is provide a tightly controlled place for them away from worthy students.' The purpose of education presented in *The Bell Curve* is to restore standards by carefully testing and efficiently sorting the genetically inferior from the genetically superior. In this way the social role of education can be fulfilled; that is, the production of an adequate workforce for American business and industry. Indeed, *The Bell Curve* reflects this educational agenda in that much of the literature used by the authors is taken from studies attempting to produce increasingly efficient tests for forecasting worker productivity – an agenda closely tied to the needs of businesses and corporations. In this context Herrnstein and Murray see their role as protecting private firms from the non-white and poor incompetents who cost businesses as much as $80 billion a year (Herrnstein and Murray's figure). Once again individuals with low IQs constitute the threat to American progress, in this case educational and economic productivity. Never is the question raised that it is possible that what IQ measures is a narrow social, racial and class status – not aptitude or merit. Herrnstein and Murray push on full steam ahead; after all they have scapegoats to construct.

In Herrnstein and Murray's world the concept of justice is conspicuously missing from the realms of education and economics. Corporate need for short-term profits takes precedence over any attempt to integrate ethics and science. Reading *The Bell Curve*, one would never get the sense that America is a democratic nation or that equality is a treasured American value. The authors find silly the proposition that the best education for any student is the best education for every student. The idea that education could be used for something other than adjusting students to the workplace needs of corporate America never enters the realm of possibility for Herrnstein and Murray. A focus on suffering and its causes, a study of the responsibilities of citizenship or an analysis of the meaning of civic courage are not concerns of Herrnstein and Murray's schools. Social criticism, the authors contend along with politicians such as Newt Gingrich, is for losers who are jealous of the success of others. Such an argument employs the same logic as the absurd proposition that feminism is for the ugly girls no one finds desirable. The idea that school might serve as a social location where students from all social and ethnic backgrounds might find empowerment to recognize and act to overcome the forces that shape their lives does not exist in the authors' right-wing, corporatist universe. Indeed, *Bell Curve*-driven schools work to impede rather than foster responsible democratic participation. From our reading of Herrnstein and Murray and their neo-scientific racist compadres, the effort to produce an educated citizenry for democracy, who are capable of analysis, imagination and a keen sense of fairness, is an impediment to the neo-fascist, pseudo-meritocracy they envision.

In these and other ways Herrnstein and Murray's social vision mutates into a yearning for an earlier period in history, an era marked by the legal and economic subordination of non-whites. They look back fondly to a time of racial segregation when non-white 'mental deficients' found a productive place in their low-status, low-paid social roles. *The Bell Curve* proudly takes its place in the tradition of both American racism and in the international eugenics tradition created by the British in the late nineteenth century to control reproduction among the 'inferior' Irish. The British wanted to manage the Irish, who were seen as a threat to Anglo-Saxons with their low intelligence and high birthrate. Americans in the early years of the twentieth century picked up on the British notion of genetic management and contemplated its usage in relation to not only the African American population but the growing numbers of Italians, Asians and especially Jews whom they considered incompetent and oversexed. The British continued their work in eugenics during the first three decades of the century. Led by British psychologist Sir Cyril Burt (whom Herrnstein and Murray revere), IQ advocates preached their racist gospel, winning many converts to the practice of sterilizing the 'genetically inferior'.

So successful was the movement in America that, by the early 1930s, thirty American states had adopted laws requiring the sterilization of individuals from the low end of the bell curve. By the Second World War over 20,000 Americans had undergone mandatory sterilization. It was in Nazi Germany, however, that eugenics reached its highest expression, as the Third Reich sought to create a world in which those at the high end of the bell curve would breed prodigiously and the inferior would not be allowed to perpetuate themselves genetically. After the fall of the Nazis and the discovery of all they had undertaken in the name of eugenics, the belief fell out of public favour. But the proponents of eugenics have kept on working, periodically revealing themselves to public view and then fading once again into obscurity. One of the reasons why *The Bell Curve* demands attention from critical multiculturalists is that its publication represents the re-emergence of eugenics into the mainstream of scientific, political policy and educational discourse. If it weren't so dangerous, it would be humorous to watch Murray after the publication of the book scramble to deny that he and the late Herrnstein support a strategy of eugenics. The dark humour emanates from the fact that practically every page of *The Bell Curve* leads the reader to the acceptance of a eugenics-based political and educational system. Their argument is simple:

1 Blacks and Latinos are less cognitively capable than whites.
2 Such incapability contributes to greater black and Latino crime, poverty,

births out of wedlock, welfare dependency, unemployment, poor work-place performance and injury.

3 Blacks and Latinos breed faster than do whites, thus reducing the average intelligence of Americans.

4 This reduction of national intelligence contributes to the nation's most debilitating social problems.

5 Thus, we must cut off the support for women from these incompetent groups who have babies.

6 We must make available birth control mechanisms for such women that are increasingly foolproof.

7 We must alter our immigration policies to keep such incompetents out of the country (House and Haug 1995; Jones 1995; Judis 1995; Miller 1995; Sautman 1995; Staples 1995; Carspecken 1996; Cary 1996; Giroux and Searles 1996; Lugg 1996; McCarthy *et al.* 1996; Pagano 1996; Tanaka 1996).

Any effort to make life better or more just for these incompetents is seen by Herrnstein, Murray and their supporters as the perpetuation of bad genes. Since blacks, Latinos and poor whites are inferior why give them welfare and perpetuate the inferiority – not to mention waste our money? Since interventions into the lives of the incompetents do more harm than good, the authors maintain that money that funds school programmes aimed at the disadvantaged should be reappropriated for gifted children. In addition the authors call for the end of income support for working elderly people, Medicaid, food stamps, unemployment insurance, worker's compensation, subsidized housing, disability insurance and any other form of aid. All of these cuts are couched in the language of fairness, of what is best for the nation. If all of this sounds familiar, it is not merely accidental. Herrnstein and Murray's programme is very similar to the one pushed by the Republicans in the 1990s – their *Contract With America*. Not only is the spirit of the proposals similar, but Herrnstein and Murray's programme matches much of the Republican contract point for point. There is a good reason for the match, as Murray has functioned for the past decade as an apologist for conservative social policy. His 1984 book, *Losing Ground*, was viewed by many observers as Ronald Reagan's bible and the president and his aides began to refer to Murray as their favourite social scientist. Herrnstein and Murray have both reflected and shaped conservative sentiments, in the process moving them to a new height of popularity and a new depth of mean-spiritedness.

Learning to live with inequality: voodoo education

The point of *The Bell Curve*, its reason for existence, is both easy to ascertain and important for everyone to understand: a natural, biological social hierarchy exists and everyone must recognize and accept his or her place in it because there is nothing we can do about it. In other words, Herrnstein, Murray and their ideological bedmates want humans to learn to live with inequality. In this context *The Bell Curve* seeks to provide order to the revolutionary social changes engendered by our acceptance of inequality. Psychometrics and its IQ tests take on a new importance in the reconceptualized social order, as they provide us with our God-given position in the hierarchy. Such changes will not come easy and Herrnstein and Murray understand that forms of *re-education* must be developed to convince the sceptics of the sanctity of the New Cognitive Order. The success of the order depends on the ability of the re-education to accomplish its task, for the greatest enemy of the new society will be those who refuse to accept their place. Herrnstein and Murray maintain that vestiges of the old order involving advantages for the marginalized must be terminated. Grossly unfair practices such as affirmative action, low-income supplements and extra help for disadvantaged students will be erased from public memory in the New Cognitive Order. The curriculum of the re-education programme will revolve around a basic body of knowledge concerning the existence and nature of the social hierarchy and a series of standardized tests to determine precisely where one fits in it. Those at the low end will cheerfully accept their place as the servants, gardeners and cleaning men and women for the cognitive elite. Because they understand their lowly place and the reduced expectations that accompany it, the cognitive dregs will learn not to charge the elite too much for their services (Gardner 1995; House and Haug 1995; Judis 1995; Kamin 1995; Lind 1995; Reed 1995; Britzman and Pitt 1996; Haymes 1996; Vidal 1996).

Rhetorically, Herrnstein and Murray use *The Bell Curve* as the opening volume in the re-education reading material, as they set up an Us (the cognitive elite) versus Them (the poor and non-white cognitive dregs) dichotomy. As the book progresses, the Us versus Them evolves into an Us-against-them binarism replete with the authors speaking directly to 'Us' – the self-selected elite capable of reading the book. We (Us), Herrnstein and Murray maintain, have friends who are almost exclusively from the top of the bell curve. These cognitively elite individuals are law abiding, dedicated to their work, morally decent and relatively racially and ethically homogeneous (read, almost all white). The 'others' (Them) are untrustworthy, undeserving, undermining our national vitality, absorbing our nation's resources and ruining our traditional moral fabric. Such dichotomizing reads easily to those cognitive elite who bought the book with an Us versus Them mental model already in place. Such readers suspected that the world would work better if the dregs were re-educated to seek happiness in their low status. This 'wise ethnocentrism', as Murray calls it, understands that the real cause of oppression of the poor and non-white involves their attempts to climb the social ladder. Their inevitable failure, the argument continues, destroys their self-esteem by inducing them to judge themselves by the standards of the cognitive elite. In the New Cognitive Order such problems will be solved by re-education's celebration of inequality; that is, its *pacification process*. Special education as it is often practised at the end of the twentieth century attempts such a re-education as it teaches students they are abnormal. Herrnstein and Murray understand the reasoning behind existing special education but argue that re-education can be accomplished much more quickly and cheaply. In their New Cognitive Order funding of special education would be ended simply because it is a waste of time (Marsh 1993; Gardner 1995; Wieseltier 1995; Apple 1996; Lincoln 1996).

To protect themselves from liberal criticism Herrnstein and Murray bemoan the creeping socio-economic stratification that exists in contemporary America – 'crocodile tears for the poor', Phil Carspecken (1996) labels their weeping. Of course, as the last teardrop falls, the authors are busy constructing a New Cognitive Order which makes the status quo look like a Great Society tea party. Despite their expressions of concern, Herrnstein and Murray quickly assume a disdainful and condescending tone towards the people with the low IQs. Tomorrow belongs to the Aryans and *The Bell Curve* wants those best and brightest to feel good about their recovery of America. The authors want the cognitive elite to experience a giddy joy that their children and grandchildren will be blessed with a well funded gifted education. Herrnstein and Murray justify such elite privilege in the same way Ronald Reagan and his cronies in the 1980s and 1990s have defended trickle-down economics: everyone benefits from a well educated cognitive elite. Trickle-down economics is converted into trickle-down education (Jacoby and Glauberman 1995). If presidential candidate George Bush could refer to trickle-down economics as voodoo economics in 1980, might we label trickle-down education with the same moniker? Voodoo education? Herrnstein and Murray's reasoning destroys the hope for a multicultural education and a racially just society. Deploying a form of pseudo-logic, Herrnstein and Murray create an anti-matter Robin Hood who steals from the poor to reward the privileged.

Covert operations: the power of crypto-racism

Despite the seemingly obviousness of white-recovery works such as *The Bell Curve*, Herrnstein and Murray, Dinesh D'Souza, Rush Limbaugh, Pat Buchanan, Bob Dole and many others vociferously deny their racist intent. Murray, speaking to a wide television audience about the book, has from a public relations perspective been relatively successful with the claim that he is not a racist. Thus, we have come to a historical juncture when the claim of black and Latino cognitive inferiority can be made without the taint of a racist label. Obviously, the rules of racial talk have changed, as we enter a so-called post-racist era where the only form of racism left is discrimination directed at whites. Critical multiculturalism's attempt to track mutating forms of racism is analogous to the CDC's (Center for Disease Control's) effort to track the ebola virus with new outbreaks popping up in diverse venues. An important feature of contemporary mutations of racism involves their cryptic nature – thus, it can be described as a crypto-racism (crypto meaning concealed, secret, not visible to the naked eye). Often, such a racist form employs thinly veiled racialized code words that evoke images of white superiority (Nightingale 1993).

Steve Haymes (1995) uncovers the virus and its damage to the public conversation about education concealed in discussions of issues of illiteracy and basic skills with their cryptic identification of non-whites with these problems. The subliminal message conveyed involves the depiction of illiteracy and lack of basic skills as a black and Latino problem so severe that educational resources needed for students who could make good use of them (read white students) are dramatically reduced. Thus, shortfalls in educational funds for middle and upper-middle class white students are not the sins of communities and the political leaders who have cut educational funding in general – such deficits are the direct fault of minority groups. Drawing upon social scientists such as Herrnstein and Murray, white supremists make the argument that such funds are wasted because the non-white and the poor are not capable of profiting from them. The story of white victimization is extended – fuel is added to the fire of white anger. All of this takes place as proponents of such perspectives deny their racism, making claim to a colour blindness relative to social, political and educational policy (Wickham 1995; Giroux and Searles 1996).

Crypto-racism produces a form of double-speak that not only transforms whites into the victims of racism but redefines the word itself. Anti-racism, in this new discourse, becomes racism. References to the existence of racism and the call for its eradication are redefined by crypto-racists as racist practices; that is, 'playing the race card' or 'evoking the tired cries of discrimination'. So pervasive has this neo-racism become that many workers are afraid to make reference to racism on the job. Workers know that merely bringing up issues of race in the workplace can undermine their chances for advancement (Macedo 1994). Crypto-racism has developed a 'proper syntax' of racial reference that involves an encoding manoeuvre that escapes identification as racism. It is a language of white supremacy that constantly denies its racist undercurrent. As it engages in the language of denial, crypto-racism aligns itself with notions of: (a) *common culture*, i.e. all solid citizens hold particular, sacred values and understandings (implicit in the assertion is that many non-whites do not share these values and understandings); (b) *urban troubles*, i.e. the cities present mammoth and unsolvable problems in the late twentieth century (unstated here is the recognition that since urban demographics have changed so fundamentally over the past thirty years – non-whites now constitute the majority of many urban populations – urban troubles can be directly blamed on non-white social pathology); (c) *family values*, i.e. the West is in decline because of the breakdown of family values (the unsaid in this discourse involves reference to the pathology of the non-white, especially the black family); (d) *the epidemics of drugs and violence*, i.e. something must be done to end this attack on communities formulated by unscrupulous drug dealers (the message encoded here involves the connection between drugs and the non-white: drugs and the violence that surrounds them are products of the ghetto, of black and Latino gangs).

What is amazing about the crypto-racist coding of these four assertions is their distortion of the truth. The first assertion concerning common culture assumes that a national culture is grounded on the notion of consensus; that is, all citizens subscribe to an unchanging homogeneous culture characterized by a universally known and accepted core of uniform values. National cultures, especially the American variety, have never been constructed on this level. The second assertion blaming non-whites for urban troubles is consummately misleading. The flight of middle class residents and corporate interests from the inner city has spawned an economic/political/social crisis for the people left behind. The refusal of citizens and politicians to address the problems and needs resulting from the flight has contributed to their hopelessness. Who is at fault here? The third assertion concerning the decline of family values fails to account for the amazing strength of black family structures historically. Regardless of historical context black families have often produced individuals who were equipped to cope with and often transcend violence, poverty and other manifestations of their powerlessness. The fourth assertion, concerning drugs and violence, ignores the sociological data that refute the myth that inner-city non-whites are primarily responsible for drug use and violence. White women are statistically more likely to use and abuse drugs than non-white women – despite the reality that black female drug users are ten times more likely to be reported than white women users. Almost 80 per cent of illegal drug use in America takes place outside of inner-city non-white communities. The prototypical crack addict is a white middle class man between the ages of forty and fifty. At the same time FBI statistics indicate that while the proportion of African Americans arrested for aggravated assault is three times greater than the proportion for whites, the National Crime Survey which studies victims of assault has found black and white aggravated assault statistics to be almost the same. Crypto-racist codes portray a misleading picture of the world (Coontz 1992; Rizvi 1993; Haymes 1995).

Encoded racism well serves the interests of power wielders. Indeed, critical multiculturalists understand that the recovery of white supremacy is in the interests of corporate and political leaders, who still overwhelmingly tend to be white. The economic and political advantages of white recovery were specifically outlined by political analyst Kevin Phillips in his *The New Republican Majority* published in 1969. Phillips understood the power to be derived from exploiting the developing perception of white workers that minority groups were unjustifiably gaining too large a percentage of the economic pie. Struggling to retain corporate profit margins of the 1950s and 1960s, many corporate leaders and their political allies in the USA employed the rhetoric of white recovery to gain the electoral cooperation of their *natural* adversaries, the (in this case white) working class. So strong were the white working class's racial concerns that they were induced to support economic and political policies contrary to their own interests. Employing the crypto-racist codes of welfare, drugs, crime in the streets, family values and the liberal assault on Western/Judaeo-Christian values, right-wing and centrist political candidates began the process of creating favourable business climates with their lower corporate taxes, reduced governmental regulations, lower wages for workers, higher public expenditures for defence-related business contracts etc. (Amott 1993; West 1993).

It is not difficult to trace this political and economic trajectory throughout the last three decades of the twentieth century. Nixon deployed 'busing' as a crypto-racist term as early as 1968. Quickly, the Republican Party became adept at using the language of white male recovery to woo white voters away from the labour-identified Democrats. By no means is this designed to absolve the Democratic Party from complicity in the recovery efforts. Like Thatcher's Conservatives in Britain the Republicans perfected the politics of white recovery using race and gender codes to divert white worker attention from the politics of the workplace. Ronald Reagan with the help of advisors Mike Deaver and Roger Ailes was the master of crypto-racist recovery, with his ability to elicit worker support of a no-tax business policy and government grants to corporations.

Lacking Reagan's charm, George Bush was forced to employ negative black visual imagery such as the picture of rapist Willie Horton in his 1988 campaign TV ads to link the recovery rhetoric to his (Bush's) persona. The racial imagery worked so well that by 1990 North Carolina Republican Senator Jesse Helms's TV ads in his race against a black challenger could make references to minorities taking white working class jobs – all the while denying racist intent. Of course, such references had little to do with reality – job loss in North Carolina involved corporate flight to the Third World. Such flight was made possible by tax incentives passed by the business-friendly Senator Helms and his corporate-financed colleagues in government. The success of such strategies kept raising the racial ante, proving that racial scapegoating works. How far can we go, candidates began to ask.

What are the most effective ways of conveying the codes? By the early 1990s such questions prepared the American political landscape for more radical and daring crypto-racists. David Duke – former essentialist racist Ku Klux Klan and Nazi Party leader – pushed the racist envelop. The work of Nixon, Reagan, Bush and Helms had ploughed the ideological and cultural terrain so as to make it more acceptable to racist seeds; Duke, for example, in a gubernatorial race in Louisiana in 1991 received nearly two-thirds of the white working class vote (Marable 1992). By the middle of the decade the rhetoric of white recovery was a common element in political campaigns in all regions of America. By the late 1990s it has become the working language of politics for both Republicans and Democrats.

Crypto-racism: the hegemonic ideology of white recovery

Returning to our discussion of hegemony in Chapter 4, our understanding of crypto-racism can be extended when it is seen in the light of hegemony and ideology. Hegemony and ideology are inseparable, in that hegemonic power blocs deploy ideologies to help to win the consent of the hegemonized. More specifically, ideology is an ambiguous concept that refers to the ways our ideas, values and beliefs are shaped and the manner in which we incorporate them into our everyday lives, our ways of being in the world (McLaren 1994a). Individuals use ideologies to organize their lived experience, to make sense of their predicaments. This organizational and sense making process is never stable, as it changes from context to context. Thus, the process is contradictory and disjointed, with sometimes bizarre and paradoxical belief structures cohabiting in our consciousness. When hegemonized, the oppressed are induced to buy into ideologies that are not in their best interests; for example, workers who grant their consent to corporate leaders around issues of race are induced to support business policies that ultimately cut employee wages and limit their input into the organization of their work lives. The central form that hegemonic action has taken over the past decades has involved the corporate winning of working people's consent to the politics of racial and corporate recovery. Thus, their private, public and work lives are structured in part by the hegemonic ideologies they internalize.

The way this structuring takes place cannot be separated from the workings of the existing hegemonic ideology. This way of seeing is successful in helping working people to make sense of their lives to the degree that it renders power-driven depictions of the world natural. Crypto-racism naturalizes the relationships that structure racial relations in a way that erases the historical processes that have helped to mould the present social order in general, and existing racial dynamics in particular. In this context we come to believe that the world could only exist in the way that it does today. Our sense of the possibility of a better social order, of racial harmony between people, is undermined. Please do not infer from these descriptions some simple process by which hegemonic ideology is transmitted into the consciousness of white people. Individuals acquire their racist orientations and their connection of these ways of seeing to corporate ideologies not through a simple duplication of the ideas to which they are exposed. The process is one of reception, construction and reconstruction that helps them make sense of, *deal with* and act in their lived worlds. Political depictions of crypto-racist blame of, for example, unqualified minority workers for taking white jobs helps white workers to organize their realities and focus their anger.

Conflicting forms of consciousness in this process are not unusual. Studies indicate that students who sincerely ascribe to tenets of multiculturalism and racial justice are untroubled by patterns of isolation between racially different students, a rhetoric of us (whites) and them (non-whites) and the perception that school values are and should be our (white people's) values. The crypto-racism that is encoded here has been described as 'aversive racism', a liberal form of race consciousness that denies its tendency for discrimination at the same instance it asserts its low opinion of the racially different. These reasonable *paradoxes* are expressed in a common and recognizable rhetorical style: rejection of racism is asserted in preliminary phrase ('I am not a racist but . . . ') followed by the delineation of an explicitly racist characterization ('these Cubans are so pushy and arrogant'). Of course, the ability to identify the various ways racism manifests itself is extremely important for critical multiculturalists. At the same time it is important for such analysts to understand that no matter what guise racism assumes, its structural consequences are similar. Victims of discrimination are marginalized, excluded and denied equal access and treatment by institutions.

Crypto-racism and Hispanics/Latinos

Latinos are profoundly affected by the racist forces we have analysed. Any examination of the relationship among racism, Hispanics/Latinos and education must begin with a recognition of the diversity within the umbrella term Hispanic/Latino. Five principal population groups are represented: Mexican Americans, 63 per cent; Puerto Ricans, 12 per cent; Central and South Americans, 11 per cent; other Hispanics/Latinos, 8 per cent; and Cubans, 5 per cent. Hispanics/Latinos constitute the fastest growing demographic group in the contemporary USA. Over one-third of them are tracked into vocational education, most of the time without any counselling as to the social and educational consequences resulting from such a placement. In Los

Angeles, for example, Mexicans, Salvadorans and Guatemalans struggle in school and in the job market. When Latinos find jobs, they will on the average make 53 cents for every dollar earned by white males. Hispanic/Latino students are victimized by crypto-racist educational practices that are represented as anti-racist, multicultural and equal-opportunity oriented. Though couched in the language of democracy, these practices exclude Hispanic/Latino students from honours and higher-level programmes, making them more likely to drop out or be enrolled below grade level and less likely to attend post-secondary programmes than any ethnic/racial group in America. Given the proliferation of these ostensibly helpful programmes, Hispanic/Latino students have lost educational ground in respect of measurements such as rates of high school graduation over the past three decades (Rendon and Nora 1991; Perez 1993; McLaren 1994a).

Rarely do educators set out to impede the educational progress of Hispanic/Latino students – crypto-racism simply does not work that way. Vocational counsellors do not think, 'Oh, here's a Salvadoran; I'm going to put him in metal work in the vocational department.' The process is much more complex, but the dynamics of social regulation of the poor and non-white do come into play. Studies indicate that minority students and/or their parents often have little input into curricular track placement. Counsellors and teachers take responsibility for these decisions, typically basing their judgements on the student's grades and test scores. Interpretation of test scores rarely takes into account the fact that many Hispanic/Latino students employ English as a second language. For the large number of Hispanic/Latino students who are recent immigrants, testing takes place long before students have had an opportunity to integrate themselves into North American life. Decontextualized assessment procedures fail to account for these and other mitigating factors, guaranteeing unmediated placements of Hispanic/Latino students into low-ability tracks on the basis of their understandably low scores.

Before they realize it many Hispanic/Latino students find themselves being trained for low-pay, low-status jobs traditionally held by the poor and non-white. The process is perpetuated year after year by counsellors operating within the modernist blinders of their profession, grounding their counselling activity with crypto-codes such as the 'cultural deficiency' of Hispanic/Latino students. Given such a degraded situation, the only realistic form of vocational counselling must involve lowering illusory professional aspirations and in the process inducing them into a curricular track that prepares such students for low-status roles commensurate with their talents (or lack thereof) (Oakes 1985; Banfield 1991; McLaren 1994a). In his historical contextualization of such unjust practices, Clinton Allison (1995) describes the historical reactions of educators to poor, minority and immigrant parents who refused to accept teachers' descriptions of their children's cognitive/academic limitations. Throughout the twentieth century educators have looked contemptuously at parents who failed to recognize 'scientifically validated' assessments of their children's limited aptitudes. Educators understood that one of the most important aspects of their professional role was to dispel poor and minority parents of their delusional hopes of upward mobility eventuating in professional careers for their children.

Critical educator Donaldo Macedo (1994), entering the Boston public schools with Portuguese as his first language, describes his encounter with a vocational guidance counsellor. Though Macedo's interest had nothing to do with the job, his counsellor advised him to become a TV repairman. As one who was pushed by his high school guidance counsellor to become a piano tuner (a vocation in which he had absolutely no interest), Joe Kincheloe can empathize with Macedo and the tens of thousands of Hispanic/Latino students whose counsellors relegate them to an educational track based on encoded perceptions of them as incapable students. Donna Gaines describes an all-too-common encounter between a marginalized student and the vocational counsellor:

'So, Roy, what do you see yourself doing five years from now?' And Roy is thinking what did I do wrong, what does she want me to say, what is going to come down on me now? And then the guidance counselor will say something about Roy's lack of spectacular grades – 'not on any teams or in any clubs, are you, Roy?' And Roy starts feeling stupid and maybe he fiddles with himself nervously and says the first thing that comes to his head, like how much he enjoys working on this car. Like she shouldn't think he's a total loser. And that's that! He's never really given much thought before now, but today, the future is laid out before him and now Roy's going to vocational high school and he's going to learn about cars.

(Gaines 1990: 145–6)

Latinas, of course, face special forms of cryptic encodement, as literature and media depict them as powerless and sometimes pathological. As subjugated, subservient, loyal daughters, wives and mothers, they are blamed for their own victimization. They are portrayed as unresistant to their positioning as sex objects and befrilled consorts with a proclivity to excessive praying. Obviously, teachers and counsellors need to understand these cryptic codes and reformulate their teaching and counselling to address them. Critical multiculturalists must help Latinas to learn to confront such ethnic encoding by developing strategies of resistance. Latinas and their teachers and counsellors must insist that they: not be excluded from academic courses; be provided access to programmes that teach them about career and life options that are available and the curricula necessary for access to them; understand the power and ethnic dynamics that force them into dead-end careers and life choices. Schools at various levels need to connect these racial, ethnic and cultural appreciations into educational curricula, building, when and where needed, centres designed to help all marginalized people (Latina students in particular) to cope with the unnerving stress, role conflicts, financial problems and crypto-racism that they will inevitably face in contemporary society. Such centres might specifically provide such services as child care, apprenticeships with Latina workers, mathematics anxiety reduction classes, economics education seminars, financial aid and community empowerment programmes (Rendon and Nora 1991).

The racial polarization of wealth

In Western societies whites and non-whites grow further and further apart both spatially and economically. A resegregation process is occurring, in part because many white people seem to feel more comfortable when non-whites are not around. The most important force promoting this segregation involves the growing disparity of wealth between different racial groups. Again, race intersects with class, producing outlandish inequities in terms of material well-being. White people who claim to be the victims of racial preferences in hiring and other forms of special privilege for blacks and other non-whites should consider these economic realities: the net worth of the average white family is $46,706 compared to the average black family's $4,054; a white female-headed family has an average wealth of $26,853 compared to a *black married couple* family's average holdings of $15,588. The great redistribution of power and wealth that conservatives insist took place over the past thirty years between whites and non-whites simply never happened (Cotton 1992). Minority children, of course, are hardest hit by this disparity of wealth, as almost half of all black children are poor as compared to one in six white children. Black children who live in homes with two parents are twice as likely as white children in the same familial arrangement to live below the poverty line. The unemployment rate for black high school graduates is 25 per cent higher than is the rate for white students who dropped out of high school. In some urban areas the drop out rate for non-white students is seventy per cent (McLaren 1994a; Giroux 1997a).

Right-wing commentators, as we have noted, ascribe the cause of this disparity to the incompetence or even genetic inferiority of non-white peoples. They fail to take into account social environmental issues such as access to jobs, cultural capital, family resources and influence, corporate job migration to low-wage developing countries, the decline of unions and the vilification of non-whites and the white fear that accompanies it. People are less likely to support individuals in need if they are scared of them. In the light of these issues, take, for example, the right-wing representation of Asians as the model minority: they score high on IQ tests, perform well in schools on average and in the minds of many white people make good citizens. If intelligence and strong academic performance are rewarded in Western meritocracies and people are poor because of their lack of ability, then why do Asians have substantially lower incomes than whites? Many Asians living in Western societies are quite poor, with little access to linguistically appropriate voter assistance, health care or job counselling and training. A large percentage of Asians live in crumbling substandard housing projects and send their children to run-down, underfunded schools. Asians in Western societies experience these hardships because of racism – viewed as outsiders who are different, they suffer many of the institutional/structural exclusions experienced by other non-whites (Chon 1995; Judis 1995; Raspberry 1995).

In the USA students from different races consistently experience different levels of funding for the schools they attend. Since schools are financed by property taxes and state revenues, and since some states and school districts are much more wealthy than others, poor areas receive much less school funding than wealthy areas. Minority groups tend, of course, to live in poor areas – once again the deadly intersection of class and race. Unfortunately, it is an intersection that assures that black, Latino and Native American children are underserved by American schools. Only about one in three students who don't speak English or have English deficiencies have access to any form of linguistic assistance; only one in ten Hispanic/Latino students with limited English proficiencies are enrolled in bilingual programmes. Equally harmful are the psychic wounds such students experience when they are induced by the culture of the school to reject their cultural and home identities. Black students are taught to give up their personal forms of peer interaction and interpersonal give and take – to act more 'white'. Proper academic behaviour is continuously defined in white terms, relegating any 'ethnic' behaviour to the realm of inappropriateness.

Mismatch: non-white students in white schools

Classroom researchers find that black and Latino students in elementary and secondary schools are too often ignored. When they are noticed, researchers find that they are misidentified for special intervention programmes, misassessed as mentally retarded or behaviourally disturbed, misplaced in special education classes and misinstructed on the assumption they are incapable. In these contexts school does little more than educate for failure. Many teachers, having been raised and acculturated in white, middle class homes, schools and neighbourhoods, have difficulty understanding the cultural capital, the ethical values and the symbols and signifiers that black and Latino students bring to their classrooms. After Spike Lee's *Malcolm X* was released, for example, many black students wore X-caps to school. Many teachers failed to understand the caps other than as a mere fashion statement or a vague reference to Malcolm via Lee's movie. They missed the dramatic significance of the 'X' signifier in African American history, the reference to the white-directed legal erasure/unnaming of Americans of African descent. What a compelling unit of study the X-cap could have initiated, with historical analysis of African American names, the etymology of the 'X', the biography of Malcolm, his relation to other black leaders of his day and the meaning of his legacy in both African American and American history (Obiakor 1992; Baker 1993; McLaren 1994b).

Without special attention to the racial dynamics of a critical multiculturalism too many teachers continue to misunderstand their non-white students. Educational anthropologist Rosalie Wax tells a fascinating story about white misunderstanding of Native Americans. White teachers on Indian reservations have complained for decades about the dirty appearance of their Native American students. 'Their parents just don't care enough about their children to clean them up for school – Indian parents are lazy and don't care about their children's learning,' they argued. As Wax and her colleagues began their research on reservation schools, they got out of bed at 6 a.m., washed, brushed and groomed themselves vigorously. No matter how hard they tried, Wax reported, they could never get themselves to look presentable in a middle class way. The prairie dust was everywhere, blanketing both their clothes and their toilet articles. The researchers had no closets in which to protect their clothes, no irons, no clean water, no hot water for shaving, no mirrors etc. Wax reported that the attempt to present a middle class appearance exhausted the researchers. Most teachers who work on the reservation had not experienced living without particular conveniences, living for the most part off the reservation or in on-reservation teacher houses equipped with such middle class accoutrements. Such teachers lacked the experiential background to understand emotionally why many of their Indian students and parents looked the way they did (Wax 1971). This experiential gap between teacher and student plays itself out daily in Native American and other non-white contexts. Critical multiculturalists insist that teachers must gain both academic and experiential understandings of racism and various ethnic experiences, including, of course, an appreciation of whiteness as an ethnicity.

As black, Latino and indigenous students enter the school, they often experience an alien culture in which they don't fit. Their experiences are rarely taken into account in the activities and assignments they are induced to complete. Students who live outside the white mainstream are asked to learn to read and write about culturally unfamiliar topics and abide by behavioural rules that often seem alien to them. A two-fold silencing process occurs in these cultural mismatch situations: the first involves the loss of voice of those culturally different from the unnamed white school culture; the second involves the silencing of any discussion or naming of racism within the school. Schools are not good places to engage in a conversation about the effects of racism on the egalitarian, democratic purposes of education. Like many other 'dangerous' topics, racism is expelled from the curriculum on the grounds that it is divisive and demoralizing – the inclusion of racism as an object of school study, many school leaders argue, would provide non-white students with an excuse not to try. In such a culturally hostile circumstance is it any wonder that many non-white students resent attempts to induce them to absorb information and values that they consider suspect, of little worth and contrary to their own? Is it hard to understand why they would reject trying because working hard at school often appears to their peers as an abandonment of the values of the racial/ethnic group – as turning white? Such issues are dramatically important but to raise them and suggest ways of dealing with them at the end of the twentieth century is to face accusations by conservatives of politicizing the curriculum. In this context political neutrality is framed as maintaining the silence (Gomez 1992; Williams 1993; Merleman 1994).

eight

SO PURELY WHITE . . . WHITENESS IN CRITICAL MULTICULTURALISM

Critical multiculturalists believe that systems of domination and subordination work to racialize everyone, regardless of social location. As racialized subjects, we take our places in the social web, constantly dealing with the effects of our racial privilege and/or oppression. In conservative and liberal varieties of multiculturalism, analysts believe that only non-whites are racialized, in the process ignoring the way whiteness as an ethnicity shapes the way white people interact with and interpret the world. Indeed, whiteness shapes lives in complex and contradictory ways, depending – as does any racial position – on the way it intersects with the power axes of class, gender and a plethora of other forces. Obviously, some white people challenge racism, while others draw upon white supremist logics in making sense of the world and their own lives. Confronting racism is not a matter of choice for white people, critical multiculturalists maintain, for it is a force that shapes their experience and identities whether they like it or not. In this context whiteness may be considered a standpoint, a location in the web of reality from which white people view themselves and racial others. Whites constitute a dominant group who deserve scrutiny around issues of their privilege and their complicity in domination.

Individuals cannot separate where they stand in the web of reality from what they perceive. In contemporary critical social theory this statement lays the foundation for the concept of 'positionality'. Positionality involves the notion that since our understanding of the world and ourselves is socially constructed, we must devote special attention to the differing ways individuals from diverse social backgrounds construct knowledge and make meaning. Critical multiculturalists, thus, are fervently concerned with white positionality. In this context they examine the various ways that social forces, including language, knowledge and ideology, shape white identity in contemporary American life. Drawing upon a critical educational tradition that is dedicated to an analysis of the construction of 'self', critical scholars hope to help readers to rethink the construction of the white self and the social, moral and political implications of such an act at the end of the twentieth century (Carby 1992; Frankenberg 1993; McMillen 1995).

Even though no one at this point really knows what whiteness is, most observers agree that it is intimately involved with issues of power and power differences between white and non-white people. Whiteness cannot be separated from hegemony and is profoundly influenced by demographic changes, political realignments and economic cycles. Situationally specific, whiteness is always shifting, always reinscribing itself around changing meanings of race in the larger society. As with race in general, whiteness holds material/economic implications – indeed, white supremacy has its financial rewards. The Federal Housing Administration, for example, has traditionally favoured housing loans for white suburbs instead of 'ethnic' inner cities. Banks have ensured that blacks have severely limited access to property ownership and capital acquisition compared to whites. Unions over the decades following the Second World War ignored the struggle for full employment and universal medical care, opting for contracts that provided private medical coverage, pensions and job security to predominantly white organized workers in mass production industries. Undoubtedly, there continue to be unearned wages of whiteness. Indeed, critical multiculturalists understand that questions of whiteness permeate almost every major issue facing Westerners at the end of the twentieth century, from affirmative action, intelligence testing and the deterioration of public space, to the growing disparity of wealth. In this context the study of whiteness becomes a central feature of any critical pedagogy or multicultural education for the twenty-first century (Fiske 1994; Gallagher 1994; Keating 1995; Nakayama and Krizek 1995; Yudice 1995).

In the context of multicultural education the study of whiteness is used to ground a pedagogy of whiteness, a form of teaching that engages students in an examination of the social, political and psychological dimensions of membership in a racial group. Our critical imperative demands that such an examination be considered in relation to power and the ideological dynamics of white supremacy. As we develop a pedagogy of whiteness for a critical multiculturalism in this chapter we will focus our efforts on three general tasks: (a) understanding the positionality of whiteness; (b) identifying and abandoning the practice of white racism; and (c) developing a critical and progressive white identity. Such a pedagogy is possible only if we understand in great specificity the multiple meanings of whiteness and their effects on the way white people's consciousness is historically structured and socially inscribed. Without such appreciations and the meta-consciousness they ground, awareness of the privilege and dominance of white Northern European vantage points is buried in the cemetery of power evasion. Our understanding that race is not biological but social or that racial classifications have inflicted pain and suffering on non-whites should not move us to reject the necessity of new forms of racial analysis.

The white privilege of universalizing its characteristics as the 'proper ways to be' has continuously undermined the efforts of non-whites in a variety of spheres. At times such universal norms have produced self-loathing among individual members of minority groups, as they internalize the shibboleths of the white tradition – 'I wish my eyes were blue and my hair blond and silky.' Invisible white norms in these cases alienate non-whites to the point that they sometimes come to live 'outside themselves'. A pedagogy of whiteness reveals such power-related processes to both whites and non-whites alike, exposing how members of both these groups are stripped of self-knowledge. As whites, white students in particular, come to see themselves through the eyes of blacks, Latinos, Asians and indigenous peoples, they begin to move away from the conservative constructions of the dominant culture. Such an encounter with minority perspectives moves many white individuals to rethink their tendency to dismiss the continued existence of racism and embrace the belief that racial inequality results from unequal abilities among racial groups. The effects of a critical pedagogy of whiteness can be powerfully emancipatory (Frankenberg 1993; Tatum 1994; Alcoff 1995; Sleeter 1995).

White reason: the colonial power of whiteness

While no one knows exactly what constitutes whiteness, we can historicize the concept and offer some general statements about the dynamics it signifies. Even this process is difficult, as whiteness as a socio-historical construct is constantly shifting in the light of new circumstances and changing interactions with various manifestations of power. With these qualifications in mind we believe that a dominant impulse of whiteness took shape around the European Enlightenment's notion of rationality, with its privileged construction of a transcendental white, male, rational subject who operated at the recesses of power while concurrently giving every indication that he escaped the confines of time and space. In this context whiteness was naturalized as a universal entity that operated as more than a mere ethnic positionality emerging from a particular time, the late seventeenth and eighteenth centuries and a particular space, Western Europe. Reason in this historical configuration is whitened and human nature itself is grounded upon this reasoning capacity. Lost in the defining process is the socially constructed nature of reason itself, not to mention its emergence as a signifier of whiteness. Thus, in its rationalistic womb whiteness begins to establish itself as a norm that represents an authoritative, delimited and hierarchical mode of thought. In the emerging colonial contexts in which whites would increasingly find themselves in the decades and centuries following the Enlightenment, the encounter with non-whiteness would be framed in rationalistic terms – whiteness representing orderliness, rationality and self-control, and non-whiteness as chaos, irrationality, violence and the breakdown of self-regulation. Rationality emerged as the conceptual base around which civilization and savagery could be delineated (Giroux 1992; Alcoff 1995; Keating 1995).

This rationalistic modernist whiteness is shaped and confirmed by its close association with science. As a scientific construct whiteness privileges mind over body, intellectual over experiential ways of knowing, mental abstractions over passion, bodily sensations and tactile understanding. In the study of multicultural education such epistemological tendencies take on dramatic importance. In educators' efforts to understand the forces that drive the curriculum and the purposes of Western education, modernist whiteness is a central player. The insight it provides into the social construction of schooling, intelligence and the disciplines of psychology and educational psychology in general opens a gateway into white consciousness and its reactions to the world around it. Objectivity and masculinity as signs of stability and the highest expression of white achievement still work to construct everyday life and social relations at the end of the twentieth century. Because such dynamics have been naturalized and universalized, whiteness assumes an invisible power, unlike previous forms of domination in human history. Such an invisible power can be deployed by those individuals and groups who are able to identify themselves within the boundaries of reason and to project irrationality, sensuality and spontaneity on to the other.

Thus, European ethnic groups such as the Irish in nineteenth-century industrializing America were able to differentiate themselves from passionate ethnic groups who were supposedly unable to regulate their own emotional predispositions and gain a rational and objective view of the world. Such peoples – who were being colonized, exploited, enslaved and eliminated by Europeans during their Enlightenment and post-Enlightenment eras – were viewed as irrational and, thus, inferior in their status as human beings. As inferior beings, they had no claim to the same rights as Europeans – hence, white racism and colonialism were morally justified around the conflation of whiteness and reason. In order for whiteness to place itself in the privileged seat of rationality and superiority, it would have to construct pervasive portraits of non-whites, Africans in particular, as irrational, disorderly and prone to uncivilized behaviour (Alcoff 1995; Nakayama and Krizek 1995; Haymes 1996; Stowe 1996). As a rock of rationality in a sea of chaos and disorder, whiteness presented itself as a non-coloured, non-blemished pure category. Even a mere drop of non-white blood was enough historically to relegate a person to the category of 'coloured'. Being white, thus, meant possessing the privilege of being uncontaminated by any other blood line. A mixed race child in this context has often been rejected by the white side of his or her heritage – the rhetorical construct of race purity demands that the mixed race individual be identified by allusion to the non-white group; for example, she's half Latina or half Chinese. Individuals are rarely half white.

As Michel Foucault often argued, reason is a form of disciplinary power. Around Foucault's axiom, critical multiculturalists contend that reason can never be separated from power. Those without reason defined in the Western scientific way are excluded from power and are relegated to the position of unreasonable other. Whites in their racial purity understood the dictates of the 'white man's burden' and became the beneficent teachers of the barbarians. To Western eyes the contrast between white and non-white culture was stark: reason as opposed to ignorance; scientific knowledge instead of indigenous knowledge; philosophies of mind versus folk psychologies; religious truth in lieu of primitive superstition; and professional history as opposed to oral mythologies. Thus, rationality was inscribed in a variety of hierarchical relations between European colonizers and their colonies early on and between Western multinationals and their 'underdeveloped' markets in later days. Such power relations were erased by the white claim of cultural neutrality around the transhistorical norm of reason – in this construction rationality was not assumed to be the intellectual commodity of any specific culture. Indeed, colonial hierarchies immersed in exploitation were justified around the interplay of pure whiteness, impure non-whiteness and neutral reason.

Traditional colonialism was grounded on colonialized people's deviation from the norm of rationality, thus making colonization a rational response to inequality. In the twentieth century this white norm of rationality was extended to the economic sphere, where the philosophy of the free market and exchange values were universalized into signifiers of civilization. Once all the nations on earth are drawn into the white reason of the market economy, then all land can be subdivided into real estate, all human beings' worth can be monetarily calculated, values of abstract individualism and financial success can be embraced by every community in every country and education can be reformulated around the cultivation of human capital. When these dynamics come to pass, the white millennium will have commenced – white power will have been consolidated around land and money. The Western ability to regulate diverse peoples through their inclusion in data banks filled with information about their credit histories, institutional affiliations, psychological 'health', academic credentials, work experiences and family backgrounds will reach unprecedented levels. The accomplishment of this ultimate global colonial task will mark the end of white history in the familiar end-of-history parlance. This does not mean that white supremacy ends, but that it has produced a hegemony so seamless that the need for further structural or ideological change becomes unnecessary. The science, reason and technology of white culture will have achieved their inevitable triumph (Giroux 1992; MacCannell 1992; Alcoff 1995; Nakayama and Krizek 1995).

Whatever the complexity of the concept whiteness, at least one feature is discernible – whiteness cannot escape the materiality of its history, its effects on the everyday lives of those who fall outside its conceptual net as well as on white people themselves. This chapter – indeed, scholarship on whiteness in general – should focus attention on the documentation of such effects. Whiteness study in a critical multicultural educational context should delineate the various ways such material effects shape cultural and institutional pedagogies and position individuals in relation to the power of white reason. Understanding these dynamics is central to the curricula of black studies, Chicano studies, post-colonialism and indigenous studies, not to mention educational reform movements in elementary, secondary and higher education. The history of the world's diverse peoples in general as well as minority groups in Western societies in particular has often been told from a white historiographical perspective. Such accounts erased the values, epistemologies and belief systems that grounded the cultural practices of diverse peoples. Without such cultural grounding students have often been unable to appreciate the manifestations of brilliance displayed by non-white cultural groups. Caught in the white interpretive filter they were unable to make sense of diverse historical and contemporary cultural productions as anything other than proof of white historical success. The fact that one of the most important themes of the last half of the twentieth century – the revolt of the 'irrationals' against white historical domination – has not been presented as a salient part of the white (or non-white) story is revealing, a testimony to the continuing power of whiteness and its concurrent fragility (Banfield 1991; Vattimo 1991; Frankenberg 1993; Stowe 1996).

What's white? Whiteness as a social construction

As with any racial category, whiteness is a social construction in that it can be invented, lived, analysed, modified and discarded. While Western reason is a crucial dynamic associated with whiteness over the past three centuries, there are many other social forces that sometimes work to construct its meaning. Whiteness, thus, is not an unchanging, fixed, biological category impervious to its cultural, economic, political and psychological context. There are many ways to be white, as whiteness interacts with class, gender and a range of other race-related and cultural dynamics. The ephemeral nature of whiteness as a social construction begins to reveal itself when we understand that the Irish, Italians and Jews have all been viewed as non-white in particular places at specific moments in history. Indeed, Europeans prior to the late 1600s did not use the label black to refer to any race of people, Africans included. Only after the racialization of slavery by around 1680 did whiteness and blackness come to represent racial categories. Only at this historical juncture did the concept of a discrete white race begin to take shape. Slowly in the eighteenth and nineteenth centuries the association with rationality and orderliness developed and in this context whiteness came to signify an elite racial group. Viewed as a position of power, white identity was often sought by those who did not possess it. Immigrant workers in the new American industrial workplaces of the mid-nineteenth century from Southern and Eastern Europe aspired to and eventually procured whiteness, viewing its status as payment for the exploitation of their labour. Such shifts in the nature and boundaries of whiteness continued into the twentieth century. One of the reasons why whiteness has become an object of analysis in the 1990s and is included in this book revolves around the profound shifts in the construction of whiteness, blackness and other racial identities that have taken place in the last years of the twentieth century.

How are students and other individuals to make sense of the assertion that whiteness is a social construction? How does such a concept inform the democratic goals of a critical multiculturalism? These questions form the conceptual basis of our discussion of whiteness, our attempt to construct a pedagogy of whiteness. In order to answer them in a manner that is helpful for whites and other racial groups, it is important to focus on the nature of the social construction process. In this context John Fiske's notion of a power bloc is once again helpful. The discourses that shape whiteness are not unified and singular but diverse and contradictory. If one is looking for logical consistency from the social construction of whiteness, one is not going to find it. The discursive construction of whiteness, like the work of any power bloc, aligns and dealigns itself around particular issues of race. For example, the discourse of white victimization that has emerged over the past two decades appears in response to particular historical moments, such as the attempt to compensate for the oppression of non-whites through preferential hiring and admissions policies. The future of such policies will help to shape the discourses that will realign to structure whiteness in the twenty-first century. These discourses, of course, hold profound material consequences for Western cultures, as they fashion and refashion power relations between differing social groups. Any pedagogy of critical multiculturalism or of whiteness itself involves engaging students in a rigorous tracking of this construction process. Such an operation, when informed by critical notions of social justice, community and democracy, allows individuals insights into the inner workings of racialization, identity formation and the etymology of racism. In the fashion of a critical multiculturalism students and teachers are empowered by such knowledge. Armed with such understandings, they gain the ability to challenge and rethink whiteness around issues of racism and privilege. In this context questions about a white student's own identity begin to arise (Gallagher 1994; Keating 1995; McMillen 1995; Nakayama and Krizek 1995).

Such questioning and renegotiating induce us to consider whiteness in relation to other social forces – non-whiteness in particular. Stephen Haymes (1996) argues that to understand racial identity formation, we need to appreciate the way white is discursively represented as the polar opposite of black – a reflection of the Western tendency to privilege one concept in a binary opposition to another. The darkness–light, angel–devil discursive binarism – like other discursive constructions – has reproduced itself in the establishment of racial and ethnic categories. Through its relationship with blackness, whiteness configured itself as different, as not enslaved, as powerful, as aligned with destiny. In this bizarre manner blackness or Africanness empowered whiteness to gain self-consciousness, often via the racist depiction of the other. Such representations affirm the superiority and power of whiteness: again, its rationality, productivity and orderliness *vis-à-vis* the chaos, laziness and primitiveness of Africans and other non-whites. Through their relation with Africanism, whites gained knowledge of themselves as the racial barometer by which other groups were measured. Yet, in our understanding of the diversity within whiteness, this knowledge has meant more to some whites than to others. Historically, poor whites have undoubtedly reaped the psychological wages of whiteness, but talk of white economic privilege in the late twentieth century leaves them with a feeling of puzzlement increasingly expressed as anger. Thus, to speak of white privilege unproblematically in a pedagogy of whiteness ignores the reality of diversity in whiteness. The critical multiculturalist axiom appears once more: we must examine racial matters in relation to other social factors – class in particular (Morrison 1993; Fiske 1994; Keating 1995).

Avoiding essentialism: the instability of whiteness

Diversity in whiteness demands our attention. Critical multiculturalists must carefully attend to the subtle but crucial distinction between whiteness with its power to signify and white people. The diversity among white people makes sweeping generalizations about them dangerous and highly counterproductive to the goals of a critical pedagogy of whiteness. Whiteness study must be maintained in the critical multicultural paradigm – it must not be allowed to escape into an essentialist multiculturalism that reduces analysis to the romantic delineation of good Africans/Native Americans and bad whites. Indeed, it is not contradictory to argue that whiteness is a marker of privilege but all white people are not able to take advantage of that privilege. It is difficult to convince a working class white student of the ubiquity of white privilege when he or she is going to school, accumulating school debts, working at McDonald's for minimum wage and unable to get married because of financial stress and holds little hope of upward socio-economic mobility. The lived experiences and anxieties of such individuals cannot be dismissed in a pedagogy of whiteness.

How, then, in the study and teaching of whiteness do we avoid essentializing white people as privileged, rationalistic, emotionally alienated people? Understanding the social/discursive construction of whiteness, students of whiteness refuse to search for its essential nature or its authentic core. Instead, critical multiculturalists study the social, historical, rhetorical and discursive context of whiteness, mapping the ways it makes itself visible and invisible, manifests its power and shapes larger socio-political structures in relation to the micro-dynamics of everyday life. This, of course, is no easy task – indeed, it should keep us busy for a while. Its complexity and its recognition of ambiguity are central to the project's success. Since there is no fixed essence of whiteness, different white people can debate both the meaning of whiteness in general and its meaning in their own lives. Critical multiculturalists believe that such debates should take place in the context of racial history and analyses of power asymmetries in order to gain more than a superficial acquaintance with the issues. Nevertheless, diversity in whiteness is a fact of life, as various white people negotiate their relationship to whiteness in different ways. Yet whiteness scholarship to this point has sometimes failed to recognize that its greatest problem is the lapse into essentialism.

In its most essentialistic manifestations whiteness study has operated under the assumption that racial categories were permanent and fixed. In their attempt to deconstruct race in this context, essentialistic whiteness scholars tend to reinscribe the fixity of racial difference. The pessimism emerging here is constructed by a form of racial determinism – white people will act in white ways because they are 'just that way'. A critical pedagogy of whiteness understands the contingency of the connection between rationalistic modernist whiteness and the actions of people with light-coloured skin. The same, of course, is true with people with dark coloured skin – they may not 'act black'. They may even 'act white'. Such anti-essentialistic appreciations are central to whiteness study in critical multiculturalism, as scholars historically contextualize their contemporary insights with references to the traditional confusion over racial delineations. Throughout US history, for example, many federal and state agencies used only three racial categories: white, negro and Indian. Who fit where? How were Latinos to be classified? What about Asians? Originally, the state of California classified Mexicans as white and Chinese as Indian. Later Chinese Americans were grouped as Orientals, then Asians, then Pan Asians and then Asian Pacific Americans. Analysis of such categorization indicates both the slipperiness of racial grouping and the American attempt to force heterogeneous racial configurations into a single category around similarities in skin tone, hair texture and eye shape. Such biological criteria simply don't work in any logically consistent manner, thus frustrating the state's regulatory efforts to impose a rationalistic racial order (Fiske 1994; Gallagher 1994; Rubin 1994; Keating 1995).

Thus, critical multiculturalists in their formulation of a pedagogy of whiteness refuse to use race as an essentialist grounding of identity, since it is not a natural category. Not only is race an unnatural category, but its cultural boundaries are constantly negotiated and transgressed as individuals engage the forces and discourses that shape them. If we are not careful when using race as a social category, we can reify the perceived differences between black and white and lose sight of the cultural hybridity we all share. When teaching about whiteness we need always to view the concept in historical context, keeping in mind the situationally specific nature of the term. Our emphasis should continuously revolve around rewriting racial identity, as we point out the inaccuracies embedded in present racial configurations. Such an emphasis undermines fixed notions of racial identity that separate peoples from various racial and ethnic backgrounds. Identity politics grounded on such fixed positions have often supported a form of authority garnered from membership in subordinated groups. This privilege derived from oppression assumes that particular forms of analysis can be spoken only by individuals who share a specific identity. In this essentialist cosmos it is inappropriate for a white man ever to criticize a black man, a Jew ever to disagree with a lesbian Latina. Such politics quickly destroy any solidarity among individuals from a variety of groups who want to pursue an egalitarian, democratic vision.

If we are unable to get beyond these fixed definitions of black and white identity, a pedagogy of whiteness in particular and multicultural education in general may construct impressions that racism is an inevitable feature of the human condition. Thus, the question emerges: can the multicultural analysis of racialized identities such as whiteness serve a democratic outcome? Critical multiculturalists take the question seriously, even though they strongly believe that such analysis is necessary in a multiracial, multicultural society. They take the question seriously because they have too often seen the divisive outcomes of essentialist forms of identity politics. The question induces us to scan carefully the cultural landscape for the negative consequences of multicultural analysis, learning in the process to recognize and anticipate the unexpected problems such activities may help to create. The meaning of whiteness in late twentieth-century societies is volatile. As such, a pedagogy of whiteness must walk a tightrope between racial essentialism on one side and a liberal colour-blindness on the other. Critical multiculturalists understand that the only antidote to racial essentialism is not a fatuous embrace of racial erasure. They embrace a middle ground position that, first, explores the socially constructed, artificial, ephemeral nature of racial identities and, second, carefully traces the all-too-real effects of such identities.

As such a pedagogy separates whiteness from white people, it understands the changing meaning of whiteness for young working class whites. In this context it analyses such individuals' view of themselves as racial victims and their resulting efforts to build an emotional community around their whiteness. Here critical multiculturalists explore the sobering consequences such tendencies may hold for twenty-first century race relations. Ever aware of the ambiguities of whiteness, a critical pedagogy of whiteness appreciates the plight and pain of the young white working class while concurrently exposing the ways whiteness developed in such a context works to hide racial forms of socio-political and economic inequality. In the global culture of hyperreality with its increasingly dynamic forms of hybrid identities, the critical work of tracing these constructions of self *vis-à-vis* group becomes progressively more difficult. As hope of finding discrete bounded notions of self fades, so too do traditional sociological and educational methodologies of inquiry, with their antiquated assumptions of national, occupational and kinship-directed identity. In the postmodern condition individuals must wear several identities, as they travel in and out of multiple cultural locales. Gone is the memory of 'genuine cultures' who pass along their mores and folkways unchanged to the next generation. In this configuration the Scots would still wear kilts and the Sioux their warbonnets. In this new, more complex world critical multiculturalists understand the need to refigure racial analysis and identity formation after the crutch and safety of essentialism is removed (Gallagher 1994; Luke 1994; Keating 1995; Thompson 1996; Wellman 1996).

Whiteness is the norm

The reason why the study of whiteness has become so important at the end of the twentieth century is that so few white people have seen a problem with it over the past couple of decades. As a common-sense norm, whiteness – like all hegemonic impulses – is able to represent itself as conventional and safe. Such normality is delineated by what it is not: in this case, blackness. The common-sense norm aspect of whiteness is what is typically erased in the minds of white and non-white people. Thus, whiteness operates as an invisible norm; this does not mean that whiteness as a race is invisible. The racial politics of the 1980s and 1990s have made whiteness as a racial designation quite visible. As a norm, however, whiteness is 'not ethnic'. Ethnic in this situation operates as a signifier for strange deviations from the norm – white music is 'regular', Caribbean music is ethnic. In this context white people, except for overt white supremists, are still uneasy talking about their whiteness and its meaning. When whites are asked to speak about their race, conversations are tenuous and often turn to the more familiar terrain of blackness, where stereotypes of black people can be validated and/or refuted. The specificities of white cultural identity are still very fuzzy for many whites and their ability to speak of the way their whiteness shapes their views of self and world is quite limited (Darder 1991; Frankenberg 1993; Haymes 1996).

This limited view of white people's awareness of the meaning of whiteness as an ethnic dynamic in their lives manifests itself in a variety of ways. One important manifestation is the equation of whiteness with nationality – whiteness equals Americanness and whiteness equals Britishness. There is nothing new with this equation, as the first Congress convened under the US Constitution voted in 1790 to stipulate that an individual be white in order to be naturalized as a citizen. I don't believe in racial and ethnic labels, many whites argue, I'm an American. Such a formulation often designates blackness and Americanness as mutually exclusive concepts and, as such, works to marginalize the role of blacks and other non-whites in national life and to shape political policies such as immigration and international relations. This conflation of Americanness and the non-ethnic norm of whiteness indicates to many whites that the formulation of America – its politics, music and literature – has had little to do with blacks, Latinos, Native Americans or Asians. While this equation of white and American may be changing, the modification is not greeted warmly by many whites. Indeed, the feeling is pervasive among them that non-whites have 'taken away' what was traditionally the province of whites. And in the process they (the non-whites) have undermined the quality/purity of what once existed.

A critical multiculturalist pedagogy of whiteness must engage whites around this normalization of whiteness in a manner that avoids inducing them simply to reject and turn off what is being discussed. Such an educational strategy must carefully work to create a non-threatening atmosphere where whites who are uncomfortable with talk about race (their own in particular) can begin to discuss the role of whiteness in their lives. Teachers of whiteness might want to introduce such a curriculum with an examination of the effects of the dominant ideology of individualism that removes the process of one's identity formation from the social arena. Such an analysis might alert individuals to the way our affiliation with a larger group shapes our consciousness, constructs our subjectivity no matter what our racial/ethnic designation. Understanding the social construction of their own identity and the ethnic nature of their own perspectives, white people may become more sensitive to the power of whiteness. Exposing the ethnic nature of whiteness in this way, teachers may be able to cultivate an awareness of it among white students as an implicit norm. Critical multicultural teachers may be able to demonstrate the ways in which power groups such as whites may propagate the impression that they are less ethnic, less ethnically shaped than the marginalized – in this case, non-whites (MacCannell 1992; Morrison 1993; Gallagher 1994; Nakayama and Krizek 1995).

When whiteness is allowed to remain unchallenged as a tacit norm, whites are free to separate issues of race from their everyday lives. In this formulation race shapes the lives of racialized peoples (non-whites) – not 'normal', non-racialized peoples (whites). The concepts of whiteness as norm or white privilege never penetrate the discursive boundaries of this formulation of whiteness. Even among many white people who think in terms of their ethnicity and tie it to European ancestry, there is a tendency to view its personal effects only within a symbolic realm. Outside of an isolated ethnic ritual or two – if even that – such symbolic white ethnic awareness rarely intersects with everyday life; nor does it promote insight into the power relations at work within the historical formation. Peter McLaren (1993) maintains that white people in this psychological state must be pushed to examine their own ethnic etymologies so that they can move beyond the tendency to normalize and universalize their ethnic experiences. A pedagogy of whiteness dedicated to the exposé of the tacit white norm understands the hegemonic features of both the macro-production and the micro-reception of the de-racialization of whiteness and the racialization of non-whiteness. Convincing whites of their normality and non-whites of their abnormality, this hegemonic strategy when left unchallenged props up the power of the privileged as it demoralizes those outside the orbit of the norm. In this context the ideology of meritocracy with its justification of inequality is perpetuated.

The socio-political magic of whiteness: the power of nothingness

In these ways whiteness – an entity that refuses specific definition – deploys its powerful socio-political magic. As the measure of all others, whiteness is unhyphenated, undepicted in 'cultures of the world', in no need of introduction and absent in most multicultural texts. Undoubtedly, it is one of the most powerful 'nothings' we can conjure. Toni Morrison (1993: 59) refers to the nothingness of whiteness as 'mute, meaningless, unfathomable, pointless, frozen, veiled, curtained, dreaded, senseless, implacable'. Again, it is important to specify that the white nothingness we are describing does not imply that white people are not seen as white. Instead, it asserts the inability of individuals to understand exactly what whiteness entails. It is the nature of whiteness and its effects – e.g. its status as norm and the privilege it bestows – that are invisible in end-of-century Western societies. In the Western white collective (un)consciousness whiteness has been used to signify not as much a culture as the non-presence of a culture, the absence of a 'distasteful and annoying' ethnicity. In this same collective (un)consciousness, Stephen Haymes (1996) astutely observes, this white nothingness assumes a superior shadow that transforms it into whiteness as a 'transcendental consciousness'. Such a higher order of being, Haymes continues, involves at some level the privileging of reason over culture. Like the science that grounds white reason, this white consciousness has been so far unable to reflect upon its own etymology, to confront its own particular assumptions (Frankenberg 1993; Morrison 1993; McIntosh 1995; Nakayama and Krizek 1995; Stowe 1996).

This power of white nothingness reveals itself in everyday life, casual conversations and political discourses. When Republican politician Patrick Buchanan implores his audience to 'take back our cities . . . take back our culture and take back our country', the 'our' in question signifies whites. When Bob Dole, Jack Kemp and William Bennett refer to family values, they are speaking of a white entity, a white norm missing in non-white homes. Television reporting of politics refuses to engage questions of whiteness in relation to such public pronouncements. Indeed, schooling and cultural pedagogy in general provide no lessons on the existence, not to mention the effects, of whiteness on life in Western culture. Even some forms of academic anti-racist multiculturalism fall victim to the power of whiteness, as they fail to appreciate the ways in which academic discourse is structured by Western forms of rationality – white reason. Whiteness is further erased in schools by the reticence of many teachers to discuss whites as a racialized group and white racism. Many teachers see value in multicultural education workshops and seminars only if such programmes provide them with new information about minority groups they didn't already know about. Many complain that they already know about minority groups such as blacks and Latinos – a comment that grants insight into their theoretical schemata regarding multicultural education.

Faced with teachers who are often reluctant to speak of whiteness and whose conceptual mapping of multiculturalism induces them to see no value in such a pedagogy, critical multiculturalists have a terrific task in front of them. Though it will be difficult, critical educators must be intellectually equipped to make a convincing case for the need to expose the fingerprints of whiteness on the academy. The white power of nothingness must no longer be allowed to shape tacitly the knowledge production and the academic canon of Western schooling. In this context a critical pedagogy of whiteness produces a counter-history grounded upon a deconstruction of a whitewashed official history. Such a counter-history opens for discussion and research questions about the deracialization of early Christianity, the possible whitening of ancient Egypt, with its appropriation of the culture's innovations in writing, medicine, mathematics and religion into a white European framework, and the bleaching of particular authors of African descent in the European literary canon, including Alexandre Dumas, Spinoza and Aesop. Such historical whitewashing conveys debilitating messages to contemporary blacks and other non-whites, as it teaches them to believe that they are intellectually inferior to whites. In addition to the specific understandings about black contributions to history, Western white history in particular, such counter-historical study engages students in an analysis of the hegemonic *process* of white supremacy.

Such an analysis is central to a critical multiculturalism, as it focuses student and teacher attention on the subtle ways racism works to shape our consciousness and produce our identity. No matter what one's racial/ethnic background, such a process is complicit in the construction of one's subjectivity. Indeed, it can be argued that the conversation about education in Western societies has always, at one level, been about whiteness in the sense that education was geared to make an individual more rational and to separate him (traditionally a male) from the uneducated, unreasonable other. Academic whitewashing allows the white magic of nothingness to rob non-whites of their culture, contributions and identities – a historical process that holds significant contemporary consequences. Recognizing these socio-pedagogical dynamics, whiteness education works to produce counter-hegemonic identities among whites and non-whites alike. Such identity production is a crucial step in the development of an anti-racist counter-future that refuses to allow whiteness to continue its role as an oppressive hidden norm (Fiske 1993, 1994; Sleeter 1993; McIntosh 1995; Tanaka 1996).

Extending the analysis of white power: defining the dominant culture

As the erased norm, whiteness holds the peculiar privilege of constituting both the dominant culture and a non-culture. Within this contradiction resides the basis of white power: whiteness can be deployed differently depending on the contextual dynamics it encounters. Students of whiteness can zealously chronicle the workings of whiteness, though not in some complete way, because it is always developing new methods of asserting itself. Our concern in this chapter is not to explore white power as it pertains to the Aryan Nation or white militias, even though these are very disturbing expressions of white power and merit detailed treatment. Our purpose here, however, is to focus more upon a mainstream, homespun, 'good taste' white power that tacitly shapes everyday life – a socially acceptable white power. Dean MacCannell (1992) provides insight into the way such tacit white power shapes the way the social world operates. In an article in the real estate section of the *Los Angeles Times* about the Cahuilla Indians and their ownership of land around Palm Springs, the author (D. Campbell) describes how the tribe leases land to white investors who build condominiums and resorts on it. The article speaks of the 'crazy quilt' legal complexity of the division of land ownership, characterizing it as 'half Indian controlled, half free'.

The discursive use of 'free' emerges unfiltered from the white unconsciousness – an unintentional rhetorical device to erase white ownership in particular and white power in general. As the author of newspaper article continues his or her description of the situation, the Cahuilla are variously described as falling into the 'catbird seat', 'forty rag-tail Indians', irresponsible in their handling of money, 'living in complete isolation from any large group of civilized humans' and 'primitive'. Such discursive positioning of the Cahuilla puts them in an unusual position as landowners. According to Campbell: (a) even though they live in a money economy that values profit making, the Cahuilla don't deserve to make a profit from their land; (b) perhaps white renters should not honour their debts to the Indians since their fiscal irresponsibility is so pronounced that they probably wouldn't know what to do with the cash once they procured it. The power of whiteness permeates this article, as the Cahuilla are positioned as the primitive, irrational other. Without referring overtly to whiteness, the author makes it clear that whiteness is the powerful norm from which judgements about the Indians' unwarranted financial position can be issued. Speaking from the mountain top of civilization, the author deploys his or her whiteness as means of declaring the Indians uncivilized. Readers can discern in this context traces of white reason that justify unequal treatment of those who fall too far from the Enlightenment tree of rationality.

Thus, any analysis of white power should recognize the privileged social position whites occupy. As the advertisement for the luxury cruise line teases its privileged potential customers with the notion that 'the rules are different here', we gain insight into the fact that the rules are different for whites whether they are dealing with irresponsible Indian landlords or attempting to secure a home loan from the bank. White power exists; it may be at times rhetorically or discursively masked, but it is still quite apparent to anyone who cares to look. Whites, white males in particular, control Western finances, information, corporate boards, unions, police departments and officer ranks in the military. White males make up the majority of doctors and lawyers and occupy most political offices. There is nothing too complex about these data: white power rules. Yet, despite this obvious reality, whiteness maintains the ability to erase itself, even at times portraying itself as a position of victimization by a politically correct cadre of multiculturalist zealots. As the dominant culture, whiteness is capable of sophisticated measures of self-justification that work best when social inequities in the power of various groups are hidden from view – inequities from which whites profit unjustly (Merleman 1986; Fiske 1994; Jordan 1995; Nakayama and Krizek 1995).

In this context whiteness develops a bag of tricks to mask its social location, making use of disguises, euphemisms, silences and avoidances. Knowing this, it makes more sense when whiteness uses concepts such as equal opportunity, assuming that in no way does the term challenge white supremacy. In this situation whites can speak publicly (in racially mixed groups) about their belief in granting everyone a fair chance at success, but understanding all the while at a tacit level that such assertions are 'just talk'. In reality they know that whites will always be better qualified – or at least appear better qualified and more comfortable to work with than non-whites. This tacit dynamic of whiteness works because whites continue to hang on to negative stereotypes about non-whites. A majority of whites believe that African Americans, for example, are more violent, less intelligent and not as hard working as whites. In this articulation of white power the reason for white racism towards non-whites is the behaviour of non-whites themselves. Of course, African Americans take special blame for such white perspectives, as the horror after all is Africa. In this context whiteness not only fears Africanism but is particularly terrified by the Africanism within itself. Modernist whiteness buoyed by its white reason is afraid of Africa's signification of the instinctual, the libidinal, the primitive (Merleman 1994; Rubin 1994; Gresson 1995).

The complexity of white power: white fear/desire of/for blackness

As a contamination of white purity, Africanness in the white collective unconscious is positioned as not totally horrible and repulsive. White slave-masters, for example, were not merely frightened by African women (and sometimes men); they also desired them and their concomitant exotica. A quick perusal of the history of slavery makes this point very clear, with its documentation of the midnight visits to the quarters. Such contradictions within whiteness's view of blackness can be traced to the present, with advertisers' commodification of black exotica, positioning individuals of African descent as objects of both fear and desire (Pinar 1991). The representation of African American sports figures as part animal and part jungle predator simultaneously elicits condescending, guilt-saturated, uneasy, impassioned and envious emotions from whiteness. The notion that whites can't jump like blacks is fed by and feeds whiteness's ambiguous relationship

with blackness, for as the stereotype is often invoked as an admirable quality it also ascribes the animalistic primitive signifier to athletes of African
heritage. Thus, whiteness as the dominant culture holds no fixed, permanent
relationship with non-whiteness. Constantly shifting, pushing away and
drawing close and degrading and desiring, the dominant culture in Western
societies cannot be essentialized in its self-perceptions and its relationship
with non-whiteness.

The dynamic of white desire for blackness has raised a range of socio-
political dynamics that shape the nature and expression of white power. The
important dissonance between white women and black men of the last
decades of the twentieth century has tapped into a long-flowing and jarring
historical current. Ever since the first interactions between European and
African civilizations this particular current has shaped the way black males
have been positioned. George Bush, for example, was able to use Willie
Horton as an affective signifier of white fear of blacks and the need for white
power to assert itself, because Horton had allegedly raped a white woman.
Understanding the fear/desire dialectic, white men were called to moral
action against this primitive challenge to their power, their manhood – they
voted for George Bush overwhelmingly in the 1988 election. This white
moral panic connects this anxiety over black sexuality to the growing crisis
of social, economic and political life. Such a connection is cemented together
by darkened images of O. J. Simpson on the cover of *Time*, magazine pieces
on welfare illustrated by pictures of black women and photographs of Mexicans illegally streaming across the California border in articles on Proposition 187 and other immigration issues (DuPlessis 1995; Giroux 1997;
Gresson 1995, 1997).

In this panicky form of whiteness, violence and hypersexuality become the
defining traits of African Americans. Following its historical predisposition,
white reason often socially and economically decontextualizes the causes of
black violence, positioning it as a natural characteristic of Africanism.
Simultaneously decontextualizing the reproductive practices of black
women, white power often deploys the hypersexual representation as an
excuse for the history of their sexual abuse by white men. The construction
of the image of the purity of white women is central to the justification of
the need for the (re)assertion of white power for the protection of whiteness
under threat. Such a discursive construction allows white power and white
racism to appear as a brave defensive effort – not a new articulation of traditional white imperialistic power. Thus, postmodern white power often
valorizes blackness as exotic, desirable and capable of great corporal feats
but simultaneously vilifies it as a threat to be controlled so that racial power
hierarchies can be maintained. This ambiguous valorization is often used at
the end of the twentieth century to prove the end of white racism. There is
no more racism toward blacks in America, the narrative asserts. How could

a racist society glamorize and so richly compensate Michael Jordan, Bill Cosby, Colin Powell and Ken Griffey Jr? Very complexly, we answer the difficult question. But as has traditionally been the case, such complexity has been a key to the success of whiteness. To work its magic, white power must always be complex, shadowy and enigmatic.

White power's positioning of the black threat in the contemporary social order has used the commodification of blackness to accomplish its project. Not too long ago the erasure of blackness in the public space and in the media space was used to illustrate one dynamic of white racism. With the increasing inclusivity/commodification of blackness in the media, whites increasingly can be heard to mutter, in response to black faces on TV, 'They're taking over'. This siege mentality makes the unjustified assumption that increased visibility translates to increased black/non-white power. As black media visibility increased in the 1980s and 1990s, the disparity of wealth between whites and blacks intensified. Panicky whiteness's vilification of non-whites – blacks and Latinos in particular – holds very specific material consequences. The power of whiteness simply cannot be separated from its control of the economy and the gatekeeping function it plays in relation to the job hiring and promotion decisions made daily (Fiske 1994; Merleman 1995; Yudice 1995; Haymes 1996).

Reasserting white power: deploying border patrols

One dynamic of the power of whiteness that is frequently missed by contemporary whites is that white power matters more to blacks than black power to whites. Few whites depend upon blacks for their job security – even if blacks and other non-whites hate them, they are only marginally affected. Yet, in an interesting Mickey Spillane twist, whites do unconsciously depend upon a black presence in their economic lives. Historically white people have habituated themselves to the availability of enslaved or cheap black labour. Such dependence continues into the present era, albeit in less dramatic terms, as whites continue to reap benefits from economic racism. (Many might argue that affirmative action might be justified on the basis of this persistent financial advantage of whiteness.) Such dependency must always ideologically be erased in the cultural production of whiteness – in school curriculums, textbooks, television news and popular culture. Since white wealth and power shape the ever more influential popular culture, the signifiers, concepts and images that are used to position social differences reflect hegemonic whiteness, even sometimes in the name of inclusivity. Popular culture's silence in regard to the economic relationship between whites and non-whites is deafening. Using the media, academia and popular culture, whiteness is able to make material differences between races seem natural, common-sensical and reasonable when such asymmetries inadvertently manifest themselves.

It is for just these reasons that a pedagogy of whiteness must always examine institutions, policies and alignments that produce knowledge. Critical multiculturalists inform students of whiteness about the less than politically/racially innocent nature of academic discourses and objective scholarly reports. As we have written elsewhere (Kincheloe and Steinberg 1993), objective educational scholarship and disinterested psychological analyses are politicized and racialized documents often saturated by the invisible power of whiteness – a power that serves to validate white experience while denigrating the experience and knowledge that students of African descent, Latinos and indigenous peoples bring to school. Academia is soaked by whiteness through and through, in its policies, its grading of students, its interpersonal relationships, its lived culture, its disciplinary discourses and its knowledge production. White reason with its white epistemology reproduces linear, capital-driven knowledge forms that in their removal of analysis from a humanized context reinforce the naturalization of white power. Indeed, white power patrols its boundaries, on the lookout for threats to its supremacy. White power relinquishes very little not demanded by localizing powers. If critical multiculturalists are not vigilant, white power takes back hegemonic forms previously challenged and abandoned.

Of course, Herrnstein and Murray's *The Bell Curve* – discussed throughout this book and in detail in Chapter 7 – constitutes an excellent example of this reclaiming of white hegemonic forms. Just as social Darwinism supplied a legitimating ideology for whites in the late nineteenth century, Herrnstein and Murray (along with many helpmates) brought it back for a centennial redeployment in 1994. Positioning non-whites and the poor as occupying a lower rung on the evolutionary ladder in relation to both intelligence (reason) and moral development, white social Darwinists of both the nineteenth and twentieth centuries patrolled national borders by barring the immigration of 'inferior' peoples. Included in whiteness's (re)deployment of social Darwinism was the ideological notion that Western social systems are open and that anyone who has ability and works hard will experience upward mobility. Thus, those who don't make it have only their own absence of ability and effort to blame. It is not a long leap from such positions, of course, to an embrace of a neo-essentialist form of racism. As we have previously discussed, such white racist essentialism assumes that as a permanent characteristic of Western life race implies a set of natural biological and genetic differences between people (Giroux 1988; Sleeter 1993; Fiske 1994; Gresson 1995; Haymes 1995; Merleman 1995; Nakayama and Krizek 1995).

A critical pedagogy of whiteness, as it maps these redeployments of long discredited forms of white power, stands ready to refute the 'common sense' of the heartland. For example, the neo-essentialist racist discourse relies on the mythology of scientifically delineated discrete categories of race. Critical multiculturalists focusing on the nature of white power are quick to point out that biologists are unable to validate genetic racial divisions between humans because the genetic differences between Africans and Europeans are not significantly greater than variations within these groups. Yet upon these shaky categories white power is established, in the process buttressing whiteness's ability to place itself in the role of the moral arbitrator and evaluator of black deportment in Western societies. Such evaluations are made on the basis of how faithfully non-white peoples adapt to the values and ideologies of whiteness. But whiteness as moral arbitrator focuses its regulatory gaze on white people as well. Establishing plain-clothes cultural border patrols, white power disciplines white transgressors who work to expose the artificial boundaries that separate races, the ways that whiteness assumes a tyrannical stance, the hegemonic nature of whiteness and the ways it harms those who fall outside of its parameters (Keating 1995; Wellman 1996; Giroux 1997; McLaren and Morris 1997). Critical multiculturalists make themselves aware of these cultural dynamics, viewing them as central features in a pedagogy of whiteness.

When push comes to shove: white privilege

One of the central features of the scholarship on whiteness of the last few years has been the emphasis on the documentation and expose of white privilege (see Roediger 1991; Frankenberg 1993). White people often understand white privilege in an ambiguous and complex manner – sometimes unable to articulate their understanding into specific words but able to acknowledge it with knowing looks, particular actions and throwaway comments in everyday life. Such tacit recognition of white privilege takes place in micro-rituals of white racial bonding. Whites buying a car choosing the white not the black salesperson, the looks exchanged by two whites in an elevator when a black male gets in, the eye contact made by two white strangers when a well dressed black male walks confidently by them in a cafeteria line or a joke about black people told among a group of white men in a barber shop all tacitly imply that white people understand that they are white and do not want to be black. A white respondent to Thomas Nakayama and Robert Krizek's (1995: 298) interview questions about white knowledge of their racial privilege confided that we (whites) look at each other 'and just know that we've got it better'. Nevertheless, many whites have great difficulty admitting in the public conversation about race at the end of the twentieth century that such racial privilege exists; a significant number of whites seem to believe strongly that it does not exist any more.

There is nothing new about the conversation about white privilege in Western societies. Decades ago W. E. B. DuBois spoke of such privilege, specifying it in relation to the public deference granted whites, their unimpeded admittance to all public functions, the tendency of police officers to be drawn from the ranks of white people, their lenient treatment in court and their access to the best school houses in any bi- or multi-racial community (Roediger 1991). Yet the complexity of this issue is belied by the sincere protestations by many whites, white students in particular, that they know of no such racial privilege. How does the tacit understanding of white privilege among whites coexist with this effective erasure of knowledge of white privilege? Such a question becomes extremely important in a study of whiteness or any white pedagogy. The stakes in Western societies – the USA in particular – are increasingly high as citizens are rated as winners and losers and social safety nets continue to be dismantled, leaving the losers in greater and greater danger.

With this question in mind an examination of white privilege is in order. When the nature of racism has been studied and taught in Western institutional and cultural pedagogies, individuals learn that racism places its victims in a disempowered position. In this educational context, however, until the past few years little has been said about the privileges accrued from racial oppression. Some argue that traditional pedagogies have actually taught white people not to recognize white privilege (McIntosh 1995). Described as a secret cache of special tools – much like Batman's collection of helpful gizmos – white privilege grants its holders passage where others are detained. In a hyperreality saturated with existential insecurity the teaching of white privilege is inscribed with psychic danger for whites (especially working class whites) already insecure with their identities, their economic futures and the meaning of life itself in the postmodern mediascape. One can sense in this context that the absence of a pedagogy of white privilege in multicultural education, sociology and the public conversation about race in general may reference a deeper unconscious defence mechanism protecting collective whiteness in these times of trouble.

In this angst-ridden, ambiguous context the attempt to pin down white privilege is further complicated by its situational specificity, its tendency to change in relation to different times and places. Though it still exists, the nature of white privilege is very different at the end from how it was at the beginning of the twentieth century. Undoubtedly, white immigrants from places such as Ireland, Russia, Poland or Italy in the nineteenth and early twentieth centuries suffered prejudice and oppression during the first years of their lives in the new country. As bad as things were, however, they were able to acquire the mantle of whiteness and its accompanying access to socio-economic mobility. In this process a social dynamic emerged that is as important to the historiography of whiteness as Frederick Jackson Turner's 'frontier thesis' was to American historiography in general. Ethnic groups such as the Irish, for example, proclaimed their own whiteness by taking on the racism of other whites. Indeed, to prove their commitment to whiteness the Irish in the second half of the nineteenth century in the USA often led the charge against African Americans. The Irish are not an isolated case, for in colonial Virginia poor white settlers were granted political and economic rights by the planter elite only in exchange for their support of black slavery and its accompanying ideology. Poor southern whites accepted this bargain throughout the slave holding South, and like their northern brothers and sisters have accepted an ever-changing articulation of it ever since. Thus, the Devil's Pact mandated that white privilege could be won only through the acceptance of a white racism designed to control non-whites by precluding any possibility of a political alliance between them and the white (or proto-white) poor (Rubin 1994; Yudice 1995; Stowe 1996).

In DuBois's famous phrase, 'the wages of whiteness' were earned by signing the pact. Whites were psychologically comforted by the knowledge that no matter how far they fell down the socio-economic ladder, they were still white. No matter how alienating and exploitative their work lives might be, they were still 'not slaves'. Around this theme the whiteness scholarship of the 1990s coalesced, designed to induce white people to 'get in touch with' their privilege and listen to the wisdom of those people that whiteness tended to silence. Whiteness scholars asked whites to see themselves as the oppressed have viewed them in order to gain a new frame of reference. Such a perspective, it was hoped, would induce white people to consider the fact that the efforts white and non-white individuals make in the attempt to succeed do not pay off equally. Because they spend so much of their time with other white people, whites are often unfamiliar with the obstacles blacks, Latinos and indigenous peoples face on a daily basis. Such exposure, the scholars maintained, would induce whites to think about race in a way previous multicultural scholarship had failed to accomplish. What many whiteness scholars did not consider was the resistance to such ideas that many whites would muster. The question often left unaddressed involved how to formulate a pedagogy of whiteness that would engage white people in an understanding of their white privilege in a way that would not simply anger them to the point they shut down conversation. Obviously, such a question is exceedingly difficult to answer, since the very nature of whiteness scholarship is designed to undermine practices and ways of seeing that work to protect white privilege (Roediger 1991; Sleeter 1993; McLaren 1994b; Rubin 1994; Stowe 1996).

In the most direct manner possible a pedagogy of whiteness addresses white resistance by pointing to the reality of white privilege: white males still overwhelmingly dominate the economic realm, the political sphere, academia, the press, TV and Hollywood and leadership and ownership in sports. Teachers can be as specific with statistical data and various domains as they want, the story is still the same: white males control the institutions and organizations of power at the end of the twentieth century (Yudice 1995). The continuation of white male social domination is one of the few simple understandings we can grasp in the socio-psychological complexity of white people's reaction to the discussion of whiteness and white privilege. The paradox of the tacit understanding of white privilege and the white politics of denial/erasure of white privilege produces a racial pain that must be delicately approached by critical multiculturalists. It is safe to conclude that those teachers of a whiteness curriculum who don't attempt to understand and empathize with the complexity of this white pain and the anger that often accompanies it will find themselves faced with a corps of sullen and alienated white students. Such empathy doesn't mean that white students should be pampered and indulged or protected from the knowledge of the privilege of whiteness – it does mean that teachers should be sensitive to the dynamics of being young and white at the end of the century. Indeed, we maintain that a successful pedagogy that engages white privilege is possible only if teachers are knowledgeable of contemporary white racial understandings and the white identity crisis that has developed in recent years.

nine

THE CURRICULUM OF CRITICAL MULTICULTURALISM: HISTORICIZING, ANALYSING AND AFFIRMING

The kind of humanities, history and social sciences curriculum conservative, liberal and pluralist multiculturalist have advocated refuses to recognize culture as a terrain of struggle. The relationship between knowledge and power is ignored, while concern with domination is buried alongside other skeletons of the past. The attempt to win the consent of the governed is used in the effort to diffuse the social conflict that inevitably emerges from domination. Of course, the creation of a one-dimensional national interest is one strategy employed to win the consent of the people – a national interest, it must be added, that often excludes black, East Indian, Hispanic, female and other minority communities. For example, the dominant definition of the classics in music, art and literature that forms the cultural basis of the nation consistently excludes the contributions of non-white, non-European men and most women. The underlying message of such a definition implies that these 'other' people are not a part of their country's cultural heritage; they are outside the national interest. Framed in egalitarian rhetoric while excluding the histories and cultures of different communities, the struggle for consent masks the reality of a society stratified along race, gender and class lines (Carby 1982; Staples 1984).

The surface harmony heralded by the media, the government and education is merely an image in the minds of those individuals who are shielded by privilege from the injustice experienced by dominated peoples. Such a pseudo-harmony idealizes the future as it covers up the historical forces that have structured the present disharmony that it denies (Giroux 1988). The governed will not deliver their consent if the presence of the conflict becomes too obvious, too overbearing. In the USA, where the economic disparity between white and non-white is great and continues to grow, the appeal to national unity is heard more frequently. It is our argument in this chapter that any critical multicultural curriculum must be grounded on rigorous historical scholarship that explores not only excluded race, class and gender histories but also the construction of the public memory about both subjugated and dominant cultural groups. Too many of the multicultural curricula we have observed have been taught by teachers not conversant with the discourse of Western historiography. The critical project cannot be accomplished outside the grounding such familiarity provides.

Eviscerated multiculturalism history

Monoculturalists do not attempt to hide their position that non-white and female history, especially the history of racial and gender conflict and oppression, should not be emphasized in the curriculum. Conservative spokesperson Russell Kirk, for example, has argued unabashedly that the purpose of education is to lift a minority student out of his or her subculture rather than immerse him or her in the 'trivialities' of ethnic history. What is to be gained by black studies? What is to be learned by women's studies? Latino/a studies? Answering his own question, Kirk argues that the only advantage derived from these curricular studies is that a student might possibly find a job somewhere as a professor in these studies (Brittan and Maynard 1984). Thus, the fact that the conquered and oppressed are not remembered is justified – their memory is not marketable in industrial capitalism. 'Official history' grows even more amnesiac with regard to black people and the past and present come to be seen as the inevitable triumph of the deserving. The European experience is assumed to be universally applicable, the only valid historical experience – an idea that tacitly permeates E. D. Hirsch's *Cultural Literacy*. No account is taken of the historiographical idea that history cannot be relayed by a single method, that the differences in experience between non-European and European cultures necessitate methodological alterations, not to mention different purposes for pursuing history in the first place (Dussel 1981; Harrison 1985). The result of such perspectives serves to exclude non-European history from the public school curriculum. This does not mean that these histories are not mentioned – one finds more coverage in the texts of the 1990s than in the 1950s. Nevertheless, the nature of the coverage is so superficial, so decontextualized, so devoid of conflict that the essence of these experiences is concealed even as liberal and pluralist multiculturalists boast of 'progress' in the area. By the use of one designated day per year, or celebratory bulletin boards and 'ethnic' meals, many schools assume they are meeting the needs of the multicultural curriculum by teaching diversity in these ways.

When non-white history is taught without a critical edge, students gain little insight into the problems facing different peoples in their culture's history and how these problems affected history in general. Black history, for instance, has often been represented in the curriculum as a set of isolated events: slaves as bit players in the larger portrayal of the Civil War; brief 'personality profiles' of Sojourner Truth, Booker T. Washington as 'a credit to his race', George Washington Carver and the peanut; Martin Luther King Jr as the one-dimensional leader of a decontextualized civil rights movement now relegated to the past, *c.*1955 to *c.*1970. The black history taught in public schools has not really induced students to ask the question: what does it mean to be an individual of African descent? Indeed, the perfunctory manner in which black history has been included in the curriculum has served as a means of defusing the rising tide of black student consciousness in school settings (Brittan and Maynard 1984). This uncritical co-option of black history has allowed school leaders to point with pride to the 'multicultural' nature of their curriculum, while at the same time maintaining a static view of the purpose of education in general. Pasted on to the curriculum in a marginal manner, black history is separated from the larger conversation about the curriculum and thus exerts no effect upon it. The 'knowledge' transmitted in schools is untouched by a consciousness of black history.

Women's history is similarly taught. The liberal and pluralist chronicles of the past acknowledge the contributions of certain women, many of whom were seen as supplementary to the history being made by males. Florence Nightingale, Clara Barton, Betsy Ross and even Harriet Tubman are added to the curriculum as 'stick-ons', reminders that 'these' people also contributed, at least marginally. We interviewed several graduate and undergraduate teacher education classes about the history of Rosa Parks and the desegregation of Montgomery's buses. Without exception, the story began something like, 'Rosa was tired from a long day at work and didn't want to move all the way to the back of the bus.' No one mentioned that Parks was involved deeply in the Civil Rights movement and that her actions on that day in Montgomery, Alabama, were planned by the movement. Describing Parks as 'tired' devalues the entire purpose of the civil action and her commitment to social justice.

Non-white, non-male and lower class history must be integrated into the curriculum on two fronts: (a) to transcend these supplementary roles, many historical perspectives must be brought to existing courses in social studies, government, history, literature, science, art and music; and (b) these perspectives should be studied as areas in their own right. History of nonwhites and females as simply integrated aspects of the general curriculum would undermine the attempt to devise black, Hispanic and female oriented conceptual frameworks and epistemologies (Sleeter and Grant 1988). Sulayman Nyang and Abdulai Vandi, for example, provide an excellent example of how an understanding of black history would affect the way mainstream educators teach the European Age of Exploration in the fifteenth and sixteenth centuries. Traditionally, the era has been taught uncritically as an age of heroes whose names were to be memorized along with their 'discoveries'. Nyang and Vandi place the 'discoveries' in broader historical context, examining the assumptions of the Europeans about themselves and other peoples and the effects of European 'heroics' on Africans and Asians. Not only do the authors examine the specifics of the Age of Exploration, but they trace the effects of the era on the lives of Europeans, Africans, Asians and colonized peoples (Nyang and Vandi 1980). Bringing a new and additional perspective to bear on the Age of Discovery changes the entire tenor of the pedagogical act. The rote-based memorization of the 'discoveries' of Columbus, Cortez, Balboa, de Gama *et al.* would give way to a thematic conceptualization of the reasons for European expansionism and the effect of such actions on African, Asian and indigenous peoples. The traditional curricular preoccupation with Europe would expand into a study of non-European cultures. The view of the Age of Exploration as an isolated historical event would be replaced by an understanding of the connections between the past and the present – especially the European past and the African diasporic present. The study of the Age of Exploration would lead naturally into an examination of colonialism and its effects on the daily events of the late twentieth century. Thus, questions generated by critical multiculturalism would fundamentally change what mainstream educators and standardized test makers have labelled 'basic knowledge' about Western civilization.

Uncritical history

Multiple histories will not only uncover new dimensions of many experiences but also reveal new ways of seeing dominant culture and dominant education. Having been situated in a state of oppression for so long, these experiences may point the way to more sophisticated definitions of social theory and ethical authority. Oppressed groups often gain unique insights into the forces that move history. They comprehend the culture of their oppressors better than do the oppressors themselves. Such subjugated insights may dramatically alter that which we refer to as knowledge. Yet schools continue to teach multiculturalism uncritically; units of study are added on to existing curricula that are otherwise unaltered. The uncritical presentation of slavery or stories from the 'homeland' often estrange students from their history more than they connect them. Such material is taught in lieu of thematic connections between past and present or the development of a sense of the problems that have faced non-whites. Writing of her own public school experience, bell hooks describes this detachment: 'We are taught to love the system that oppressed us' (hooks 1981).

Non-critical, mainstream education has confused traditionalism with a critical conception of tradition. Distinguishing between the two concepts, Enrique Dussel argues that traditionalism ends with superficial comprehension. Superficial traditionalism does indeed transmit something, but what it tells conceals more than it reveals. It dwells on the surface, thus hiding the critical dimension, inner nature and lived experience. To be critical in a historical context means to 'de-present' the present; that is, to take the mundane, hold it up to the light and look at it from another angle. Critically grounded, tradition never lets history slip by unquestioned; it requires that we really test and interrogate what tradition transmits, to uncover what has been concealed in the obvious (Dussel 1976). For example, blacks know they are African descendants, but the important point is to know what that means. It is one thing to know that black people gained educational opportunities in the last portion of the nineteenth and the first part of the twentieth century; it is another idea entirely to understand what the dominant culture perceived the purpose of that education to be.

Textbooks inform students that America, for example, from the beginning was a melting pot, a land without great conflict. No history books, bell hooks writes, mentioned racial imperialism. The minds of Americans were filled with romantic notions of the new world, the American dream, America as the land where all the races lived together as one (hooks 1981). Fearful of dangerous tradition and the reality of oppression and conflict, many textbook publishers and curriculum developers do not believe that students need to understand the role of racism in America over the past four centuries. With their emphasis on national unity, spokespeople such as William Bennett and Diane Ravitch contend that emphasis on matters such as race and culture are inappropriate. We should concentrate less on racial concerns in the modern curriculum, they maintain and focus our attention on the great facts of American history; that is, a sanitized, 'white'-washed view of America, the 'greatest' nation in history (Kincheloe 1989).

Ravitch's and Bennett's perspectives are not unlike the positions taken by mainstream curriculum developers since the origins of public schools. A survey of modern public school social studies texts reveals that the word racism does not appear in their indexes. When this central theme of the African American experience is not raised, serious political consequences result. Indeed, any measured treatment of racism in American history would need to focus on the variety of forms it takes at different historical moments. Racism is not a fixed principle but a contradictory phenomenon that is constantly changing its form in relation to the alterations of wider political and economic structures (Solomos *et al.* 1982; Hale-Benson 1986). No American public school textbook, for example, examines the history of the northern urban African American experience. As a result no textbook studies the evolution of institutional racism and its dramatic impact on northern black communities. If the question of racism is raised, it is viewed in a southern slavery or Jim Crow context where it was mandated by law and quite overt. Such was not the case in the North. Left without historical explanations of the nature of racism that developed in the urban, industrialized North, students have no conceptual experience that might help them to understand why blacks in Chicago could not gain the same employment and educational opportunities as immigrants from Poland. An understanding of the black experience in the labour markets of the North is critical in modern America, where children of immigrants from Europe ask: 'We worked hard and succeeded in America, why didn't blacks?' Thus, as James Anderson concludes, it is easy for such students to buy into popular theories of black social pathology and blame the black victim of racism for the difference in status between African Americans and white immigrants in the urban North (Anderson 1986).

Liberal and pluralist forms of multiculturalism have often framed racism as simply a struggle over representation, an imagistic battle that effectively serves to hide the social relations of domination in which racism is situated. A central function of non-white and women's history as a component of the school curriculum must involve their ability to expose naive notions about the nature of racism and sexism, such as the belief that they are simply attitudes that need to be changed. Such treatment of racism and sexism perpetuates a cultural blindness that submerges the recognition of the social relations of the lived world. Historical myths of 'progress', the success of racial integration and women's rights and the conquest of prejudices eclipse the power relationships that sustain institutional racism and reproduce inequality in the very classrooms that point out the decline of prejudice (Carby 1980, 1982; Harrison 1985). Although curricular reformation has often concerned itself with the removal of race and gender stereotyping from textbooks or with the artefacts produced in specific cultural sites, such as art, religion, music, dance and food, a decline in racial and gender oppression has not followed.

The critical multicultural intervention

Here is where non-white and women's history intervenes; here is where it plays a particularly critical role in the effort to develop a critical consciousness. The histories of racism, sexism and classism reveal tendencies for virus-like mutations. In the past fifty years the dominant form of expression has moved from individual '-isms' involving overt acts by individual whites towards individual non-whites to institutional racism that takes the form of public policies and socio-economic arrangements that deny non-whites access to legal, medical or educational facilities. Institutional racism, of course, is particularly insidious because it perpetuates policies that are promoted as racially neutral but exert a discriminatory impact.

A critical multiculturalism reveals these mutations, their geneses and their contextual development. Such revelations set the stage for the deconstruction of the meanings embedded in words such as merit, quality education, reverse discrimination, tuition tax credits, 'bad' neighbourhoods, at-risk students, family values and law and order. Proceeding from these understandings, we come to realize that people are not just viewed in terms of stereotypes but also in relationship to their power and status (Brittan and Maynard 1984; Piliawsky 1984; Bowser 1985). Thus, inequality is not simply a matter of prejudice, a cultural phenomenon – it is also grounded in the way certain groups are economically and politically located in society.

Understanding this political-economic location of marginalized groups, this evolution of prejudice, this critical tradition, permits those who are historically conscious to move closer to an awareness of non-white and female visions, philosophies and pedagogies. Subjugated peoples have to establish their own visions – visions that stand in stark contrast to the world views assumed by those established in the current centres of power. The ultimate power of any history is in its truth telling. As history is removed from the afternoon shadows cast by the dominant culture, its truth telling reshapes the present as it creates new visions of the future. The historiographical assumption embedded in this concept is that the future is somehow imprinted in the past (Holt 1986). It is not just the subjugated consciousness that stands to be remoulded but dominant consciousness as well. The possibility offered by critical multiculturalism confronts teachers with the question of what constitutes official knowledge (Inglis 1985). If successful, critical multiculturalism will force teachers, curriculum developers and, it is hoped, the public to ask where knowledge does come from, who certifies it and what its political impact involves.

Michel Foucault's notion of subjugated knowledges (discussed in Chapter 2) helps us to theorize the possible curricular roles of non-white and female history. Foucault would resurrect these subjugated knowledges: (a) history that has been buried or disguised, typically a history of subjugation, conflict and oppression lost in a dominant theoretical framework or wiped out by a triumphant history of ideas; and (b) knowledges that have been disqualified as inferior to the dominant definitions of scientificity, knowledges regarded as primitive by mainstream intellectuals (Foucault 1980). The knowledges of the culturally different fall into this latter meaning, since Western intellectuals have traditionally viewed non-Western epistemologies as illogical, not worthy of serious philosophical analysis. One theme runs through both meanings: the historical consciousness of conflict. Foucault admonishes the dominant culture to end its suppression of the role of conflict in history, in discourse – a role that is suppressed in a variety of contexts, the mainstream curriculum included. Foucault used the term genealogy to describe the process of remembering and incorporating these memories of subjugated knowledges, conflict and the dimensions of power they reveal into active contemporary struggles (Welch 1985).

Foucault's genealogy is reminiscent of Herbert Marcuse's concept of 'dereification', which implied a certain type of remembering. Something extraordinarily important had been forgotten in the modern world, Marcuse argued. What had to be retrieved were the human origins of a socially constructed world that had been buried by industrialization and the power of Enlightenment rationality (Jay 1982). Foucault's genealogy picks up where Marcuse left off. Specifying the nature of excluded contents and meanings, Foucault prepares us for the strategic struggle between the subjugated and the dominant knowledges. He begins with the realization that the insurrection of subjugated knowledges exists among the oppressed, as in his study of prisons and prisoners. The insurrection is not something that dominant intellectuals can theorize into existence – historians simply acknowledge its reality. Obviously, women's and non-white knowledges are prime examples of Foucault's notion of subjugated knowledges. No intellectual systematically theorized it – it was already there. W. E. B. DuBois recognized its existence decades prior to Foucault. To understand ourselves as black people, he wrote in 1946, we must understand African history and social development – one of the most sophisticated world views, he added, the planet has witnessed (DuBois 1973).

How might a teacher build his or her practice on the foundation provided by such understandings and theoretical insights? A practice grounded on an understanding of a history of subjugated knowledge would be aware of the way schools are structured around specific silences and omissions (Giroux 1988). Teachers would thus seek to incorporate subjugated knowledge by forging links with those marginalized communities – not just the dominant culture's definition of the 'successful' elements of those communities but a variety of groups and subgroups within them. The diverse resources to be found in each community open the school to a variety of community traditions, histories and cultures discredited within the culture of the school. The stories, the worldviews, the music, the politics, the humour, the art of the marginalized community become a central part of everyday school life, never viewed in isolation or as supplements to the 'real work' of the school but always viewed in the context of the general curriculum. How do these knowledges, teachers would ask, fit with the dominant knowledge? What dynamics are at work in their interrelationship? The attempt to answer such questions lays the foundation for a critical curriculum, an education that takes the non-white and female experience seriously. The dominant curriculum, with its non-problematic, standardized definitions of knowledge and its standardized tests, has no room for such activities – it is too busy being accountable. The isolation from community that results eventually sets up adversarial relationships between teachers and non-white parents, citizens and political leaders.

Educators informed by Foucault's notion of subjugated knowledges thus rewrite history in their classrooms – not in the sense of a totalitarian regime (China's official account of the Tiananmen massacre, as an example) that manufactures a pseudo-history to control its people. This critical rewriting of history involves the inclusion of subjugated knowledges and the new perspectives such counter-memories provide. E. P. Thompson in *The Making of the English Working Class* alludes to this process of historical rewriting as he describes the task of the labour leaders in the nineteenth century who were struggling to cope with the problems of an industrializing Britain. They had to write a new past, Thompson tells his readers, create forms of unprecedented political organization and draw upon this new history to invent class traditions from a largely invisible past. There is something pedagogically important here, something that provides a peek at the subtle and complex ways history influences curriculum theory and political practice. Nineteenth-century labour leaders took the subjugated historical experience of the working class and theorized it into knowledge – a knowledge that affected the consciousness and pedagogical and political practice of those who grasped it. A solidarity between those who understood the new knowledge was forged and thereby a community of learning was established (Inglis 1985). The subjugated history, the counter-memory of the English working class, like the historical experience of African Americans, was not just 'dead old history'; within it were found the origins of the problems, the debates, the oppression of the present. This is what happens when the oppressed draw upon their subjugated knowledges and speak for themselves. Insurrections of subjugated knowledges elicit critical interpretations of educational and school codes, symbols and texts, institutional structures of public education and the possibility of an educational praxis built on the wisdom gleaned from these recognitions (Welch 1985).

Critical multiculturalism and public memory

Critical multicultural history, in its essence, is concerned with repressed memory, subjugated knowledge and the influence of such repression on the life of the present. The power of the memory of repression is nowhere better represented than in the African diasporic experience. Memory finds itself intimately connected to the present as its cultivation helps to liberate the knowledges of peoples long separated from their pasts. With oppressed groups memory engenders consciousness that leads to a panoply of possible futures. Black historians must draw upon its power in the attempt to secure a place in the public discourse about education.

Thus, once the often eclipsed relationship between past and present is recognized, the ties between history and politics can be exposed. History is a discourse that exists in a dialectical relationship with political thought (Kaye 1987). If such a relationship seems paradoxical or dangerous, it is because we often hold such a narrow view of politics. In the popular sense of the term, politics typically refers to public office seeking at the least and the great public issues at the most. If the definition is expanded to include the larger moral and ethical dimensions of power sharing in a society, the relationship between history and politics is rendered less threatening. In the dialectical interplay between history and politics (and education), the way one makes sense of the past is essential in the determination of what political (or educational) perspective one will view as realistic or socially responsible (White 1987). Indeed, some would argue that all political and educational reasoning is basically a form of historical argument (Popular Memory Group 1982). Thus, history – no matter who writes it – is never disinterested. Disinterested history is a luxury only dominant groups can afford. When W. E. B. DuBois viewed the past, he saw a useful chronicle of methods employed by his black ancestors to fight slavery and oppression – methods, he believed, that could be put to use in present struggles against racial tyranny. The blueprints for the black future, he theorized, must be built on a base of our problems, dreams and frustrations; they will not appear out of thin air or based exclusively on the experience of others (DuBois 1973). Echoing this theme, Maulana Karenga argued almost forty years later that African American history is a reflection not only of what black people have done but of what they can do (Karenga 1982). The black past holds out possibilities because it served the political function of destabilizing the existing order by revealing its social construction and thus its bogus supra-historical character.

This critical multiculturalist notion of historical memory confronts academics and teachers with a Eurocentric objectivist historiographical problem. Historians have long wrung their hands over the relationship between past and present. Obviously, many professional historians would find the concept of critical historical memory incompatible with their idea of disinterested scholarship. Pure scholarship, modernist objectivists would argue, is best served by a consistent resistance to the attempt to compare historical events to the present. Tell the story as it was, many write, and stay away from too much theory. Uncomfortable with the perceived distortion of an *histoire engagé*, such historians urge their colleagues to understand the past on its own ground, according to the criteria of its own time.

If we are to pursue critical history as subjugated memory, critical multiculturalism must confront these questions and carefully analyse the nature of the past–present relationship. Objectivist historians are correct when they point to the often dishonourable heritage that has attempted to appropriate the past for some desirable end. In many hands history has become little more than a repository of relevant anecdotes, moralist admonitions and precedents to be invoked at will by jurists and politicians. The intent of critical history is not to reduce the project of history to an *immediate* political utility – immediate in the sense that specific civics lessons with step by step instructions for social amelioration can be drawn from historical scholarship. Reagan, Bush, Gingrich, Thatcher, Major and the New Right serve as excellent examples of how the conception of immediate utility eventuates in the abuse of history (Kaye 1987). A critical multicultural history attempts to move the dialogue between memory and the present to a more subtle level – a realm where admittedly history is used, but the use involves the acquisition of critical insight into existing situations and a sensitivity to the values historically embedded within these present realities. Such a task inevitably evokes charges of presentism. The admonition to avoid presentist history is at best a negative injunction, failing even to bestow insight into the attempt to ascertain what a particular segment of the past was like. It does not recognize the fact that the historian's knowledge and experience of the present is necessary to his or her understanding of the past. The appreciation of a historical form rests on a recognition of the interplay between past and present. Indeed, the past can be understood only insofar as it has continued to live in the present (White 1987).

History as subjugated memory eschews antiquarianism. As French historian Marc Bloch, a victim of the holocaust, wrote during the Second World War, antiquarians revere buildings and institutions and romanticize the past. Historians are citizens of the here and now who love life. Following Bloch's imperative, historians must avoid the production of past images for *passive* consumption only by other historians. Historians' knowledge is necessary to our attempt to understand the workings of social, psychological and educational processes and their subtle interrelationships. The historian's approach to his or her task, however, must always be informed by dedication to accuracy and infused with a larger social purpose. Historians, more than other scholars, must be aware of the consequences of historical ignorance and amnesia. Our modern unconsciousness of history does not free us from the past, but, to the contrary, traps us in the snare of an unconscious destiny. When the past is forgotten, its power over the present is hidden from view. We are victimized by an amnesia that makes 'what is' seem as if 'it had to be'. Contrary to what antiquarians might argue, historians will be judged by the contributions they make in putting their knowledge of the past to work in the attempt to understand the present and to shape the future. The point is so obvious that it might not be worth stressing, except for the fact that historians have worked so diligently to deny it.

Critical multicultural history forces us to confront two questions: (a) what is the role of critical historians as transmitters of culture; and (b) what is the role of historians in the larger society? These two questions involve the concept of memory, both in a social and an individual sense. To answer these questions historians must explore the role that memory and historical knowledge play in our lives. The word memory directs the attention of historians away from an exclusive concern with the past and towards a concern with the past–present relationship (Popular Memory Group 1982). Memory, unlike history, has a verb form – to remember. Because the past lives in the present – and certainly in the minds of people who live in the present – public memory becomes a focus of political struggle. How it is approached by historians as well as by other social actors is intrinsically a political act. How we remember matters because it informs our existence in the present and our vision of the future. Yet, because of their commitment to particular notions of objectivity and methods of verification, memory has always proven to be a difficult concept for historians to confront.

What does it mean to remember history? What must we do with memories of such history to make them active and alive rather than mere antiques or quaint curiosities? One of the social roles of any historian is to peddle the idea that memory is a vital resource in political life, in social action or in education. Memory counters the oppressive 'presence' of late twentieth-century life as it helps us to make sense of the nature and changeability of our current conditions. Memory is the means by which we gain self-consciousness about the genesis of our own common-sense beliefs, derived as they are from our social and cultural milieu (Popular Memory Group 1982). This self-consciousness applies not only to individuals but to institutions as well. The collective memory of educators, for example, aids understanding of a shared social reality that underlies perception of purpose. In other words, it matters if we forget, for example, John Dewey or the race, class and gender-influenced origins of public schooling or the historical justifications for vocational education.

What makes it matter so much is that the relationship between memory and history is so fractured in the late twentieth century (Giroux 1997b). The repair of this fracture must be a central role for critical historians concerned with the world of the present. Our audiences must be confronted not only with the past, but with what has happened to the memory of it. Educational leaders and teachers can benefit from an understanding of the phenomenon of historical disengagement which has destroyed our memories of how curricula were developed and why schools have assumed their present forms. Critical multiculturalists in all domains must reunite memory and history in order to address the ideological distortions that daily confront us in various expressions of popular culture. Power wielders have never had such access to the reshaping of public memory. Blacks, Latinos, women, working class people and indigenous peoples must constantly monitor the ways their pasts are inserted into the collective historical (un)consciousness of Western societies.

Christopher Lasch writes of history that remembers and history that arises from the need to forget (Kaye 1987). Historians need to concern themselves with exposing the *functional* dimension of this need to forget. When the bloodstains are bleached out of the historical record, established power is justified and shored up. The production of what might be called dominant memory is a central historical task. When dominant memory serves to structure consent and build alliances in the functioning of formal politics, the power of memory is revealed (Popular Memory Group 1982). Such power is illustrated by the American public's memory of the United States' relations with Iran. Most Americans remember only angry Iranians chanting anti-American slogans in the streets of Tehran, a crazed Ayatollah preaching martyrdom and hostages torn away from their families. Not included in the dominant memory are images of the CIA working to overthrow the government of Iranian Premier Mohammed Mossedegh in 1953 and replacing it with the 'friendly' Pahlavi Dynasty represented by the young Shah. The structuring of such memories makes a difference. The power of memory in education is revealed by the rewriting of the history of the Educational Testing Service to exclude the eugenicist origins of and influence on what passes as a value neutral, objective testing service (Owen 1985). The form that public memory takes is always a struggle between imperializing and localizing powers. Critical multiculturalists must be informed historical scholars capable of filling in the omissions and offering a sense of possibility to oppressed and dominant groups.

The possibility that critical multiculturalism holds does not involve the presentation of past heroics, resistances and dreams for simple imitation. The past cannot be repeated; present circumstances are unique and will not allow such a tack. The mere repetition of a past formula is bogus – the possibility of a critical multicultural curriculum rests in its fresh restatement for each new age and new generation. This obviously, is no panacea; it simply immerses students in the vital flow, the white water of tradition – in the process they come to see the possibilities for liberation in the everyday stream of events. Because history does not lead automatically to our finding the right strategy for the present, several other steps of emancipatory socioethical analysis must be pursued if individuals are to come to a reflective sense of what they are to do. These steps, Beverly Harrison writes, include the delineation of our solidarities and loyalties. Every political and curricular stance is influenced by the solidarities and loyalties to groups it aims to serve (Harrison 1985). As Rebecca Chopp agrees, arguing that since there are no purely individual categories for meaning, freedom or reason, solidarity forms the basis for ideological critique and historiographical theory.

Solidarity with marginalized and oppressed groups forms the cornerstone of history – the multicultural curriculum holds little meaning outside the bounds of such solidarity (Chopp 1986).

Drawing upon the insights of Chopp and Harrison, oppositional educators have come to realize that insight into oppressed history alone does not provide a pedagogy sufficient for the emancipatory task. An emancipatory pedagogy must begin with critical traditions, confirm them as subjugated knowledges and interrogate them in order to understand their relationship to present realities and mutated forms of racism, sexism and other oppressions. A critical multicultural history becomes a starting point for curriculum theorizing about what students and others need to learn in addition to their own cultural, racial, gender and class experiences; that is, the relationship between dominant and subjugated knowledges. William Pinar (1988) clarifies the issue when he writes, 'After self-revelation, the question becomes, what do I make of what is revealed?' (p. 272). All people are more than just their history, their experiences, what they have been conditioned to be. In other words, once a critical multicultural curriculum with its new histories and new voices is laid bare, what are we to make of this knowledge? How are we to connect it to our own lives and the lives of others?

Constructing the subjugated curriculum: including the multiple perspectives of the marginalized

Once we understand the mainstream curriculum's tendency to use narrow guidelines to exclude non-white, lower socio-economic class and women's experiences, how do critical multiculturalists begin the process of curriculum development in both school and cultural locations? Western societies have been, are now and always will be Eurocentric, monoculturalists proclaim. Concluding that nothing about such a position is racist, conservatives such as E. D. Hirsch maintain that in a nation such as the USA, the Eurocentric nature of America was intact by 1776. What about the cultural exchanges that have occurred in the USA before and after 1776? Hirsch conveniently ignores the important contributions to the national culture by a pot pourri of immigrants from all corners of the globe, not to mention the indigenous peoples who lived in America before the arrival of the Europeans. Certainly we have made this point throughout the book and it needs no more elaboration here. Critical multiculturalism, at this point, works to devise a curriculum that connects these historical understandings to the lives of individuals from both dominant and subordinate groups.

Joyce King and Carolyn Mitchell (1995), in their book *Black Mothers to Sons: Juxtaposing African American Literature with Social Practice*, provide profound insights into ways of shaping the historically contextualized subjugated (in this case, Afrocentric) curriculum. Concerned with the personal experiences of black mothers with their sons, King and Mitchell brought black mothers together for a group conversation where they discussed, compared and analysed their lived worlds in the light of vignettes from African American literature. Using literature as a mirror for life and, thus, a generative pedagogical activity rubbed against the grain of traditional Eurocentric literary criticism, with its privileging of art/literature as an aesthetic not a political dynamic. Thus, literature was not being used as a universal aesthetic but as an evocative device in the socio-political context of the black microcosm. What King and Mitchell were developing in this process was an innovative research methodology into the black experience that held profound curricular and pedagogical implications. When black literature was examined *vis-à-vis* social practice, the authors found a valuable strategy to enlighten educators about the vicissitudes of black life and the false and misleading nature of popular stereotypes of black mothers and black families.

King and Mitchell were concerned with providing a setting where the literary encounter evoked a group conversation about the relevant topics. As researchers, King and Mitchell made no attempt to cultivate detachment, seeking instead personal interaction with the participants. Drawing upon the method, critical multiculturalists use their historical and power-related understandings to ground this coming together of students, teachers and members of the community in exploring the meaning of such concepts in their lives. Critical teachers work to help students gain self-knowledge through the awareness of the social etymology of their mutual emotions and traumas. Using King and Mitchell's mothers as a model, the critical groups identify shared problems and work to solve them. This research-for-change model is central to a critical pedagogy and can be used to enable conversations among a variety of groups about many different topics. As a means of examining how individuals and groups receive knowledge, the method engages group members in a process of rewriting knowledge. One can imagine many possibilities for deploying the method in the critical multicultural context, including group analysis of film and TV representations of African Americans or the methods by which academic knowledge about blacks and other oppressed groups is produced.

What King and Mitchell are proposing involves a form of paradigmatic analysis – an examination of knowledge production, in this case a Eurocentric knowledge production about individuals of African heritage. As we discussed in Chapter 2, modernist Eurocentric forms of epistemology separate spirit and emotion from reason and intellect, in the process promoting the superiority of reason and intellect. The Eurocentric paradigm posits that the knowledge emerging from its epistemological assumptions is universal, neutral and objective. King and Mitchell's Afrocentric paradigmatic analysis claims, however, that such knowledge tacitly reflects a Eurocentric world view and covertly reifies the status quo. An epistemology and research methodology constructed by the dominant powers within a society sees the world from that dominant vantage point. From this perspective blacks and other marginalized groups are often objectified as members of sub-cultures who don't share dominant values. Eurocentric ways of seeing produce an epistemological power that induces individuals to acquiesce to modernist criteria for judging what is of worth in human experience. This epistemological colonialism moved Europeans across the centuries to see themselves as producers and purveyors of truth. Through their science and rationality they often came to think that they possessed the solutions to all earthly (and sometimes unearthly) problems. As agents of truth, Europeans were able to justify a variety of crimes against humanity – especially non-white humanity (Dion-Buffalo and Mohawk 1992). It is the effects of this Eurocentric one-truth research paradigm that King and Mitchell's method seeks to analyse. Obviously such analysis is central to critical multiculturalism and grounds the basis of its curriculum.

The core of the critical multicultural curriculum involves the effort to understand the world as seen from the margins, the marginalized. Some have referred to this dynamic as decentring the centre, viewing subjugated experience as well as whiteness from an outsider's vantage point. The pedagogical implications of such a move are dramatic, as multiple accounts replace the 'Truth'. In the light of the ways black, Latino, Asian and indigenous lives are misrepresented in both academia and the media, such a curriculum is profoundly needed by non-white students with understandably low self-esteem, not to mention students from the dominant culture whose anger towards the marginalized grows daily. A curriculum that *sees* from the margins operates differently from the dominant curriculum, starting, for example, a study of race in the USA not with slavery but with the pre-fifteenth-century civilizations in West Africa. Such an approach tells a different story, as it frames the African American struggle as one to regain its original strength, not as a story of a traditionally weak, enslaved people trying to *develop* a sense of dignity.

The critical multicultural curriculum of the marginalized does not attempt merely to replace Eurocentrism with Afrocentrism or androcentrism with gynocentrism. Proponents do maintain, however, that the study of various marginalized peoples should be emphasized because they have been ignored or distorted. They also contend that dominant groups such as white people should be viewed from other angles, from non-Eurocentric epistemological assumptions. Such analysis, as we cautioned in Chapter 8, does not mean that we simply demonize whiteness; it does mean that we treasure subjugated ways of knowing. Subjugated stories become a valuable resource to be used to build a better future for individuals from diverse groups, a collective future based on the principles of communitarianism, power sharing and social justice. With these understandings a critical multicultural curriculum might start a study of Mexican Americans, for example, before the Mexican War in 1846 – the point where many liberal and pluralist curricula begin their study. Such a critical curriculum would investigate what was occurring in Mexico before the USA conquered the northern half of the nation. It would also appreciate that from a Mexican and/or Indian perspective the study of Mexican Americans would include gaining a familiarity with the ancient Aztec and Mayan civilizations. In the Anglocentric US history curriculum the study of the conditions in England that led to the Pilgrims' migration is commonplace. Such is not the case with non-white American immigrants (West 1993; Sleeter and Grant 1994).

A multicultural curriculum that valued marginalized perspectives would search for new ways of seeing in a variety of pedagogical spaces. It is a basic premise of historiography that historical analyses of the past often tell readers as much about the time in which they were authored as about the epoch they chronicle. Joel Taxel (1994) points out that teachers must be aware of these dynamics in children's literature, maintaining that a comparative reading of books such as Yates's *Amos Fortune, Free Man* (1950), Hamilton's *Anthony Burns: the Defeat and Triumph of a Fugitive Slave* (1988) and Lyons's *Letters from a Slave Girl: the Story of Harriet Jacobs* (1992) provide a unique insight into changing white perspectives towards African Americans. Indeed, they are probably more important in this way than they are as studies of slaves' lives. In a similar vein, Toni Morrison (1993) explores racial points of view in literature, analysing the racial imagination of white mainstream authors and readers. In this context she exposes the ways the dominant power of whiteness exercises its hegemony in literature, film and various forms of popular culture. Such hegemonic dynamics induce readers to accept the unjust social status quo, the exclusions of academic disciplines and the curriculum as it stands. Indeed, the dominant racial imagination is built into the production and organization of knowledge itself (King and Mitchell 1995).

Albeit from different directions, Afrocentrism and critical theory come together for social and curricular transformation

When we use marginalized perspectives as a key ingredient in a critical multicultural curriculum, by definition we study ways of improving the lives of oppressed peoples. Both critical theory/critical pedagogy and Afrocentrism, though from different cultural traditions, agree on that socio-educational objective and are willing to work tirelessly to achieve it. Both theoretical positions have much to learn from one another, although in our positions as privileged white analysts we make no attempt to *teach* African Americans who claim Afrocentric credentials how critical perspectives can extend the Afrocentric project. This is not our role – the development of Afrocentrism is a black concern at this historical juncture. Our purpose here is simply to point out the ways the theories converge in a manner that informs critical multiculturalism. Afrocentrism provides a unique challenge to liberal and pluralist multicultural curricula that hide their Eurocentric ideological features. In this context Afrocentrism understands the intimate connection between the economic and social stresses that afflict black communities in Western societies and the crises of knowledge and human meaning that subvert the culture's ability and/or willingness to respond to the chaos.

The drums of black protest and pain sound loudly in the music of young rappers and reggae artists who provide Afrocentrism with its most audible oppositional voice. Such forms of protest are revered by many non-white (and white) youths and virtually ignored – except for efforts to curb the music's obscenity or violent expressions – by the dominant culture and the mainstream curriculum. Such Afrocentric protests are validated by critical scholars of black economics who ground their scholarship on the concept of 'market failure' – the inability of free-market economies to provide the goods, services or capital needed by the black community. This critical theory of black economics goes on to maintain that a lack of material well-being among individuals and groups within the economy exerts negative economic and cultural consequences for the society as a whole. Thus, all members of society benefit, not just blacks, from the economic development and vitalization of the black community. Critical multiculturalists learn from young rappers, Afrocentrists, critical black economists and many other marginalized voices more than just a chronicle of misery. They gain insight from such voices into ways of producing students of power who become wielders of oppositional power: cultural workers who upset the stasis of economic, political and educational systems that have rested comfortably despite the omnipresence of glaring racial inequality. In these ways they gain unique perspectives into the process of curriculum development that takes seriously the knowledge of the marginalized.

A critical multiculturalism informed by Afrocentrism gains the ominous realization that in the late twentieth century curricular issues cannot be separated from black survival. As they elicit group reaction to various black texts, King and Mitchell (1995) refer to the psychic holocaust faced by black people, young black males in particular. The curriculum of critical multiculturalism cannot ignore contemporary media representations of black men as animalistic and criminal and their psychological effects on black males themselves. The unfair political and economic realities black men face in late twentieth-century Western societies cannot be separated from the violence, anger and destructiveness often turned upon themselves. Like King and Mitchell's cadre of black mothers of black sons, critical multicultural-ists worry about the safety of young black men. In an era when young black men in some areas are twice as as likely to end up in prison as in college, black male survival becomes a serious question.

Because of the severity of the social environment young black men must negotiate, King, Mitchell and the black mothers understand that lessons must sometimes be taught harshly, albeit lovingly. Critical multiculturalism learns from this dynamic, as it provides a power literacy that helps students to gain insight into the ways the world works in reality rather than the sani-tized version depicted in mainstream introduction to democracy textbooks and Disney movies. A curriculum that teaches black males the nature of racism and provides maps of the socio-economic terrain is far more valuable for our threatened black sons than a pedagogy of denial. Such a critical cur-riculum pulls no punches as it studies racial codes as embodied in concepts such as 'good neighbourhoods', 'quality education' and the Los Angeles judicial and law enforcement's use of NHI (no humans involved) to refer to young urban black males. While it is unfortunate that we must tell our young black male students (and other marginalized students) that they must 'be better' intellectually and ethically than their white middle/upper-middle class peers if they want to escape poverty and its accompanying danger, it is none the less a necessity. Such cold revelations must always be accompanied by affirmations of the brilliance of the African diasporic tradition and the profound knowledge and talents young black men bring with them to school.

A curriculum of affirmation

As a critical multiculturalist curriculum explores the degradation of Africanness in Western societies, it concurrently looks at the genius of things African for the purpose of providing affirmational experiences for black students. Critical multiculturalists want children of African descent (and children from other cultural/racial backgrounds as well) to understand African history, philosophy and culture. In the spirituality and communi-tarianism expressed through its art, storytelling and lived culture, the African tradition affirms both individuality and collectivity. The brilliance of black men and women in the diasporic tradition involved their ability to avoid nihilism in spite of the despair of their enslaved position. Through their cultural constructions of meaning, feeling and love, they created a psy-chic armour that protected them from the hopelessness and cruelty of slav-ery and oppression. Such armour remained in place from the seventeenth century to the 1970s, when it began to disintegrate. Despite the trials and tribulations of black life, black suicide rates in the USA were the lowest of any group. By the 1990s young black Americans' suicide rate was the highest of any ethnic group. Critical multiculturalists drawing upon the knowledge of the Afrocentric tradition want to understand the psychological power of black ancestors to deal with inequality and oppression as one portion of a larger strategy of social transformation (Hall 1992; West 1992, 1993; King and Mitchell 1995).

In addition to Stuart Hall's (1992) three unique features of the African diasporic tradition – style, music and the use of the body (each of which deserves volumes of analysis) – the black academic/literary tradition can help individuals to survive and make sense of their lives. The chills and tears we have seen elicited in class by Paul Laurence Dunbar's 'The Haunted Oak', with its literally overwhelming 'take' on the history of violence against black men in the USA, has opened pathways to liberation from the meaningless and violence of oppression. From the perspective of the hanging tree, Dunbar writes of the emotions elicited by the innumerable lynchings of black innocents. The charismatic power of haunted oaks, autobiographies of figures such as Malcolm X and the stories of authors such as Ralph Ellison, Toni Morrison, Alice Walker, Richard Wright, Claude Brown and Zora Neale Hurston have changed the lives of many black males – interestingly, prison journals often speak of the magic of such literature. Obviously, such literature should be found in school curricula as well as prison libraries.

The critical multicultural curriculum of black affirmation is a black studies programme that overtly forges connections between academia and everyday black life, black cultural production. Drawing upon the collective black experience in life and literature, the curriculum induces students to re-examine their lives from an Afrocentric perspective. The knowledge produced in this reflective activity can provide basic understandings needed to transform Western culture. Such a critical black pedagogy pays special attention to the cultural production of black youth: rap, reggae, hip hop etc. Houston Baker Jr (1993) maintains that reggae, for example, has extended black studies to the young. Understanding the role of reggae and rap artists as public intellectuals, Baker describes his use of rap to gain pedagogical entree to a group of poor, racially and ethnically diverse British secondary students. Describing Shakespeare's *Henry V* as a rapper – 'a cold dissing, def con man, tougher-than-leather and smoother-than-ice, an artisan of words', – Baker took students on a pedagogical journey back and forth and between *Henry V* and Public Enemy's 'Don't Believe the Hype'. In this context a cultural hybridity was developed that affirmed black racial identities and cultural production, while at the same time teaching a valuable traditional lesson in the Eurocentric canon. As we have argued throughout the book, our notion of critical multiculturalism in its embrace of the margins makes no effort to exclude and degrade all that is Eurocentric. In Baker's case

Afrocentricity was used as a vehicle for the exploration of the traditional canon. Neither Baker nor we would always use black cultural production to get to a European concept – often we would explore the Afrocentric for its own intrinsic merit as a way to take us to yet another Afrocentric point (King and Mitchell 1995).

Drawing on the black experience induces teachers and other cultural workers to address the black aesthetic. Such a perspective turns everyday life into aesthetic objects of perception; in such a context people, lived activities, tragedies and celebrations can all be viewed in moral, political and ethical context. The symbolic realm is connected to lived reality in a manner that helps to construct a new consciousness – one that we have referred to elsewhere as post-formal thinking (Kincheloe and Steinberg 1993; Kincheloe 1995). The black aesthetic provides the possibility for a pedagogy of affirmation of students of African descent. As the metaphor of jazz is introduced as a curricular principle, black and white students are drawn into African ways of seeing and being. Jazz, as it is used here, is not only a musical form but an approach to life, with its improvisational flexibility and resistance to the positivist-like certainty of either/or epistemologies. Like a jazz pianist, the improvisor operates both individually and in concert with the group – indeed, the pianist's individuality catalyses the creative tension within the group, leading it to previously unimagined accomplishments. No other culture has produced a musical or aesthetic form comparable to jazz.

This jazz motif is employed in Afrocentric pedagogies, curriculum development and research strategies. Just as jazz musicians play a split second before the beat and tease the note as an unstable sonic frequency, teachers and other cultural workers develop new takes on old assumptions. Thus, what has been called the 'tragic magic' of jazz becomes an omnipresent dynamic within the Afrocentric imperative and its production of a scholarly method that is grounded on a understanding of oppressed people's pain and frustration. Critical multiculturalists understand that merely teaching students about great black people and their accomplishments is insufficient in the quest for affirmation. A key aspect of the pedagogy of affirmation involves the ability of students both to understand and to act on a set of ever-evolving moral, ethical and scholarly principles. The tragic magic of jazz is directly connected to black pain and anguish. So is the curriculum of affirmation, as it induces children and young adults to identify and make sense of the pain they confront daily in the nihilism that surrounds them. As they come to understand their pain, oppressed students are nurtured in the effort to express their understandings creatively and therapeutically (Jafa 1992; Nightingale 1993; West 1993).

Rap and the black aesthetic

Black resistance to the right-wing resurgence and what Aaron Gresson (1995) has termed the recovery of white supremacy has emerged in the 1980s and 1990s not as much in the academic and political spheres but in popular cultural expressions such as black literature, black film, black music videos and especially rap. The black aesthetic fuelled this counter-hegemonic cultural moment, as rappers responded to the pain of racism in a variety of creative ways. A critical multicultural curriculum of affirmation takes these cultural expressions very seriously, studying and learning from them insights into the issues they address as well as the experiences that shaped the lives of the individuals who produced them. Emerging from the economic crisis of young African Americans in New York in the 1970s, rap addressed the vilification of black youth. Bringing together the language skills of black ministers and the African polyrhymic tradition, rap uses black rage to construct a new popular cultural art form. Cornel West (1993) believes that rap is the first step on the way to something great, as it strives to create a social vision of a better future. Always contradictory, rap's sometime violence, misogyny and homophobia cannot be excused. As we listen to interpret rap, multicultural scholars must not fall into an all or nothing glorification or romanticization. Cultural workers can comfortably point out the contradictions of rap, as they encourage those around them always to listen with a critical ear (Nightingale 1993; Gray 1995).

In many ways it can be claimed that the most compelling and politically conscious expressions of the black aesthetic in the last two decades of the twentieth century have come from rap. Truly a black art form, rap cannot be easily 'covered' (appropriated) by white musicians – the short-lived career of Vanilla Ice being no exception. The urban blackness of the form seems to necessitate a style accessible mainly to African American youth – a quality that undermines its acceptance as a serious musical form. As with other popular cultural forms, the power of rap involves its ability to construct fields of interest that are connected to affective dynamics such as desire and anger. Critical multiculturalists know that the understanding of the way rap (and other forms of popular culture) constructs fields of interest is extremely important. Anyone who teaches young people should possess an awareness of rap that can be deployed at many different times for many different reasons. Too often we talk to teachers and teacher educators who dismiss rap and its cultural/pedagogical importance – such educators are often the ones who possess little visceral identification with the pain and hopelessness experienced by many of their black students.

The positive sites of rap are full of energy – sometimes rage – but always concerned with injustice. The obscenity of white male corporate profit-taking, for example, is a common political theme in a genre that relentlessly pursues the wrongs of the state. As a source of racial pride and a condemnation of racism, rap negotiates gansta rage with stop-the-violence appeals. Within the rap cosmos there are works devoted to the rights of black women, opposed to child abuse and rape, dedicated to teaching an Afrocentric curriculum, critical of police officers who don't respect the rights of individuals etc. While the types of rap continue to expand, almost all of them maintain their connection to the black aesthetic (Baker 1993; Gray 1995; Giroux 1997a). We conclude this book with rap and the black aesthetic as an example of the sources critical multiculturalists insist on studying in the reconceptualized curriculum. Obviously, students of African descent can profit from the study of such alternative sources, but we want students and individuals from all backgrounds to understand the issues raised by rappers and their relationship to the production of well educated, well informed and civically courageous people. Critical multiculturalism, with its power literacy, social vision, pedagogical imagination and radical commitment to democracy and justice, can build a new curriculum for both the educational and political spheres in the dangerous new times Western societies face.

REFERENCES

Adler, S. (1991) Forming a critical pedagogy in the social studies methods class: The use of imaginative literature, in B. Tabachnick and K. Zeichner (eds) *Issues and Practices in Inquiry-oriented Teacher Education*. New York: Falmer Press.

Airaksinen, T. (1992) The rhetoric of domination, in T. Wartenberg (ed.) *Rethinking Power*. Albany, NY: SUNY Press.

Alcoff, L. (1995) Mestizo identity, in N. Zack (ed.) *American Mixed Race: the Culture of Microdiversity*. Lanham, MD: Rowman and Littlefield.

Allison, C. (1995) *Present and Past: Essays for Teachers in the History of Education*. New York: Peter Lang.

Amott, T. (1993) *Caught in the Crisis: Women and the US Economy Today*. New York: Monthly Review Press.

Amott, T. and Matthaei, J. (1991) *Race, Gender, and Work: a Multicultural Economic History of Women in the US*. Boston: South End Press.

Anderson, E. (1987) Gender as a variable in teacher thinking, in R. Thomas (ed.) *Higher Order Thinking: Definition, Meaning and Instructional Approaches*. Washington, DC: Home Economics Education Association.

Anderson, J. D. (1986) Secondary school history textbooks and the treatment of Black history, in D. Clark Hine (ed.) *The State of African American History: Past, Present, and Future*. Baton Rouge, LA: Louisiana State University Press.

Anthias, F. and Yuval-Davis, N. (1992) *Racialized Boundaries: Race, Nation, Gender, Colour and Class and the Anti-racist Struggle*. New York: Routledge.

Appiah, K. (1995) Straightening out The Bell Curve, in R. Jacoby and N. Glauberman (eds) *The Bell Curve Debate: History, Documents, and Opinion*. New York: Random House.

Apple, M. (1992) Constructing the captive audience: Channel One and the political economy of the text. Unpublished manuscript.

Apple, M. (1996) Dominance and dependency: situating The Bell Curve within the conservative restoration, in J. Kincheloe, S. Steinberg and A. Gresson (eds) *Measured Lies: The Bell Curve Examined*. New York: St Martin's Press.

Arnot, M. (1992) Schools and families: a feminist perspective, in K. Weiler and C. Mitchell (eds) *What Schools Can Do: Critical Pedagogy and Practice*. Albany, NY: SUNY Press.

Aronowitz, S. (1993) The relativity of theory, *The Village Voice*, 27, 60.

Aronowitz, S. and DiFazio, W. (1994) *The Jobless Future: Sci-tech and the Dogma of Work*. Minneapolis: University of Minnesota Press.

Aronowitz, S. and Giroux, H. (1991) *Postmodern Education: Politics, Culture and Social Criticism*. Minneapolis, University of Minnesota Press.

Ayers, W. (1992) Disturbances from the field: recovering the voice of the early childhood teacher, in S. Kessler and B. Swadener (eds) *Reconceptualizing the Early Childhood Curriculum*. New York: Teachers College Press.

Balsamo, A. (1985) Beyond female as variable: constructing a feminist perspective on organizational analysis, paper presented to the Conference 'Critical Perspectives in Organizational Analysis', New York.

Baker, H. Jr (1993) *Rap: Black Studies and the Academy*. Chicago: University of Chicago Press.

Banfield, B. (1991) Honoring cultural diversity and building on its strengths: a case for national action, in L. Wolfe (ed.) *Women, Work, and the Role of Education*. Boulder, CO: Westview Press.

Banks, J. (1988) *Multiethnic Education: Theory and Practice*, 2nd edn. Boston: Allyn and Bacon.

Baudrillard, J. (1983) *Simulations*. New York: SemioText(e).

Beardsley, T. (1995) For whom The Bell Curve really tolls, in R. Jacoby and N. Glauberman (eds) *The Bell Curve Debate: History, Documents, and Opinion*. New York: Random House.

Beck, U. (1992) *Risk Society: towards a New Modernity*. London: Sage.

Bellah, R. (1991) *The Good Society*. New York: Vintage Books.

Berger, B. (1995) Methodological fetishism, in R. Jacoby and N. Glauberman (eds) *The Bell Curve Debate: History, Documents, and Opinion*. New York: Random House.

Bhatnagar, D. (1988) Professional women in organizations: New paradigms for research and action, *Sex Roles*, 18(5–6): 343–55.

Bizzell, P. (1991) Power, authority, and critical pedagogy, *Journal of Basic Writing*, 10(2): 54–70.

Block, F. (1990) *Postindustrial Possibilities: a Critique of Economic Discourse*. Berkeley: University of California Press.

Bluestone, B. and Harrison, B. (1982) *The Deindustrialization of America: Plant Closings, Community Abandonment, and the Dismantling of Basic Industry*. New York: Basic Books.

Bluestone, I and Brown, A. (1983) Foreword, in A. Wirth, *Productive Work – In Industry and Schools: Becoming Persons Again*. Lanham, MD: University Press of America.

Bohm, D. and Peat, F. (1987) *Science, Order, and Creativity*. New York: Bantam Books.

Borgmann, A. (1992) *Crossing the Postmodern Divide*, Chicago: University of Chicago Press.

Bourricaud, F. (1979) Individualistic mobilization and the crisis of professional authority, *Daedalus*, 108(2): 1–20.

Bowers, C. and Flinders, D. (1990) *Responsive Teaching: An Ecological Approach to Classroom Patterns of Language, Culture, and Thought*. New York: Teachers College Press.

Bowser, B. P. (1985) Race relations in the 1980's: the case of the United States, *Journal of Black Studies*, 15(4): 307–24.

Bozik, M. (1987) Critical thinking through creative thinking, paper presented to the Speech Communication Association, Boston.

Brimelow, P. (1995) Restoration man, in R. Jacoby and N. Glauberman (eds) *The Bell Curve Debate: History, Documents, and Opinion*. New York: Random House.

Brittan, A. and Maynard, M. (1984) *Sexism, Racism, and Oppression*. New York: Basil Blackwell.

Britzman, D. (1991) *Practice Makes Practice: a Critical Study of Learning to Teach*. Albany, NY: SUNY Press.

Britzman, D. and Pitt, A. (1996) On refusing one's place: the ditchdigger's dream, in J. Kincheloe, S. Steinberg and A. Gresson (eds) *Measured Lies: The Bell Curve Examined*. New York: St Martin's Press.

Brooks, M. (1984) A constructivist approach to staff development, *Educational Leadership*, 32: 23–27.

Brosio, R. (1994) *The Radical Democratic Critique of Capitalist Education*. New York: Peter Lang.

Brown, R. (1993) Cultural representation and ideological domination, *Social Forces*, 71(3): 657–76.

Business Week (1995) IQ is not destiny, in R. Jacoby and N. Glauberman (eds) *The Bell Curve Debate: History, Documents, and Opinion*. New York: Random House.

Butler, J. (1992) Contingent foundations: feminism and the question of 'postmodernism', in J. Butler and J. Scott (eds) *Feminists Theorize the Political*. New York: Routledge.

Capra, F. (1982) *The Turning Point: Science, Society, and the Rising Culture*. New York: Simon and Shuster.

Carby, H. (1980) Multiculture, *Screen Education*, 34: 62–70.

Carby, H. V. (1982) Schooling in Babylon, in Centre for Contemporary Cultural Studies, *The Empire Strikes Back: Race and Racism in 70s Britain*. London: Hutchinson.

Carby, H. (1992) The multicultural wars, in G. Dent (ed.) *Black Popular Culture*. Seattle: Bay Press.

Carlson, D. (1991) *Teachers and Crisis: Urban School Reform and Teachers' Work Culture*. New York: Routledge.

Carnevale, A. (1992) Skills for the New World Order, *The American School Board Journal*, 179(5): 28–30.

Carspecken, P. (1996) The set-up: crocodile tears for the poor, in J. Kincheloe, S.

Steinberg and A. Gresson (eds) *Measured Lies: The Bell Curve Examined*. New York: St Martin's Press.

Cary, R. (1996) IQ as commodity: the 'new' economics of intelligence, in J. Kincheloe, S. Steinberg and A. Gresson (eds) *Measured Lies: The Bell Curve Examined*. New York: St Martin's Press.

Cherryholmes, C. (1988) *Power and Criticism: Poststructural Investigations in Education*. New York: Teachers College Press.

Chesneaux, J. (1992) *Brave Modern World: the Prospects for Survival*. New York: Thames and Hudson.

Chidley, J. (1995) The heart of the matter, in R. Jacoby and N. Glauberman (eds) *The Bell Curve Debate: History, Documents and Opinion*. New York: Random House.

Chon, M. (1995) The truth about Asian Americans, in R. Jacoby and N. Glauberman (eds) *The Bell Curve Debate: History, Documents, and Opinion*. New York: Random House.

Chopp, R. S. (1986) *The Praxis of Suffering*. Maryknoll, NY: Orbis Books.

Christian-Smith, L. and Erdman, J. (1997) Mom, it's not real: children constructing childhood through reading horror fiction, in S. Steinberg and J. Kincheloe (eds) *Kinderculture: Corporate Constructions of Childhood*. Boulder, CO: Westview Press.

Codd, J. (1984) Introduction, in J. Codd (ed.) *Philosophy, Common Sense, and Action in Educational Administration*. Victoria, Australia: Deakin University Press.

Collins, G. and Sandell, R. (1992) The politics of multicultural art education, *Art Education*, 45(6): 8–13.

Coontz, S. (1992) *The Way We Never Were: American Families and the Nostalgia Trap*. New York: Basic Books.

Cooper, D. (1994) Productive, relational, and everywhere? Conceptualizing power and resistance within Foucauldian feminism, *Sociology*, 28(2): 435–54.

Copa, G. and Tebbenhoff, E. (1990) *Subject Matter of Vocational Education: in Pursuit of Foundations*. Berkeley, CA: NCRVE.

Cotton, J. (1992) Towards a theory and strategy for black economists development, in J. Jennings (ed.) *Race, Politics, and Economic Development: Community Perspectives*. New York: Verso.

Critical Art Ensemble (1994) *The Electronic Disturbance*. Brooklyn, NY: Autonomedia.

Cross, W. (1996) The Bell Curve and transracial adoption studies, in J. Kincheloe, S. Steinberg and A. Gresson (eds) *Measured Lies: The Bell Curve Examined*. New York: St Martin's Press.

Daines, J. (1987) Can higher order thinking skills be taught? By what strategies?, in R. Thomas (ed.) *Higher Order Thinking: Definition, Meaning and Instructional Approaches*. Washington, DC: Home Economics Education Association.

Darder, A. (1991) *Culture and Power in the Classroom: a Critical Foundation for Bicultural Education*. Westport, CT: Bergin and Garvey.

Denzin, N. (1987) Postmodern children, *Caring for Children/Society*, A32–9.

DeYoung, A. (1989) *Economics and American Education*. New York: Longman.

DiLeonardo, M. (1994) White ethnicities, identity politics, and baby bear's chair, *Social Text*, 41: 5–33.

Dion-Buffalo, Y. and Mohawk, J. (1992) Thoughts from an autochthonous center: postmodernism and cultural studies, *Akwe: kon Journal*, 9(4): 16–21.

Dionne, E. Jr (1995) A long tradition, in R. Jacoby and N. Glauberman (eds) *The Bell Curve Debate: History, Documents, and Opinion*. New York: Random House.

Doyle, W. (1977) Paradigms for research on teacher effectiveness, *Review of Research in Education*, 5: 163–98.

DuBois, W. (1973) *The Education of Black People: Ten Critiques, 1906–1960*. New York: Monthly Review Press.

DuPlessis, R. (1995) Hoo, hoo, hoo: Some episodes in the construction of modern whiteness, *American Literature*, 67(4): 667–700.

Dussel, E. (1976) *History and the Theology of Liberation*. Maryknoll, NY: Orbis.

Dussel, E. (1981) *A History of the Church in Latin America*. Grand Rapids, MI: William B. Eerdmans.

Easterbrook, G. (1995) Blacktop basketball and The Bell Curve, in R. Jacoby and N. Glauberman (eds) *The Bell Curve Debate: History, Documents and Opinion*. New York: Random House.

Edson, C. H. (1979) Sociocultural perspectives on work and schooling in urban America, *The Urban Review*, 11(3): 127–48.

Eisner, E. (1984) Can educational research inform educational practice?, *Phi Delta Kappan*, 65(7): 447–52.

Ellwood, D. (1988) *Poor Support: Poverty in the American Family*. New York: Basic Books.

Evetts, J. (1994) Introduction, in J. Evetts (ed.) *Women and Career: Themes and Issues in Advanced Industrial Societies*. New York: Longman.

Falk, W. and Lyson, T. (1988) *High Tech, Low Tech, No Tech: Recent Industrial and Occupational Change in the South*. Albany, NY: SUNY Press.

Fee, E. (1982) Is feminism a threat to scientific objectivity?, *International Journal of Women's Studies*, 4(4): 378–92.

Feinberg, W. and Horowitz, B. (1990) Vocational education and the equality of opportunity, *Journal of Curriculum Studies*, 22(2): 188–92.

Ferguson, A. (1991) *Sexual democracy: Women, Oppression, and Revolution*. Boulder, CO: Westview Press.

Ferguson, K. (1984) *The Feminist Case against Bureaucracy*. Philadelphia: Temple University Press.

Ferguson, M. (1980) *The Aquarian Conspiracy: Personal and Social Transformation in Our Time*, Los Angeles: J. P. Tarcher, Inc.

Fine, M. (1993) Sexuality, schooling, and adolescent families: the missing discourse of desire, in M. Fine and L. Weis, *Beyond Silenced Voices: Class, Race, and Gender in United States Schools*. Albany, NY: SUNY Press.

Fiske, D. (1986) Specificity of method and knowledge in social science, in D. Fiske and R. Shweder, *Metatheory in Social Science: Pluralisms and Subjectivities*. Chicago: University of Chicago Press.

Fiske, J. (1993) *Power Plays, Power Works*. New York: Verso.

Fiske, J. (1994) *Media Matters: Everyday Culture and Political Change*. Minneapolis: University of Minnesota Press.

Fosnot, C. (1988) The dance of education, paper presented to the Annual Conference of the Association for Educational Communication and Technology, New Orleans.

Foucault, M. (1980) Two lectures, in *Power/Knowledge: Selected Interviews and Other Writings*. New York: Pantheon.

Frankenberg, R. (1993) *The Social Construction of Whiteness: White Women, Race Matters*. Minneapolis: University of Minnesota Press.

Frankenstein, M. and Powell, A. (1994) Toward liberatory mathematics: Paulo Freire's epistemology and ethnomathematics, in P. McLaren and C. Lankshear (eds) *Politics of Liberation: Paths from Freire*. New York: Routledge.

Franklin, G. and Heath, I. (1992) School haze: a response to Louis Menand's view on multicultural education, *Viewpoints*, 120: 2–22.

Fraser, S. (1995) Introduction, in S. Fraser (ed.) *The Bell Curve Wars: Race, Intelligence, and the Future of America*. New York: Basic Books.

Freire, P. (1970) *Cultural Action for Freedom*. Cambridge, MA: Harvard Educational Review Monographs.

Freire, P. and Macedo, D. (1996) Scientism as a form of racism: a dialogue, in J. Kincheloe, S. Steinberg and A. Gresson (eds) *Measured Lies: The Bell Curve Examined*. New York: St Martin's Press.

Fusco, C. (1992) Pan-American postnationalism: another world order, in G. Dent (ed.) *Black Popular Culture*. Seattle: Bay Press.

Fuss, D. (1989) *Essentially Speaking: Feminism, Nature, and Difference*. New York: Routledge, Chapman and Hall.

Gaines, D. (1990) *Teenage Wasteland: Suburbia's Dead End Kids*. New York: Harper Perennial.

Gallagher, C. (1994) White reconstruction in the university, *Socialist Review*, 24(1–2): 165–87.

Gardner, H. (1995) Cracking open the IQ box, in S. Fraser (ed.) *The Bell Curve Wars: Race, Intelligence, and the Future of America*. New York: Basic Books.

Gaskell, J. (1987) Gender and skill, in D. Livingstone (ed.) *Critical Pedagogy and Cultural Power*. South Hadley, MA: Bergin and Garvey.

Genovese, E. (1995) Living with inequality, in S. Fraser (ed.) *The Bell Curve Wars: Race, Intelligence, and the Future of America*. New York: Basic Books.

Gergen, K. (1991) *The Saturated Self: Dilemmas of Identity in Contemporary Life*. New York: Basic Books.

Giddens, A. (1986) *Central Problems in Social Theory: Action, Structure, and Contradictions in Social Analysis*. Berkeley: University of California Press.

Gilligan, C. (1981) *In a Different Voice: Psychological Theory and Women's Development*. Cambridge, MA: Harvard University Press.

Gilman, S. (1996) The Bell Curve, intelligence, and virtuous Jews, in J. Kincheloe, S. Steinberg and A. Gresson (eds) *Measured Lies: The Bell Curve Examined*. New York: St Martin's Press.

Giroux, H. (1988) *Schooling and the Struggle for Public Life*. Minneapolis: University of Minnesota Press.

Giroux, H. (1991) Introduction. Modernism, postmodernism, and feminism: rethinking the boundaries of educational discourse, in H. Giroux (ed.) *Post-*

modernism, Feminism, and Cultural Politics: Redrawing Educational Boundaries. Albany, NY: State University of New York Press.

Giroux, H. (1992) *Border Crossings: Cultural Workers and the Politics of Education*. New York: Routledge.

Giroux, H. (1993) *Living Dangerously: Multiculturalism and the Politics of Difference*. New York: Peter Lang.

Giroux, H. (1997a) *Pedagogy and the Politics of Hope: Theory, Culture, and Schooling*. Boulder, CO: Westview Press.

Giroux, H. (1997b) Are Disney movies good for your kids? in S. Steinberg and J. Kincheloe (eds) *Kinderculture: Corporate Constructions of Childhood*. Boulder, CO: Westview Press.

Giroux, H. and McLaren, P. (1988) Teacher education and the politics of democratic reform, in H. Giroux (ed.) *Teachers as Intellectuals: toward a Critical Pedagogy of Learning*. Granby, MA: Bergin and Garvey.

Giroux, H. and Searls, S. (1996) The Bell Curve debate and the crisis of public intellectuals, in J. Kincheloe, S. Steinberg and A. Gresson (eds) *Measured Lies: the Bell Curve Examined*. New York: St Martin's Press.

Goldman, R. (1992) *Reading Ads Socially*. New York: Routledge.

Gomez, M. (1992) Breaking silences: building new stories of classroom life through teacher transformation, in S. Kessler and B. Swadener (eds) *Reconceptualizing the Early Childhood Curriculum*. New York: Teachers College Press.

Gould, S. (1995) Curveball, in S. Fraser (ed.) *The Bell Curve Wars: Race, Intelligence, and the Future of America*. New York: Basic Books.

Gramsci, A. (1988) *An Antonio Gramsci Reader*. New York: Schocken Books.

Grant, L. (1994) Helpers, enforcers, and go-betweeners: black females in elementary school classrooms, in M. Zinn and B. Dill (eds) *Women in Color in US Society*. Philadelphia: Temple University Press.

Gray, H. (1995) *Watching Race: Television and the Struggle for Blackness*. Minneapolis: University of Minnesota Press.

Greene, M. (1988) *The Dialectic of Freedom*. New York: Teachers College Press.

Gresson, A. (1995) *The Recovery of Race in America*. Minneapolis: University of Minnesota Press.

Gresson, A. (1996) Postmodern America and the multicultural crisis: reading *Forrest Gump* as the call back to whiteness, *Taboo: The Journal of Culture and Education*, 3: 11–34.

Gresson, A. (1997) Professional wrestling and youth culture: teasing, taunting, and the containment of civility, in J. Kincheloe and S. Steinberg (eds) *Kinderculture: Corporate Constructions of Childhood*. Boulder, CO: Westview Press.

Grossberg, L. (1992) *We Gotta Get out of This Place*. New York: Routledge.

Grossberg, L. (1995) What's in a name (one more time)?, *Taboo: The Journal of Culture and Education*, 1: 1–37.

Grubb, N., Davis, G., Lum, J., Phihal, J. and Morgaine, C. (1991) *The Cunning Hand, the Cultured Mind: Models for Integrating Vocational and Academic Education*. Berkeley, CA: NCRVE.

Hacker, A. (1992) *Two Nations: Black and White, Separate, Hostile, Unequal*. New York: Ballantine Books.

Hacker, S. (1989) *Pleasure, Power, and Technology: Some Tales of Gender, Engineering, and the Cooperative Workplace.* New York: Routledge.

Hale-Benson, J. E. (1986) *Black Children: Their Roots, Culture, and Learning Styles.* Baltimore: Johns Hopkins University Press.

Hall, S. (1992) What is this 'black' in black popular culture?, in G. Dent (ed.) *Black Popular Culture.* Seattle: Bay Press.

Hamper, B. (1992) *Rivethead,* New York: Warner.

Harred, J. (1991) Collaborative learning in the literature classroom: old problems revisited, paper presented at the Conference on College Composition and Communication, Boston.

Harris, K. (1984) Philosophers of education: detached spectators or political practitioners, in J. Codd (ed.) *Philosophy, Common Sense, and Action in Educational Administration.* Victoria, Australia: Deakin University Press.

Harrison, B. W. (1985) *Making the Connections: Essays in Feminist Social Ethics.* Boston: Beacon Press.

Harvey, D. (1989) *The Condition of Postmodernity.* Cambridge, MA: Basil Blackwell.

Hauser, J. (1991) Critical inquiries, uncertainties and not faking it with students, paper presented at the Annual Conference of the Center for Critical Thinking and Moral Critique, Rohnert Park, CA.

Haymes, S. (1995) Educational reform: what have been the effects of the attempts to improve education over the last decade?, in J. Kincheloe and S. Steinberg (eds) *Thirteen Questions: Reframing Education's Conversation.* New York: Peter Lang.

Haymes, S. (1996) Race, repression, and the politics of crime and punishment in The Bell Curve, in J. Kincheloe, S. Steinberg and A. Gresson (eds) *Measured Lies: The Bell Curve Examined.* New York: St Martin's Press.

Hebdige, D. (1989) *Hiding in the Light.* New York: Routledge.

Held, D. (1980) *Introduction to Critical Theory: Horkheimer to Habermas.* London: Hutchison.

Herrnstein, R. and Murray, C. (1994) *The Bell Curve: Intelligence and Class Structure in American Life.* New York: The Free Press.

Hitchens, C. (1995) Minority report, in R. Jacoby and N. Gluberman (eds) *The Bell Curve Debate: History, Documents, and Opinion.* New York: Random House.

Holmes, S. (1995) Defining race, in R. Jacoby and N. Glauberman (eds) *The Bell Curve Debate: History, Documents, and Opinion.* New York: Random House.

Holt, T. C. (1986) Whither now and why?, in D. Clark Hine (ed.) *The State of African American History: Past, Present, and Future.* Baton Rouge: Louisiana State University Press.

hooks, b. (1981) *Ain't I a Woman: Black Women and Feminism.* Boston: South End Press.

hooks, b. (1992) *Black Looks: Race and Representation.* Boston: Beacon Press.

hooks, b. (1993) *Sisters of the Yam: Black Women and Self-recovery.* Boston: South End Press.

Horne, D. (1986) *The Public Culture.* Dover, DE: Pluto Press.

Hossfeld, K. (1994) Hiring immigrant women: Silicon Valley's simple formula, in M. Zinn and B. Dill (eds) *Women of Color in US Society*. Philadelphia: Temple University Press.

House, E. and Haug, C. (1995) Riding the bell curve: a review, *Educational Evaluation and Political Analysis*, 17(2): 263–72.

Hultgren, F. (1987) Critical thinking: phenomenalogical and critical foundations, in R. G. Thomas (ed.) *Higher-order Thinking: Definition, Meaning and Instructional Approaches*. Washington, DC: Home Economics Education Association.

Inglis, F. (1985) *The Management of Ignorance: a Political Theory of the Curriculum*. New York: Basil Blackwell.

Jacoby, R. and Glauberman, N. (1995) Introduction, in R. Jacoby and N. Glauberman (eds) *The Bell Curve Debate: History, Documents, and Opinion*. New York: Random House.

Jacques, R. (1992) Critique and theory building: producing knowledge from the kitchen, *Academy of Management Review*, 17(3): 582–606.

Jafa, A. (1992) 69, in G. Dent (ed.) *Black Popular Culture*. Seattle: Bay Press.

Jay, M. (1982) Anamnestic totalization, *Theory and Society*, 7, 116.

Jayaratne, T. (1982) The value of quantitative methodology for feminist research, in G. Bowles and R. Klein (eds) *Theories of Women's Studies*. Boston: Routledge and Kegan Paul.

Jennings, J. (1992) Blacks, politics, and the human service crisis, in J. Jennings (ed.) *Race, Politics, and Economic Development: Community Perspectives*. New York: Verso.

Jipson, J. and Reynolds, U. (1997) Anything you want: women and children in popular culture, in S. Steinberg and J. Kincheloe (eds) *Kinderculture: Corporate Constructions of Childhood*. Boulder, CO: Westview Press.

Johnson, W. (1991) Model programs prepare women for skilled trades, in L. Wolfe (ed.) *Women, Work and School: Occupational Segregation and the Role of Education*. Boulder, CO: Westview Press.

Jonathan, R. (1996) The curriculum and the new vocationalism, *Journal of Curriculum Studies*, 22(2): 184–8.

Jones, J. (1995) Back to the future with The Bell Curve: Jim Crow, slavery, and G, in S. Fraser (ed.) *The Bell Curve Wars: Race, Intelligence, and the Future of America*. New York: Basic Books.

Jones, M. (1992) The black underclass as systematic phenomenon, in J. Jennings (ed.) *Race, Politics, and Economic Development: Community Perspectives*. New York: Verso.

Jordan, J. (1995) In the land of white supremacy, in C. Berlet (ed.) *Eyes Right: Challenging the Right Wing Backlash*. Boston: South End Press.

Judis, J. (1995) Hearts of darkness, in S. Fraser (ed.) *The Bell Curve Wars: Race, Intelligence, and the Future of America*. New York: Basic Books.

Kamin, L. (1995) Lies, damned lies, and statistics, in R. Jacoby and N. Glauberman (eds) *The Bell Curve Debate: History, Documents, and Opinion*. New York: Random House.

Karenga, M. (1982) *Introduction to Black Studies*. Los Angeles: Kawaida Publications.

Kaufman, B. (1978) Piaget, Marx, and the political ideology of schooling, *Journal of Curriculum Studies*, 10(1): 19–44.

Kaus, M. (1995) The it matters-little gambit, in S. Fraser (ed.) *The Bell Curve Wars: Race, Intelligence and the Future of America*. New York: Basic Books.

Kaye, H. J. (1987) The use and abuse of the past: the new right and the crisis of history, *Socialist Register*, 33: 23–65.

Keat, R. (1994) Skepticism, authority, and the market, in R. Keat, N. Whitely and N. Abercrombie (eds) *The Authority of the Consumer*. New York: Routledge.

Keating, A. (1995) Interrogating 'whiteness,' (de) constructing 'race', *College English*, 57(8): 901–18.

Kellner, D. (1989) *Critical Theory, Marxism, and Modernity*. Baltimore: Johns Hopkins University Press.

Kellner, D. (1990) *Television and the Crisis of Democracy*. Boulder, CO: Westview Press.

Kennedy, R. (1995) The phony war, in S. Fraser (ed.) *The Bell Curve Wars: Race, Intelligence and the Future of America*. New York: Basic Books.

Kincheloe, J. L. (1989) *Getting Beyond the Facts: Teaching Social Studies in the Late Twentieth Century*. New York: Peter Lang.

Kincheloe, J. (1991) *Teachers as Researchers: Qualitative Paths to Empowerment*. New York: Falmer Press.

Kincheloe, J. (1993) *Toward a Critical Politics of Teacher Thinking: Mapping the Postmodern*. Westport, CT: Bergin and Garvey.

Kincheloe, J. (1995) *Toil and Trouble: Good Work, Smart Workers, and the Integration of Academic and Vocational Education*. New York: Peter Lang.

Kincheloe, J. and Pinar, W. (eds) (1991) *Curriculum as Social Psychoanalysis: Essays on the Significance of Place*. Albany, NY: SUNY Press.

Kincheloe, J. and Steinberg, S. (eds) (1995) *Thirteen Questions: Reframing Education's Conversation*. New York: Peter Lang.

Kincheloe, J., Steinberg, S. and Tippins, D. (1992) *The Stigma of Genius: Einstein and Beyond Modern Education*. Wakefield, NH: Hollowbrook.

King, J. (1996) Bad luck, bad blood, bad faith: ideological hegemony and the oppressive language of hoodoo social science, in J. Kincheloe, S. Steinberg and A. Gresson (eds) *Measured Lies: The Bell Curve Examined*. New York: St Martin's Press.

King, J. and Mitchell, C. (1995) *Black Mothers to Sons: Juxtaposing African American Literature with Social Practice*. New York: Peter Lang.

Koetting, J. (1988) Educational connoisseurship and educational criticism: Pushing beyond information and effectiveness, paper presented to the Association for Educational Communications and Technology, New Orleans.

Kohlberg, W. and Smith, F. (1992) *Rebuilding America's Workforce: Business Strategies to Close the Competitive Gap*. Homewood, IL: Business One Irwin.

Kroc, R. (1977) *Grinding It Out: the Making of McDonald's*. New York: St Martin's Press.

Lamphere, L. (1985) Bringing the family to work: women's culture on the shop floor, *Feminist Studies*, 11(3): 519–39.

Lather, P. (1991) *Getting Smart: Feminist Research and Pedagogy with/in the Postmodern*. New York: Routledge.

Lavine, T. (1984) *From Socrates to Sartre: the Philosophic Quest.* New York: Bantam Books.

Lawler, J. (1975) Dialectical philosophy and developmental psychology: Hegel and Piaget on contradiction, *Human Development,* 18: 1–17.

Leshan, L. and Margeneu, H. (1982) *Einstein's Space and Van Gogh's Sky: Physical Reality and Beyond.* New York: Macmillan Publishing Company.

Lincoln, Y. (1995) If I am not just one person, but many, why should I write just one text?, paper presented at the American Educational Research Association, San Francisco.

Lincoln, Y. (1996) For whom *The Bell* tolls: a cognitive or educated elite?, in J. Kincheloe, S. Steinberg and A. Gresson (eds) *Measured Lies: The Bell Curve Examined.* New York: St Martin's Press.

Lind, M. (1995) Brave new right, in S. Fraser (ed.) *The Bell Curve Wars: Race, Intelligence, and the Future of America.* New York: Basic Books.

Liston, D. and Zeichner, K. (1988) Critical pedagogy and teacher education, paper presented to the American Educational Research Association, New Orleans.

Livingstone, D. and Luxton, M. (1988) Gender consciousness at work: Modification of the male breadwinner norm among steelworkers and their spouses, unpublished manuscript.

Loury, G. (1995) Dispirited, in R. Jacoby and N. Glauberman (eds) *The Bell Curve Debate: History, Documents, and Opinion.* New York: Random House.

Lowe, D. (1982) *History of Bourgeois Perception.* Chicago: University of Chicago Press.

Lugg, C. (1996) Attacking affirmative action: social Darwinism as public policy, in J. Kincheloe, S. Steinberg and A. Gresson (eds) *Measured Lies: The Bell Curve Examined.* New York: St Martin's Press.

Luke, C. (1994) White women in interracial families: reflections on hybridization, feminine identities, and racialized othering, *Feminist Issues,* 14(2): 49–72.

Luke, T. (1991) Touring hyperreality: critical theory confronts informational society, in P. Wexler (ed.) *Critical Theory Now.* New York: Falmer.

Luttrell, W. (1993) Working class women's ways of knowing: effects of gender, race and class, in L. Castenell and W. Pinar (eds) *Understanding Curriculum as a Racial Text: Representations of Identity and Difference in Education.* Albany, NY: SUNY Press.

MacCannell, D. (1992) *Empty Meeting Grounds.* New York: Routledge.

McCarthy, C. and Apple, M. (1988) Race, class and gender in American educational research: toward a nonsychronous parallelist position, in L. Weis (ed.) *Class, Race, and Gender in American Education.* Albany, NY: State University of New York Press.

McCarthy, C., Buendia, E., Mills, C., *et al.* (1996) The last rational men: citizenship, morality, and the pursuit of human perfection, in J. Kincheloe, S. Steinberg and A. Gresson (eds) *Measured Lies: The Bell Curve Examined.* New York: St Martin's Press.

McCarthy, T. (1992) The critique of impure reason: Foucault and the Frankfurt School, in T. Wartenberg (ed.) *Rethinking Power.* Albany, NY: SUNY Press.

Macedo, D. (1994) *Literacies of Power: What Americans Are Not Allowed to Know.* Boulder, CO: Westview Press.

McIntosh, P. (1995) White privilege and male privilege: a personal account of work in women's studies, in M. Anderson and P. Collins (eds) *Race, Class and Gender: an Anthology*. Belmont, CA: Wadsworth.

McLaren, P. (1986) *Schooling as Ritual Performance: toward a Political Economy of Educational Symbols and Gestures*. London: Routledge and Kegan Paul.

McLaren, P. (1991) Decentering culture: postmodernism, resistance, and critical pedagogy, in Nancy B. Wyner (ed.) *Current Perspectives on the Culture of Schools*. Boston: Brookline Books.

McLaren, P. (1993) Multiculturalism and the postmodern critique: towards a pedagogy of resistance and transformation, *Cultural Studies*, 7(1): 118–46.

McLaren, P. (1994a) *Life in Schools: an Introduction to Critical Pedagogy in the Foundations of Education*. White Plains, NY: Longman.

McLaren, P. (1994b) White terror and oppositional agency: toward a critical multiculturalism, in D. Goldberg (ed.) *Multiculturalism: a Critical Reader*. Cambridge, MA: Basil Blackwell.

McLaren, P. (1995) *Critical Pedagogy and Predatory Culture: Oppositional Politics in a Postmodern Culture*. New York: Routledge.

McLaren, P. (1996) White supremacy and the politics of fear and loathing, in J. Kincheloe, S. Steinberg and A. Gresson (eds) *Measured Lies: The Bell Curve Examined*. New York: St Martin's Press.

McLaren, P., Hammer, R. Reilly, S. and Sholle, D. (1995) *Rethinking Media Literacy: a Critical Pedagogy of Representation*. New York: Peter Lang.

McLaren, P. and Morris, J. (1997) Mighty Morphin Power Rangers: the aesthetics of macho-militaristic justice, in S. Steinberg and J. Kincheloe (eds) *Kinderculture: Corporate Constructions of Childhood*. Boulder, CO: Westview Press.

MacLeod, J. (1987) *Ain't No Making It*. Boulder, CO: Westview Press.

McMillen, L. (1995) Lifting the veil from whiteness: Growing body of scholarship challenges a racial 'norm', *The Chronicle of Higher Education*, 8 September, A23.

Maher, F. and Rathbone, C. (1986) Teacher education and feminist theory: some implications for practice, *American Journal of Education*, 94(2): 214–35.

Maher, M. (1992) Men do and women are: sixth grade girls, media messages, and identity, paper presented at the Center for the Study of Communication's Mainstream(s) and Margins Conference, Amherst, Massachusetts.

Mahoney, M. and Lyddon, W. (1988) Recent developments in cognitive approaches to counseling and psychotherapy, *The Counseling Psychologist*, 16(2): 190–234.

Malveaux, J. (1992) Popular culture and the economics of alienation, in G. Dent (ed.) *Black Popular Culture*. Seattle: Bay Press.

Marable, M. (1992) Race, identity, and political culture, in G. Dent (ed.) *Black Popular Culture*. Seattle: Bay Press.

Marsh, D. (1993) Freire, Vygotsky, special education, and me, *British Columbia Journal of Special Education*, 17(2): 119–34.

Meissner, M. (1989) The reproduction of women's domination in organizational communication, in L. Thayer (ed.) *Organization, Communication*. Norwood, NJ: Ablex Publishing.

Merleman, R. (1986) Domination, self-justification, and self-doubt: some social-psychological consideration, *Journal of Politics*, 48: 276–99.

Merleman, R. (1994) Racial conflict and cultural politics in the US, *Journal of Politics*, 56(1): 1–20.

Merleman, R. (1995) *Representing Black Culture: Racial Conflict and Cultural Politics in the United States*. New York: Routledge.

Metzger, E. and Bryant, L. (1993) Portfolio assessment: pedagogy, power, and the student, *Teaching English in the Two Year College*, 20(4): 279–88.

Mies, M. (1982) Towards a methodology for feminist research, in G. Bowles and R. Klein (eds) *Theories of Women's Studies*. Boston: Routledge and Kegan Paul.

Miller, A. (1995) Professors of hate, in R. Jacoby and N. Glauberman (eds) *The Bell Curve Debate: History, Documents, and Opinion*. New York: Random House.

Moore, E. (1986) Family socialization and the IQ test performance of traditionally and transracially adopted black children, *Developmental Psychology*, 22: 317–26.

Morrison, T. (1993) *Playing in the Dark: Whiteness and the Literary Imagination*. New York: Vintage.

Mullings, L. (1994) Images, ideology, and women of color, in M. Zinn and B. Dill (eds) *Women of Color in US Society*. Philadelphia: Temple University Press.

Mumby, D. (1989) Ideology and the social construction of meaning: a communication perspective, *Communication Quarterly*, 37(4): 291–304.

Murray, R. (1992) Fordism and post-Fordism, in C. Jencks (ed.) *The Post-modern Reader*. New York: St Martin's Press.

Murray, J. and Ozanne, J. (1991) The critical imagination: emancipatory interests in consumer research, *Journal of Consumer Research*, 18(2): 129–44.

Musolf, R. (1992) Structure, institutions, power, and ideology: new directions within symbolic interactionism, *The Sociological Quarterly*, 33(2): 171–89.

Muwakkil, S. (1995) Timing is everything, in R. Jacoby and N. Glauberman (eds) *The Bell Curve Debate: History, Documents, and Opinion*. New York: Random House.

Nakayama, T. and Krizek, R. (1995) Whiteness: a strategic rhetoric, *Quarterly Journal of Speech*, 81: 291–309.

Nieto, S. (1996) *Affirming Diversity: the Sociopolitical Context of Multicultural Education*. White Plains, NY: Longman.

Nightingale, C. (1993) *On the Edge: a History of Poor Black Children and Their American Dreams*. New York: Basic Books.

Nisbett, R. (1995) Race, IQ, and scientism, in S. Fraser (ed.) *The Bell Curve Wars: Race, Intelligence, and the Future of America*. New York: Basic Books.

Noffke, S. and Brennan, M. (1991) Student teachers use action research: issues and examples, in B. Tabachnick and K. Zeichner (eds) *Issues and Practices in Inquiry-oriented Teacher Education*. New York: Falmer.

Nyang, S. S. and Vandi, A. S. (1980) PanAfricanism in world history, in M. K. Asante and A. S. Vandi (eds) *Contemporary Black Thought: Alternative Analyses in Social and Behavioral Science*. Beverly Hills, CA: Sage.

Oakes, J. (1985) *Keeping Track: How Schools Structure Inequality*. New Haven, CT: Yale University Press.

Obiakor, F. (1992) The myth of socio-economic dissonance: implications for African American exceptional students, paper presented at the Council for Exceptional Children, Minneapolis.

Owen, D. (1985) *None of the Above: Behind the Myth of Scholastic Aptitude.* Boston: Houghton Mifflin.

Pagano, J. (1996) Speculation based on speculation: the problem of The Bell Curve and the question of schooling, in J. Kincheloe, S. Steinberg and A. Gresson (eds) *Measured Lies: The Bell Curve Examined.* New York: St Martin's Press.

Palmer, P. and Spalter-Roth, R. (1991) Gender practices and employment: the Sears case and the issue of choice, in L. Wolfe (ed.) *Women, Work, and School: Occupational Segregation and the Role of Education.* Boulder, CO: Westview Press.

Pascall, G. (1994) Women in professional careers: social policy developments, in J. Evetts (ed.) *Women and Career: Themes and Issues in Advanced Industrial Societies.* New York: Longman.

Pearson, H. (1995) Breaking ranks, in R. Jacoby and N. Glauberman (eds) *The Bell Curve Debate: History, Documents, and Opinion.* New York: Random House.

Perez, L. (1993) Opposition and the education of Chicana/os, in C. McCarthy and W. Crichlow (eds) *Race, Identity, and Reproduction in Education.* New York: Routledge.

Perry, T. and Fraser, J. (1993) Reconstructing schools as multiracial/multicultural democracies: toward a theoretical perspective, in T. Perry and J. Fraser (eds) *Freedom's Plow: Teaching in the Multicultural Classroom.* New York: Routledge.

Piliawsky, M. (1984) Racial equality in the United States: from institutionalized racism to 'respectable' racism. *Phylon*, 45(2): 135–43.

Pinar, W. F. (1988) Time, place, and voice: curriculum theory and the history moment, in W. F. Pinar (ed.) *Contemporary Curriculum Discourses.* Scottsdale, AZ: Gorsuch Scarisbrick.

Pinar, W. (1991) Curriculum as social psychoanalysis: on the significance of place, in J. Kincheloe and W. Pinar (eds) *Curriculum as Social Psychoanalysis: Essays on the Significance of Place.* Albany, NY: State University of New York Press.

Pollin, R. and Cockburn, A. (1991) The world, the free market, and the left, *The Nation*, 252(7): 224–36.

Popular Memory Group (1982) Popular memory: theory, politics, and method, in Centre for Contemporary Cultural Studies, *Making Histories: Studies in Historywriting and Politics.* Minneapolis: University of Minnesota Press.

Pruyn, M. (1994) Becoming subjects through critical practice: how students in an elementary classroom critically read and write their world, *International Journal of Educational Reform*, 3(1): 37–50.

Pullin, D. (1994) Learning to work: the impact of the curriculum and assessment standards on educational opportunity, *Harvard Educational Review*, 64(1): 31–54.

Raspberry, W. (1995) Only racists will cheer this, *Centre Daily Times* (State College, Pennsylvania) 23 September, A2.

Reed, A. Jr (1995) Intellectual brown shirts, in R. Jacoby and N. Glauberman (eds) *The Bell Curve Debate: History, Documents, and Opinion.* New York: Random House.

Reinharz, S. (1979) *On Becoming a Social Scientist.* San Francisco: Jossey-Bass.

Reinharz, S. (1982) Experimental analysis: a contribution to feminist research, in G. Bowles and R. Klein (eds) *Theories of Women's Studies*. Boston: Routledge and Kegan Paul.

Reinharz, S. (1992) *Feminist Methods in Social Research*. New York: Oxford University Press.

Rendon, L. and Nora, A. (1991) Hispanic women in college and careers: preparing for success, in L. Wolfe (ed.) *Women, Work, and School: Occupational Segregation and the Role of Education*. Boulder, CO: Westview Press.

Richmond, S. (1986) The white paper, education, and the crafts: an assessment of values, *Journal of Educational Thought*, 20(3): 143–55.

Rizvi, F. (1993) Children and the grammar of popular racism, in C. McCarthy and W. Crichlow (eds) *Race, Identity, and Reproduction in Education*. New York: Routledge.

Roediger, D. (1991) *The Wages of Whiteness: Race and the Making of the American Working Class*. New York: Verso.

Rorty, A. (1992) Power and powers: a dialogue between buff and rebuff, in T. Wartenberg (ed.) *Rethinking Power*. Albany, NY: SUNY Press.

Rubin, L. (1994) *Families on the Faultline: America's Working Class Speaks about the Family, the Economy, Race, and Ethnicity*. New York: Harper Collins.

Ruddick, S. (1980) Material thinking. *Feminist Studies*, 6(2): 342–67.

Rumberger, R. (1984) The growing imbalance between education and work, *Phi Delta Kappan*, 65(5): 342–6.

Ryan, A. (1995) Apocalypse now? in R. Jacoby and N. Glauberman (eds) *The Bell Curve Debate: History, Documents, and Opinion*. New York: Random House.

Sadker, D. and Sadker, M. (1991) Sexism in American education: the hidden curriculum, in L. Wolfe (ed.) *Women, Work, and School: Occupational Segregation and the Role of Education*. Boulder, CO: Westview Press.

Sautman, B. (1995) Theories of East Asian superiority, in R. Jacoby and N. Glauberman (eds) *The Bell Curve Debate: History, Documents, and Opinion*. New York: Random House.

Schön, D. (1987) *Educating the Reflective Practitioner*. San Francisco: Jossey-Bass.

Semali, L. (1997) *Literacy in Multimedia America: Integrating Media Across the Curriculum*. New York: Garland Publishing.

Shiva, V. (1993) *Monocultures of the Mind*. London: Zed Books.

Shor, I. (1992) *Empowering Education: Critical Teaching for Social Change*. Chicago: University of Chicago Press.

Shor, I. and Freire, P. (1987) *A Pedagogy for Liberation: Dialogues on Transforming Education*. South Hadley, MA: Bergin and Garvey.

Shrubsall, V. (1994) Equal opportunities at work: EC and UK law, in J. Evetts (ed.) *Women and Careers: Themes and Issues in Advanced Industrial Societies*. New York: Longman.

Sidel, R. (1992) *Women and Children Last: the Plight of Poor Women in Affluent America*. New York: Penguin Books.

Simon, R., Dippo, D. and Schneke, A. (1991) *Learning Work: a Critical Pedagogy of Work Education*. Westport, CT: Bergin and Garvey.

Slaughter, R. (1989) Cultural reconstruction in the postmodern world. *Journal of Curriculum Studies*, 3: 255–70.

Sleeter, C. (1993) How white teachers construct race, in C. McCarthy and W.

Crichlow (eds) *Race, Identity, and Reproduction in Education*. New York: Routledge.

Sleeter, C. (1995) Reflections on my use of multicultural and critical pedagogy when students are white, in C. Sleeter and P. McLaren (eds) *Multicultural Education, Critical Pedagogy, and the Politics of Difference*. Albany, NY: State University of New York Press.

Sleeter, C. and Grant, C. (1994) *Making Choices from Multicultural Education: Five Approaches to Race, Class, and Gender*. New York: Merrill.

Smart, B. (1992) *Modern Conditions, Postmodern Controversies*. New York: Routledge.

Solomos, J., Findlay, B., Jones, S. and Gilroy, P. (1982) The organic crisis of British capitalism and race: the experience of the seventies, in Centre for Contemporary Cultural Studies, *The Empire Strikes Back: Race and Racism in 70s Britain*. London: Hutchinson.

Solorzano, D. (1989) Teaching and social change: reflections on a Freirean approach in a college classroom, *Teaching Sociology*, 17: 218–25.

Stack, C. (1994) Different voices, different visions: gender, culture, and moral reasoning, in M. Zinn and B. Dill (eds) *Women of Color in US Society*. Philadelphia: Temple University Press.

Stafford, W. (1992) Whither the great neo-conservative experiment in New York City, in J. Jennings (ed.) *Race, Politics, and Economic Development: Community Perspectives*. New York: Verso.

Staples, B. (1995) The IQ cult, in R. Jacoby and N. Glauberman (eds) *The Bell Curve Debate: History, Documents, and Opinion*. New York: Random House.

Staples, R. (1984) Racial ideology and intellectual racism: blacks in academia, *The Black Scholar*, 15(2): 217.

Steinberg, S. and Kincheloe, J. (1997) *Kinderculture: Corporate Constructions of Childhood*. Boulder, CO: Westview Press.

Stowe, D. (1996) Uncolored people: the rise of whiteness studies, *Lingua Franca*, 6(6): 68–77.

Swartz, E. (1993) Multicultural education: disrupting patterns of supremacy in school curricula, practices, and pedagogy, *Journal of Negro Education*, 62(4): 493–506.

Tanaka, G. (1996) Dysgenesis and white culture, in J. Kincheloe, S. Steinberg and A. Gresson (eds) *Measured Lies: The Bell Curve Examined*. New York: St Martin's Press.

Tatum, B. (1994) Teaching white students about racism: the search for white allies and the restoration of hope, *Teachers College Record*, 95(4): 462–75.

Taxel, J. (1994) Political correctness, cultural politics, and writing for young people, *The New Advocate*, 7(2): 93–108.

Thiele, L. (1986) Foucault's triple murder and the modern development of power, *Canadian Journal of Political Science*, 19(2): 243–60.

Thompson, B. (1996) Time traveling and border crossing: reflections on white identity, in B. Thompson and S. Tyagi (eds) *Names We Call Home: Autobiography on Racial Identity*. New York: Routledge.

Thompson, E. P. (1963) *The Making of the English Working Class*. London: Gollancz.

Thompson, J. (1987) Language and ideology: a framework for analysis, *The Socio-logical Review*, 35: 516–36.

Torres, C. (1993) From the 'pedagogy of the oppressed' to 'a luta continua': the political pedagogy of Paulo Freire, in P. McLaren and P. Leonard (eds), *Paulo Freire: a Critical Encounter*. London: Routledge.

Tripp, D. (1988) Teaching journals in collaborative classroom research, paper presented to the American Educational Research Association, New Orleans.

Tucker, C. (1995) Resurgent racism, in R. Jacoby and N. Glauberman (eds) *The Bell Curve Wars: Race, Intelligence, and the Future of America*. New York: Basic Books.

Ulmer, G. (1989) Mystory: the law of idiom in applied grammatology, in R. Cohen (ed.) *Future Literary Theory*. New York: Routledge.

Valli, L. (1987) Gender identity and the technology of office education, in L. Weis (ed.) *Class, Race, and Gender in American Education*. Albany, NY: SUNY Press.

Van den Berg, O. and Nicholson, S. (1989) Teacher transformation in the South African context: an action research approach, paper presented to the International Conference on School-based Innovations: Looking Forward to the 1990s, Hong Kong.

Vattimo, G. (1991) *The End of Modernity*. Baltimore: Johns Hopkins University Press.

Vidal, M. (1996) Genetic rationalizations and public policy: Herrnstein and Murray on intelligence and welfare dependency, in J. Kincheloe, S. Steinberg and A. Gresson (eds) *Measured Lies: The Bell Curve Examined*. New York: St Martin's Press.

Walkerdine, V. (1984) Developmental psychology and the child-centered pedagogy: the insertion of Piaget into early education, in J. Henriques, W. Holloway, C. Urwin, C. Venn and V. Walkerdine (eds) *Changing the Subject*. New York: Methuen.

Wallace, M. (1992) Boyz N the Hood and Jungle Fever, in G. Dent (ed.) *Black Popular Culture*. Seattle: Bay Press.

Walsh, D. (1993) The role of ideology in cultural reproduction, in C. Jenks (ed.) *Cultural Reproduction*. New York: Routledge.

Wartenberg, T. (1992a) Introduction, in T. Wartenberg (ed.) *Rethinking Power*. Albany, NY: SUNY Press.

Wartenberg, T. (1992b) Situated social power, in T. Wartenberg (ed.) *Rethinking Power*. Albany, NY: SUNY Press.

Wax, R. (1971) *Doing Fieldwork: Warnings and Advice*. Chicago: University of Chicago Press.

Weiler, K. (1988) *Women Teaching for Change*. South Hadley, MA: Bergin and Garvey.

Weinberg, R., Scarr, S. and Waldman, I. (1992) The Minnesota transracial adoption study: a follow-up of IQ test performance at adolescence, *Intelligence*, 16: 117–35.

Weis, L. (1987) High school girls in a de-industrializing economy, in L. Weis (ed.) *Class, Race, and Gender in American Education*. Albany, NY: SUNY Press.

Welch, S. D. (1985) *Communities of Resistance and Solidarity*. Maryknoll, NY: Orbis Books.

Welch, S. (1991) An ethic of solidarity and difference, in H. Giroux (ed.) *Post-modernism, Feminism, and Cultural Politics: Redrawing Educational Bound-aries*. Albany, NY: SUNY Press.

Wellman, D. (1996) Red and black in white America: Discovering cross-border identities and other subversive activities, in B. Thompson and S. Tyagi (eds) *Names We Call Home: Autobiography on Racial Identity.* New York: Routledge.

Wertsch, J. (1991) *Voices of the Mind: a Sociocultural Approach to Mediated Action.* Cambridge, MA: Harvard University Press.

West, C. (1992) Nihilism in black America, in G. Dent (ed.) *Black Popular Culture.* Seattle: Bay Press.

West, C. (1993) *Race Matters.* Boston: Beacon Press.

White, H. (1978) *Topics of Discourse: Essays in Cultural Criticism.* Baltimore: Johns Hopkins University Press.

White, H. (1987) *The Content of the Form.* Baltimore: Johns Hopkins University Press.

Wickham, D. (1995) Born to lose, in R. Jacoby and N. Glauberman (eds) *The Bell Curve Debate: History, Documents, and Opinion.* New York: Random House.

Wieseltier, L. (1995) The lowerers, in S. Fraser (ed.) *The Bell Curve Wars: Race, Intelligence, and the Future of America.* New York: Basic Books.

Williams, S. (1992) Two words on music: black community, in G. Dent (ed.) *Black Popular Culture.* Seattle: Bay Press.

Williams, S. (1993) Social injustice: the vital ingredient of a democratic curriculum, *Thresholds in Education,* 19(1–2): 7–13.

Willis, E. (1995) The median is the message, in R. Jacoby and N. Glauberman (eds) *The Bell Curve Debate: History, Documents, and Opinion.* New York: Random House.

Willis, P. (1977) *Learning to Labour: How Working Class Kids get Working Class Jobs.* Farnborough: Saxon House.

Winant, H. (1994) Racial formation and hegemony: global and local developments, in A. Rattans and S. Westwood (eds) *Racism, Modernity, and Identity on the Western Front.* Cambridge: Polity Press.

Wirth, A. (1983) *Productive Work – In Industry and Schools.* Lanham, MD: University Press of America.

Wolfe, A. (1995) Has there been a cognitive revolution in America? The flawed sociology of The Bell Curve, in S. Fraser (ed.) *The Bell Curve Wars: Race, Intelligence, and the Future of America.* New York: Basic Books.

Wolff, J. (1977) Women in organizations, in S. Clegg and D. Dunkerly (eds) *Critical Issues in Organizations.* London: Routledge Direct Editions.

Young, I. (1992) Five faces of oppression, in T. Wartenberg (ed.) *Rethinking Power.* Albany, NY: SUNY Press.

Young, R. (1990) *A Critical Theory of Education: Habermas and Our Children's Future.* New York: Teachers College Press.

Yudice, G. (1995) Neither impugning nor disavowing whiteness does a viable politics make: the limits of identity politics, in C. Newfield and R. Strickland (eds) *After Political Correctness.* Boulder, CO: Westview Press.

Zinn, M. (1994) Feminist rethinking from racial-ethnic families, in M. Zinn and B. Dill (eds) *Women of Color in US Society.* Philadelphia: Temple University Press.

Zinn, M. and Dill, B. (1994) Difference and domination, in M. Zinn and B. Dill (eds) *Women of Color in US Society.* Philadelphia: Temple University Press.

Zweigenhaft, R. and Domhoff, G. (1991) *Blacks in White Establishment.* New Haven, CT: Yale University Press.

INDEX